THE STORY *of* DUNBAR

VOICES OF A VANCOUVER NEIGHBOURHOOD

EDITED BY

PEGGY SCHOFIELD

RONSDALE PRESS

THE STORY OF DUNBAR
Copyright © 2007 Dunbar Residents' Association
Text copyright © 2007 by the authors

RONSDALE PRESS
3350 West 21st Avenue
Vancouver, B.C., Canada V6S 1G7
www.ronsdalepress.com

Editing: Naomi Pauls, Paper Trail Publishing
Cover art: Paul Ohannesian, "The Dunbar Theatre"
    (Alert readers will have noted that the streetcar motorman seems
    to have forgotten to change his sign. Normally for the return trip
    headed north on Dunbar, this streetcar would be marked 3–Main.
    The numbers 7–Dunbar and 3–Main were introduced in 1949.
    Before then, the Dunbar streetcar ran as 14–Dunbar and
    13–Hastings E. By 1951 the Dunbar streetcar was history.)
Cover design: Julie Cochrane
Text design and typesetting: Julie Cochrane, in Adobe Garamond 12 pt on 15
Frontispiece: Joseph Wilson, his daughter, Ethel, and son-in-law, James Albinson,
    stand on the Albinsons' newly purchased lot, 3728 West 20th Avenue, in 1911.
    Courtesy of Fred and Betty Albinson.
Dedication photo: Peggy Schofield (p. v) courtesy of Wilf Schofield
Maps: Louise Phillips (pp. x, 24, 30); Ron Simpson (p. 233)
Index: Bookmark Editing & Indexing

Ronsdale Press wishes to thank the following for their support of its publishing program: the Canada Council for the Arts, the Government of Canada through the Book Publishing Industry Development Program (BPIDP), and the Province of British Columbia through the Book Publishing Tax Credit program and the British Columbia Arts Council.

Library and Archives Canada Cataloguing in Publication

   The story of Dunbar: voices of a Vancouver neighbourhood / edited by Peggy Schofield.

Includes bibliographical references and index.
ISBN-13: 978-1-55380-040-8
ISBN-10: 1-55380-040-0

   1. Dunbar-Southlands (Vancouver, B.C.) — History. 2. Dunbar-Southlands (Vancouver, B.C.) — Anecdotes. I. Schofield, Peggy, 1931–2005

FC3847.52.S865 2007   971.1'33   C2006-904895-9

Printed in China

TO PEGGY SCHOFIELD (1931–2005),
WHO BROUGHT US TOGETHER
AND KEPT US THERE.
THERE IS A BIT OF PEGGY
IN EVERY CHAPTER.

Contents

Maps

Preface

A city is a pattern in time.
— STEVEN JOHNSON, *Emergence*

How long after events should we wait before we write their history? Some aspects of history require the perspective provided only after a considerable period of time has elapsed. A history such as this one, on the other hand, deals with the lives of inhabitants of a small geographic area during a relatively short period of time. It is best written while it is still possible to document personal recollections describing people's lives and their everyday activities and while we still have remnants of a population whose grandparents arrived before British Columbia joined the rest of Canada in 1871. Some of us heard first-hand about clearing land to make a farm and when, if you lived on the riverfront of Point Grey, "going to town" meant going to New Westminster by ferry, canoe or rowboat.

This book has its roots in the sense of place felt by members of the Dunbar/Southlands community. Part of this sense derives from living on an edge — both literal and figurative — a concept that reappears in different guises throughout the book. Our sense of place is accompanied by a sense of pride; our patient editor Naomi Pauls had to warn the authors it was inappropriate to engage in "boosterism" in our writings.

The Story of Dunbar traces the establishment of dwellings, businesses, schools, churches, parks and transportation networks in Dunbar/Southlands, and describes family life, trends, customs and concerns within this framework. The experiences and perspectives described are based upon many interviews with people from all walks of life, of all ages — pioneer descendants, long-time residents and newcomers. The stories are full of grit, humour and determination — stories about people and events that have created the Dunbar legacy.

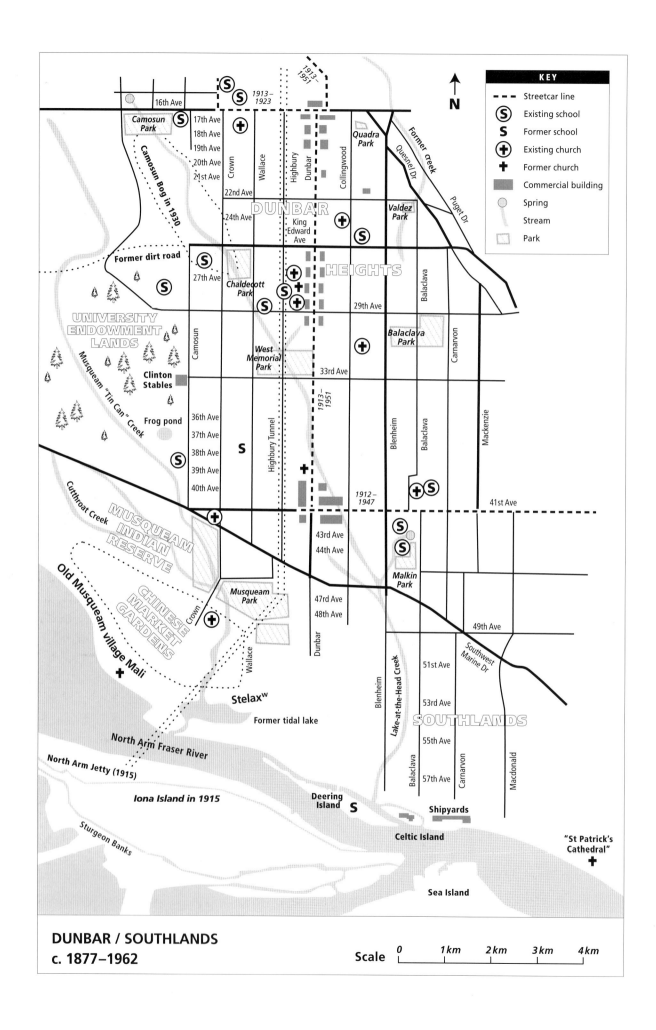

KEY

- - - - Streetcar line
Ⓢ Existing school
S Former school
✚ Existing church
✝ Former church
▬ Commercial building
● Spring
～ Stream
▱ Park

N

1913–1951

16th Ave
Camosun Park
17th Ave
18th Ave
19th Ave
20th Ave
21st Ave
22nd Ave
24th Ave

1913–1923

Camosun Bog in 1930

Crown
Wallace
Highbury
Dunbar
Collingwood

Quadra Park

Former creek

Quesnel Dr

Puget Dr

DUNBAR

King Edward Ave

Valdez Park

HEIGHTS

Former dirt road

27th Ave

Chaldecott Park

29th Ave

Balaclava

UNIVERSITY ENDOWMENT LANDS

Musqueam "Tin Can" Creek

Camosun

West Memorial Park

33rd Ave

Balaclava Park

Carnarvon

Mackenzie

Clinton Stables

Frog pond

36th Ave
37th Ave
38th Ave
39th Ave
40th Ave

S

Highbury Tunnel

1913–1951

Blenheim

Balaclava

Cutthroat Creek

MUSQUEAM INDIAN RESERVE

1912–1947

41st Ave

✝

43rd Ave
44th Ave

Malkin Park

CHINESE MARKET GARDENS

Musqueam Park

Crown

Old Musqueam village Mali

✚

Wallace

47rd Ave
48th Ave

49th Ave

Southwest Marine Dr

Stelax^w

Former tidal lake

Blenheim

Lake-at-the-Head Creek

SOUTHLANDS

North Arm Fraser River

51st Ave

53rd Ave

North Arm Jetty (1915)

55th Ave

Iona Island in 1915

Balaclava

Carnarvon

57th Ave

Macdonald

Sturgeon Banks

Deering Island S

Shipyards

Celtic Island

"St Patrick's Cathedral"
✝

Sea Island

DUNBAR / SOUTHLANDS
c. 1877–1962

Scale 0   1km   2km   3km   4km

Introduction

The area of Vancouver now known as Dunbar has been home to the Musqueam First Nations people for over 3,000 years. *The Story of Dunbar* records the history of a period that is little more than one hundred years, a period when Dunbar became home to people from all over the world and all walks of life. This short period saw the transformation of a forest at the mouth of the Fraser River into a middle-class suburb of 21,000 people located at Vancouver's western edge. Here are the stories of people who fished the river, cleared the land, started farms, and worked and lived in Dunbar through a century wracked by two world wars, the Great Depression and continuing changes in the life of the community.

The Dunbar/Southlands neighbourhood lies on the southern half of the Point Grey peninsula from 16th Avenue to the north arm of the Fraser River, east to Mackenzie Street and west to Camosun Street. From the perspective of geologic time, this land as recently as 15,000 years ago was buried under a sheet of glacial ice. Boulders that had been driven by the ice and deposited when it melted can still be seen on the beaches of Point Grey. Similar large rocks had to be dealt with as settlers cleared the land, which is formed of glacial deposits compacted in layers impervious to water. These layers and the streams that ran over them provided a source of water for early settlers. They also provided a challenge in clearing the land and in constructing the huge sewage conduit, the Highbury Tunnel, in the early 1960s.

About 11,500 years ago, a bog formed on top of one of these compacted layers of glacial till. It became an area where the Musqueam

◄ Map 1: Dunbar/Southlands, c. 1877–1962. Map by Louise Phillips, based on extensive preliminary work by Ron Simpson

trapped elk, deer and birds, and later where children floated on home-made rafts and skated in winter. Point Grey was covered with a forest of ancient Douglas fir, cedar, hemlock and spruce intersected by Native trails that led from the Musqueam village to a seasonal camp at Locarno Beach.

In 1858, a brief gold rush in the Fraser Canyon left some disappoint-ed miners to look for other means of earning a living. The government of the mainland Colony of British Columbia enticed these newcomers with offers of inexpensive land to settle in the Fraser River delta. At the time, the colony's centre was New Westminster, then just a collection of wooden stores, sheds and tents. An 1860 law allowed settlers to "pre-empt" parcels of up to 160 acres if they would clear and farm the land.

The first such settlers on the north arm of the Fraser River were two prospectors from Ireland, brothers Samuel and Fitzgerald McCleery. Nearby, lots were snapped up and settled south of what was to become Dunbar by E. John Betts and Henry Mole. These farmers supplied dairy products, meat and vegetables to the mainland colony's sawmills and Point Grey residents until the 1920s.

The majority of the settlers were from the British Isles, living along-side the Musqueam, whose reserve was established in 1864. In 1877, Chinese farmers were brought in by the federal government to raise vege-tables on the fertile delta soil on land leased from the small First Nations band. In the 1890s a Japanese community was established on the river's edge at Deering and Celtic Islands after fishermen were encouraged to come from Tottori, Japan, to help harvest the huge Fraser salmon runs.

In 1885 the Canadian Pacific Railway announced that it would build its western terminal in "Granville," the future City of Vancouver. This decision unleashed a flood of development, although it would not reach Dunbar for several decades. The City of Vancouver was incorporated in 1886, but by 1892 the city's southern boundary still extended only to West 16th Avenue. The area south of that, extending eastward to Burnaby, was part of the municipality of South Vancouver. Both McCleery and Mole served on its council and were active in building roads on the south slope.

After 1900, the sprawling municipality began to differentiate into several distinct neighbourhoods. Labourers and artisans had moved onto small lots in the eastern area of South Vancouver and were unwilling to pass money bylaws for improvements, while the more affluent men of the future Point Grey wanted the area serviced and laid out for development. However, there were still on this western edge a large number of lower wage earners who could afford the new 33-foot lots in Point Grey, where many hand-built their own homes. A story was told of a Dunbar man employed at the downtown peninsula's Hastings Sawmill wheeling barrowloads of salvaged lumber all the way home to Dunbar to use in building his house.

In 1908, the new municipality of Point Grey, including Dunbar/ Southlands, was formed, which remained a separate municipality until 1929. Long-time Dunbar resident Bob Jones remembered going with his mother in the early 1920s to pay taxes at the Point Grey Municipal Hall, which stood at West 42nd Avenue at the present site of the Kerrisdale Community Centre. Development in the new municipality came in all shapes and sizes: a large farmhouse on 10 acres at 40th and Johnson Road (now Blenheim Street), fine houses built on stone foundations in Dunbar Heights, and log cabins built as early as 1910. This was the start of a building boom that was to last only two years.

Charles Trott Dunbar, a developer from the United States, lost his $50,000 investment in lots on the hill even after he had paid B.C. Electric $35,000 to run a shuttle between the 41st Avenue streetcar and the line to the north at 10th Avenue and Crown. Although Dunbar Heights is probably named for C.T. Dunbar, there is no evidence that Dunbar Street is named for him. Street names in the area commemorate European battles, including the battle in 1650 at Dunbar, Scotland. In 1909 the new municipality laid out its main thoroughfares half a mile apart, running north-south as well as east-west. That was also the year that the municipality of Point Grey issued its first tax notices and passed bylaws to borrow funds for local improvements and road building. Until then there were no municipal water supplies or services such as sewage, lighting or finished roads.

In 1922 Point Grey municipality enacted Canada's first zoning bylaw, restricting building to residences only, thanks to the advisory work of Frank Buck, a Point Grey resident and professor who did the initial landscape design for the University of British Columbia. In 1925 alderman Warner Loat, a resident of the area, extolled the advantages of Dunbar Heights as a residential district, writing in an article published in the *Point Grey Gazette*: "An earnest invitation is extended to the man or woman who appreciates the beautiful, to locate among us out here on the Dunbar Highlands, where the sun seems to shine a little brighter than anywhere else, where the folks seem a little bit more friendly toward the newcomer."

By 1925, when Helen MacDonald's family moved to Blenheim Street to be near the newly established university, more than 90 homes were available for sale. This may have been because of the entrepreneurial spirit of Jack Wood, who built the first real estate office in Dunbar at 29th Avenue. In 1926 the Point Grey Town Planning Commission was established with Frank Buck as chairman, further advancing Point Grey's vision of becoming a city "in which the best type of home could not only be built, but also adequately safeguarded from the encroachments of undesirable types of development." Point Grey was firmly a single-family district and Dunbar was still a part of Point Grey.

The Point Grey planners had done much groundwork by the time a consulting firm from Missouri was asked to draft for Vancouver what was to become known as the Bartholomew Plan. It was completed in 1928 and revised in 1929 to include the newly amalgamated districts South Vancouver and Point Grey. This plan, although never formally adopted by the City of Vancouver, influenced city planning for years to come, and many of its recommendations for parks and other amenities were realized. Numerous provisions in the bylaws of the Point Grey municipality were respected as well, including Point Grey's single-family zoning.

Citizen participation in town planning was one provision in the Point Grey bylaws that was not adopted by the City of Vancouver. The Bartholomew Plan was entirely professionally developed, whereas the Point Grey Zoning By-law No. 727 (1927) had explicitly acknowledged the right of citizens to have a say. In the coming decades there would frequently be tension between town planning as envisioned by qualified professionals, the desire of local citizens to have a greater role in shaping their neighbourhoods, and the continuing efforts of developers to increase the housing stock in the area. This gave rise to the formation of "ratepayers' associations," which rallied against unpopular development proposals, and also to a series of municipal plans shaping the futures of communities. Dunbar, fiercely defensive of its right to maintain its distinctive character, was one of the first Vancouver neighbourhoods chosen to develop a *Community Vision* document.

Beneath the tree-lined streets and comfortable single-family homes of Dunbar, the vestiges of logging and farming and the courses of underground streams are still present. They are featured each spring during the history walks and talks of the neighbourhood's month-long Salmonberry Days festival. Natural habitats are being painstakingly restored in Camosun Bog and on the north arm of the Fraser River, thanks to the efforts of environmentalists. Like the layers of glacial till that make up Dunbar's geology, Dunbar's character reflects the contributions of many different people over time. Alongside the original residents of the peninsula, these people have come, settled, and enjoyed the abundance that the land and the community have to offer, leaving traces that enrich the lives of those who come after them.

CHAPTER I

The First People

⁓ Peggy Schofield

The first people living in the area we know today as Dunbar/South-lands were the Musqueam. The Musqueam's main village was — and still is — located at the mouth of the north arm of the Fraser River. Carbon dating of basket fragments discovered by a team of researchers working under UBC anthropologists Charles Borden and David Archer in 1973 and 1974 showed that people had been living at this place for at least 3,000 years. The Musqueam define their unceded territory as the Fraser River Delta, Burrard Inlet, English Bay and the City of Vancouver. Many of their descendants still live on the Musqueam Indian Reserve No. 2, a reserve that represents only a small portion of the traditional territory.

Since the 1860s, the Musqueam have persistently and continuously protested for recognition of their aboriginal rights and title. Their comprehensive land claim submitted to the federal government in 1984 highlights that the Musqueam hold aboriginal title to their territorial lands. In addition, the Musqueam have launched many important legal actions that have confirmed and clarified aboriginal rights issues in British Columbia and Canada. More recently, in October 2004, the Musqueam argued successfully in the B.C. Court of Appeal that the provincial government arranged to sell the University Golf Course land to the University of British Columbia without consulting with the band. Today the Musqueam are negotiating these claims in the British Columbia treaty process.

▲ This 2,300-year-old antler pendant was found on the Musqueam reserve in 1973. It was named *xwanaimus*, or "Smiling Man," by Musqueam elder James Point when it was discovered. It is considered one of the finest artistic compositions of the Late Marpole period. Dimensions: 7.2 x 2.2 x 1.2 cm. Courtesy of Rose Point.

◄ Debra Sparrow and her grandfather and mentor Ed Sparrow. It was common for Musqueam elders to impart their knowledge of the world to the young members of the community. Courtesy of Debra Sparrow.

The name Musqueam is thought to mean "People of the River Grass." A story passed down from generation to generation explains that the people living by the river grass called *m-uh-th-kwi* flourished or declined from plague or war, just like the marsh grass that came and went. The Musqueam's long and complicated history cannot be covered in full in this chapter. However, in the interest of understanding their culture, it is touched on here as related by Musqueam Band members and people from Dunbar who have interacted with them. Information presented also comes from scholarly research and the Musqueam Web site, www.musqueam.bc.ca. A chronology in this chapter gives insight into the issues faced by the Musqueam Nation and its non-aboriginal neighbours.

Early Contact with the Newcomers

The first known white man to encounter the Musqueam on the Fraser River and record his experiences was Simon Fraser. In July 1808 the explorer had come down the Fraser (which he thought was the Columbia River) in search of a trade route to the Pacific. He reached a Native village near present-day New Westminster and intended to proceed downriver, but his canoes were in bad condition. He appealed to a local chief to borrow canoes, but the river Natives were reluctant to lend them.

Musqueam elder Delbert Guerin tells the story as it was passed down to him from the elder James Point: "Fraser pulled out his rum rations and was being very nice and gave them drinks of it, and . . . never having had alcohol before in their lives, it hit them like a ton of bricks. Naturally they slept in the next morning. Being used to it, Fraser got up with his crew and took the canoes of those people." However, aboriginal runners went in relays to each family settlement ahead of Fraser's party, travelling along what became known as the North Arm Trail, and warned the Musqueam about the theft of the canoes. At their village, the Musqueam turned back Fraser and his party. Because of this episode with the canoes, Fraser would have trouble with aboriginal communities when he retraced his journey up the river. James Point's grandfather said that Fraser returned the canoes; he never intended to keep them in the first place.

At the time of Fraser's visit, the Musqueam village consisted mainly of individual row houses arranged side by side in two house groups, with some larger rectangular plank dwellings, housing several families, behind them. The houses were next to each other lined up facing the water, looking very much like the 500-metre-long "fort" described by the explorer Fraser.

Today, there is some uncertainty regarding the population of the Musqueam in 1808, but it is generally understood that a smallpox epidemic had swept up from Mexico and greatly affected coastal Native

◄ Musqueam village area of Mali, c. 1927–28. The three posts formerly supported a platform from which potlatch hosts threw blankets and other gifts to their guests, until the custom of the potlatch was outlawed in 1884. UBC Museum of Anthropology photo. Courtesy of Rose Point.

communities, including these two village areas called Mali and Stelaxʷ. The area known as Stelaxʷ was built around a small bay located near present-day 51st Avenue and Wallace. Because it was inundated by flood-water that came with high tides and wind, it was eventually abandoned. In 1951–52 its cemetery contents were moved to the west, to the site of the present Musqueam cemetery, known as Mali.

When the mainland colony of British Columbia was established in 1858, the colonial government began to set aside small plots of land as Indian reserves at the same time as they surveyed land for European settlement. The person the Musqueam put forward to speak to colonial officials, according to Delbert Guerin, was called Tsumlan. The government surveyors assumed Tsumlan was a "chief." In traditional society, however, there were no hereditary chiefs; rather, respected people became important family leaders because of their behaviour, knowledge and status. Delbert Guerin explains: "In each house they basically looked at the issues that were on the table, so to speak, and they appointed the one they thought would be the most capable of representing the family. So these people were the chiefs." In the late 1800s, certain heads of household became spokespeople for the band because they could speak the trade language Chinook and communicate with the new white immigrants. Tsumlan was descended from a guide who had accompanied Simon Fraser and had learned some English.

Tsumlan kept his position until the 1890s, when Chief Johnny, Xwixwayluq, took his place and held the position of chief until 1914. Chief Johnny was replaced by Jack Stogan, known as Tsimlenuxw. These leaders were put in their positions by the men of the community, women having no say until the Indian Act was revised in 1951. The first band elections were held in 1952, and John Sparrow (son of Ed), Bill Guerin and Andrew Charles Jr. were elected as the band's new chief and council. They were the youngest band council in Canada, all being just twenty-one years of age.

Community Connections and Celebrations

According to the elders of the band, their culture is Coast Salish, a linguistic group that includes more than 50 bands living in a circle around the Strait of Georgia — from Campbell River south to southern Oregon, including those in Nanaimo, Cowichan, Sechelt, Burrard Inlet, Ladner, Tsawwassen, Lummi and east in Stó:lō ("People of the River") territory as far as Chilliwack. These communities shared the Halkomelem language, but the Musqueam also spoke Hulquminum, their own dialect. The ceremonial life of this circle of tribes is passed down through spirit and mask dancing in the longhouse. (For more on Musqueam spirituality, see chapter 10.)

Historically there was much interaction between family groups related by marriage or blood, as well as between the bands as a whole. Such networks were complex, and the benefits were many. There was the expectation of sharing of food and material goods, help with hosting potlatches or naming ceremonies and, more recently, money loans. From time to time, individuals would live with others from their extended family either in the same community or in more distant communities. For this reason, Musqueam houses can even today be filled to overflowing with long-term guests.

Among traditional Stó:lō people and Coast Salish bands, including the Musqueam, large gatherings were opportunities to mingle with people from beyond their immediate village and to exchange goods and certain hereditary privileges. Such gatherings included naming ceremonies, the celebration of the first salmon of the season, coming-of-age ceremonies, potlatches and canoe races. At memorials, revered tools and ownership of resource gathering sites were handed over to chosen descendants. Special personal items were burned when the owner died. These traditions are carried on into the twenty-first century with only slight variations, and include gift exchanges.

The Musqueam did not forgo potlatches following their prohibition by the federal government in 1884 or even after the prohibition's enforcement in 1921. Winnifred (Mole) Challenger, the daughter of John Mole who farmed on the river until the mid-1920s, attended one of these winter events on the reserve with her parents:

> We went in the evening. The Indians were gathered in a big longhouse. I remember it was very dark in there, and the smoke and sparks went

◄ This model of a longhouse was made by Dominic Point from the wood of one of the Seven Sisters, old-growth cedars in Stanley Park that fell during Typhoon Frieda in October 1962. The large rectangular structures featured a peaked roof with smoke holes. Some of the larger houses accommodated as many as four families. The population of the two areas in Musqueam, Mali and Stelax", was estimated by elders to have been about a thousand people. Photo by Joan Tyldesley.

up through a hole in the roof. Some men were beating drums, while others kept time by slapping their hands on boards. The dancers came out from a very dark corner and danced around the fire until they were exhausted. In another corner was a smaller fire with a huge black pot boiling on it. The Indian women were squatting around this, cutting up meat and vegetables and throwing them in the pot. . . . Often in the summer months, after we went to bed, we could hear them beating their drums and singing.

In 2000, elder and mask dancer Andrew Charles recalled that when he was a child in the 1930s and '40s, the people at Musqueam were very traditional: "The longhouse was a very important part of our existence. . . . Before prohibitive legislation, spirit dancing was a winter function. It had very strong religious connotations. The mask dancing [for the men] was usually celebrating the spring, summer and fall; it [was held] out-of-doors when there was good weather. And that's where potlatching happened, where a lot of gifts were given away."

Living Off the Land

Until trade began with the Hudson's Bay Company at Fort Langley in 1827, clothing worn by the Musqueam was woven of the inner bark of red cedar and dog hair. Andrew Charles explained: "We had dogs. Little white dogs. And we'd often use the 'woof' — the fine hair from those dogs. We wouldn't kill them, but we would pluck or cut [the hair]. And we also used mountain goat wool. . . . The fine wool would be on the bush and things, and they would gather it from there. The best time to

▲ Basket made by Dominic Point's grandmother around 1900. Artifacts held on the Musqueam reserve. Photo by Joan Tyldesley.

harvest the wool would be when it was shed, and that was what they used to make blankets."

Woven goods, including baskets and cradles, were decorated in a characteristic checkerboard pattern. Wooden spindle whorls featured carved motifs. Mats woven with cattails divided the large dwellings into family apartments. The Musqueam made costume accessories using feathers, bones, antlers, shells and also grey slate beads obtained in trade from the community living near what is now known as Marpole. By the mid-1800s, the people had adopted European clothing and blankets supplied by the Hudson's Bay Company at Fort Langley in exchange for salmon and pelts. The Salish weaving tradition was almost lost, but was revived in the 1960s by Stó:lō women at Sardis and in other Coast Salish communities (see also chapter 7).

Food and medicinal plants were found locally. Musqueam women gathered the plants and were responsible for monitoring the gathering sites. They delineated them by natural landmarks and kept them viable by periodic weeding and burning. Root crops were wrapped in skunk cabbage leaves and steamed in pits, then stored in mesh bags that were hung indoors.

In keeping with Coast Salish practice, the Musqueam did not share their harvest sites outside the extended family. Exceptions were salmon and clams, although eddies in the river could be claimed as hereditary. Huge aerial nets were used to snare birds in the intertidal zone, and game was snared or hunted by bow and arrow. In 1912, when Chief Johnny planned marriages for his daughters, he sent his men out into what became the University Endowment Lands area and was able to get enough game for the feasts. Some game was trapped or hunted beside a lake where Camosun Bog is now.

During salmon runs, fish camps peopled by other tribes would be set up, often on what is now Iona Island. Sturgeon were found in that area; clams, crabs, blue mussels and oysters were obtained all around the Point Grey shoreline. A network of trails led through the woods from Musqueam to a spring and summer camp located at what is now called Locarno Beach. There, starry flounder, herring and other varieties of fish and sea mammals could be caught. While archaeologists have found no evidence of a year-round camp, they have established that the site was used actively from as early as 2,500 to 3,000 years ago until at least 1,600 years ago. Harpoons and ornaments of wood, shell, bone and stone have been discovered there. The Halkomelem name for this camp was Ee'yullmough, or "good spring water."

The Musqueam were fearful of the tribes of the northern coast, and their situation at the mouth of the river was an especially vulnerable one. Andrew Charles said: "We had trails . . . all the way up the river. We had

runners who would deliver messages. We had two outlooks out here in Point Grey in case of invasion. We used to get invaded by the Kwakiutls and the Haida at times. So we would have lookouts . . . , or we'd travel over to English Bay. There would be marked trails leading that way — regular trails just like animal trails — well defined."

In the early 1800s raids were made on Musqueam to bolster the status of northern raiders' heads of households. During these often violent confrontations, slaves and material goods would be seized, whether for settling disputes, fulfilling obligations or supplying goods for the next potlatch. Journals written at Fort Langley in 1827 reported: "Several families of Misqueam passed [going] up. Shunton, their chief, has just arrived from the Yeukelta, where he went to try to recover his wife and daughter who were taken along with 30 more women and children in the last attack. He did not get them, as they were already sold to Indians further to the northward." As recently as the 1960s evidence of quick burial after tribal warfare was uncovered by Chinese tenant farmers. Linda Fong, the

▲ Stewart and Aaron Point, aged nine and eleven, with an eulachon dip net in the spring of 1974. The eulachon (also spelled oolichan) is a small smelt with a high (20 percent) fat content. The Musqueam smoked eulachon for eating, especially at potlatch ceremonies, and the oily fish was also used to produce valuable fat that was traded. The eulachon is the first fish to arrive at the river after the long winter and was traditionally welcomed as a sign of spring. However, like other local fisheries, the eulachon is in trouble today, with much-reduced runs compared to its historic numbers. Courtesy of Rose Point.

daughter of Eddie Chan, who arrived in the area in the 1950s, said, "Dad told me they uncovered hundreds of human bones when they ploughed the fields." Elder Rose (Pettis) Point said these bones, which were those of invading armies, were sent to UBC.

Farming in the Post-settlement Period

The Musqueam reserve was established in 1864 and then reduced in size to 314 acres in 1870 on the eve of B.C.'s entry into Confederation. When Indian Superintendent I.W. Powell tried to enlarge it to 1,400 acres in 1873, on the basis of 20 acres for each of the 70 families then at Musqueam, the provincial government refused to agree. In 1876 the Joint Indian Reserve Commission added some acreage on Sea Island to the Musqueam reserve, but the reserve has remained an insufficient size to support the Musqueam's population.

In 1877 a number of Chinese men from Guangdong Province were invited to Canada by the federal government and allowed to operate farms on the Musqueam reserve. This occupation of Musqueam land by tenant farmers was intended to demonstrate to the Natives that agriculture was the way to earn one's way in the world. The Department of Indian Affairs collected rent from the farmers, and that was given in turn to the Musqueam landowners. Some Musqueam families pastured cattle, but the agricultural experiment never did "take" at the village. Seasonal fishing was the main occupation of the people, and there was not enough land available to raise more than a few head of cattle. As well, some Musqueam families had horses, and their young men helped the Dunbar newcomers in the 1920s by working in logging operations and digging basements.

Leila (Yung) Chu, of Chinese descent, was born in 1916 on her father's farm at the most western edge of the reserve, near Wreck Beach. She remembered the Musqueam families and estimated that the Native population was about 250 in 1930:

> They were very nice, hard-working people. We got along quite well. The owner of the land was an Indian named Jack [Stogan]. He had four or five children. Every farm had a different owner, and some landlords lived at the back of the farmhouse, while the majority lived on the reserve. The rent was a source of income for them. They cut and sold wood to the farmers and did jobs on the farm. They traded us salmon for rice and vegetables, because they weren't allowed to sell the fish. Jack [Stogan] fished all year, grew potatoes, hunted duck and smoked salmon. They traded fish all the time. The Indians cut wood: one cord for two dollars. Our pig troughs were made of wood bought from the Indians. We were very poor, but the Indians were even poorer.

Pre-contact Resources

This list of local natural resources used and traded by the Musqueam is of necessity brief, but it gives an idea what they used before contact to carry on life from day to day. The list of medicinal plants, just a sample of the more important ones, was provided by Jerilynn Sparrow, director of the Healing Centre at Musqueam.

Food plants
Camas roots
Sword fern rhizomes
Swamp potato or *wapato*
Salmonberry shoots and berries
Black raspberries or blackcaps
Huckleberries, blueberries,
    blackberries
Salal berries, wild strawberries
Stinging nettles (spring), rose hips
Wild hazelnuts, acorns

Fish and game
Muskrat, elk, deer, bear
Waterfowl
Eulachon and sturgeon
Salmon: spring, coho, sockeye,
    chum, pink
Starry flounder and sea mammals
Clams, crabs, oysters and blue
    mussels
Herring, halibut
Seabirds, eagles, hawks (netted)
Seaweed with herring roe

Medicinal plants
Devil's club, the most useful plant, for diabetes,
    arthritis, infection, etc.
Oregon grape root (natural antibiotic)
Stinging nettles for asthma, arthritis
Huckleberry and salmonberry roots for
    chest and lungs
Hawthorn for heart, lungs, asthma
Plantago for sore throat, cuts, burns

Other raw materials
Red cedar for planks, canoes and paddles
Cedar bark and white dog hair for blankets
Cedar bark and cattails for baskets, mats,
    hats and capes
Cottonwood fluff for soft woven goods
Fireweed fluff for diapers
Fireweed stems, cedar twigs (withes), stinging nettle
    fibres for nets and rope
Tools of antler, ground stone, bone for awls
Obsidian, quartz arrowheads (trade item)
Thimbleberry leaves for toilet paper
Skunk cabbage for wrapping food during steaming
Vine maple for bows and arrows

The women baked bread and made their own food. They didn't leave the reserve very much and didn't go downtown often. If they were sick, they went to [the Native hospital at] Chilliwack. They also went out there in the summer to pick hops. Jack [Stogan] died when he was one hundred years old. They kept track of their age by making marks on a stick.

Chu mentioned that Mary Seymour, a Native woman, married a Chinese farmer whose name was Hong. To retain membership in the Musqueam Band, they took the Musqueam family name of Grant. However, at the time no one realized that Gordon Hong already had a wife in China. This complicated the subsequent applications of the descendants of that union many years later when they sought Musqueam acceptance and then Canadian citizenship. The large Grant farm property was near the northwestern edge of the present-day Shaughnessy Golf and Country Club.

Growing Up Musqueam, 1900–1950

Into the 1920s, the children of European and Canadian settlers reported that they had Musqueam children as their playmates — fishing alongside them in the little lakes at Camosun Bog, near St. Philip's Church and in what became Memorial West Park. Ken Jessiman said that when his family moved to 21st Avenue and Blenheim Street in 1921, they saw Natives scooping trout with lacrosse sticks from the stream running along Blenheim. However, after the Musqueam children started living at the residential schools in 1923, they seldom spent time in the rapidly developing community up the hill. The women of the reserve, however, visited frequently, especially during the Depression, to sell berries and baskets in exchange for food and clothing.

At the time the non-aboriginals settled in Dunbar/Southlands, a Native child's education bore little resemblance to the formal system that was familiar to the settlers. Wendy (Sparrow) Grant-John described it this way: "What happened to a large degree is that the whole community educated each child. The aunts and uncles and the extended family had a responsibility to ensure that the child was following the kind of path that had been chosen for him or her, and so there was communal guidance given. [Once] I was picking flowers when an old woman talked to me about what the flowers meant and how important it was to do what I was doing, which was to pick different flowers and identify them." Grant-John pointed out that because children were educated by members of their extended family, they received different perspectives from different people. For Howard Grant, who did not go to residential school,

The mural of swimming salmon at the entranceway to Southlands school was created by students under the direction of Debra Sparrow. It acknowledges both the Musqueam people whose land the school stands on and the disappearance of many streams in the nearby area. Courtesy of Joan Tyldesley. ▶

this meant that in the 1950s, in an age when there was no television, he learned from the elders' daily "table talk" when he returned home from the local public school.

The residential school system, which began in 1884, was enforced in collaboration with various religious groups. Aimed at speeding up the assimilation of aboriginals into white society, this educational system destroyed family life as the Musqueam knew it. Andrew Charles shared his experience of going to Coqualeetza near Chilliwack at the age of seven in the late 1930s. He came home only two months out of the year.

> We went by tram from Vancouver. It took two and a half hours to get to Chilliwack, and once we got off the tram we heard our names being called. So the lady who came to fetch us brought us to school, and my sister was immediately taken to the girls' side, and I was taken to the boys' side — up to the fourth floor into the primary dormitory. Once undressed and into school clothes, I went down to the basement, where I was absolutely frightened. The kids came up to me, you know, curious, and I wailed like a two-year-old. I remembered that from going to school. But once I acclimated to the system, then of course a lot of us tried to make the best of it.

By the time Native children were allowed into the public and private school system in the 1950s, a disconnection had occurred within the community. The elders on the reserve were often no longer serving as

Slahal, a gambling game with sticks and bones, being played at Musqueam in 1954. This game has been played since before contact by aboriginal people across North America. A carved bone figure is passed from hand to hand with the accompaniment of the drum. The game involves the accumulation of sticks, and appropriate gestures are made to make people guess left or right. Andrew Charles Sr. beating drum, Cagney Point and Stan Charles hold bones, Lyall Sparrow and Daniel Dan seated behind. Photo by Della (Charles) Kew. Courtesy of Pam Chambers. ▼

Musqueam Chronology from Contact

1772 First smallpox epidemic spreads from Mexico and kills two-thirds of aboriginal Stó:lō people in six weeks.

1792 Capt. George Vancouver sails into Burrard Inlet and names Point Grey Peninsula for Capt. George Grey, a friend.

1808 Simon Fraser and his men are turned back from Musqueam.

1827 Musqueam trade furs and fish for blankets, guns, buttons and other metal items at Fort Langley.

1850 Surveyors come from the government.

1860 First Catholic Mass in B.C. is held at Musqueam by Oblate Fathers forced northward by tribes in the Oregon Territory.

1862 Neighbouring flatland on the North Arm settled by the McCleery brothers.

1867 Dominion of Canada declared.

1870 Musqueam allotted 314 acres for the 70 families living on the reserve.

1871 Province of British Columbia joins the Dominion of Canada.

1873 Indian reserves are registered. Indians are not allowed to own land outside their reserves and cannot develop district lots.

1877 Chinese farmers are allowed to farm on Musqueam reserve land; they establish more than 13 farms.

1884 Anti-potlatch law is declared by the federal government.

1888 Legislation is passed to limit fishing by Musqueam and other First Nations people. Food fishing is allowed, but no trade or barter.

1897 Musqueam men and women are employed at the Celtic Cannery and McCleery farm. Native men work in the logging industry in Point Grey and fish for the cannery. Japanese are allowed to enter the salmon fishing industry.

1900 Musqueam population is 92 – down because of an influenza epidemic. Jack Stogan, Tsimlenuxw, is chosen as chief by the men of the community.

1914 Hell's Gate slide, in the Fraser Canyon, is caused by debris from railway construction. A ban on fishing is declared, because the Indian chiefs refuse to stop catching the fish trapped at the slide. According to some accounts, they were trying to move them to the other side of the slide so the fish could spawn.

1916 Allied Tribes of B.C. is formed to pursue legal cases on aboriginal rights.

1919 Natives are allowed commercial saltwater fishing licences.

1919–23 Complete fishing closure declared on the Fraser River because of the slide.

1921 London Privy Council decrees that aboriginal title is a pre-existing communal right that must be continued unless the contrary is established.

1923 Residential schools forced on Musqueam families. Principal locations are Coqualeetza at Chilliwack, St. Mary's in Mission, and the Alberni and Sechelt residential schools. They provide instruction through Grade 8.

1923 John L. George withdraws from Musqueam and establishes a longhouse in Burrard Band territory.

1925 The trade of salmon for vegetables to non-Natives is allowed.

1927 The federal government brings in legislation to prevent Native organizations from filing lawsuits. Lawyers caught helping aboriginals are disbarred.

1930 A second Musqueam village, Stelax̌ʷ, north of Mali, complete with cemetery, is documented.

1942 Tsimlenuxw dies, and James Point is elected chief by one vote.

1949 The provincial vote is given to aboriginal, Chinese and Japanese citizens.

1950s Musqueam children are allowed to enter public and private schools. First archaeological dig takes place in Musqueam.

1951 Parliament lifts bans on potlatches and the hiring of lawyers by Natives.

1952 John Sparrow becomes the first elected chief of Musqueam under the revised Indian Act.

1958 Shaughnessy golf club receives permission from the band to lease the land just west of Southwest Marine Drive on the strength of certain guarantees. These are altered unilaterally and kept from the band for 20 years.

1959 Gertrude Guerin of Musqueam becomes the first elected female chief of a First Nations band in Canada.

1960 Reserve aboriginals are permitted to vote in federal elections.

1961 Shaughnessy golf club establishes next to Block Brothers Realty residential leases on reserve land. Chinese farms in this area are closed.

1962 Highbury Tunnel for Vancouver sewerage is routed through the reserve to Iona Island in exchange for $1 in perpetuity and one connection for the Musqueam.

1964 Dominic Point makes a canoe from downed tree of the Seven Sisters in Stanley Park. Population of Musqueam is 294.

1965 Large lots next to Marine Drive are leased from the Musqueam Band.

1966 Old homes on the reserve begin to be replaced with the help of Central Mortgage and Housing and Indian Affairs. A preschool starts at Musqueam.

1968 Natives are allowed to access provincial health facilities.

1970 Local administration is transferred to the bands.

1976 Musqueam Declaration claims aboriginal title to much of the Lower Mainland.

1982 The Constitution Act (sec. 35.1) specifies that aboriginal people have a right to self-government: "The existing aboriginal and treaty rights of the aboriginal peoples of Canada are hereby recognized and affirmed."

1983 Musqueam weaving school is started by Wendy Sparrow. The old methods of weaving are followed, along with both original and traditional motifs.

1984 The Supreme Court of Canada rules that it was a breach of fiduciary duty for the owners of the Shaughnessy golf club to change the lease of Musqueam land without consultation with the band, which is awarded $10 million. In the Guerin case brought by the band under Chief Delbert Guerin (*Guerin v. the Queen* [1984] 2S.C.R. 335), the Supreme Court of Canada rules that the federal government must protect the interests of aboriginal people and also recognizes that these aboriginal rights were pre-existing.

1986 Bill C-31, a controversial amendment to the Indian Act, states that those reserve women who had married whites may return to the band as members, thereby increasing band membership.

1988 Musqueam are allowed to use Celtic shipyards for their own boat building and repair facility.

1989 The University Endowment Lands, claimed as Musqueam territory, is turned over to the Greater Vancouver Regional District by the provincial government under Premier Vander Zalm as a park and renamed Pacific Spirit Park.

1990 In the *Sparrow* decision (*Sparrow v. the Queen* [1990] 1S.C.R. 1075), the Supreme Court of Canada rules that section 35 of the Constitution Act of 1982 provides a strong measure of protection for aboriginal rights. Thus, the court overrules the 1980 decision against Ed Sparrow (who challenged the government by fishing with too large a net) and at the same time establishes aboriginal rights across Canada.

1992 Stó:lō are allowed to sell their allotted food catch. The last Chinese farmer leaves Musqueam.

1993 Musqueam Band begins work on treaty negotiations with federal and provincial governments.

1998 Musqueam Band challenges interpretation of "fair market value" for large lease properties near Southwest Marine Drive.

2000 Appeals and counter-appeals continue in the leasehold/current market value conflict.

2002 The last fluent speaker of the Musqueam dialect, Adeline Point, dies at age ninety-two.

2003 A new education centre opens at Musqueam, teaching the Hulquminum language to children again.

mentors. For this and other reasons, Wendy Grant-John observed that the parents of Musqueam children who attended Southlands, Kerrisdale and Immaculate Conception elementary schools were largely unable to become involved in the white community. She also recalled the humiliation of being told by a fellow student in Grade 1 at Southlands school that "Indians are not allowed in this way. You have to go in the other entrance." They did not really have to line up separately, according to Wendy, but it was the perception. "It was the feeling of the other people about who we were." These feelings and perceptions continued even to the period when her youngest son was attending high school.

In the early Coast Salish tradition, girls and boys sought a "spirit guide" through undertaking a solitary journey into the woods. This private search for spirituality was made public to others in the community through a spirit dance in the longhouse. Musqueam youths went through rigorous physical training in order to avoid being seen as lazy — a tradition carried on more recently in canoe racing and soccer.

As recently as the 1950s, Native girls, as counselled by the Catholic Church, were given a special experience at puberty. Rose Pettis from Seabird Island, who married Cagney Point from Musqueam, explained: "At puberty they taught you things about the reproductive cycles and the importance of being clean. They got girls to witness a birth at age eleven so that they'd know the significance of childbearing." Point said that in her experience she had to bathe the baby right after it was born.

Arranged marriages occurred between different families within the same community as well as among members of distant bands. The latter practice was especially common in the 1970s, when more boys than girls were living on the reserve. Common-law unions between members of different bands were sometimes preferred, because the woman retained her own band membership, and the union had to be recognized by the chief and council of the man's band. The Native marriage ceremony is much like a naming ceremony, involving an exchange of material goods.

The Catholic Church, which had a following on the reserve as early as the late 1800s, enforced a policy during the 1950s to ensure that teenagers did not marry too young. The Church decreed that young Native couples should not go out together without a chaperone until they turned eighteen, and that girls should not marry until they had had two years of employment experience.

Over time, the Musqueam youth began to spend some of their leisure time in the emerging commercial areas in Dunbar. Andrew Charles remembered the Cathay Café as a favourite hangout for Musqueam teens in South Dunbar: "Coming out of residential school as teenagers, [we went to] a restaurant on 41st and Dunbar called . . . well, we referred to it as Gus's. And we would quite often assemble there in the afternoon to

▲ Chris Guerin looks on while his twelve-year-old niece Janet casts on to handmade wooden knitting needles for a Cowichan sweater resembling the one he is wearing. It was made by Janet's mother, Amy (Mrs. Edward) Guerin. The photo appeared with a feature article written by Pam Chambers for the *Vancouver Sun* in 1954. The newspaper was sent to Sweden to a former logger from Vancouver, who asked to have a sweater like the one in the picture. A cheque was duly sent, and Amy Guerin, an expert spinner and knitter, quickly filled the order. Photo by Pam Chambers.

play the jukebox and have a snack or two. We were perhaps the best clients he had, because we were always there, you know, in the winter months." John Rome, who grew up on nearby Alma Street, remembered seeing Musqueam women nursing their babies at the bus stop at 41st and Dunbar in the late 1940s or early '50s. It was a wooden shed, open to the north, with benches on three sides that provided a place to sit, chat and be out in the wider community.

Addressing Challenges

In the 1950s, the Musqueam hoped to establish a new industry involving knitted Cowichan sweaters, but the planned outlet never materialized. By the 1980s, artists or their young family members sold wood carvings door to door in exchange for cash. These carvings exhibit influences of popular North Coast designs, and the materials came from local wood wholesalers.

As the neighbouring non-aboriginal population increased, there was no commensurate improvement in living conditions on the reserve. New measures in the 1950s designed to give the band material comforts were ineffectual. In 1968, only 73 percent of the homes in Musqueam had electricity, only 24 percent had running water, and only 19 percent had indoor plumbing. Liquor and drugs had contributed to many Musqueam members experiencing a continuing sense of detachment from both the Native and immigrant societies. In 2000 it was estimated that there was 70 percent unemployment on the reserve, and a new residential development in 1960 on Marine Drive did not seem to provide lasting benefits, in part because the band received so little for the land leases. Accidents were a leading cause of death in the community, reducing the number of mentors for a growing youth population. What did improve after 1930, however, was the availability of medical care. Before that time, diseases such as smallpox, measles, flu and tuberculosis were a serious problem. Andrew Charles was in a family of 13 children, of whom only five survived — the youngest ones born after 1930. Sadly, he recalled, "Our older siblings did not go to Indian residential school, because they all died when they were young."

When it became obvious that the transition from reserve life to that of the nearby elementary schools was difficult, mothers including Gertrude Guerin, her daughter-in-law Fran Guerin and Rose Point sought a special program for preschoolers through the First Citizens Fund, established by the provincial government under W.A.C. Bennett. Although they met some opposition from the band, former chief Delbert Guerin and his wife Fran worked hard to promote the preschool, inspired by the preschool their son was attending at the church at 39th and Dunbar.

They started in an abandoned home on the reserve, then moved to a new building designed by Southlands architect Barry Downs.

Classes were started in 1966 under Joyce Brown, a non-Native teacher, who carried on a successful program for several years. Later, Grace Mearns (Fran's sister), who had raised 12 children, was convinced by the Guerins to take over. To make this happen, she worked for her teaching certification. Delbert Guerin said the early childhood education provided by the preschool definitely had an impact. "Up till then our kids were dropping out of school in the early grades and were looking for jobs, because jobs were plentiful then, but they were all labour jobs. . . . After the preschool started you could see a change. Not as big as we'd like to have seen, but there was a change."

In 2004 the Musqueam developed a new education centre with programs that are making children aware of their own culture and language. Adults who had gone to residential school (which did not go beyond Grade 8) were now able to complete high-school credits. A graduation ceremony in 2004 celebrated the successful graduation from Grade 12 of 15 Musqueam students, as well as several others who had graduated from university with B.A. and M.A. degrees.

Since the 1940s, a growing number of Musqueam women and men have entered civic and Native politics. Ed Sparrow and his grandchildren, including Leona, Debra, Robyn, Wendy and Gail Sparrow, the late Gertrude Guerin, her son Delbert, Rose Point, Andrew Charles Jr. and his sister the late Della (Charles) Kew, and Mary Roberts at Southlands School have contributed much to education, cultural awareness and the arts in Musqueam. More recently Victor Guerin and Larry Grant have been teaching Hulquminum to children and adults.

From the time of the first settlement by the white men on the southern shore of Point Grey, the "People of the River Grass" have struggled to maintain their traditional lives, while at the same time gaining respect from the immigrants who live next door. The struggle continues as the Musqueam Band develops local programs to make the community stable and prosperous.

CHAPTER 2

Early Settlement and Industry

—⌐ Helen Spiegelman

The first European settlements in Dunbar/Southlands are part of the larger story of colonial history in North America. The riverfront farms established in Southlands, which were among the earliest European settlements in what was to become Vancouver, served as symbols of Britain's colonial hegemony over the area. Although Britain and the United States had settled their long dispute over possession of "Oregon Country" with a treaty in 1846, and Britain had established the Colony of Vancouver Island three years later, the unoccupied territory on the mainland was still unclaimed. In 1858 the Cariboo gold rush brought 25,000 American prospectors streaming across the 49th parallel, and Britain established a second colony on the mainland in the same year. (The two colonies would be united and become the Colony of British Columbia in 1866, and the united colony would become a province of Canada in 1871.)

The mainland colony's capital was established at New Westminster. One hundred and fifty Royal Engineers were sent out from Britain to survey the land and begin developing roads and bridges to serve the gold-fields of the Interior. American encroachment in the Lower Mainland, meanwhile, could be prevented by clear indications of private land owner-ship and agricultural development. Accordingly, in 1860 British subjects were offered an opportunity to "pre-empt" parcels of 160 acres along the

Fraser River for agricultural use. A notice in the *Victoria Colonist* enticed disappointed gold-seekers with the promise of riches from agriculture: "Digging no deeper than six inches from the surface the farmer may realize as handsome a return as the miner who delves in the creeks of the Cariboo."

A "Land Rush"

The original fee for pre-emption was about $2 per acre. This was reduced to $1 per acre as further inducement. The proviso was that there should be evidence of some improvement such as land clearing and construction of a house before the land could be sold or mortgaged. The Land Registry Office in New Westminster did a brisk business. Betty (McCleery) McQueen, who is a descendant of three of the earliest European settlers in Southlands, called it a "land rush": "It was like a gold rush. They would rush to register a piece [of land] whether they were going to develop it or not. To hold it, you had to move onto it within two years. A lot of people who got their name on [a piece of land] gave it up because they found another piece which suited their needs better."

Such a forfeiting of title was how McQueen's great-uncle Fitzgerald McCleery acquired his holding in Southlands, which became the first operating farm in what would become the city of Vancouver. Fitzgerald McCleery and his brother Samuel were Irishmen who had come to British Columbia to find their fortune in the goldfields. Their uncle Hugh McRoberts had pre-empted a piece of land in Southlands, identified as District Lot 315 (DL 315). In addition, McRoberts had used "government scrip" that he had earned by working on the Fraser Canyon Road to acquire another piece of land, a large portion of the present Sea Island, and had begun developing that land. (Sea Island was first locally known as "McRoberts Island.") Betty McQueen recounted: "So when . . . the McCleery boys came, their uncle said, 'I got that District Lot 315 right across the river from me. If you boys want it, you can have it.' "

On 26 September 1862, DL 315 was transferred to Fitzgerald McCleery. The following day, Fitzgerald's brother Samuel registered pre-emption of DL 316. The two riverfront lots extended from the present-day Carnarvon Street eastward to the eastern edge of today's Marine Drive golf course. In July 1941 a land location stake was recovered from beneath the roots of a large maple tree 135 feet south of Marine Drive. This rough, axe-hewn cedar stake marked the northern boundary of DL 315. It is now housed in the Vancouver Museum.

According to Betty McQueen, Hugh McRoberts had a contract to build a trail from the Musqueam village to New Westminster, and he hired the McCleery brothers to work on the trail, making it possible for

◄ Churning butter at the McCleery farm, c. 1898. The women are Greta McCleery (right), the second daughter of Fitzgerald McCleery, and her cousin Nannie, the second child of John B. McCleery. Courtesy of Betty McQueen.

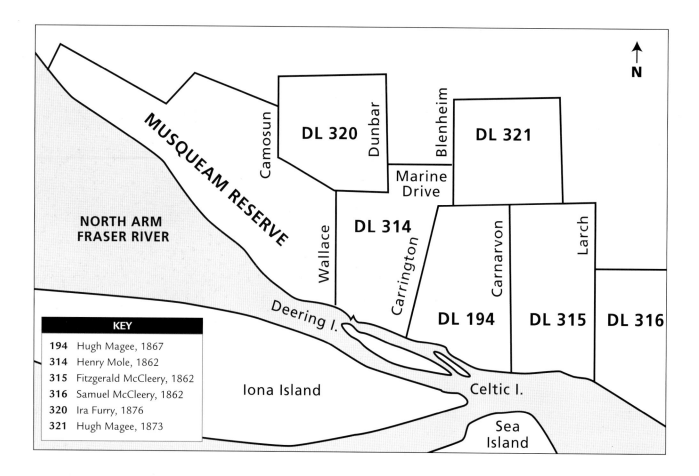

KEY
194 Hugh Magee, 1867
314 Henry Mole, 1862
315 Fitzgerald McCleery, 1862
316 Samuel McCleery, 1862
320 Ira Furry, 1876
321 Hugh Magee, 1873

▲ Map 2: District Lots on the North Arm, 1860s–1880s. Not to scale. This map shows property ownership in Dunbar/Southlands from 1870. The lot lines became the streets that are indicated. Map by Louise Phillips, based on a sketch by Beryl March.

them to begin development of their land right away. Fitzgerald McCleery kept a diary detailing his activities as the farms were developed. One of the first tasks was the construction of a small cabin on the riverbank at the southwest corner of DL 316. Fitzgerald's diary records on 1 April 1863: "Commenced to build the house today," and on 2 April 1863: "Finished the house today." Betty McQueen remarked: "Obviously it was a very small and simple structure. It was built of lumber floated down the river from nearby mills." The cabin was referred to later as St. Patrick's Cathedral because it served as the local church to a variety of parishioners. A larger McCleery farmhouse would be built somewhat back from the river later on, followed by a second house on higher land overlooking the river. (These houses are described in chapter 6.)

The second major landholder in Southlands was Henry Mole, Betty McQueen's maternal grandfather. Mole and his business partner E. John Betts registered a claim on DL 314 in 1862, when a Mr. Transfield gave up his pre-emption. Mole and Betts were living and working in New Westminster at the time. By 1864 they had earned some cash and were able to move onto DL 314 just before the pre-emption expiry date. That same year, Henry Mole pre-empted additional properties. The island on the north arm of the river known today as Deering Island used to be called "Mole Island." In 1882 Mole bought out John Betts's share in

▲ The McCleery farm as it appeared from the "bottom farmhouse" around 1900, looking south towards the river. The Welsh brothers' Celtic Cannery is in the distance. Courtesy of Harry Fitzgerald McCleery Logan, from a thesis submitted in 1947 to UBC.

DL 314. (Betts would later drown while travelling by boat on the Fraser River, as described in chapter 5.)

A third large riverfront farm was established in 1867 by Hugh Magee. Magee's farm was on District Lot 194, which lay between the McCleery farm and the Mole farm. Hugh Magee was a man remembered by some as a difficult neighbour, known as the "pig-headed Irishman," according to Kayce White, in Chuck Davis's *Greater Vancouver Book*, but he was nonetheless a successful farmer and became a large land-owner in the area. Elizabeth Bell-Irving, while researching the history of Crofton House School, which stands on land formerly held by Hugh Magee, found a write-up on Hugh Magee's farm in an agricultural publication from the 1860s: "Mr. Magee, late of [the Province of] Canada, has an excellent part-prairie-grass, part-woodland claim. He has several cows and expects to import more soon."

Henry Mole's farm, directly to the west of Magee's, was described by his granddaughter Winnifred Margaret (Mole) Challenger, who transcribed Mole's diaries: "The low land was nothing but a series of sloughs and ridges, at times covered with tidal water. The high land was timbered with cedar, fir and a stand of maple trees. There was a large creek down the east side of the property."

This spring-fed creek, Betty McQueen explained, was the source of fresh water for the farm and was obtained with special effort. It was intended that each district lot should be provided with a creek fed from a spring on higher land. As it happened, DL 194 (Magee's land) had two such streams, whereas DL 314 (Mole's land) had none. The property line of DL 314 was therefore adjusted at the northeast corner to encroach on DL 194, so that Mole's land could tap into a spring-fed creek. That creek still runs, mostly underground, from Camosun Bog to the Fraser River. It has been referred to by Terry Slack and others as Lake-at-the-Head Creek or Blenheim Creek.

Clearing, Building and Ploughing

The rich alluvial soil on the riverfront held great promise, but there was much work to be done before it would produce crops. The early settlers spent their time cutting trees and brush, chopping wood, splitting rails and sawing and splitting shakes. They also had to build shelters for themselves and their animals and covered storage for hay and grain. Also, because the farms were situated in the floodplain, high tides regularly flowed over the prairie grass. Therefore, extensive diking and ditching were among the first requirements for establishing agriculture in the area. Once the ditches and dikes were in place, the final piece of work was a "flood box," which helped to control the water level in the ditches as the tides changed. Betty McQueen marvelled at the settlers' achievement: "It was all done by shovels and men — and there weren't very many men!"

Once the dike system was in place, repairing damage by wildlife was a perennial chore. Beavers and muskrats were a constant problem for farmers, blocking drainage ditches and tunnelling through river dikes. As recently as 1900, an entry in Mole's diary recorded: "January tides [are] very high and pour over dikes between [Musqueam] reserve and the old farm. Flood gates in bad condition, muskrats making holes in the dike."

Expanding Production

The first crops recorded on Southlands farms were potatoes and hay. Wild grasses were probably the first hay crops; diaries provide a record of seeding timothy grass and clover. Oats was the most common grain grown at first, with barley and wheat harvested in later years. In 1867, Fitzgerald McCleery recorded that he was moving fruit trees from the river to the hill and that he had bought currant and grape sets; by 1880 he wrote in his diary about "the orchard."

The settlers had to acquire animals and transport them to the farms — by water, of course. Fitzgerald McCleery's diary describes a cattle-buying trip, bringing back cattle from Oregon in 1864. First there was a long and arduous cattle drive during which calves were born, animals were lost and animals died. At the town of Steilacoom near Olympia,

Harvesting grain on the McCleery farm. The machines cut the stalks, laid them straight, then bound them with twine into sheaves. After binding, the sheaves were "stooked," leaned together with the stem end down and the grain heads up to dry. McCleery's second farmhouse is just visible on the ridge. Courtesy of Betty McQueen. ▶

Washington, the cattle were loaded onto a schooner that sailed to Port Townsend, made a stopover, then finally anchored two days later at Garry Point (today a popular kite-flying site in Steveston). There, McCleery off-loaded the animals from the schooner to a scow for the last leg of the trip, around Sea Island to his farm on the North Arm. He recorded that this last leg of the trip began on a Saturday, 26 March, and it took until Tuesday, 5 April, with many further distressing events before most of the cattle were finally delivered safely to the farm.

The Southlands farms were essentially mixed farms, although a degree of specialization evolved. Betty McQueen noted that Henry Mole's land was covered with grass, lending itself at first to the raising of beef cattle. Mole applied in 1865 to buy DL 236 (Iona Island) to pasture his cattle because his farm in Southlands turned out to be too wet. The land was finally granted in 1877. Winnifred Challenger wrote: "He took his cattle back and forth on a scow using tides, wind and his own strength. Sometimes the tide was not high enough to unload them, so he had to anchor the scow and wait until the scow and the wharf were at the same level." Mole did his own butchering, probably in the river barn so that the meat could be loaded easily into the large Indian canoe that he used to deliver his produce. In later years Mole raised dairy cows. His diary records deliveries of butter to Vancouver city markets.

The McCleery and Magee farms eventually became primarily dairy farms. In the days before mandatory pasteurization, farmers with a few head of cattle could sell milk straight from the farm. Refrigeration was provided by a spring-fed stream that ran down from Kerrisdale. The milkhouse was built over the stream, with a cement trough where the milk cans were kept cool. Bottles were sterilized with steam generated by a boiler housed in a separate shed. The McCleery farm was retailing 60 gallons of milk per day by 1916. (That was the year Betty McQueen's

father began operating McCleery's farm. McQueen spent her early childhood playing in the farm's fields.)

The first draught animals on the farms were oxen. Mrs. Greta Mackie, Fitzgerald and Mary McCleery's second daughter, recalled that the oxen used for ploughing on their farm were named "Bright" and "Jerry." Oxen were gradually replaced by horses, and as farming activities expanded, machinery was acquired to augment the work of animals. Diaries report time spent repairing a crusher or a thresher. In a diary entry in 1879, Henry Mole noted the acquisition of a new mowing machine and binder, with the comment that the "oxen did not take to these and at first refused to move."

The Mole farm had the distinction of possessing a water wheel to run a grinder for grain. This had long been a cherished ambition of Henry Mole's son John, who took over operation of the farm in the early 1900s. In 1904 a wheelwright opportunely appeared at the farm looking for work and John's dream was realized. The itinerant wheelwright, Sam Mitchell, constructed a 16-foot-diameter wheel from timbers cut on the farm; a Pelton turbine, shafting and flanges were purchased from Vancouver Engineering Works. The wheel was fed with water flowing from a high wooden flume. Betty McQueen explained that the flume took water from Blenheim Creek on higher land near the present Marine Drive and carried it across to the top of the wheel, which was placed on lower ground. The water would pour from the flume into buckets on the wheel, generating enough power to run machinery to chop feed and perform other tasks.

▲ Threshing grain, probably oats, on the McCleery farm, c. 1919. Just at the edge of the frame to the left is the steam engine with its long belt that drove the threshing machine, seen blowing straw onto the large pile. Teams of horses are hitched to the hayracks, one rack almost empty by the straw pile and the other, already emptied, being pulled in the background. In the foreground, a full rack waits for its turn at the thresher. The old Buick has just brought tea from the farmhouse and some of the workers are taking a break. Courtesy of Betty McQueen.

▲ The remains of the Pelton water wheel from the Mole farm. Built in 1904, this wheel used the current of Blenheim Creek (also known as Lake-at-the-Head Creek) to power farm machinery. The wheel is gone, but the creek still runs underground at the spot where this wheel used to operate, just below the present Southwest Marine Drive at Blenheim Street. Courtesy of Betty McQueen.

McQueen said the water wheel was no longer in use by the time she was living on the farm between 1916 and 1926. The wooden flume was dismantled, but the old wheel remained in place after the farm had become the Point Grey golf course, according to Clare Cruise, who grew up in the area and is a long-time member of the Point Grey Golf and Country Club. Cruise said the grown-ups always warned the kids not to play around the old water wheel. McQueen agreed, saying that two people had lost their lives, one of them while operating the wheel.

Getting Produce to Market

There was a good local market for farm produce, but it had to be delivered by boat. In October 1867, Fitzgerald McCleery wrote that he travelled by boat around to Burrard Inlet to call at different sawmills, mentioning Jeremiah Rogers's mill located at Jericho and Jonathan Miller's on the military reserve at what is now Stanley Park. Similarly, Henry Mole would work with the tides and the wind, paddling or putting up sail to travel around Point Grey and make deliveries of meat to logging camps and sawmills in Vancouver and on the North Shore. Betty McQueen recalled one of Mole's stories about getting caught in a heavy fog coming around the inlet heading for home: "He couldn't see a thing, so he got out and walked along the shoreline, floating his canoe behind him. Every time I look down from the First Narrows Bridge, I think of that! It was a very difficult life. People today have no idea."

In the late 1880s Hugh Magee obtained permission to clear a new road so that he and Henry Mole could transport their milk into the city by wagon. That road was known as Magee Road until 1911, when it was renamed West 49th Avenue. When it was built, it was the only east-west road in the area and joined up with the old "North Arm Road," now called Granville Street.

The easiest way to deliver produce and receive goods from the colonial capital in New Westminster was by water, along the north arm of the Fraser River. McCleery's diary describes a trip to New Westminster with a scow that went up the river loaded with oats, wheat and carrots and then back down the river loaded with lumber. The farms along the river had "river barns" with boat landings and flags that signalled to the ferries to pick up passengers or goods.

The three original Southlands farms are all gone today. Hugh Magee's property was farmed only until he died in 1909. Magee's holdings included many other lots in addition to DL 194 where the farm was located, all of which were subdivided over time and developed for residential uses. Henry Mole's farm was acquired by the Point Grey Golf and Country Club in the 1920s and is the present site of the club's golf course. When Fitzgerald McCleery died in 1921 the farm passed to his son-in-law,

Harry Logan, becoming known as "Logan's Farm." The Logans' son Gerry later joined his parents in working the farm. The McCleery farm was thus both the first and the last operating farm within the City of Vancouver. In the late 1950s Fitzgerald McCleery's land (DL 315) became the McCleery public golf course. Fitzgerald's brother Samuel's land (DL 316) became the Marine Drive Golf Club.

Chinese Market Gardens

A different form of farming in Southlands began in the late 1870s when the Department of Indian Affairs began leasing small plots of arable Musqueam reserve land to Chinese immigrant farmers. Eleven parcels of land, ranging from one acre to five acres in size, were rented to Chinese tenant farmers in west Southlands. The original tenant farmers were all relatives, mainly unmarried men, who came from the war-ravaged and

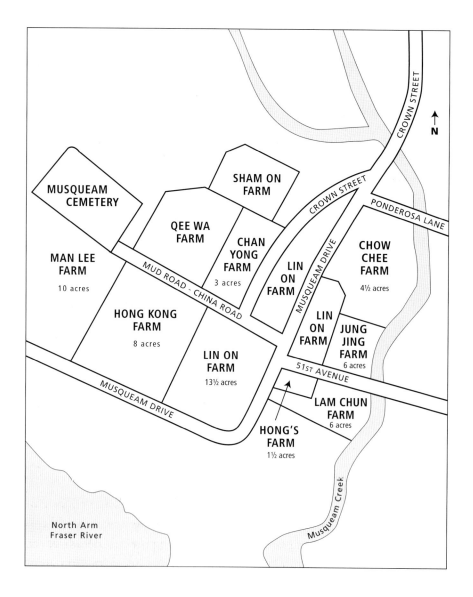

◄ Map 3: Chinese Market Gardens, 1954–67. Not to scale. Map by Louise Phillips, based on a sketch by Peggy Schofield.

Eddie (Senyow) Chan's rented farm on "China Lane" in Southlands. Chan belonged to several generations of Chinese immigrant farmers who leased land from the Musqueam and raised vegetables. Chan farmed this land until 1969. Courtesy of Rose Point. ▶

overcrowded Guangdong province in China. Leila Chu's father was one of the later immigrant farmers. She was born in 1916 and grew up on her father's rented farm near the present Shaughnessy golf course, living there until her marriage in 1935. She recalled: "We paid $30 a month for the whole farm. An Indian Agent came and collected the rent." She also recalled the hard work operating a small farm:

> My dad raised pigs, ducks and chickens. We sold eggs. Dad killed our own pigs. We had a deep well but in the summer there were only two or three feet of water in the well. There was a stream for vegetables and there was a pump to pump water to the vegetables. I also moved water on my shoulders to water the vegetables. My shoulders were covered in blisters. . . . We dug in the fields using a claw tool with five to seven fingers, digging and hoeing the ground. We had a horse plough to do the work, and a sleigh.

The Chinese farmers were able to harvest vegetables very early in the season. Chu recalled: "There was lots of sun in this location and no wind blew in. We were protected from the north wind." Chu's father sold produce to local grocers as well as to three big Chinese grocery stores downtown, earning cash to pay for staples. "There was a Red and White Store on Dunbar and 41st Avenue. We sold vegetables in Kerrisdale. Kerrisdale was very small back then and rich people lived there. We worked 10 to 14 hours a day and made no money because we had to pay for rent, food, rice and fertilizer. We bought 20-pound bags of rice shipped from China in straw-woven sacks. Dad bought 20 sacks per year."

Some of the Chinese tenant farmers maintained families in China and made the arduous journey back to visit them. Eddie (Senyow) Chan's father and uncle had immigrated to Canada during the first decade of the twentieth century, but Eddie was born in China's Guangdong province in 1936 and lived there until he reached the age of sixteen. Then Eddie Chan followed his father and uncle, arriving in Canada in 1952. He settled down to work on a farm plot rented by his uncle (his father's farm, he explained, had enough help at the time). As described in chapter 1, there was no electricity or sewage hookup on the Musqueam reserve in the early 1950s. The only running water was a single tap used for drinking only. The farmers pumped water from the river at high tide and ran it in ditches to irrigate their crops.

In 1957 Eddie Chan married in Hong Kong and brought his wife back with him to Canada. That year he leased a farm of his own. He described it as an "early farm," with southern exposure and shelter from tall cottonwood trees at the top of the bank. Because of these optimum conditions, he was able to sell all his crops before the other farms. He built two greenhouses, which ensured an even earlier start for the plants. He grew lettuce, bok choy and celery. When the four children were in elementary school, Chan moved his family to a house in East Vancouver. Eddie and his wife continued to travel to the farm and worked it until 1969. Musqueam elder Rose Point referred to the little Chinese farm community in Southlands as "China Lane."

In the 1950s Chinese growers were also renting truck farms in the easterly part of Southlands by then known as the Blenheim Flats (the Magee and McCleery properties). The Blenheim Flats area of Southlands also supported non-Chinese family farm plots raising livestock and vegetables. Sharon Slack, whose family lived there during the 1940s, recalled that Fitzgerald McCleery's grandson Gerry Logan (Harry Fitzgerald McCleery Logan) was working part of McCleery's farm, known then as "Logan's Farm." Slack remembered that her father used Logan's team of horses to plough their back property where they grew potatoes. She said that at various times her family raised chickens, geese and turkeys for their own use. She also recalled that some large greenhouses abandoned by the truck farmers were still there and that "asparagus kept sprouting in the fields long after the truck farmers had left."

Logging the Point Grey Peninsula

Farms helped establish a British presence in the new colony, but stable industries were also needed to support the economy. Coal deposits (at "Coal Harbour") did not prove out, but the forests on the peninsula of Point Grey provided huge returns. When the colony was proclaimed in 1858, Point Grey was forested with enormous Douglas fir, cedar and hemlock as well as trees of lesser economic importance. The only remnants of this original forest are a small stand of ancient trees at the tip of Point Grey near Booming Ground Creek. There was no shortage of markets

A growing shed at the Chan farm in Southlands, c. 1965. Eddie Chan's children Linda, Murray, Murphy and Manley are in the foreground. By the 1960s, Chan's family residence was in East Vancouver but he and his wife continued to operate the farm in Southlands. Courtesy of Rose Point. ▶

for the wood in these forests. The American Civil War had stopped the supply of Mississippi lumber to Britain. Lumber could be shipped to Valparaiso, Chile, which was being rebuilt after being flattened by the Spanish navy in 1866. There were additional sales to be made in Hawaii and in Shanghai.

These prospects brought a number of entrepreneurs to the area, including Capt. Edward Stamp, who obtained a timber lease in 1865 extending from the south shore of Burrard Inlet across the entire Point Grey peninsula to the north arm of the Fraser River. One condition of the 21-year lease was that a sawmill be built and maintained in steady and constant operation, ensuring that the land would be logged and not held idle. The first logging on Point Grey was selective, referred to by sawmill owners and loggers as "high-grading." The straight, tall Douglas firs growing in the area were admirably suited to meet the demand for masts and spars for the sailing ships of the day. Later, the demand for red cedar roof and siding shingles and cedar shakes resulted in logging contractors such as Daggett and Furry (mentioned below) cutting most of Dunbar/Southlands' first-growth forest.

The loggers lived in camps near where the timber was being felled. The cut logs were hauled on "skid roads," which were constructed of small logs ("skids") about 10 inches in diameter and 10 feet long, laid 2 feet apart along the trails and smeared with dogfish oil to make the logs slide more easily behind the teams of oxen. The man who oiled the skids, called the "dauber," would walk along the skid road with his

dogfish oil in a can. With a wave of his swab he would slap the oil on the skids, first one side and then the other, the oil splashing onto his clothes. The dauber had a cabin to himself at the camp; the other men would not bunk with him because of the stench of the oil. The amount of oil required for these operations was sufficient to warrant the construction of a fish "reduction" (rendering) plant on Burrard Inlet.

The northern slopes of Point Grey were logged first, because access to the water was easier. Towards the end of Stamp's timber lease, in the 1870s and 1880s, the southern slope of the Point Grey peninsula began to be aggressively exploited. Logging camps and skid roads were most active in Dunbar between 1865 and 1885. However, the Southlands floodplain presented a challenge, it being impossible to skid the logs across the long stretch of soft, waterlogged ground to the river. In 1880 Henry Furry and Charles Daggett were cutting Hastings Sawmill timber from a camp just above the Musqueam village. They made arrangements to dig ditches so that the logs could be floated across the flats to the river. One such ditch was dug across the Magee farm. Magee was paid $500 for the right-of-way through his farm. One of Magee's cows managed to get onto a log boom and kill herself, whereupon Magee sued Charles Daggett. Two of these floodable ditches are still visible, one on the west side of Point Grey golf course near the west end of Deering Island, and the other on the Musqueam reserve. After floating or skidding to the shore, the logs were dumped into the deep water in an operation known as a "log roll."

The Hastings Sawmill timber lease expired in 1891. After the best timber had been cut, considerable lower-grade timber remained on the

Crown land. This was cut for cordwood and for milling into lumber and shingles through separate timber sales. In 1912, the British Columbia Forestry Branch offered to sell timber at the eastern edge of the present Pacific Spirit Park south of West 16th Avenue, including Camosun Bog. A condition of the tenders was that all saleable timber was to be removed within two years in order to prepare the land for a planned residential subdivision. (That new subdivision, which was not completed, would have included all of today's parkland east of Blanca Street and south of West 16th Avenue down to the Musqueam reserve.) In 1913, Timber Sale X4 was sold to Young, Scott and Company. Permission was granted to build a temporary sawmill near where Clinton Stables was later established. The portable mill cut both lumber and shingles. It was apparently the largest and most mechanized operation in the Point Grey area. Nevertheless Young, Scott and Company ended in bankruptcy.

Between 1912 and 1923 there were about 30 timber sales in the area between West 16th Avenue and Marine Drive. Sawmills operated at the present intersections of West 41st Avenue and Arbutus Street and Blenheim and West King Edward. The timber permits were resold frequently. The public notice of Timber Sale X788 in November 1916 provides some insight why. "Reproduction" refers to second growth:

> 39 acres of logged and burned over land. Logged 20 years ago. Apparently burned six years ago. No reproduction of value. Can only be considered a cordwood proposition. . . . Green fir cordwood: 50 cords, shingle bolts: 25 cords. Fir cordwood is old growth, large trees with dead tops, and windfalls. Timber classed as dead fir is down timber badly burned and must be picked up from a large percentage of rotten material which would be unusable. Cedar bolts are windfalls, badly burned and small, apparently 50% of this is worm-eaten. Reproduction alder and brush with some clumps of good hemlock and fir second-growth.

It was obvious that by 1916 the Point Grey peninsula had been logged over to the point that cutting for sawmills was no longer economic. By then most of the timber processed in local sawmills was coming from forests farther away.

Stump Farms in Dunbar

Up the hill in Dunbar, the removal of valuable timber in the early twentieth century left the area covered with brush and stumps. Small farms began appearing as the logging operations wrapped up. The term "stump farm" aptly describes these properties. They were mostly small subsistence farms that could not be considered commercial farms in size or economic importance. Some of these small holdings were developed by loggers and sailors who elected to stay in the area. Some were doubtless squatters who were able to eke out a living by cutting stove wood and splitting shakes. Dr. Bert Brink remembered one such farm. It was owned by two bachelor brothers named McKenzie who had come to British Columbia from the Orkney Islands. One came to mine the placer fields in Cassiar and the other to fish. (The second brother later became fire chief for the municipality of Point Grey.) When the two brothers retired they cleared a few acres of land near 16th Avenue, planting a good-sized orchard and a garden that not only supplied their personal needs but allowed for some modest sales. Two of their fruit trees still survive on a lot on Camosun Street.

At Highbury Street and West 37th Avenue, a sizeable poultry farm was established by Charles E. Tryon. Several old-timers interviewed for this book mentioned the "Sies farm" located near 24th Avenue. As recently as 1938, residents in Dunbar complained to the city about a neighbour who kept 3 dogs, a bull, 20 cows, 50 pigs and hundreds of chickens. During the Depression the Vancouver Park Board approved livestock grazing and vegetable growing in undeveloped city parks.

The Booming Grounds

Log booms on the north arm of the Fraser River have been a familiar sight for more than a century. The Iona Island rock jetty extending west from Iona Island took four years to build (1915–19). The jetty provided shelter for storage of logs, and fresh water inside the jetty offered protection from the marine shipworm (teredo).

A little community of "boom men" — log salvagers, fishers and beachcombers — lived with their families in floathouses on the Iona Jetty. Terry Slack's grandfather and uncle settled in this Iona Jetty community in the 1930s, joined in 1948 by his family, eight members in all, who emigrated from the coal-mining town of Nottingham, England. Two years later, prompted by a water shortage on the Iona Jetty and a desire to be closer to schools, the little community moved across the North Arm and settled at the bottom of the cliffs of Point Grey. There, MacMillan Bloedel Ltd. held a "water lease" and used the area for scaling, sorting and booming logs before they were towed to sawmills. Some of the company crew also lived in floathouses at these booming grounds. In all, there were four floathouses and a MacMillan Bloedel office float.

After the move, the Slack family continued their own salvage and fishing activities. The little community drew its water from Booming Ground Creek and also accumulated water from springs in large oak barrels mounted halfway up the cliff. Milk was delivered by the local dairy to the top of the cliff at Marine Drive. The families kept fowl and

The Point Grey booming grounds covered in snow, c. 1950s, viewed from the Simon Fraser monument on Marine Drive. The Iona Island jetty, built over a period of four years from 1915 to 1919, is visible beyond the log booms. The jetty provides shelter and protection from the marine shipworm. In the 1930s, the Iona Island jetty was home to a small community of log salvagers, including Terry Slack's grandfather. The community later relocated to the riverfront near the booming grounds. Courtesy of Beryl March. ▶

had to cover the coops with netting to protect the birds from bald eagles. Today, eagles are recovering to their historic numbers since the 1969 ban on DDT. A 2004 survey of Booming Ground Creek indicated the return of salmon and trout to this historic stream.

Terry Slack said that the "river kids" in the early 1950s, with pike poles and peaveys in their hands, were accomplished at walking on the booms and catwalks. They were expected to "dog up" stray logs and they knew how to rack salmon nets. Slack said: "When I go down now and see our old winch lying on the beach I think to myself: 'Well, this is where we pulled our boats to shore.' You can see the little depression in the mud where our houseboat used to be."

Bob Jones was a log scaler employed at the booming grounds and living three miles away in Dunbar. Jones recalled that the family had only one car so he acquired a bicycle to ride to work along Marine Drive: "I remember I had a six-foot scale rule for measuring logs. I'd put that on my bike with my little bag. I could park at the top of one of those lookout places [on Marine Drive overlooking the booming grounds]."

After parking his bike, Jones would hike down Booming Ground Trail just west of the present-day Simon Fraser monument on Marine Drive. The trail led through the woods and down the cliff to the shore. Jones's company, R.E. Jones Log Scaling Ltd., was still in business in British Columbia in 2005, but the MacMillan booming ground had been abandoned during the 1960s when log sorting began to be carried out at the logging camps. Today the Fraser Estuary Management Program (an intergovernmental partnership) attempts to keep log boom moorage offshore to protect the sensitive marsh habitat at the shoreline. Maintaining the quality of an estuary area is vital for the survival of young salmon and other fish species migrating from fresh water to the sea.

A "Salmon Rush"

Long before the arrival of Europeans and other migrants, fishing was a mainstay of the Native peoples of British Columbia, including the Musqueam people in the villages at the mouth of the Fraser River. The abundance of salmon in the Fraser River is literally the stuff of legends. The following tall tale was told by Native people and then retold by Japanese Canadians in a written history about the fishery: "In the early days during peak season the river was [such] a mass of salmon that a tree placed among the salmon would stay upright and would be carried upstream without falling, and a dog running on the backs of the salmon was able to cross the river to the other side."

During the nineteenth century the Hudson's Bay Company (HBC) exercised a monopoly on salmon fishing in the Fraser River. The HBC exported salted salmon packed in barrels from Fort Langley to the Hawaiian Islands in the 1830s. But in 1858 the HBC's exclusive licence was revoked by the Crown. With the loss of that monopoly, the development of a modern salmon canning industry on the Fraser began in earnest. The "salmon rush" was on.

By the end of the 1870s ten canneries were operating on the Fraser River. But it was not until 1896 that Edward B. Welsh, Robert A. Welsh and William L. Tait purchased land from farmer Hugh Magee and built the first cannery on the north arm of the Fraser. The following year their cannery, known then as the Welsh Brothers Cannery, began operations on a riverfront site on Celtic Island located between the present Blenheim and Balaclava Streets. According to Betty McQueen, the cannery's name was changed to Celtic Cannery, and then the spelling changed from "Celtic" to "Keltic." But shortly thereafter there was a dreadful mishap when a crate of kerosene, marked with the letter "K," was shipped to England with a shipment of "Keltic Island" salmon marked with a similar "K." McQueen said the cannery was quickly renamed Celtic again.

Canneries were the hub of an industry that provided employment to a diverse local workforce that included Europeans, Musqueam, Chinese and Japanese. In the early days, Musqueam fishermen supplied the canneries with fish, using dugout canoes. Over time they faced competition from other groups of fishers, notably Japanese, who soon outnumbered the other salmon harvesting groups supplying Fraser River canneries with fish. Japanese fishermen faced official policies of exclusion, which were described as follows in a history of the Japanese immigrant experience written by Kaiji Endo and Bungo Kadonaga:

> Japanese fishermen tried to operate their own canneries but were un-
> able to get the necessary permits. Therefore they were in essence sub-

Flat-bottom North Arm gillnet skiffs in Celtic Slough, c. late 1800s. The view looking downriver shows Deering Island to the left and the Point Grey escarpment to the right. There was no decking under the net racks; the men had to walk along open beams to work on the nets. The closer buildings beyond the net racks are bunkhouses. Courtesy of City of Richmond Archives. ▶

contractors selling the salmon to the canneries. The people making the largest profits were the white people who operated the canneries, while the Japanese were actually common labourers merely fishing for salmon. . . . Income was governed by the market price of salmon at the time, and the practice was for the fish companies to remunerate the labourers in one lump sum at the end of employment.

The following detailed description of a typical Fraser River cannery building appeared in the same written account: "The canneries were simply built with half the building resting on pilings placed in the water and planks of the floor widely spaced. Workers would stand on platforms and remove the heads and entrails of the salmon and dump them through the openings into the water below. Canneries used steam power and free-flowing water as a method of operation."

With mechanization, the appetite of the Fraser River canneries outstripped the supply of fish. As long ago as the 1880s, declining runs of salmon prompted the federal government to limit the number of fishing licences. But when the restrictions were lifted in the 1890s a fishing "boom" occurred, with more canneries and salmon boats joining the industry. In 1902 the owner of the Celtic Cannery complained: "The fishing grounds extend for only about 25 miles up the River's mouth and in this distance 48 canning operations are in operation. The industry is in a deplorable condition."

In that same year the Fraser River canning industry consolidated, with 29 canneries merging their operations to form the British Columbia Packers Association. This resulted in closure of some of the salmon canneries, and their licences were handed over to larger canneries with mechanized operations that could process more fish. After 1905 the

Celtic Cannery was operated only every fourth year, following the cycle of huge runs of Stuart Lake sockeye.

In 1914 the fishery suffered a further setback owing to a massive rock slide on the Fraser River at Hell's Gate between the towns of Hope and Lytton. The slide, caused by blasting along a railway route, cut off the largest sockeye salmon run from their spawning grounds. The fishery did not recover. In 1917, B.C. Packers closed the Celtic Cannery, using it only as a buying station for its Imperial Plant at Steveston. There was a complete fishing closure on the Fraser from 1919 to 1923.

The collapse of the commercial fishery profoundly affected the Musqueam. In a letter dated 28 September 1938, Ed Sparrow wrote to the Indian Agent:

> I was over to New Westminster to get a permit to fish for my own use and was refused. . . . I heard they were going to give out permits to the Indians after the first week off close season [*sic*] so I went up and tried to do what's right and was refuse and denied on my own food [*sic*]. Not only would [I] like to get a fish to eat. There are a lot more Indians that would like to get a fish to eat. I don't see is fair [th]at all the upper Fraser Indians are fishing and getting plenty for their winter supplies and us Indians down in this commercial fishing District are denied the rights to fish for our winter supply. If this fishing is going to be close[d] much longer and [we] can't fish to eat it's going to be pretty hard on some of the Indians.

A half-century later, on 25 May 1984, Ronald Edward Sparrow put to test in court the Natives' aboriginal right to fish under the Canadian Constitution. The landmark *Sparrow* decision handed down by the Supreme Court of Canada on 3 May 1990 affirmed that aboriginal fishing rights are protected under section 35(1) of the Canadian Constitution and that provincial governments must provide compelling justification for any infringement of these rights.

Japanese Internment

After the Celtic Cannery shut down, some small-scale salting of salmon and boat building by the Japanese-Canadian fishing families continued. This group had been living in a small community of stilt houses along Celtic Slough starting in the late 1890s. Later, Japanese families built homes on Blenheim Flats on land purchased or leased from the pioneer farming families. But their lives were disrupted when their fishing boats were among the more than 1,200 Japanese-Canadian boats seized in British Columbia during the Second World War. Like other people of Japanese descent on the west coast of North America, they were forced from their community and interned in camps in B.C.'s interior, losing their homes and their livelihoods. The Japanese of Celtic Cannery and Blenheim Flats did not return to their community. A historic board-and-batten Japanese net storage and drying shed on Celtic Slough was the last building to stand as a reminder of the community. It burned on 20 July 1995, leaving surviving members of the little Japanese community with only their memories.

Boat Builders on the North Arm

In 1926–27, B.C. Packers built a shipyard on the site of the former Celtic Cannery on Celtic Island. This new shipyard had marine railways for hauling the boats out of the water, a machine shop and a warehouse for storage of equipment. It provided year-round repair and maintenance for B.C. Packers' fleet of boats and construction of new seine boats, including the *B.C.P. 41* and *B.C.P. 42*, which were launched in 1928. Boat building ceased during the Depression and did not resume until 1939, when the Celtic Shipyards constructed its first large vessel. The MV *NorthIsle* was 66 feet long and was considered to be one of the finest sea-going fishing vessels built in the area.

Celtic Shipyards was enlarged in 1940. It and other small shipyards were important during World War II, when the larger shipyards were fully engaged with war contracts. As many as 95 men were employed in the shipyard during the war, but working conditions were not always

A 1961 scene looking downriver on Celtic Slough, with Deering Island on the left and the B.C. Packers small commercial fishboat moorage to the right. In the centre are log net floats spread with nets. In the distance is the original bridge to Deering Island, built in 1928 to provide access to the Shell gas station, one of the first marine gas stations. Courtesy of Terry Slack. ▶

healthy. Rose Point remembered that many of the workers, including her husband, Cagney, had lung problems. She is convinced this was because they were "always spraying inside with lead-based paints." Terry Slack noted that copper-based paints used on the boat bottoms must also have been a health threat.

In the 1940s, the bridge entrance to Celtic Shipyards was the site of a violent clash between striking union members and strikebreakers, resulting in injuries to two men, the arrest of a union member and enduring bitterness.

In May 1950, a dramatic fire at Celtic Shipyards made front-page news in the *Vancouver Daily Province*. The fire touched off drums of gas and oil "with cannon-like explosions" and engulfed the entire area in "a solid sheet of flame." The old cannery building, then being used as a warehouse, was destroyed along with the valuable marine equipment stored inside. A seine boat moored at the site was also lost, and many other boats suffered damage.

One striking feature on the B.C. Packers site is a tall shed covering a marine way high enough to allow a boat to go under without stepping the mast. Terry Slack said that this west marine way building is built with flying buttresses to provide stability against the winds. Today the shed is privately owned, used by boys from St. George's School for pole-vaulting practice.

The eastern end of Deering Island was subleased to Shell Oil in 1929 so that Shell could provide a fuelling station for boats that used the local

◄ This covered marine railway, built about 1942 by B.C. Packers, still stands as a landmark on the north arm of the river. Constructed with flying buttresses, it is tall enough that a boat can enter without stepping the mast. Courtesy of Joan Tyldesley.

Seiners in Celtic Slough, looking upriver, c. 1950s. These boats were gearing up for the huge Adams River sockeye run that year, loading their nets at the new B.C. Packers seine net facility on Deering Island. Courtesy of Rose Point. ▶

shipyards. In 1934 the lease was extended for another five years and the facility was upgraded with the construction of a wharf. Terry Slack recalled that the popular gillnet fishing area on the North Arm down-stream from the Shell fuelling station was called the "gas station drift."

B.C. Packers built a net loft on Deering Island in the 1950s. This was the largest net facility on the B.C. coast and was popularly nicknamed "The Maple Leaf Gardens." The facility was upgraded in 1960 with a heavy wooden truck bridge from the south foot of Carrington Street and a large loading ramp to provide water access for seine boats on the south side of the island. Today, these industrial facilities are gone, replaced with spacious single-family homes and pleasure-boat moorages.

Terry Slack remembered that between 1962 and 1967 whaling ships used to be moored on the north arm of the Fraser during the off-season and serviced at Celtic Shipyards. The ships were part of operations off the coast of British Columbia by the Western Canada Whaling Company, which was owned jointly by B.C. Packers and a Japanese company.

Rum-Running in Southlands

The 18th Amendment to the U.S. Constitution gave rise to an informal Canadian export industry, rum-running, which flourished in B.C.'s coastal waters from 1921 to 1933, when the Prohibition Act was repealed. It is rumoured that some of the local fishing fleet in Southlands partic-ipated in rum-running activity. Terry Slack said that a local boat called

Shimoiget, which looked like a fish packer or small freight boat, may have acted as a mother ship in the rum-running operation. The mother ships would be stationed outside U.S. territorial waters loaded with cases of liquor. The liquor would be off-loaded from these mother ships onto smaller, faster rum boats (locally called "cigar boats"), which would transport the liquor to the shore.

Many of the cigar boats were outfitted with a famous World War 1-era engine called the Liberty Engine. These were 400-horsepower engines weighing more than 800 pounds, and they could usually outrun whatever was chasing them. Prohibition-era expert Douglas Hamilton described how the American military turned out, ironically, to become a supplier to the rum-running industry: "[The Liberty Engine was] designed by two American motorcar engineers in 1917 to power warplanes. The war ended before they could be put to use and thousands were sold after the war as surplus — for as little as $200 each. It was not uncommon to cram as many as four of these v-12 behemoths into a narrow speedboat, which could then reach speeds in excess of 40 knots. Some of these vessels were protected with steel plate to fend off U.S. coast guard machine guns and hijackers."

Penland's Boatyard

C.F. ("Fritz") Penland operated a small boatyard for B.C. Packers during the 1940s and 1950s on the dike at the south foot of Blenheim Street south of Celtic Avenue. Penland's fishing boat shipyard had two narrow-tracked marine railways that lifted boats onshore for winter storage. The old marine ways and shed timbers from this boatyard can still be seen from the waterfront walkway by the old willow tree just west of Blenheim Street.

The Penland yard became famous for adapting "Columbia River hulled" fishboat sterns, replacing the rounded stern with yellow cedar block-and-plank straight sterns. Penland's yard was equipped with a unique 30-foot wood-fired steam box that made the bending of oak ribs and cedar planking an easy job. Three local Blenheim Flats boat builders, the Hoey brothers, worked there. The winter work, carried out under the boat shed, required an early morning shot of whiskey as a starter, and then the three brothers would use brute force to ram the steamed boat planking into place. After about three months of such work, a fine gillnet boat would be born.

In addition to operating his boatyard, Mr. Penland reared European bullfrogs and a few sheep. The frogs were raised in a pond that used to exist between the slough and Celtic Avenue, the estuary of Lake-at-the-Head Creek. Penland sold frogs to markets in Chinatown.

▲ The B.C. Forest Service Fraser Marine Station, at the foot of Carnarvon Street, as it appeared in 1952. The facility built boats that were used for carrying out forest surveys in the days before helicopters or airplanes did this work. The long "river boats" on dry land to the right were able to navigate shallow creeks deep into forested land, while the smaller skiffs to their left patrolled the coastline. Note the two barges of granite and the protective pilings sheltering the moored boats and wharves from damage and river erosion. B.C. Archives, photograph #NA-13440.

B.C. Forest Service Marine Station

East of Penland's boatyard, the B.C. Forest Service built a marine station in 1941 on property purchased from farmer Gerry Logan. The new station replaced an older facility located in Thurston Bay on Sonora Island, which had become isolated from marine traffic. The big new station included a machine shop, carpenter's shop, three boat ways, and a pump and outboard motor shop upstairs. More buildings were added about 1950.

More than one hundred boats were built at the station for the Forest Service, and existing boats were rebuilt and refitted. Terry Slack worked there as a shipwright at a time when the Forest Service marine fleet was well known up and down the coast of British Columbia. The boats, he said, were built "way above the regulations." They were such quality boats, and so well maintained, that the work attracted shipwrights from many countries. The last boat built at the Forest Service marine station was a double-ender called the *Coast Ranger*, and its completion marked the end of a skilled trade on the North Arm. "We were the people who started from the keel and built the boat to the very top," said Slack. "It takes a certain person to build a boat. With the end of the wooden boats the practice of my trade came to an end."

The tiny dock on the west side of the Forest Service marine station was the home port tie-up for an unusual ship with a long and eventful life of service. The 29.9-metre *Syrene* was built at a shipyard on the River Thames in England in 1921 for a Greek billionaire. In 1933, the neglected ship was acquired by the British Columbia Coast Mission, repaired, renamed the *John Antle* after her captain, the Rev. John Antle. After a hair-raising two-ocean voyage from London by way of the Cape, the *John Antle* arrived in Victoria on 14 November 1933. The first task was to remove the ship's figurehead, an alluring nude in black and gold, which was donated to the Royal Vancouver Yacht Club. The teak and copper planked ship served as a mission ship for only three years. In 1942 it was purchased by the Forest Service and its name, once again the *Syrene*, was carved on the bow. The ship was not without marine accidents on the coast. One time the *Syrene's* bowsprit found its way through the wheelhouse window of a passing fishing boat, lifting up the fishing boat's cabin, to the surprise of its sleeping skipper. After the Forest Service station closed in 1988, the *Syrene* was sold to a private owner.

The Forest Service property was purchased by the Musqueam Band in 1988. The band operated it briefly as a commercial shipyard under the name Celtic Shipyards 88. In 2005 the property was approved for rezoning and subdivision into lots for 12 luxurious single-family residences, bringing another chapter of Southlands' industrial history to an end. However, the city and the Southlands community negotiated an agreement with the developer that would secure public access to the riverfront. When the property is redeveloped, there will be a public riverfront trail with signage, and the pioneer farming families, Chinese tenant farmers, Musqueam and Japanese fishermen, rum-runners, log scalers and wooden boat builders who are all part of Southlands' past will have their stories told.

CHAPTER 3

Forging a New Community

—∾ Pam Chambers, Peggy Schofield
and Helen Spiegelman

D unbar's short history is a compressed journey from rugged bachelor farmers breaking soil in a new colony to a busy modern city neighbourhood coping with densification and traffic jams. Through the years, the people who have lived this journey express over and over again their appreciation of a neighbourhood that has retained an old-fashioned sense of community. The connections between people, both locally and with loved ones far away, facing the challenges of daily life, are the strength of the neighbourhood and a secret to its enduring charm.

Life along the Riverfront

Betty McQueen, who descended from pioneer settlers in Southlands, reminded us that initially, except for the Musqueam, there was no "community." A handful of bachelor farmers settled the land, and in the early years they worked hard to establish farms on virgin soil. McQueen suggested that even the layout of these farms hinted at a closer connection to distant markets than to each other: "The farms fronted on the river and each farm had its own river barn and river dock. The little river boats serviced them and took the produce to New Westminster and into Granville because the mills were there." But it was not long before the bachelor farmers in Southlands began to marry and establish families, and only

then did a sense of community begin to grow. It was a community based on family ties and shared hard work. The farmhouse would be the heart of the community, and farm women the heart of the home. Farm life was strenuous for women as well as men. At threshing time, when farmers and their crews would help bring in each other's crops, the farm women were expected to provide the meals for the farm workers, on top of their other household chores.

Perhaps the defining moment for a sense of community to emerge in the non-Musqueam area of Southlands was when Mary Wood came alone to British Columbia from her family home in Ontario, following in the footsteps of a brother and a cousin. In 1873, she and Fitzgerald McCleery married and started life together in the "lower" farmhouse (described in chapter 6), which Fitzgerald had completed just in time for the wedding. In the next few years, two sons would die in infancy, and then two daughters were born, Theodora (Dora) in 1878 and Margareta (Greta) in 1880. Mary (Wood) McCleery was remembered as the model of a hard-working farm wife. Betty McQueen said that her great-aunt made everyone feel welcome at the family home. "The McCleery house was like a community centre. No fancy tea parties. Just biscuits always ready if someone (usually workmen) dropped by. Mary McCleery kept in close touch with the fishermen and the Musqueam families. She was the one who made soup for them and sent by horseback for a doctor when they were sick."

Along with offering warm hospitality to farm workers, fishers and Musqueam neighbours, Mary McCleery provided another kind of community support: temporary accommodation to family members in need. Fitzgerald's sister Esther, for instance, who was married to a man named McKee, gave birth to baby Maggie at the McCleery house before the couple went on to settle in Fort Langley. Fitzgerald's older brother John, who had stayed in Ireland when his brothers and sisters emigrated, found himself widowed at the age of sixty, with four young children. At Mary's insistence, John and the children — a boy and three girls — made the trip to the new land in 1890. They were invited to settle on a farm that Fitzgerald had acquired near Armstrong, an estate the family called Lansdowne.

In the early days, unmarried girls would often become the mainstay of families that lost their female heads of household. For example, Mary McCleery arranged for Fitzgerald's niece Maggie, by then eighteen, to move up to Lansdowne and look after the house and children for John. A few years later, when Maggie's mother died, Maggie was called back to her family home in Fort Langley to keep house for her father. As well, Lizzie, John and Fitzgerald McCleery's unmarried sister, came to keep house for Fitzgerald and his daughters Dora and Greta after Mary died in 1903.

◄ Three McCleery girls, Dora, Agnes Mary (Nannie) and Greta, are in costume, practising a play in the parlour of the big house, c. 1898. The girls did many chores on the farm, but mostly in the house or the dairy. They used their spare time to write and perform plays as well as to take photographs that they processed themselves. Courtesy of Betty McQueen.

When John McCleery and the children lost their housekeeping support at Lansdowne, Mary McCleery insisted that they come back down to the Southlands farm, which they did, and the community circle in Southlands was again enlarged. John and the children moved in with Fitzgerald and Mary, by now living at their new farmhouse up the hill. Their original farmhouse was temporarily leased to another farmer.

Fitzgerald's brother Samuel, who had pre-empted land in Southlands at the same time as Fitzgerald, also married and started a family, but Samuel died when the couple's only child, a daughter named Eva, was one year old. Eva's mother remarried, but the link to the McCleery family was strong, and Eva spent a lot of time with the growing number of girl cousins on the Fitzgerald McCleery farm. Eventually there were six, all confusingly referred to by outsiders as "Miss McCleery."

Another link in the growing Southlands community was forged when the McCleerys' neighbour Henry Mole married in 1881. His bride was Elizabeth Ann Paull, a widow with two children. Her late husband, a tugboat captain, had died of a heart attack the previous year. One year after their marriage, Henry and Elizabeth Ann had twins, Jack and Annie, bringing the household to six. Mole was a deeply religious man and also very musical. He spent his evenings and Sundays playing hymns on a concertina, a small accordion. One of his early diary entries mentions practising with "two ladies," one of whom was the Miss Mary Wood who would later wed Fitzgerald McCleery. Church services, a vital community

▲ Tea party at the McCleerys' for Mr. Charles Cridland, who had just delivered the new maple burl table he had made for Fitzgerald and Mary McCleery. The couple are seated in the chairs on the right, holding Ross, infant son of Tina Wood. In the photo are Emma Wood, with the guitar, a niece of Mary (Wood) McCleery; Theodora McCleery, who inherited Sam's eastern farm at Angus lands and later married Harry Logan; John B. McCleery, widower brother of Sam and Fitzgerald and grandfather of Betty McQueen; Tina Wood, niece-in-law of Mary; Fitzgerald's daughter Margareta (Greta), who later managed the farm; Jennie McCleery, youngest daughter of John; and Aunt Lizzie, eldest daughter of John. Courtesy of Betty McQueen.

link for the pioneers, were held in the settlers' homes or in the Wesleyan Methodist church at Eburne, the present-day Marpole. Mole used to make the trip upriver by boat, so he would need an incoming tide to make it easier. His diary records that on 11 February 1872, in a "slight frost with heavy wind from the northwest and a high tide," he arrived at church and made preparations for holding service. "We waited there until noon, but no one came," the diary recorded.

Community life in Southlands was altered when Henry Mole leased out his farm in 1889 and moved his family downtown for a period of time. Elizabeth Ann had serious health problems, and Henry moved from his beloved farm to be near medical care for his wife and also to obtain proper schooling for the children. The family's household goods were transported in a scow that Mole navigated around Point Grey and into English Bay. The area near St. Paul's Hospital where their new house was built is today known as Mole Hill. Here the family would benefit from a much more developed community, with closer neighbours and easier access to services.

Henry, however, had remarkable energy and maintained close ties with the Southlands community even while enjoying cultural and recreational activities in his new surroundings. He continued an active role in the operation of the riverfront farm. His diary recorded an occasion when he walked for more than four hours from downtown to the farm. He was also an attentive father to his growing children. His diary for 1890 records:

19 July: I have bought some cotton to make a boat sail, and cut it out and begun to sew it.
20 July: I worked on the sail and finished the sewing today.
21 July: I was working on a mast for the boat today.
22 July: I was fixing at the sail and mast most of the day.
23 July: John [his son] and I went on English Bay for a sail in the afternoon.

McCleery girls on a river picnic, c. 1898, with friends who worked in the nearby cannery. The skiff had a homemade canvas sail. Girls left to right: Emma Wood, niece of Mrs. Fitzgerald McCleery; Agnes Mary McCleery, daughter of John McCleery; Theodora McCleery, daughter of Fitzgerald McCleery; and Elizabeth McCleery, daughter of John McCleery. Courtesy of Betty McQueen. ▶

◄ The Mole family on the front porch of the family cottage in the 1880s. Left to right: John (Jack) Mole, Henry's son and Annie Mole's twin; their friend George Hooper; "Donzie" Teague, a cousin from Cornwall; Henry Mole; Annie Mole; and Mary Louise Paull, Henry Mole's step-daughter, who was elected to be the family housekeeper after her mother died. Courtesy of Betty McQueen.

Mole also found time to bake the bread for his family and to maintain his active interest in music. He purchased a piano (see chapter 7) and escorted his wife Elizabeth Ann to concerts. However, Elizabeth Ann's health continued to decline. After removal of an eye, she still required further treatment, and Henry travelled with her by train to Toronto for expert help. Several weeks after their return from Toronto, Henry recorded in his diary simply: "August 11, 1893: My dear E.A. passed peacefully away this evening at 10:15 p.m." Henry decided to return to the farm in Southlands, moving back to the cottage in 1898. He had a large house built for his family in front of the old cottage in 1902 (see chapter 6) and held a big housewarming.

By this time, there were quite a number of young people living in Southlands. They kept themselves busy with farm chores, but also with picnics and with plays that they wrote and performed in the billiard room of the McCleery farmhouse. The riverfront farm families celebrated Christmas royally. Henry Mole's granddaughter Winnifred (Mole) Challenger wrote about one such event:

> We would gather around the big dining room table for our Christmas dinner. If there were too many for the table, someone had to eat off the sewing machine. Every meal finished with not only plum pudding and mince pie, but saffron cake — something Elizabeth Ann had introduced to the family. It was a Cornish recipe. After our meal, we got ready for Santa Claus. Uncle Norman always played Santa Claus. . . .

Mrs. Henry Mole feeding lambs. Courtesy of Betty McQueen.

We would all gather at the dining room window to watch for his coming. Even when I got to be bigger and wasn't too sure about the Santa bit, it was very exciting.

In such holiday gatherings, the lives of the Moles and the McCleerys became closely entwined. Henry Mole's daughter Annie married John McCleery's son Samuel in 1907. The couple would have two children, a boy, Kenneth, and a girl, Jean Elizabeth ("Betty") McCleery. Because of her lifelong interest in history, in 2006 Betty (McCleery) McQueen was a living link to the early history of both families. McQueen's family heirlooms include Henry Mole's farm diary and many early photographs. The photos were taken by Emma Wood, a niece of Mary, and by Henry Mole's step-daughter Polly with a camera she received as a gift from Henry.

Relations with the Musqueam

In the early years, the interactions between the farm families and the nearby Native community were close and cordial. Betty McQueen said that Henry Mole learned how to speak the Musqueam language, and he employed Musqueam men on the farm. Mary McCleery employed Musqueam women in her house, where they helped do the laundry for the large extended family. The farm families frequently went to Musqueam gatherings to watch the dancing. "Of course, I don't remember," Betty McQueen said, "but my parents apparently took me to a gathering on the reserve. It was a very friendly gathering — they loved having neighbours over. I heard somebody say once that they [the farmers and the Musqueam] didn't get along, but they did get along."

McQueen recounted a family story about an incident in which Henry Mole's detailed farm diary prevented an injustice. The incident both illustrated and cemented the good relations that existed between Mole and his Native neighbours. McQueen related: "Well, time went by and one Indian was accused of murdering somebody, so he came to Henry and said, 'I didn't murder her because I wasn't there. I worked for you that day. Can you tell them that?' And Henry said, 'Yes, I can.' He turned out his diary, and there it was. He [Mole] was a part of their lives."

Life for Chinese Farmers on the Reserve

From the 1870s on, the federal government invited Chinese farmers, initially all bachelors, to farm rented land on the small Musqueam reserve (see also chapter 2). By the 1920s there were still many Chinese bachelors and only three families farming on the reserve. Leila (Yung) Chu's family was one of them. Chu said that her father built their house in

◀ Wai Yiu and Eddie Chan play mah jongg, a favourite family game, with some of their grandchildren in 2004. Courtesy of Linda (Chan) Fong.

1920 for $100. It was heated by wood brought from the beach and cut with handsaws. The children slept upstairs on the floor on bamboo rattan mats. A highlight of the children's lives was the trip to Chinatown. "Every two or three years, we would go downtown and stay for a week. We would go to see the Chinese opera in Shanghai Alley for 25 cents. It was 12 hours long . . . we almost fell asleep. We stayed at Dad's relatives, truck gardener neighbours back then. There were three big stores in Chinatown and we sold our vegetables to the Chinese grocery stores." Leila Chu stayed at the farm until her marriage in 1935, when she moved to Mount Pleasant.

Senyow "Eddie" Chan, whose farm is described in chapter 2, arrived in 1952 as a sixteen-year-old with his mother to join his father. Later Eddie went back to Hong Kong to find a wife. He brought Wai Yiu to live on the farm in the same household as her parents-in-law. According to their daughter Linda (Chan) Fong, Wai Yiu found it very difficult at first being so far from her own family. In those days of early airplane travel, the trip from China took 30 hours, a long time but much shorter than the earlier trips by ship. Fong remembers from her childhood the bumpy dirt roads on the farm as well as the large wooden sheds and the glass greenhouses. Life on the farm was secluded and the work was hard, but there was also lots of fun for a child living there. Fong said that visiting the home of Linda Schofield, her friend from Southlands school, gave her "a glimpse into the other world." Eddie Chan's family left Musqueam in the 1960s, farming for eight more years in Richmond. Then Chan studied for and received his real estate licence. In 2005

Linda said that most of the Chans were back in Vancouver, living in or near Dunbar, and that her children were going to school with the children of her childhood playmates from Musqueam. For the Chan family, as for many others in Dunbar/Southlands, this community exerts a strong pull that transcends generations.

The Japanese Fisher Families

Many emigrants from the Tottori region of Japan came to the mouth of the Fraser River to fish and work in the salmon canneries. By 1905, twenty-five families had settled on what they called "Middle Island" (today's Celtic Island) on the north arm of the Fraser. The late Victor Daykin was a local fisherman who had a long relationship with these families. Daykin recorded his observations of the Japanese community on Middle Island in the 1930s and early '40s, before their internment in World War II. He observed that "all the families could get by in English, although they spoke Japanese together. All were fishermen except a man by the name of Kano, who worked in downtown Vancouver. There was also a farmer by the name of Sasaki on Balaclava Street."

The strongly organized Japanese community established their own school on Celtic Cannery property on Middle Island. According to Daykin, the Japanese children walked to Kerrisdale school. He said they were very bright and always well above average in their school marks. After walking home to the river from Kerrisdale school, the children attended Japanese school in their community (see chapter 9). Daykin remembered that one Caucasian boy named Evans was attending the Japanese school just before the Japanese were forcibly removed from their homes on the coast.

The houses in this little Japanese community were rectangular cabins at the edge of the riverbank. They were built on pilings, and the tides brought the waters up to just under the floors. The outsides were finished in cedar siding laid vertically board and batten style. As the houses were heated by wood stoves, the ones located near the cannery and shipyard had fire buckets on the roof. They were not equipped with bathtubs but, in the Japanese custom, there were communal bath-houses, one for men and one for women.

Sharon Slack's family lived in one of these homes when Sharon was a young child in the late 1940s after the Japanese had been interned. She remembered that their house was quite cozy. The front with its main windows faced south and the north side was protected by a work shed used by her father, who was a pipefitter at the shipyard. There was a net loft upstairs. She remembers being cold only during one exceptional winter, when their wooden sink was full to overflowing with ice. It was

◄ The Mount family inspecting their partly framed house at 3379 West 22nd Avenue, c. 1912. Dora Mount was born in the house in 1913, the first white girl to be born in Dunbar. Courtesy of the Mount family.

served by an exposed pipe that her mother had left slightly running over-night in the hope that it would not freeze.

The little riverfront community was dispersed when all Japanese, whether Canadian citizens or not, were evicted from the coast after the bombing of Pearl Harbor on 7 December 1941. The upheaval for the families was entirely and totally devastating. Even for the children's friends at school it was a puzzling time. Eva Redmond recalled, "One day they just disappeared. . . . We were very good friends and all of a sudden she was gone. In those days you didn't question too much. . . . I could not see how they were a danger. I think that's a very bad time in our country's history."

Settlement of "the Sticks"

Long after the close-knit bonds of community based on family ties and ethnic traditions had been forged in Southlands, the recently logged-off suburb of Dunbar Heights still comprised mostly empty building lots. The pace of settlement there was governed by economic booms and busts;

during the booms building lots sold "like hotcakes," but during the busts construction would grind to a halt. In this boom-and-bust pattern, property changed hands frequently. Harold Johnson, the occupant of a house at 3256 West 27th Avenue in 1915, moved seven times in eleven years in Dunbar, having already lived in various locations in the Kitsilano area.

The earliest families to settle in Dunbar Heights experienced a very different neighbourhood from the one we see today. Their houses typically stood in isolation, surrounded by logged-off forest, and there was still much of the rugged self-sufficiency that characterized the earliest settlers on the river. The Mounts built a "shack" at 3379 West 22nd Avenue in 1912, after they cleared the land of discarded logs, stumps, rocks and debris left over from logging (see more photos chapter 6). In a letter written thirty-seven years later, Mr. and Mrs. Mount described their early life: "At that time it was all bush, no road, no light, no water, nothing but logs to climb over to get to the place. We had to walk to 16th and Johnson Road [the present Blenheim Street] to get water from a spring." The Mounts would not have close neighbours on the block for many years to come. Their baby Dora, born in June 1913 in the family shack, was the first white girl to be born in Dunbar.

In spite of the isolation and the lack of civic amenities, a sense of community began to grow, often because of connections among children. On Christmas Day 1913 the first white boy was born in Dunbar Heights, at a home at 33rd and Crown Street. That child, Robert Montador, later told

Mark Mount aged about six swinging on the gate at 3379 West 22nd Avenue. This "shack" was gradually modernized while the family lived there until 1929. It was demolished in December 1987. Courtesy of the Mount family. ▶

Tent Living in a Pioneer Municipality

In 1914, some families were still living in tents like those used during the gold rush. Rose Ellen Mitchell, who emigrated with her husband from Scotland, is shown standing in front of her tent home in 1918. There was hardship living in the damp, cold tent, with thick fog a constant reminder of the wood fires being used to cook and keep warm. Note the pipe to collect roof water runoff in the barrel. Carole Rochford, Mrs. Mitchell's daughter, said that her mother always thought her terrible arthritis came from living in that tent. Like many of the early settlers, Mitchell was something of an entrepreneur, buying an extra lot at 29th and Dunbar (where McDermott's Body Shop is now) as an investment. Photo courtesy of Carole Rochford.

his children that he had Musqueam children as his playmates, fishing with them in a stream near the present St. Philip's Anglican Church. Following his father's example, Robert Montador eventually worked in construction, building homes and shops for Jack Wood, the most prominent real estate developer in Dunbar. He later became a building inspector for the Vancouver engineering department.

One thing that ties communities together is stories. Mer Montador, Robert's daughter, shared a story from her grandparents from their early days. The family was preparing to put a modest meal on the table for Christmas when their chow dog appeared with a fully cooked ham in his mouth. The dog had been trained to carry their parcels of meat home from the butcher without tearing into them (see chapter 5). Not knowing whose the ham was, they decided to serve the meat for dinner. They could not ordinarily afford such fare.

Slowly residential development filled in the empty lots in Dunbar. Fred Crowhurst's family moved into a house at 4067 West 32nd Avenue in 1918, where for the next four decades they said they "watched the influx of new neighbours hem [them] in." In an early undated newspaper clipping Crowhurst described life in "a real rural community," so much so that in the early 1920s everyone chipped in to help build the community hall next door to Slim Williams' gas station on Dunbar near 29th Avenue.

Some of the early houses built in Dunbar were built with timbers logged and milled right in the neighbourhood. For example, just at the edge of Mackenzie Heights, the house at 2875 West 29th Avenue was built in 1910 from lumber that was logged in what is now Balaclava Park and milled at a sawmill on the southwest corner of 33rd Avenue and Mackenzie Street. Kathleen Richardson, who lived in the house from 1950 to 2000, said that for many years there was still a large pile of sawdust on the corner property where the mill had stood. Today that lot is the site of the Mackenzie Heights service station.

The year the Richardsons' house on West 29th was built, businessman Ollan Bugg bought six lots on the south side of the same block. The Craftsman-style house he built at 2886 West 29th Avenue, complete with a cutstone granite foundation and granite sills on the lower windows, cost $11,000. The foundation was excavated using horses belonging to the Ledingham construction company. Ledingham's employees were on strike at the time, so Bugg put it to Ledingham that he would keep the horses exercised for him, and thereby got their services for a very good price.

World War 1, 1914–1918

As the decades passed, world events would affect life in Dunbar and play a role, for better and for worse, in the community. When World War 1 broke out in Europe, for instance, Dunbar residents loyal to their British motherland did not hesitate to "join up" to defend their distant homeland. But on the darker side, closer to home, neighbours who were deemed to be "enemy aliens" bore the brunt of patriotic hostility.

The sinking of the *Lusitania* in 1914 engendered feelings of resentment against the Germans in Vancouver, sometimes expressed through trashing of businesses run by Germans. Many Germans had settled in Vancouver because of the charismatic German count, Alvo von Alvensleben, one of Dunbar's more colourful historical figures. As described elsewhere, Alvensleben established an estate in 1908 on the south side of 41st Avenue between what is now Blenheim and Balaclava Streets and entertained lavishly there. He also built Wigwam Inn at the end of Indian Arm for wealthy German tourists, conveying them there in a sternwheeler. Although these efforts had brought needed economic investment to the colony, Alvensleben became the target of anti-German hostility, and his properties were confiscated by the Dominion government. As he was visiting Berlin when the war broke out, he was unable to return to Canada. In 1917, he travelled to Seattle, where he was detained as an enemy alien and sent to a camp in Utah. Eventually he took out

American citizenship and remained in Seattle until his death in 1965. His Dunbar estate lay empty for several years before being bought by the Cromie family, owners of the *Vancouver Sun.* Eventually it became home to the Crofton House School for Girls.

For most people living in Dunbar, the war meant departures and, for the more fortunate, happy returns. The late Elfleda (Langford) Wilkinson described the scene of her father's return from the war, where he had served with the 29th Battalion. She remembered that there were huge crowds at the Denman Arena at Denman and Georgia Streets near Coal Harbour on the day the soldiers returned. At first the family could not see her father's face in the crowd; then Elfleda saw a man giving orders to the others. She said that it was natural for her father to be "bossing" people, and so she knew that it was him.

> I'll never forget the day he came back. I was ten. My mother and my brother and I had to take the streetcar to get to this place. We got there, and the men were brought in by buses or trucks or something. They were all lined up, and we were at the side, and I saw my dad . . . and he dismissed them for the last time. I can remember how they all threw their hats up they were so happy it was over. Most of those had been people put into the battalion to build it up. Only thirteen of the originals came back with the battalion.

When war broke out, John S. Adam, who had come to B.C. from Glasgow in 1910, joined the 16th Canadian Scottish Regiment. He served overseas and then went to Glasgow to marry his Scottish fiancée. Their daughter Sheila was born there before the young family returned to Vancouver, where a second daughter, Leslie, and a son, Ian, were born. Mrs. Adam had to adjust to the more informal life in her new surroundings. According to Leslie (Adam) Harlow: "My mother brought all sorts of things [from Scotland]: material, and marabou fur, all sorts of things in velvets and velveteens. She used to dress my sister and me in these. People used to see us walk down the street with little velvet coats and fur on the collars and beautiful hats and they would all look in amazement and think, 'Oh my gosh, these must be rich people.' They weren't that. They had just come back to start to make a living here." The Adam children, like their neighbourhood friends, played among stumps and empty lots, a far cry from the urban environment their parents had left behind in Glasgow.

Adam, an architect, built the family home at 3692 West 24th Avenue, where they lived for eight years. Even as the family became part of their local community, their ties to Scotland remained strong. As members of the community that founded Dunbar Heights United Church, the family billeted the new minister, Dr. Hugh Rae, and his wife, who had just been called from Scotland. The war had lasting effects. Like many Canadian soldiers serving in Europe, Adam was very badly gassed during the war. As a result he had to take early retirement and endured bronchial asthma and emphysema arising from his exposure to gas during the war.

Watching a Community Change

In 1925 the University of British Columbia moved to the tip of the Point Grey peninsula. The move attracted new families to Dunbar, and the presence of university people has contributed to the neighbourhood's distinct character ever since. Helen MacDonald's family moved to Dunbar from New Westminster when she was a teenager in 1925, so her sister could enroll at the new university campus. At the time, her father was working as superintendent of the Premier Mine at Stewart, B.C., a rich gold mine that operated from 1920 to about 1935.

When the MacDonalds moved into their new home, it was surrounded by second-growth bush. Trails led to the main streets in all directions, lined by blossoming wild currant bushes. MacDonald recalled that in the summer they could hear the crickets at night. During the day, it was a hike through the woods to the store:

> We used to go through the woods at Blenheim and 33rd to Dunbar. The store I remember was at 29th and Dunbar. Dunbar residents quite often did their major shopping at Woodward's. About once a month we would go to their store on Hastings Street and buy our supply of staple foods. Woodward's was the largest grocery store in the British Empire at that time. We would get our more perishable foods at Dunbar, or over at Mackenzie. People didn't shop in the same way. A lot of stuff you ordered by phone. For instance, we always ordered our meat from the Strathcona Meat Market on West Boulevard and had it delivered. I can remember the proprietor saying, "You know, your mother has bought meat from me for about twenty-five years, and I've never seen her."

MacDonald remembered the Chinese vegetable man who came at least once a week and that sheets, pillowcases and towels were sent to the Pioneer Laundry. The clean laundry would be delivered every Saturday afternoon. MacDonald said, "I still remember the very nice man who delivered it. My mother would often ask him if he'd like to come in and have a cup of tea, and he was always willing to."

Harold J. Chisholm was raised in the house built by his father at 3781 West 27th in 1925 — the same year the MacDonalds arrived in Dunbar. Many years after leaving Dunbar to live in an apartment in the West End, Chisholm wrote in a letter to Peggy Schofield that Dunbar was "a unique area to have lived in for 40 of my 75 years — unique in that it was small. You knew most everyone, if not by name then by sight." At the same time, Chisholm said that "*community* wasn't uppermost in my memory. You had your own family, your own friends, your church, your school." Chisholm noted was that there were no community centres as such, the way there would be in the future. "You made your own fun."

Gerald Smith, a member of Ollan Bugg's family down on West 29th, recalled the long walk to Kerrisdale school along Mackenzie Street past second-growth forest. The family's house was on the wrong side of the boundary for nearby Lord Kitchener school. On the way to school, Smith recalled, there was a house on the corner of 33rd and Mackenzie where the sawmill used to be. It had a small convenience store run by a widow who sold ice cream cones for five cents.

Robert Dale Morrisette lived with his grandparents from 1937 to 1947 at the Morrisette Farmhouse (see also chapter 6). He shared treasured memories of that remarkable house and grounds:

> This fourteen-room house was built on a ten-acre farm, along with a large barn to house a family cow and a horse and buggy. There was an orchard with King and Transparent apple trees, Bing and Queen Anne cherries. . . . Also there were prune and plum trees and a large chestnut tree near the back door with swings and a trapeze for us kids. The wood all came from the Rat Portage Sawmill — the beautiful oak beams in the dining room, living room and parlour. The parlour was a place we children could not enter unless all dressed up for a visit with Grandmother's guests or to play a tune on her Heintzman piano.

Morrisette said that his favourite place in the house was the attic, where he slept most of the time. "I used to crawl out the window onto the roof and watch the airplanes take off from Sea Island," he remembered. "The first plane I ever saw flying straight up was the *Kittyhawk* in 1940–42."

Morrisette also had memories of taking a lunch and hiking with his friends down to the Fraser River, catching salmon in Tin Can Creek, and working summers on George Heather's gillnetter on the north arm of the river. Decades later, the Morrisette house was operated until her retirement by Victoria Zabolotny as Amber Lodge, a boarding home for elderly women.

Fred Crowhurst, mentioned earlier, looked back on his childhood years in Dunbar decades earlier from the vantage point of 1949: "In the passing of years our Dunbar has grown up, and to my mind is still the grandest spot in Vancouver. But somehow I yearn for the old days when I knew everyone from 16th Avenue to 41st. I honestly don't think there was a kitchen between those two points that wasn't good for a cookie or two."

In the pioneer tradition, early residents of Dunbar Heights were self-sufficient. Many families kept animals and raised produce to help their

An Authentic Flying Ace

One block away from the house where young Robert Morrisette took pleasure in watching the planes at the airport lived one of Canada's most renowned World War I air heroes, Donald Roderick MacLaren (1893–1989). Originally from Ottawa, he enlisted in 1917 in the Royal Flying Corps and after training was posted to Britain, flying many successful sorties over enemy territory in Europe. One of Canada's most decorated pilots, he remained with the newly formed Royal Canadian Air Force after the war, attaining the rank of major.

Moving to Vancouver in 1921, MacLaren and his family lived at 3522 West 39th Avenue until the 1940s. He continued his career in civil aviation, starting Pacific Airways Ltd., which did fishery patrols and aerial surveys for provincial and federal governments. He collaborated in the first airmail service on the Prairies. Pacific Airways merged with Western Canada Airways, then with Trans-Canada Airlines. MacLaren retired as executive assistant to the president in 1958.

▲ J.P.D. Malkin in his study in 1928, participating in the first Vancouver to London telephone call. His brother, Vancouver mayor W.H. Malkin, was on the other end of the line. Cover of B.C. Telephone Company magazine courtesy of Telus.

families get by in hard times. The house at 3703 West 20th was the childhood home of retired police constable Charles "Chuck" Blythe. His mother, widowed in 1920 when Chuck was only five, was left to raise four young children alone. She became a seamstress and took in work at home. For years their house, surrounded by bush and stumps, was the only one on 20th Avenue between Dunbar and Highbury. Blythe remembered that they had four fruit trees on their 33-foot lot. They also had a white billy goat that had the run of the bush. As Blythe and his brother grew older they learned to hunt for mallards, which they would pluck and clean for their mother to cook. Blythe recalled that they kept some wild ducks to use as decoys: "We were allowed to have live decoys at the time. We would go down to the bottom of Dunbar or Blenheim Street and we would rent a boat from the Japanese fishermen down there and row over to Iona Island. That was a popular spot to hunt in those days. You set your wild birds out. You had to tie their foot around the leg so they wouldn't get away. I don't think it's legal now."

Point Grey alderman Warner Loat kept silver foxes behind the house at 3781 West 20th, near Highbury, where he owned three lots during the 1920s. The foxes were kept in small buildings with wire-fenced runs. Bred for their elegant fur, which was a popular fashion item at the time, the animals could be seen from Highbury Street. Loat was one of Dunbar's greatest boosters. He later moved to the corner of 26th Avenue and Collingwood Street, continuing his public service in 1929 as an alderman for the newly amalgamated city of Vancouver.

After the war, the 1920s were a time of optimism and growth and the development of amazing new technologies that were to pervade life in the twentieth century and bring Dunbar in closer touch with the rest of the world. Jamie Malkin, who remembers being sent across Marine Drive with a pail in his hand to get milk at the Mole farm, is the son of pioneer businessman J. Philip D. Malkin. He told the story of the large photograph hanging in the den of his Collingwood Street home. It was taken in March 1928 at his father's house near Blenheim Street and Marine Drive. "He's sitting at the desk with the telephone in his hand and he's talking to his brother Harold in England. My father's in Vancouver, Harold's in England. That's the first telephone call made from Vancouver to England. I think the call cost $75 a minute, so if you multiply that by 20, it would be $1,500 of our money per minute."

W. Harold Malkin, Jamie's uncle, who also lived near Blenheim Street and Marine Drive, was mayor of Vancouver at that time. Jamie characterized his uncle as a public-spirited person. However, his term came to an end just as the Depression was starting. "Any person who was in any position of responsibility was blamed for everything that happened," said Jamie. Harold Malkin lost the next election to veteran city politician

◄ Mrs. C.E. Tryon in 1934 hanging out the wash on the pulley line in the backyard of the farmhouse on 38th Avenue. The garments in the photo are the woollen bathing suits worn in those days. Courtesy of Marjorie Jones.

Louis D. Taylor, who based the punch line of his election speech on a send-up of the Malkin family's grocery brand name. "We'll see when the votes come in. If Taylor's the worst, it's still a little bit better than *Malkin's Best.*"

Impacts of the Great Depression

Almost overnight after the economic collapse of October 1929, many people found themselves without jobs and without money to pay for food, clothing and other essentials. Former newspaper publisher Charles Elmer Tryon had established a farm in the 3800 block of 37th Avenue in 1920, developing it into a business raising chickens. In a 1981 letter from daughter Marjorie (Tryon) Jones to Ifon Boone, the present owner of the house, Marjorie stated: "My father was very proud of his work with the chickens. (I thought they were dreadful!) He worked closely with the agriculture faculty (principally with Jacob Biely) at the University of British Columbia and was the first to produce Grade A-1 eggs in B.C." Charles's son, Elmer (Al) Tryon, said their family suffered during the

Dad

▲ Pencil sketch of farmer Charles Elmer Tryon by his daughter, art teacher Marjorie (Tryon) Jones. Courtesy of Marjorie Jones.

Depression, even though they could raise their own vegetables, cows and chickens. Marjorie remembered how often she would see her father sitting at the kitchen table, worried, his head in his hands. The children helped out on the farm with the tedious job of cleaning eggs every day after school because paid help was out of the question. During the 1940s, Tryon moved his farm to Coquitlam because Dunbar had become too built up and the West Side taxes were high.

Chuck Blythe, mentioned earlier, survived the Depression by doing motorcycle deliveries for several businesses in Dunbar, but he always wanted to work for the fire department or the police department. His chance came in March 1938, when he was accepted into the police department as a constable. Chuck's son Terry, who was born in 1948, was also accepted into the force, at age twenty-one, and in 1999 was appointed chief on a three-year commission. Chuck went to the swearing-in. "I handed him his badge," he said with pride. Both father and son are now retired.

The following story may be apocryphal, but it was mentioned in several interviews, although without specific names or an address. In the hard times of the Depression, plumbers were not being paid for the work they did in homes. One who profited eventually was a plumber whose customer could not pay the bill so he gave him the house instead. Family doctors were similarly vulnerable to not being paid. Gayle Johnson Mitchell, the daughter of Dr. E.V. Johnson who had a practice at 27th and Dunbar, provided her father's written musings on the difficulties of those times, including the following sad words written in 1938 on his 40th birthday: "Money must be an object; whether solely or indirectly it must be got. Otherwise, hardship and discomfort. Today, what is owing me is offset by what I owe. There is only one thing certain: I will have to meet my obligations, whereas my debtors can and no doubt most will, stall me off or refuse to pay for various reasons."

The late James Irvine Chambers was interviewed about the Depression at his home on West 33rd Avenue for a school project in 1981. He had lost his job in the insurance business and eventually found work in what became known as "the relief office." At that time, this was a department of the City of Vancouver, for municipalities were held responsible for their own "indigent." W.L. Mackenzie King was prime minister, and Chambers remembered vividly that King had said in Parliament that his government would give "not one penny piece for relief" (Hansard, 3 April 1930). Chambers added, "He thought people could get work if they looked for it."

Shortly afterwards King lost the election to R.B. Bennett, who had many economic plans, including an early form of unemployment insurance, but whose government was also unable to prevail against an economic disaster of such magnitude. British Columbia and the other western provinces were especially hard hit, not only because of their reliance on primary product exports, but also because an unprecedented drought had devastated the prairie farmlands. This caused a mass exodus of desperate young men who "rode the rods" across the country, especially to British Columbia, looking for any kind of work or subsistence they could find.

At first municipalities were expected to pay all the costs of financial aid, but when people began to lose their houses because they could not pay their property taxes, cities began to go bankrupt and even the city staff had to endure severe wage cuts. Both the federal and provincial governments had to come to the rescue of impoverished cities. Chambers, who retired in 1958 as director of what was then called the City Social Service Department, described the era as "an economic earthquake." He saw firsthand the desperation of people who had been self-sufficient all their lives and now had to ask for food and shelter for their families. "I had to tell new staff when they came on that when you are on this job use your head, but don't forget you've got a heart. And remember, the only thing between you and the client is the counter. If it wasn't for that you would be on the other side."

◄ Constable Chuck Blythe in front of his home at 3703 West 20th Avenue. Courtesy of Charles "Chuck" Blythe.

Depression Photo Op

In the "Dirty Thirties" people had to exercise their entrepreneurial skills in order to scrape together a meagre living. One man went door to door with a small replica of an airplane, enticing parents to pay for photos of their children sitting in it. Here the three youngest Zahar brothers, Franklin, Edward and Albert, pose in front of their house at 4727 Wallace Street. Photo courtesy of Franklin Zahar.

Chambers's wife Edith was interviewed along with her husband in 1981. Edith worked for many years as a secretary in Vancouver's relief office. She said that when the Depression got so bad that the city cut the wages of all staff, the women were already getting less than the men. "The rate was $125 per month for men and $80 for women. . . . I got down to $69 a month; that was the worst." In the relief department women investigators or social workers would be reclassified as stenographers in order to pay them the lower wages. Edith said: "It was pretty discouraging. You couldn't see any end to the Depression. You couldn't see things were going to get better. Of course, they did."

The Depression gave rise to social activism. One who railed against social injustice was a Dutch war bride of World War I who was becoming well known in the 1930s as a fiery orator and a defender of the underdog. Dorothy Gretchen Bierstecker, born in Amsterdam in 1891, had married Canadian army officer Rupert Steeves in 1919. They lived at the corner of Dunbar and 26th Avenue throughout the 1930s and '40s. Dorothy "Dolly" Steeves had studied law at Leyden University before her marriage. In Canada she became one of the founders of the Canadian Co-operative Federation (CCF), the forerunner of the NDP. She sat as a member of the B.C. legislature for the constituency of North Vancouver from 1934 to 1945 and worked tirelessly for the poor and for the rights of women.

One day many years after the Depression ended, Val Pfeiffer noticed a small group of people standing in front of the tiny house next door to her home on West 35th Avenue. They were looking intently at the little cottage. She learned that during the Depression their father had been so ashamed at being unable to support the family that he had left and was never heard from again. Their mother had then rented the property with its large lot so she could grow vegetables to feed the children, even growing runner beans hanging down from the eaves to save space in the garden. The Depression had marked these people; they came back to the scene decades later with tears in their eyes for their mother's hardships.

World War II, 1939–1945

When the Second World War started in September 1939, young people, especially women, who had grown up scrimping and making do through ten years of economic depression were suddenly able to get work right out of school. But they were not always able to choose the work they wanted. The federal government's Selective Service would assign them to work wherever it was deemed they were needed for the war effort. Leslie Harlow, mentioned earlier, was part of this work force. After graduation from Lord Byng High School she spent a year working as a cashier, then got a job at a bank. Not liking it, she quit, but when she went back to Selective Service they said, "You are just going to have to go right back into another bank." So she did. That was in 1941, and from then on banking became her career.

After the war, some of the returning servicemen were able to apply their wartime experience to successful careers. Radio pioneer Vic Waters

◄ The Gowe children listen to Santa Claus on the radio, 1941. During wartime, the radio brought news from overseas but was also a source of entertainment for children and adults alike. Courtesy of the Gowe family.

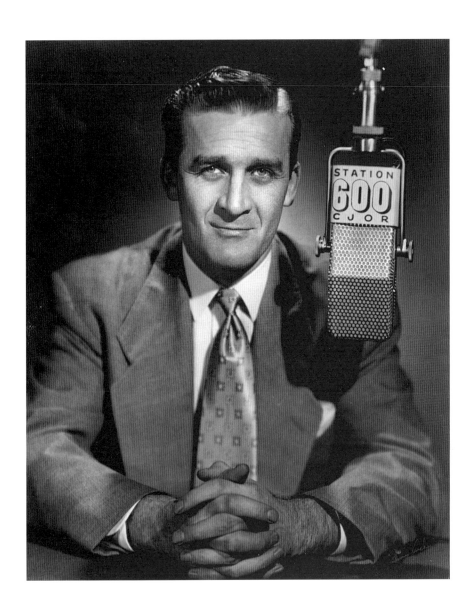

Pioneer Vancouver broadcaster
Vic Waters at CJOR in 1955.
Courtesy of Vic Waters. ▶

spent five years in special army service using his particular skill as a very
fast operator in Morse code. This he had learned in the 1930s as a ham
radio enthusiast and also at the Sprott-Shaw School of Radio and Commerce, a school started in 1903 by Marine Drive resident R.J. Sprott and
his partner W.H. Shaw. Waters was stationed with the Number One
Special Wireless Group in Darwin, Australia — "kind of spy story stuff"
— monitoring signals of the Japanese forces in Timor and New Guinea.
On his return to Vancouver in 1946, he was re-hired by his pre-war employer, George Chandler of radio station CJOR. A popular broadcaster,
"silver-voiced" Waters eventually became news editor for the station, retiring in 1968. After a lengthy retirement trip, he helped the founders of
community cablevision (Channel 4) get started and stayed on for another
five years. "We had $47,000 worth of equipment. Today that wouldn't
buy the lens on a camera." As volunteer community work he also taught
the Scouts Morse code in the 1950s.

But the Second World War, like the First, took its toll on families even when the endings were happy ones. R.G. (Bob) Ross came from a B.C. pioneer family with a long military history. At the time he was born in 1940, his father John was already serving overseas, and they did not meet until Bob was four and a half years old. "So for the first four or five years of my life my father was simply a faded brown and white photograph on my mother's chest of drawers," he said. Like many others of his generation, Bob's life was governed by the war news heard on the radio and by the rationing of commodities such as sugar, meat, butter and gasoline:

▲ John Ross, c. 1940, near the beginning of World War II, in the uniform of a captain of the 15th Field Regiment (artillery). He had the rank of major when he returned to Vancouver at the end of the war. Courtesy of Robert Ross.

> I remember sitting in the evening, we had a big console radio in the living room, one of those great big ones with tubes, and in the evening my mum and my aunt — there were a lot of women in my life when I was young, there were no men — we would sit and listen to the war news each night. It was sort of an occasion. And they would sit around knitting all the time, knitting socks, woollen gloves and things for the troops. And collecting the silver wrapping out of the cigarette boxes because they were told that would be turned into something useful for the war effort. I can't remember what it was.

The years of absence allowed no opportunity to develop a bond between father and sons. When Bob's father came home, the appearance of this stranger in uniform was alarming to Bob and his brother. In turn, the father had no realistic idea of what to expect from his two sons, who had been idealized in letters from home. Bob Ross remembered the home-coming. "He got out of the taxi and he walked up, and Mum introduced him to us, and he shook our hand! 'How do you do.' And very quickly we began to resent his presence because now we didn't get Mother's full attention. It took quite a while for us to feel comfortable with him." In addition, because of the war mentality that had developed, the brothers grew up with a great awareness of the Cold War developing in the 1950s. As young teenagers, Bob said, they and their friends built a fort in the woods beyond the Fraser booming grounds, to be safe from potential enemy atomic bombs.

Radicalism in Dunbar: Beatniks to Green Dollars

The '50s were the "McCarthy years" in the United States, and the impacts of that American phenomenon spilled over into Dunbar. When loyalty oaths were imposed on American university professors, some of those professors came north to teach at UBC. One of them was Bob Rowan, who helped found the well-known Arts One program at UBC. These young professors met a willing audience. Young people in Canada were influenced by world events of the era, the revolution in Cuba and the strug-

During the war years many high-school students trained as cadets. Lord Byng army cadets are marching west on 16th Avenue, 8 May 1942. Courtesy of Lord Byng Secondary School. ▸

gle for Black Power in the United States. "It had a profound effect on us," remembered Bryan Belfont, who became one of the instigators of a local beat scene in Dunbar in the late 1950s, a precursor to Kitsilano's flowering a decade later as a centre of hippie culture. Nothing in Canada took the attention of young people as did the issues in the country next door. "We were probably more influenced by Californian politics and culture," said Belfont, "by the war in Vietnam, draft dodgers and other influences such as women's liberation."

Belfont had arrived in Canada from England in 1958. He was eighteen and looking for a place to live. He said that when he discovered Vancouver "there was no choice after that." But he needed a way to support himself through university. "A bunch of us got together and decided we would have a coffee shop because coffee shops were the vogue then. Beatniks were on the agenda." The Black Spot coffee house opened at 4345 Dunbar Street in 1959, with Belfont and poets bill bissett and Lance Farrell living in the apartment upstairs.

The coffee shop was operated by various partners until 1962. Avantgarde music played in the background and poets and musicians came to perform. Beat poet Allen Ginsberg was teaching summer school at UBC and came by, as did actor Alan Scarfe and poets Jamie Reid, George Woodcock and George Bowering (who became Canada's Poet Laureate in 2002). "We could do our own thing there and discuss whatever topics interested us, with no censorship," said Belfont. One regular at the coffee shop was Shelagh Lindsey, a now-retired professor of architecture at UBC.

The music became rather loud, and eventually some of the neighbours petitioned City Hall to close down the coffee house. Doug Edwards

▲ Black Spot coffee house membership card. Note that it states that alcohol is not allowed. Courtesy of Bryan Belfont.

remembered thinking as a youngster that the Black Spot was some sort of weird den of iniquity. "You'd look in there and it was black as all get-out. The later hippie generation [with] the long hair and the beards and all that — the Black Spot predated all that. It was the T-shirts, sweat shirts and goatee beards, bongo drums and beat poetry."

Shelagh Lindsey went to City Hall with a delegation of supporters of the coffee shop and invited Mayor Tom Alsbury to come and see for himself that they were doing nothing illegal. The Black Spot remained in business until 1962, when it closed so its proprietors could look for better paying jobs. "Beats had a big effect on this part of the city," said Lindsey. Belfont said he still regards himself as a radical.

A generation later there was another community effort to foster alternative culture in Dunbar. In the late 1970s the Agora food co-op opened a storefront at 17th and Dunbar. Diane Marshall and her husband, dentist Donald Marshall, were among the early members. "Once a month you did your two hours of work," she said. "There was a great sense of community around that too. The people came from this part of Vancouver. I think there was only one other food co-op at the time." Marshall and her idealistic friends also experimented with an informal barter or exchange group, which was based on "green dollars." "We got together a group from all over the city, almost to Burnaby," she said, "and we met two or three times. For some reason it didn't come together. I had a sense later that people were too far flung. If you are going to do something like that, do it closer to home." The Agora Food Co-op left its Dunbar location in the mid-1980s and operated at 3420 West Broadway until it folded in the mid-1990s.

New Waves of Settlers

After half a century, the generations of early settlers who had established their roots in Dunbar had become a stable community, a community that could be described as generally homogeneous and middle-class. Then in the 1970s and 1980s, significant numbers of new arrivals came to establish their roots in Dunbar and forge connections with their new community. As was the case with the earlier settlers, their stories tell of looking back as well as looking forward, and creating bridges between Dunbar and communities far away.

Rosemary Dickinson recalled her family's immigration to Vancouver from South Africa and their settlement on Olympic Street. As English-speaking newcomers, they said their transition was "reasonably easy." There was some strangeness of terminology in the language at first, Dickinson said, and adjustments to the much freer way of life here, with a reduced emphasis on household security. As parents, they had to get used to young children staying up later in the summertime because of the longer daylight hours at this latitude. Dickinson said it was probably natural for there to be a fair amount of complaining and comparing with the old country at first. But a trip home reminded her that it was not quite as rosy as remembered, and that roots had been put down here after all. She laughingly called it the "thousand dollar cure."

Two brothers from the Punjab had a great influence on their new community. Harkirpal Singh Sara shared his vivid memories of adjusting to life in Vancouver after arriving on 19 August 1955 to live with his older brother Iqbal and his German wife Helga, already residents of Dunbar. In 1953 Iqbal Singh Sara had been the first Asian-born barrister admitted to the Canadian bar in British Columbia. Later he served on the North Fraser Harbour Commission and the National Parole Board, and he received a commemorative medal for the 125th anniversary of Confederation "in recognition of significant contribution to compatriots, the community and Canada." On Iqbal's death in December 1997, former member of Parliament Ted McWhinney paid tribute to his "intellectual vivacity and imagination" and "high style and grace."

When Harkirpal arrived he had a bachelor of arts degree and work experience as an assistant sub-inspector of police, but this did not help him find professional employment in Vancouver. He took a job as janitor at the *Province* newspaper near Victory Square and enrolled in a drafting course at Vancouver Vocational Institute across the road. While on this job he met his first Canadian friends, Dunbar residents Douglas Tyson and his wife, Jean, who become his friends for life. By 1959 he had also found a job as a draftsman. He then completed a program at UBC in elementary education and was engaged by the Vancouver School Board as a teacher.

He later qualified to teach at the high-school level and was at Lord Byng Secondary School for many years until his retirement. A month after his arrival his wife, Shobha, had joined him, and she soon found employment at a private hospital as a nurse. She later earned her registered nurse qualification and moved to pediatrics at Vancouver General Hospital. Harkirpal describes himself as a "modern Sikh." He and Shobha plunged into active community life: she volunteered in child care at the Dunbar Community Centre, and he became a member of its board of directors. He was also elected as a school board trustee. He wrote: "I have always felt humble for the wide support I got from this wonderful community. It is a remarkable locality . . . but above all, it displays its real strength through its happy and very considerate residents."

Tien Ching, owner of Omega Custom Framing and Gallery on Dunbar Street (see chapter 7), emigrated alone from Beijing to Vancouver in 1983 and later brought her two brothers. Tien married soon after she arrived and has been raising a family in addition to operating her business. She observed that for many immigrants the first generation has to compromise itself ("maybe *sacrifice* is not the right word") to make a living for the family in the new world. Tien has kept her family name first, in the Chinese custom, and has not chosen a Canadian name for herself. Her children are growing up as Canadians while keeping some Chinese customs at home. Tien said she hopes eventually to continue her education: "For many years in China after the Cultural Revolution, it was a big disaster for the whole nation. I barely finished my high school and I didn't have the opportunity to go to university because it's very much to do with your political background. Also the university closed for a few years and after it reopened it was very different." She went on: "I always feel there is something still on my mind. Here you always fulfill your dream. You can do it. You just have to wait till the right time." Meanwhile Tien is helping to fulfill dreams for young village girls in the country she left behind two decades ago. After a trip back to China, she enlisted the aid of friends in her new Vancouver community to create a foundation, Educating Girls of Rural China, which has provided financial aid to 250 elementary students and 27 university students — all girls from Gansu province who would otherwise be unable to continue in school.

Ling Chuen Leung was among those who emigrated to Canada in anticipation of the return of Hong Kong to Chinese rule in 1997, when the historic British lease was up. As a teacher and business person in Hong Kong, Ling Leung was qualified to emigrate but her husband, a medical doctor, was not. Ling Leung moved first to Montreal, where she and her daughter stayed for four and a half years. Finding the French language too difficult to learn at an older age, and life in the province of Quebec too confining, she returned to Hong Kong for another four years.

She returned to Canada in 1995, this time to Vancouver, to further the education of her daughter, who was then fifteen. When Stephanie enrolled at UBC, Ling decided to go back to school too, and graduated from UBC with a B.A. in Asian studies. Ling Leung's husband has not been permitted to practise in Canada, so until he retires, he must spend most of his time working in Hong Kong. Said Ling, "He comes here once or twice a year, and we go back once or twice a year. This is how life is. Quite a number of Chinese families are like this." Ling Leung became an active volunteer in the Dunbar Community Centre. She also served to bridge the English-speaking and Chinese-speaking communities in Dunbar by translating the Salmonberry Days calendar of events, which has encouraged participation by Chinese-speaking residents. Leung said she did not wish to remain exclusively within her own Chinese culture while living in the Dunbar community.

Growing Pains

"One of the nice things about living in Dunbar is that nothing much changes around here." This comment, appearing in the summer 2006 edition of the Dunbar Residents' Association newsletter, reflects a widely held view. The Dunbar neighbourhood basically works well. Changes, when they come, need not be radical. The streetcar suburb had turned out to be a good model for community life. Not the only one, but a good one.

In many ways, this success was the fulfillment of the community vision that was set out in the innovative zoning bylaw adopted by the municipality of Point Grey in 1922. The civic leaders who led the secession from South Vancouver in 1908 to establish Point Grey municipality envisioned a community where homeowners, through their taxes, would support civic amenities and create a modern "City Beautiful." Point Grey municipality would be an enclave of "one-family dwelling districts" supported by small "local commercial districts." The zoning explicitly excluded multiple dwellings, group houses, large sanitariums and hospitals, and light or heavy industries. After the city's amalgamation in 1929, Vancouver adopted the Point Grey zoning principles, and such pedestrian-friendly single-family neighbourhoods were built around streetcar lines all across the city. Residents enjoyed life in compact but liveable communities that were connected to downtown and to each other by transit.

Dunbar contributed its share of political leaders who promoted this community vision. In 1925, Point Grey's Ward 6 councillor Warner Loat praised Dunbar as a place where "the man or woman of moderate means and artistic tastes can, at so little expense and among people of a finer type, build up a home under . . . nearly ideal conditions."

Down through the decades to come, more and more people would seek to settle in Dunbar. Vic Waters, for instance, would use his World War II army discharge grant to buy a home on Quesnel Drive. Looking back in 2001, Waters reminisced: "Growing up in Grandview, we used to call it 'Dunbar Heights,' kind of a hoity-toity district, you know. We felt very pleased and proud to be able to get a house in Dunbar. It was nice to say you lived in Dunbar, and I think it still is."

Over time, however, the price of land in Dunbar rose dramatically, and new pressures began to be felt. To help with their mortgages, homeowners built basement suites to rent to students and others who were happy to find accommodation in Dunbar at affordable rates.

Inevitably, such a desirable neighbourhood also drew the interest of developers, who sought economic opportunities through land-use intensification. As long ago as the 1960s, the Dunbar community began to face spot rezoning proposals on single-family blocks that would introduce levels of density not envisioned under the zoning bylaw. In response, the community began to form associations such as the Dunbar Homeowners Association (1960s) and the Southlands Action Committee (1973) with "the aim of keeping the Dunbar-Southlands area a primarily single-family neighbourhood." The residents made it clear that they were not opposed to change. Rather, they objected to land speculation, spot rezoning, and conversion of single-family areas to other uses.

In the mid-1970s, the failed Penta co-operative housing project, described in greater detail in chapter 6, would have created a new cluster of dense housing in a quiet, established single-family-zoned area. At about the same time, a developer proposed to demolish single-family houses on West 41st between Collingwood and Blenheim and replace them with townhouse complexes, a proposal blocked by the Southlands Action Committee. Residents then formed the Dunbar-Southlands Planning Committee and asked the city to initiate a local area planning program in the area from 17th Avenue to the Fraser River, between Camosun and Blenheim Streets. The group wanted to discourage land speculation, among other things. During the 1980s, residents of Southlands (south of Marine Drive) helped develop a neighbourhood plan to preserve historic farm uses in their neighbourhood. But development pressures continued.

In 1991, Polygon Development Ltd. began acquiring single-family lots in a residential enclave on Alma Street between 27th and 29th Avenues. Polygon approached homeowners in the area, offering to purchase their homes. The developer's intent was to replace the houses with a 200-unit apartment and townhouse project. Sonia Wicken remembered that she was home with her grandson Trevor, a toddler at the time, when the Polygon representative knocked on her door offering to buy the family home. Wicken's community involvement had centred on her children's school and sports teams, but the Polygon proposal made her aware of broader community concerns about residential density, including unsafe traffic patterns. She started speaking with her neighbours about the project. Many of them did not feel comfortable with the Polygon proposal. Through her soccer contacts she linked up with Norm Redcliffe, who was already working on traffic concerns near the Queen Elizabeth school annex. The "Dunbar-Chaldecott Residents Association" distributed an infor-

Dunbar's "Queen Scout" Troop

In the 1950s the boys of the 25th Scout Troop at Dunbar Heights United Church often met in the kitchen of Vic and Thelma Waters' home for cocoa and cookies. Under the training of scout master Phil Gordon and his wife Helen, they all received their Queen's Scout Award in the same season. It was unusual for a whole troop to qualify at once, so they were invited to Government House in Victoria, where they were entertained by the lieutenant-governor, Gen. George Pearkes, who joined them in the garden for hot dogs and chocolate cake. During the same period, the local newspapers had been publicizing the misdeeds of the "Dunbar Gang," so Thelma insisted that they give as much attention to boys who were achieving good things. She did get their picture into the newspapers. Courtesy of Victor and Thelma Waters.

mation letter to houses on 42 blocks in the affected area. The Polygon proposal was eventually withdrawn due to neighbourhood complaints.

Even as the community was holding firm against piecemeal densification of Dunbar's residential streets, they welcomed new mixed-use low-rise developments on the commercial streets. Notwithstanding, the Dunbar community held the developers to a high standard in constructing these buildings, which would eventually define the character of the community's high street. On the corner of Dunbar and 26th Avenue, the solid-looking four-storey brick "Dunbar House" met with praise, while a building kitty-corner from Dunbar House was criticized because of its slapdash exterior detailing.

As these examples demonstrate, the Dunbar community has never been shy about asserting its right to help shape its future. When the city planning department engaged Dunbar in a "visioning" process in the mid-1990s asking the community to consider its future patterns of growth, the vision that emerged was not that different from the one enshrined in the Point Grey zoning bylaw. The message Dunbar sent to city council was that they wanted to retain single-family housing in most areas, while allowing denser development within the three main commercial areas.

In the summer of 2006, however, the Dunbar Residents' Association newsletter reported that "some developers seem to be getting second chances with the City Planning Board of Variance" even after local residents had shown that a proposal did not fit within the community. The newsletter reminded residents that "these issues were addressed in our community's City Vision Plan drawn up a decade ago and in zoning by-laws designed to protect the past and character of our community" and commented that "bureaucrats at City Hall seem to be ignoring these plans and bylaws."

The *Dunbar Community Vision* included strong support for provision of assisted housing for seniors. Long-time residents were having to leave the neighbourhood when they could no longer maintain their homes. In 2005 the city purchased a lot at the corner of Dunbar and 16th Avenue with the possible intent of providing not seniors' housing, but transitional housing for recovering addicts. The community promptly made its objections known, organizing letter-writing campaigns. The Dunbar Residents' Association urged members to share personal stories about the need for seniors' housing in letters to city staff as well as to elected representatives at all levels of government.

Although Dunbar participated in the *Vision* process, from the very beginning residents had doubts about whether the very broad principles of the document would be detailed enough to guide practical decisions in the future. Indeed, DRA president Peggy Schofield appeared before city council at this time and recommended that the *Dunbar Community*

Vision not be adopted because it was incomplete. Former city councillor Jonathan Baker was a member of the Dunbar Residents' Association board during the *Vision* process. Baker wrote in an e-mail to Schofield:

> When Visioning began I recall that Jon Ellis and I as well as several others expressed the view that the process was simply a make-work project for lower echelon bureaucrats in the Planning Department. We had both been through this thing before. In fact the City comes up with a new version every six or seven years. These so-called plans have no content. I note that the Mayor stated that the plan is not written in stone. He is correct. It is written in Jell-O. In a real sense this is planning by exhaustion. The danger is that the community may get discouraged fighting a phantom, and when something real happens, i.e., a new zoning bylaw comes along, the residents will feel you cannot fight City Hall.

Ellis repeatedly pointed out that Dunbar residents want to be involved in actual decisions, rather than in general discussions about planning ("coffee klatches," as Baker dismissed the *Vision* workshops). Ellis proposed an alternative approach that would have engaged neighbours in facilitated discussion when specific projects were proposed in their neighbourhood.

Addressing the same concern, Dunbar resident John Geddes wrote in a letter to the mayor and council:

> If the City wishes to implement changes that will significantly impact the current nature of Dunbar (i.e., zoning, density, housing mix), it must define and use a process that has more legitimacy than informal workshops and informal input from a self-selecting small group. I am not alone in this opinion. A dramatic 91% of Dunbar residents indicated in the [*Vision*] survey their concern that you develop processes for ongoing community involvement in decision making. This is the strongest approval rating given any Vision Direction. Given this feedback, I find it very surprising and disturbing that the proposal in front of you (and presented to the community at large) does not contain specific proposals for how the process of representative community input will be implemented in the future.

In the coming years, three Dunbar residents, Jon Ellis, Helen Spiegelman and Wendy Turner, would run for election to city council campaigning for reform in neighbourhood consultation. (Not affiliated with either of the two main political parties, the three would not be elected.)

The Dunbar Residents' Association continued to be the most active neighbourhood association in the city, serving as a local forum for neighbourhood concerns and a catalyst for needed improvements. When UBC-bound cars began "rat-running" through the quiet triangle bounded by 41st Avenue, Marine Drive and Camosun Street where Peggy Schofield lived, she brought her concerns to the DRA and became chair of a traffic committee. At about that time the city launched a city-wide transportation planning process, and Schofield agreed to represent the DRA on the consultation task force. She became president of the DRA in 1997, the year the Transportation Plan was adopted by council. Under Schofield's leadership, the DRA worked with other neighbourhood organizations, including the Dunbar Community Centre Association, on local initiatives to establish traffic safety measures such as speed bumps near parks and schools. Because of this joint work, pedestrian crossing lights were installed at 41st and Wallace and at 33rd and Dunbar (unfortunately, only after pedestrian deaths at those intersections). Similarly, a local action committee, the Blenheim Neighbourhood Group, worked with city engineers to develop a traffic calming plan for their street that was based on the principles adopted in the 1997 Transportation Plan. In the early 2000s property crime began to emerge as a neighbourhood concern, and the DRA formed a volunteer Dunbar Community Patrol to combat vandalism and graffiti.

Neighbour Helping Neighbour

The stories of the old-timers in this book paint a picture of a neighbourhood actively involved with the community through church, school, little-league sports, recreational activities and community improvement projects, a community where "people knew each other if not by name, then by sight." Even as the community grew, it preserved and nurtured a small-town sense of neighbourliness. Sonia Wicken remembered that a local bank manager assigned to his company's Dunbar branch after

The Dunbar Residents' Association sponsored the creation of an inviting rest area in front of the Dunbar Public Library. Volunteers planted an Eddie's White Wonder dogwood in the spring of 2001. Two wooden benches were built by Jon Ellis and sponsored by the Dunbar CIBC and the DRA. Left to right: Walter Lanz, Fred Lanz and Barry Smith. The name of the man in the foreground is unknown. Courtesy of Peggy Schofield. ▶

working in other communities across the country picked up instantly on the local spirit: "Dunbar is unique — the people really care."

Every block in Dunbar has a story to tell about neighbourliness at the very local level. One of the best examples is May Brown's block. May Brown and her late husband Lorne moved into their brand-new house in the 4000 block of 30th Avenue (described further in chapter 6) in the spring of 1950. May reminisced: "When we moved here to this newly developed block, we were all young couples, and we were pinching every nickel we had, because to get into the houses it cost us quite a bit to get what we needed, all the bare essentials. So what we used to do was buy things communally. One neighbour would buy the wheelbarrow, while the other would purchase the ladder. So we had groups of people in on gardening tools and so forth. So if one person had that tool, you didn't buy it."

The young homeowners knew nothing about gardening at that stage of their lives. They all worked together on landscaping their properties. They spent the first year picking up stones and sifting the soil. They held work parties if someone was doing a big project such as a lawn. May Brown recalled: "Everyone would come out and help, and then of course it worked vice versa. So this is how you got to know everyone on the block. We looked after each other's children when we wanted to go out. It was very friendly and definitely a great way to get to know your neighbourhood." To this day, the neighbours are still helping each other. The same ladder is still in use. A younger generation has moved in who are willing to help the older ones. Paul Reynolds, for instance, lives in his grandfather's old house on West 31st Avenue. Brown said: "If I have things in the car that I can't get out, I just wait until Paul comes home from work. There are lots of people around to help out if it's needed. It's very friendly, very neighbourly. It's pretty much why I stay; it's a great support system. If I need anything at all, I simply call the neighbours."

From the extended families that defined community life in early Southlands to the formal and informal associations that link the lives of citizens living and working in Dunbar/Southlands today, Dunbar has maintained connections within the community and with communities beyond its borders that are a source of its enduring appeal as a place to live.

CHAPTER 4

Commercial Development through the Decades

⌐ Larry Moore

From the early 1920s, when Dunbar's commercial district was developing, the three stops on the streetcar line were the centres not only of commerce, but also of community life. Until 1958, when the community centre was built, residents gathered at stores within walking distance of their homes to shop and converse. Their local buying patterns speak to a time of fewer consumer goods, more self-sufficiency, and face-to-face contact that forged bonds among a smaller population. These buying patterns also say much about changing values.

Some of the features of early commercial Dunbar are with us still. In 2002, when Jeffrey Ho was considering the purchase of Blight's Home Hardware at 3322 Dunbar, he noticed the family atmosphere that characterized Blight's and the friendliness that existed between customers and staff. Ho was convinced that a strong customer base would continue; he is now the new owner of one of the area's oldest and most successful family businesses.

This chapter looks at the development of Dunbar's business activity from the days of market gardens and horse-drawn delivery wagons to an era of increasing affluence, fast food and specialty stores. Stories of Dunbar family life and times reveal factors shaping present-day commercial Dunbar and the trends and concerns that may determine Dunbar's future commercial life.

Early Business Ventures, 1920s

In 1911 Charles T. Dunbar, a realtor, visualized a substantial new subdivision between 16th and 25th Avenues and east of Dunbar Street to Blenheim. Dunbar's contribution of $35,000 influenced the B.C. Electric Railway Company to build the streetcar line that would run south from 10th Avenue all the way to 41st Avenue. Laid in 1920, this streetcar line gave shape to Dunbar Street and led to the commercial centres that exist today.

The Dunbar area had just been logged in the early '20s, and secondary bush was beginning to cover the cleared ground. Real estate subdivisions were being approved and a few houses were beginning to appear. Jack Wood built a real estate office at Dunbar Street and 29th Avenue in 1923. Power poles for street lights and general electrical service lined the east side of Dunbar, and telephone lines were strung along the west side. Although the single streetcar track had been laid down the middle of the street, Dunbar was a dirt and gravel road until 1921 — and a long distance from downtown Vancouver.

The district's first store was Scott's Grocery, established at 29th and Dunbar in 1922. Scott's Grocery was a general or village store designed to supply local customers with small quantities of daily necessities such as food, toiletries and small hardware items. Marion (Tulloch) Funell remembers shopping near, but not on, Dunbar at another small, local store as a young girl in the early '20s. "There was a little store on 16th, the West Side Grocery store, they called it. I can't remember just when but it changed hands quite a number of times. It was a popular place to get an ice cream cone. Oh, they gave you a big scoop of ice cream for a nickel. We would run through the trail from the back of our house and it was a shortcut. Of course, you always took the shortcuts." Many of the stores along Dunbar 80 years later cater to a localized clientele.

To appreciate fully the early economic development of Dunbar, it helps to remember that the B.C. economy had been severely affected by World War I. Of about 400,000 persons living in the province when the war started, roughly 55,000 young men joined the fighting forces. Vancouver sent a higher proportion of soldiers to France than any other city in North America. Roughly half these men never returned home and Vancouver's population dropped by 26,000. With peacetime, veterans returned sick of war and eager for a normal life with jobs and families. Realtors acquired recently cleared land tracts and subdivided them into lots. Standard lot sizes in the Dunbar area were 33 x 120 feet and 42 x 120 feet, with some wider lots available. Some owners preferred to acquire two adjacent 33s or 42s, building on one and developing the second as a garden.

Between 1923 and 1933 a tremendous amount of housing construction took place. Some builders erected residences of rather similar design,

◄ Lilac Cleaners and Dressmakers, on the west side of Dunbar between 29th and 30th Avenues, about 1939. Left to right: Peggy Mizuguchi, Jack Watanabe, Mr. Watanabe and an unnamed friend. Courtesy of the Watanabe family.

mostly to be advertised and sold to blue-collar or white-collar families of Caucasian background. In many Vancouver neighbourhoods, including Dunbar, restrictions against non-white ownership of property were in force. Compared to the present, Dunbar's early inhabitants were a much less diverse socio-economic mix.

Commercial development is closely linked to income and spending patterns of consumers. Although jobs were available, most young couples settling in Dunbar in the early '20s had little capital and a meagre cash flow. Most of the wages earned went to purchase the absolute necessities for the family, and families had to be frugal. Private automobiles were uncommon in Dunbar in the '20s and '30s, and there were certainly no traffic or parking problems.

It was very rare during this period to find a family where the wife/mother worked outside the home. This fact played a major role in shaping the daily life and financial standing of the typical family and also helps explain the early commercial patterning along Dunbar. (The mother stayed close to home and shopped for daily necessities at stores in the neighbourhood, generally within walking distance.) As Ed Bowman notes: "If you had to work, there was something wrong with your husband. He could be an invalid, which you could be forgiven for, but not if he was one that stopped off and had a beer here and there and the money wasn't coming in. . . . Women seemed to be more concerned about their youngsters; really mothered them to make sure that everything was all right and where they were going and coming back from, going to school and checking out. The fathers would see the report cards and hand them over to the mother."

◀ Scott's Grocery, c. 1923, at 29th and Dunbar, was Dunbar's first store. It was also the first of a long and continuing line of convenience stores located along Dunbar Street. City of Vancouver Archives, photograph #13505.

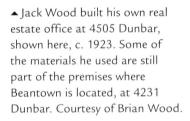

▲ Jack Wood built his own real estate office at 4505 Dunbar, shown here, c. 1923. Some of the materials he used are still part of the premises where Beantown is located, at 4231 Dunbar. Courtesy of Brian Wood.

In the early '20s, the typical husband/father had to journey a considerable distance each morning to one of the mills on Granville Street or False Creek, or to a wage earner's job in downtown Vancouver. There was very little employment in the immediate Dunbar area. Commonly, he commuted via the streetcar, which added more than an hour of travel time, each way, to his long workday. Most mothers canned fruit and vegetables raised in their backyard gardens for use in the winter, with a vacuum sealing technique and glass Mason jars. Items such as squash, carrots, pears and apples would be preserved fresh and would last until the New Year or even longer. Pears and apples were individually wrapped in newspaper and packed in crates. Carrots and other root vegetables were placed in tarpaper-lined pits dug at a suitable place in the garden. The pit was kept covered with earth to protect its contents from frost and moisture.

MARKET GARDENS

Home-grown produce was augmented in some seasons with vegetables and greens raised by market gardeners (mostly Chinese) in the Southlands area. Deliveries and sales were made on foot or by horse cart. At the south end of Dunbar along the Fraser River and in the present Musqueam Park area, there were a number of market (or truck) farms that supplied the Dunbar area with vegetables. Terry Slack recalled: "When you went along Marine Drive, you'd see a little shingle out on a tree, and it was a truck farm. And you went down a little dirt road and into the huge truck farm. Mr. Chan had one of these truck farms. He had an open-bed truck, and he put his boxes of vegetables on it. This was why he was called a 'truck farmer.'"

Barrie Lindsay also remembered the market gardens:

Two major gardens operated through at least to the end of World War II. One fronted on the south side of the 3900 block of Southwest Marine Drive between large homes on the east owned by the Mercers and on the west owned by the Buscombes. It was approximately three to four acres and reached by dirt road to the main buildings directly at the south end of Wallace Street. At the south end of the Buscombes' large property and reached by the south end of Holland Street was an elderly Occidental market gardener on a couple of acres. His name was Jones and he was a favourite of all the kids. As well as a full range of produce, he also grew wonderful gladioli. His distribution was both on-site and door-to-door by wheelbarrow throughout Southlands.

The second, and somewhat larger market garden, was reached by about a half-mile dirt road south of Marine Drive near where the present access is to Shaughnessy golf club. This was a more mysterious place for kids due to being surrounded by bush. Both locations farmed a typical range of produce, starting in late April with green onions. I remember the last big crop was cauliflower. Their produce always went out in bulk by their own solid-tired trucks, usually early in the morning. Both locations did some on-site sales but, I recall, to very limited clientele.

Lindsay said most of the Chinese workers, some of whom "lived in," were a bit scary to the kids — owing to the language barrier but also to their reaction to carrot-patch raids. "The sight of a wildly screaming Chinese man with his coolie hat and swinging a two-foot-long knife had a definite effect on us."

▲ Shops on the west side of the 3200 block of Dunbar showing delivery van, c. 1927. The cement paving along the streetcar tracks is incomplete. Courtesy of Omega Custom Framing and Gallery.

Stores on Dunbar Heights, 1927

25TH AVE.
— Lohman's Grocery
— Red's Super Service (Shell) Station

26TH AVE.
4212 – De Barre Barbers
4224 – Dunbar Cleaners/Dyers
4231 – West Point Tailors/ Cleaners
4235 – Dunbar Hardware
4236 – Dunbar Investment Co.
4238 – Dunbar Dairy
4244 – Dunbar Meat Market
4250 – McDonald's Fruit and Vegetable Market

27TH AVE.
4337 – Ideal Bakery
4339 – Dunbar Dry Goods
4345 – Morgan's Grocery

28TH AVE.
4439 – Rome's Confectionery
4441 – Rogers' Barber Shop
4443 – Dunbar Shoe Shop
4479 – Elliott's Market (meat)
4485 – Dunbar Green Grocery
4492 – McDonald's Grocery
4495 – Midway Dry Goods

29TH AVE.
4505 – Dunbar Heights Realty
4508 – Kerrisdale Motors
4517 – Dunbar Florists
4518 – Canadian Imperial Bank of Commerce
4528 – Dunbar Hairdressing Parlors
4534a – Sloan's Grocery
4534b – Dr. L.H. Webster, physician
4538 – Dunbar Delicatessen

Even-numbered addresses are on the east side of Dunbar, odd-numbered addresses on the west side.

Source: Vancouver City Directory, 1927.

Al Tryon's father, Charles E. Tryon, established a market garden to serve the Dunbar area. Tryon sold his newspaper business in Saskatoon and brought his wife and five children, including the two-and-a-half-year-old Al, to Vancouver in 1920. The family had a house and outbuildings built at 3830 West 37th Avenue, then started a small dairy and poultry business, planted 35 fruit trees and put in a vegetable garden on two and a half acres at 37th Avenue and Highbury. Their commercial venture operated for the next 20 years, selling and delivering milk, eggs and fruit before urban development forced the family to move its business to the Coquitlam area. When he became old enough, Al delivered much of the produce in his hand-pulled wagon.

A chicken coop and a pen graced many Dunbar backyards, providing a reliable supply of eggs and a Sunday treat of fried or roast "free-range" chicken on occasion. Marion Funell described chicken raising: "The chickens would be outside in their fenced-in area. Of course, with so few people around, the owners didn't have to worry about property lines. If they wanted more room for the chickens, they just moved the fence."

For most households there was no refrigeration until the late '30s. Before this time, an air-circulation cooler was usually built into the corner of the kitchen. This device was a rectangular cube with an access door in the kitchen and square, screen-covered vents to the outside. Foodstuffs could be kept for only a short time. By the mid-'20s the ice man came around in a truck. Stan Cornish, who grew up at 3983 West 33rd Avenue, told this story:

> A slab of ice was marked and it went in. We would get the chips and put them in our mouths. That was the life for us: sucking the ice. The refrigerators were a wooden box for the ice with a metal lining. We did not keep meat in the ice box. We bought every day what we wanted from the butcher store [Elliott's] in small quantities. My mother sent my sister, who was three years older than I was, so she'd get the job of running up to the store. There was a trail from our house through the bush to 31st, then there was another trail and we'd come out at 29th and Dunbar. . . . In those days the butcher store had sawdust on the floor to pick up the bits of meat and they had these chopping blocks and they were always scraping. It did not have meat displayed like they do today. If you wanted something they would cut it for you because there was no place to store it. My sister, Louise, would be given 25 cents to purchase enough ground round steak for our family of five.

Between 1927 and 1930, Dunbar Street's commercial development was mainly limited to the stretch between 25th and 30th Avenues, later called Dunbar Heights. Within this five-block area there were 28 businesses. Most of these shops catered to short-term, localized demand, because it was simply too time-consuming or expensive to travel farther afield to obtain household supplies or services.

CONVENIENCE STORES

In addition to Scott's Grocery, there were a few other small convenience stores in the Dunbar district (Heather Handy Store, est. 1926; Gibbons Store, est. 1927; Lord Byng Grocery and the Red and White, est. 1929). Located between 20th and 21st Avenues on the east side of Dunbar, with no other commercial establishment for two blocks to the north and 10 blocks to the south, Heather Handy Store is a fine example of a 1920s neighbourhood convenience store. Robert Heather purchased the store in 1926 and changed its name from the Dunbar Cake Shop to the Heather Handy Store. For the next 42 years, the store remained in the family. After their father's death in 1942, Guy and Lloyd Heather continued to operate the store seven days a week from 8:00 A.M. to 11:00 P.M., stocking most items offered by markets and featuring "customer service, first and foremost." Christmas Day was the only day the store closed!

One of the two Heather brothers was almost always behind the counter, although a part-time girl was employed to help out and one or

◄ Dunbar Cake Shop was purchased by Robert Heather in 1926 and converted to a long-lived grocery, Heather Handy Store, open 8:00 A.M. to 11:00 P.M. seven days a week. Note laying of new double tracking for streetcar in the foreground. Courtesy of Clista Heather.

▲ Lloyd Heather (son of Robert Heather) stands ready to ring up a purchase at the counter in Heather Handy Store, 1955. Courtesy of Clista Heather.

two high-school boys did the phone-order deliveries. Credit was extended to regular customers. The store was never larger than 750 square feet as a result of zoning restrictions, but it generated enough business to support two families. For a while, the store featured a counter with stools and some tables and chairs where customers could relax over a dish of ice cream, a soft drink or other confectionaries, but eventually the space was needed for shelving. Heather Handy Store sponsored Dunbar baseball teams for many years, illustrating its strong community orientation.

Clista (Davis) Heather, Guy's wife, remembers two robberies at Heather Handy Store:

Lloyd was working in the store and the robbers came in with sawed-off shotguns and they shot at him, to scare him more than to injure him. They shot into the baby food and it went all over the store. All over everything. They got away with some money that time.

Then one other time we were robbed too — I guess about a year and a half later. Our house was next door and we had it wired for burglary from the store. One night, about two in the morning the alarm went off. Our oldest was just a baby. Of course, the alarm woke her and she was screaming, so my husband, Guy, phoned the police. He could look out the window and could see men going out the back of the store, taking big cartons of cigarettes. They were loading them, or stacking them, or something. So he went outside to sort of keep an eye on them but he was keeping at a distance. He thought if they took off he would follow them. So while he was there, the police came and they grabbed him because they thought he was a robber. He said, "I'm not the robber, I phoned you!" The robbers were caught later by the police.

HOME DELIVERY

Because most families in the 1920s did not have cars, home delivery was very important. Besides the fruit and vegetable delivery operators, the ice man, and the local store delivery boys, a number of other delivery businesses served the Dunbar homemaker. Jersey Farms (later Dairyland) milk was delivered daily by horse cart (by horse and sled in snowy conditions) and later by truck to the front doorstep or to a little box built into the side of the house. The milkman opened the small outside door, removed the empty glass bottles and replaced them with full bottles, which the homemaker then retrieved through the inside door. Special or modified orders were written on scraps of paper and left with the empties.

Carol-Ann Lang wrote the following in a 1999 *Vancouver Sun* obituary for her father, Jack Lang:

Dad worked for 13 years as a milkman for Dairyland. He made home deliveries in Dunbar/West Point Grey. Because of his seniority, he drove one of Dairyland's first two milk trucks. One of my favourite stories from this time was when one of the families on his route bought a new piano. For some reason they were up at 5 a.m. when Dad came by to deliver the milk. They invited him in to try the new piano. Well, one thing led to another and pretty soon the party was underway. As the morning progressed, others on the milk route awoke to find their milk hadn't been delivered. Looking down the street they saw the milk truck parked in the middle of the block. People began to wander down with their empty bottles, tokens and coins. These they exchanged for their allotted new full bottles of milk. Upon leaving the truck they could hear the piano playing and voices singing. So, they took their bottles of milk home to the ice box where they exchanged them for cases of beer, and headed back to party. By 1 p.m. nobody cared if the new piano was in or out of tune — the party was in full swing. By 5 p.m. one of the office staff came out to see what had happened to the truck and driver. Nobody had called in to report not receiving their milk. The truck was found in the middle of the block where it had been since 5 a.m. It was in perfect order with full bottles all exchanged for empties all neatly stacked in the appropriate cartons; all the tokens and change were in the tray. Each person had taken only what she or he was entitled to and had paid honestly for what was taken. The keys were still in the ignition. The party was still going strong, for now the whole neighbourhood had joined in. Many years later when Dad left Dairy-

Horse-drawn milk wagons were used to deliver milk to Dunbar residents until the 1940s. If the snow got deep in winter, milk sleighs were seen. Vancouver Public Library, photograph #23639. ▶

A milkman from Associated Dairies serving Dunbar via motor truck, c. 1945. Milk was pasteurized, not homogenized, and packaged in quart- and pint-sized round glass bottles. Vancouver Public Library, photograph #16485. ▶

land in the 1940s . . . the customers of his milk route threw him a farewell party. The event made the *Vancouver Sun* newspaper, complete with the headline "The Most Popular Milk Man in Town."

Another merchant who made regular trips through Dunbar was the rag-and-bones man, who drove his horse and wagon in the back lanes, calling out "Any rags and bones today?" as he collected the area's reusable items — a precursor to the city's recycling program begun in the 1990s. Junk dealers had to be licensed to operate legitimately.

Door-to-door calls were made by salespeople for Fuller Brush (brushes for all purposes, polish), Watkins Products (waxes, salves and ointments) and other companies, offering many types of merchandise. The salesman would open his suitcase to reveal a wondrous assortment of items that could be purchased on the spot or ordered for delivery by mail or directly from the salesman. Often the customer would be given free samples of new products.

At the close of the 1920s, the typical Dunbar homemaker rarely ventured far from the local shopping area except to take the streetcar downtown each week or every other week for major grocery shopping or for purchasing necessary clothing and other dry goods. Purchases were usually confined to necessities and not to luxuries. Many food items were consumed within a very short time frame (two or three days). Therefore, convenience shopping and home delivery were normal and expected. For the breadwinner, generally the husband, having and holding a job assumed prime importance and occupied much of his time. Homemaking, generally the wife's primary role, meant being conscious of price and quality. In purchasing goods, money was usually scarce and needed to be spent carefully and mainly on the essentials of life.

Commerce Takes Off, 1930s

The ten years between 1930 and 1940 might be called the "takeoff" period in Dunbar's commercial evolution — despite the Depression. Most families living in the area acquired a refrigerator and many also bought an automobile. Thus the typical family was not as dependent on local shops. The homemaker did not need to shop as often, nor was she as confined to the Dunbar area to fill her shopping needs. Commonly, on Saturday, the whole family drove downtown for the weekly shopping. This was a special event for everyone. The price-conscious shopper could usually shave the food bill quite a bit by taking advantage of lower basic prices and the sales to be found on Woodward's Food Floor. Woodward's also carried a whole range of clothing, towels and sheets as well as most other household items, including appliances and furniture. For comparison shopping, the Hudson's Bay Company and Spencer's (later bought out by Eaton's)

▲ Junk peddlers were licensed to pick up discarded or donated items in the late 1920s, constituting Dunbar's first official recycling program. A rectangular brass licence plate was for a motor vehicle and a round brass plate was displayed on a horse-drawn cart. Courtesy of Tanya Cooke.

▲ Bayview Market receipt, c. 1930s. Courtesy of Larry Moore.

- Mousetraps are selling for 2 for 5 cents at the Piggly Wiggly on Dunbar Street.

- Forcing the rear door, burglars gain entry to Piggly Wiggly store No. 16 on Dunbar Street and remove a 250-pound safe containing approximately $400.

- Dunbar Heights has been proving the most popular district in Greater Vancouver for residential purposes for homes that range in value from $3,750 to $7,000.

Source: Vancouver Sun.

July 20, 1934

Sugar Crisp Corn Flakes sold for 5 cents a box at Stong's, located at this time in downtown Vancouver at Robson and Seymour.

Source: Vancouver Sun.

were also in downtown Vancouver and carried competitive merchandise at attractive prices.

Bessie (Whyte) Smith took her children Joan and Kenny with her on the streetcar downtown to Woodward's on Saturday mornings. Joan and Kenny waited on the steps inside the big store leading down from street level to the basement location of the Food Floor where their mother shopped. Many other children waited there too, and a bit of horseplay often took place. Once, trying to run down the steps two at a time, Joan slipped and fell, hitting her leg on the edge of a stone step. Sixty years later, she still had the scar and the memory of the painful incident. Bessie heard Joan's wails and returned to comfort her and take her to the soft ice cream stand for a chocolate ice cream cup before they caught the street-car home to Dunbar.

During the 1930s, in spite of the increasingly popular practice of shopping in downtown Vancouver, the number of stores on Dunbar grew from 58 to 146 — a 250 percent increase. Coincidentally, the number of residential dwellings had also more than doubled. There were now many more working- or middle-class families making their homes in Dunbar. This was Dunbar's greatest era of densification, as undeveloped lots became fewer and farther apart.

SPECIALTY STORES

Whereas in the 1920s the predominant type of Dunbar business was the convenience store, in the 1930s and '40s many more specialty stores joined the mix. In 1938, Eric Nicol bought his school supplies at Ridgewell's Lending Library at 19th and Dunbar, which was owned by the Gatenburys. Alma Welsh of 3743 West 19th borrowed books for herself and her daughter, Helen, from Ridgewell's for 5 cents a book. Alma found the lending library much more convenient than taking the streetcar all the way downtown to the Carnegie Library, Vancouver's only public library, at Main and Hastings.

By 1940 other specialty stores had emerged. There was a photographer, a dressmaker, a men's clothing store, a Parisian fashion designer, a bake shop, a candy store, a beauty shop (hair salon), a radio repair shop and six automobile service stations or garages. Ed Bowman, a young man in the '30s, described his employment as a "grease monkey" at the Signal station (Dunbar and 16th Avenue, north side of 16th). Lubrication jobs needed to be done every month or two, and car owners had their oil changed at the same time. The grease monkey had to grease perhaps 20 fittings using a pressure hose. He cleaned spark plugs with a sand blaster, and a mechanic had to adjust the carburetor as part of a tune-up job.

Bowman earned three dollars a week as a grease monkey and saved his money. Finally, he went down to a used car market on Georgia Street

and bought a 1923 Chevrolet "banger" for $15. His dad said, "You stole it." The licence plate cost as much as the car. Because he was learning how to fix cars from first-hand experience on the job, he now could keep his own car running. "Every week it was in for repairs one way or another so [my parents] knew where I was — up there doing the work on the hoist."

Three druggists also served the community by 1940 — Dunbar Pharmacy at the north end of the street, Harcus Drugs in the middle and Law's Drugs at the south end. The Dunbar Theatre opened in 1935 — the first Odeon theatre in Western Canada (see page 206). A couple of grocery chains, Safeway and Piggly Wiggly, had outlets that competed favourably with Woodward's on many grocery items — and they were closer to home. The district's first restaurant, Southlands Home Cooking, opened for business in 1935.

Patsy (McQueen) Damms, now living in Prince George, recalls child-hood pleasures — and reveals her sweet tooth:

> How many of you remember the Piggly Wiggly, Westmoreland's (*the* place to buy your mum her birthday present!), Cunningham's on the lane and the wonderful candy store beside the Dunbar Theatre? And right beside Westmoreland's was a café, I think called Irene's, where we could go to have a Pepsi when we were about twelve or so. Another candy store between 26th and 27th sold penny candy and we would, if

The commercial strip between 17th and 18th, east side of Dunbar Street, 1939, included at least two food stores and a hardware store. Vancouver Public Library, photograph #25036.

George Fisher, the Pharmacist Who Cared

According to Helen (Davidson) Robinson:

Harcus used to have a drugstore by the post office and then Fisher's store started. The first one was where Olinda's is [4305 Dunbar]. When I was pregnant with my first boy, there was an old druggist in there named Anderson, and he had a regular old drugstore with the coloured globes in the window. He just sold drugs and then he retired, and George Fisher took it over. Then he moved to where the delicatessen is. Then across to where Shoppers Drugs is. Then it was Pharmasave. Then Shoppers took it over. I went in one day and found George had retired. I sent him a card. . . . George was good for business. He was in the Shriners and knew so many people. At his funeral, I think everybody in Dunbar was there. He was awfully good when our kids were sick. He'd bring a prescription down at night. He was good that way. That store was great. My kids went there to buy

Christmas presents. There was a big store with counters down the sides and in the middle and he had everything in there, from a needle to a haystack.
Photo of Lena and George Fisher courtesy of Lena Fisher.

we were lucky, get a bag of candies that would last us all day. A very strong memory is buying a bag, going to an empty lot on 25th and lying on the ground looking at the sky and savouring the candy!

Although in 1940 her mother baked most of the family's bread, Barbara Mercer loved being sent to Jaffrey's Bakery (3350 Dunbar) for apricot and raspberry slices. These criss-cross pastries had jagged edges at the side and, Barbara remembers, they tasted wonderful. Mrs. Jaffrey was a short Scottish lady who always wore a white uniform. Mr. Jaffrey did the baking. Little Barbara thought that everything the Jaffreys made was delicious.

Terry Slack's family lived in a community of floating houses on the north arm of the Fraser River. Every week Terry and his brothers and sisters purchased "goodies" at Mr. Pyatt's confectionary store (5648 Dunbar) near 41st on the east side of the street, next to Cunningham Drugs. Henry Pyatt even gave credit until Terry and his siblings could find enough beer and pop bottles to pay their bill. Terry said:

Pyatt's was located near where Herta Flowers is today [5650 Dunbar, now Gardenia Flowers]. And he was a wonderful confectionary man. He had a little chalkboard on which he kept all his little notes about

◄ Early automobiles required frequent lube jobs, oil changes, tire repairs and tune-ups. Full-service stations were common on Dunbar, including this one at 16th, c. 1933. Vancouver Public Library, photograph #11965.

◄ Opened in 1935, the Dunbar Theatre was the first Odeon theatre to serve Western Canada. Photo by Stuart Thomson. City of Vancouver Archives, photograph #99-2889.

who owed what, and you could actually have accounts. As teenagers, we found it very interesting that we could have an account there. And we would buy a bottle of pop for a nickel or 10 cents, and "Well," he said, "you have to pay me by Friday." Then he'd put us on what he called "the slate." And he would put 10 cents against my name, then we would pay up on Friday when we came in after school. So he was a wonderful man and I'll never forget him. He knew everybody, and even Herta says that once in a while his ghost comes back to the store.

Dunbar Businesses in 1940

NORTH DUNBAR

16TH AVE.
3200 – Hillcrest Service Station
3211 – Soule & Young Grocery
3212 – Olympic Cleaners
3218 – Taylor, P., confectioner
3228 – Royal Bank of Canada
3231 – Bayview Meat Market
3289 – Art's Confectionary
3291 – North, A.J., barber
3293 – De'Lite Fruit Market
3295 – Dunbar Dry Goods
3297 – Dunbar Pharmacy
3297 – P.O. Substation #38

17TH AVE.
3308 – Safeway Stores
3322 – Gordon Hardware
3336 – Cavin Dairy Deli
3350 – Jaffrey, A., Bakery
3352 – Hoy Fruit Market, produce

18TH AVE.
3408 – Three Smart Girls
　　　　Beauty Salon
3432 – Vance, F., barber
3434 – Boothman, A.J., dentist
3444 – Point Grey Bakery
3446 – Sunrise Cleaners
3456 – Odd Bakery
3458 – Sterling Food Markets
3467 – Ohio Cleaners
3468 – B & K Economy Grocery
3469 – Elm Confectionary
3470 – Jersey Dairy Confectionary
3480 – Rose Beauty Shoppe
3482 – Paramount Shoe Repair
3494 – Ridgewell Lending Library
3496 – Young Bros. Produce

20TH AVE.
3644 – Heather, R.A., confectioner
3680 – Moise Studio, music teacher

22ND AVE.
3879 – Hoppers Homes,
　　　　building contractor

25TH AVE.
4184 – Lovegrove Service Station/
　　　　Garage
4195 – Grant's Imperial Station

DUNBAR HEIGHTS

26TH AVE.
4202 – B & K Economy Grocery
4205 – Stephens-Tully, florists
4209 – Woman's Bakery
4212 – DeBarre Barber & Beauty Shop
4229 – Safeway Stores
4230 – Dunbar Fish & Chips
4231 – Dunbar Cleaners & Dyers
4232 – Affleck, Miss J., milliner

4235 – Dunbar Cycles
4236 – O K Shoe Repair
4238 – Dunbar Dairy
4243 – Bonnie Lass Cleaner/
　　　　Dressmaker
4244 – Dunbar Meat Market
4245 – Scottish Ham Curers/Meats
4250 – Quality Fruit Market
4252 – McRae, Mrs. M.,
　　　　women's clothing
4253 – Marshall, Mrs. M.,
　　　　confectioner
4255 – Du Barry Studio,
　　　　photography
4256 – Dunbar Investment
4256 – Meyer, H.J., painter
4260 – Charm Beauty Salon
4263 – Collegiate Shop Wool Goods
4264 – Swartz, C.F., barber
4265 – Sunny Market, produce
4268 – Dunbar Children's Wear
4273 – Toggery Men's Clothing
4275 – Madelon Dress Shoppe
4288 – Parisian Designers
4290 – Dairydale, dairy products
4292 – Honey's Dress Shop
4293 – Ellen's Dairy Lunch
4294 – Sutherland, Mrs. M.,
　　　　dresssmaker
4295 – Variety Store, dry goods
4298 – Johnson, E.A., physician

27TH AVE.
4305 – Braemar Pharmacy
4311 – Dunbar Lending Library
4315 – Kelona Produce
4321 – Ideal Bakery
4335 – The Nest, eggs & poultry
4341 – Modern Sprayers, painters
4345 – Beaver Brand Fisheries
4355 – Cunningham Drug Stores
4365 – Dunbar Hardware
4385 – Dunbar Beauty Parlor
4389 – Burns, Miss J., ladies' wear

28TH AVE.
4407 – Canadian Imperial
　　　　Bank of Commerce
4408 – Verity Hair Dressing
4409 – Florine Confectionary
4410 – Harvey, Miss M., milliner
4413 – Superior Stores, grocery
4424 – Marina's Chocolate Shop
4426 – Modern Press
4439 – Sterling Markets, meats
4441 – Rogers' Barber Shop
4443 – Bagnall, J., shoe repair
4445 – Golden Sheaf Bake Shop
4454 – Community Shoe Repairs
4455 – Mayfair Dairy, confectionary
4458 – Dunbar Table Supply, deli
4464 – Home Radio Service

4465 – Palmer, L., hardware
4466 – Vroman, C., dentist
4467 – Lee Some, produce
4468 – Dunbar Community Hall
4479 – Exmoor Meat Market
4485 – Community Library
4492 – Williams Super Service
　　　　Garage
4495 – Quality Made Bakery
4497 – P.O. Substation #24
4497 – Harcus Drug

29TH AVE.
4505 – Dunbar Heights Realty
4505 – Master Craft Homes,
　　　　building contractor
4508 – Burns, B., service station
4518 – Reliable Confectionary
4528 – Southlands Realty
4531 – Sloan, R., grocer
4534 – Wilson, S., physician
4538 – Dunbar Plumbing
4543 – Lilac Cleaners
4545 – Window Maid Candy/Pastry
4555 – Dunbar Theatre
4590 – Island View Service Garage
4597 – Marine View Service Station

DUNBAR/SOUTHLANDS

39TH AVE.
5505 – B & K Economy Grocery
5515 – Sterling Markets, meats
5525 – Can Wind Bakeries
5529 – Blue Moon, confectionary
5539 – Ladyfair Beauty Shop
5549 – Reliable Shoe Repair
5555 – Dunbar Dressmakers
5557 – Point Grey Lending Library
5566 – Southlands Dry Goods
5566 – P.O. Substation #13
5569 – Stanton, H., cleaners

40TH AVE.
5607 – O K Barber Shop
5619 – McKay, Mrs. F.,
　　　　women's clothing
5620 – Macfarlane's Grocery
5621 – Southlands Family
　　　　Meat Market
5626 – Mayfair Produce
5629 – Law, W., drugs
5630 – Jean's Beauty Shoppe
5633 – So Hoy Produce
5640 – Safeway Stores
5648 – Pyatt, H., confectioner
5649 – Quick, W., hardware
5661 – Southlands Barber Shop
5687 – Southlands Home Cooking

Even-numbered addresses are on the
east side of Dunbar, odd-numbered
addresses on the west side.

Source: Vancouver City Directory, 1940.

◄ Mr. Pyatt was well known to South Dunbar teenagers in the 1940s. He sold great candy and pop and even extended credit at his Bungalow Confectionary, between 40th and 41st on the east side of Dunbar. Courtesy of Jane Pyatt Hubbard and Thelma Pyatt Perrault.

For many of the small convenience and specialty retail operators, competition was quite stiff and merchants had to be innovative. To attract and hold customers, some merchants extended credit, and then often found it impossible to collect what was owed them during the tough economic times of the '30s. Ian McGlashan, whose family operated Scottish Ham Curers from the early '30s to the early '50s, said that his father, Lyall, had to close for this reason. He found it hard to go to his customers to collect money when he knew how strapped for cash they were.

Modern Hairdressing and Beauty Culture profiled Dunbar's Ladyfair Beauty Shop in April 1941. An excerpt follows:

Appearance is the fundamental basis on which the entire hairdressing and beauty industry has been built. Women have become more conscious of their appearance and the important part it plays in the development of their personality. It is, therefore, logical that the same

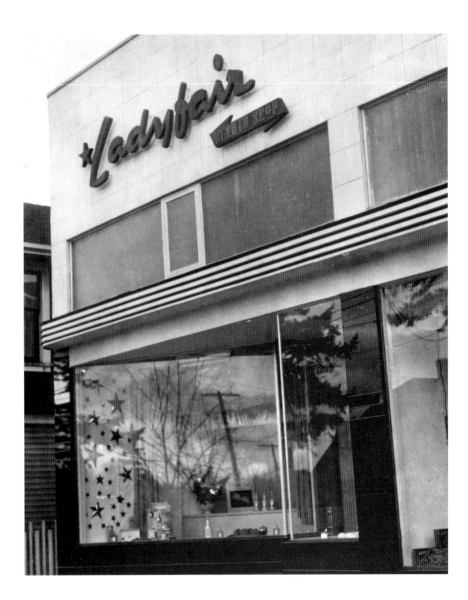

Hairdresser Florence Johnson's sensitivity to the importance of appearance and beauty was reflected in her storefront design. The name of the firm was lettered in green and red neon tubing and placed on a grey tile background with a glossy, black tile base. Courtesy of Dana (Logie) Coukell. ▶

principles of pleasing and artistic appearance when applied to a hairdressing establishment itself should play a key role in the development of business.

This theory has been tried out with definite results in the Ladyfair Beauty Shop, 5589 Dunbar Street, Vancouver. This business has been carried on for a considerable number of years and a steady increase in its clientele necessitated removal to larger premises. Miss Florence Johnson, proprietress, took advantage of this opportunity to put her ideas, which she had practised in part at her old location, into fuller operation. The result was the creation of one of the smartest beauty shops in the Canadian Pacific Coast metropolis.

- The exterior of the store is finished in black vitrolite with red relief lining and cream trim.
- The reception room is given a modernized touch by the streamlined canopy over the appointment desk and cosmetic display counter.

- CB.WAND - PHOTO - 1926
VANCOUVER, BC.

■ The uniform worn by the operators is distinctive, being of the pinafore type comprising a delicate-hued blue tunic worn over a peach blouse.

Since moving to her new premises and adopting her attractive layout, Miss Johnson has found a marked increase in her business and is firmly convinced that the investment in appearance, to be found in her shop, is thoroughly justified by results secured.

▲ Vegetables and fruits were delivered and sold in Dunbar's lanes by truck farmers with flatbed vans. Photo by C.B. Wand. Vancouver Public Library, photograph #58916.

Changing with the Times, 1940s and 1950s

Some of the commercial activities that thrived in the '20s were not faring well as the '40s drew to a close. The small logging operation and sawmill located near Crown and 33rd had run out of easily available trees and closed down in the late '20s; Clinton Stables started operating there in 1929. The Chinese vegetable and fruit gardens on the rich Southlands delta were gradually eliminated by land purchasers who turned the area into small acreages used mainly for horse pasture. The McCleery dairy farm was sold to the City of Vancouver and converted to the McCleery Golf Course in 1954 — a harbinger of the transition from a relatively unregulated rural to a more structured urban district economy.

Even so, in season, fresh produce from the Southlands market gardens was delivered on a regular basis at least until the mid-'50s. Patricia McLean has a memory of hand deliveries:

We called him Wong, which I guess we assumed was his first name. It shows our ignorance compared to the present times. I remember that he wore black pants, a black shirt and drove a small delivery van that was covered in a black canvas-like material that could be rolled up at the sides. He was extremely polite and very helpful. [Wong] was very kind to my mother and always seemed to cheer her up. When my mother had a cold he would give her a cold remedy in the form of an ointment that she would rub on her nose. My mother swore by it as a treatment! At Christmas time Wong would present my mother with some lily bulbs as a gift.

Joan Tyldesley, who lived at 3464 West 36th Avenue in the same period, has a similar memory:

I remember Wong coming up our back steps with his load of produce. . . . He held a fascination for me as a child. In his dark clothes and with his Oriental face I found him quite mysterious. I particularly found it intriguing how he would reach through the curtains at the back of his truck with his arms disappearing into the blackness and then would magically draw out a bamboo basket brimming with vegetables. In my childhood imagination I was sure that there were all sorts of exotic things in the back of that truck!

INCREASED CONSUMER SPENDING

Compared to the severe depression that crippled the B.C. economy in the 1930s, the economic picture immediately after World War II was characterized by pent-up demand. Wartime wage and price controls were removed. Most veterans returning to Dunbar were able to find good full-time employment, and their families soon had more disposable income than ever before. Wartime rationing restrictions were lifted, and there were exciting new goods and services available for purchase.

Sometimes, however, it took a while for the manufacturer-wholesale-retail linkage to begin to function efficiently. Harry Blight, partner in Pulham and Blight's Hardware at 3322 Dunbar (now Blight's Home Hardware), recalls how he and Mr. Pulham met the post-war demand for certain building materials by purchasing and selling used nails and other items because new ones were not yet available from the wholesaler.

Kathleen German, owner of the Dunbar Lending Library and Gift Shop at 4311 Dunbar (now Ashley Gift Shop) remembers that people were eager to obtain fine china at the end of the war. She received from her supplier a barrel of teacups so big it would not go through the shop's front door. People clustered around at 9:00 P.M. when she and her staff were unpacking outside and bought half the barrel's contents before the cups were even taken into the shop.

By the mid-'40s a revolutionary new quick-freeze process was providing homemakers with fresh-frozen rather than canned fruits and vegetables every month of the year. Quick-freeze facilities at the wholesale level had now been extended to scores of Vancouver retail merchants. A constant supply of frozen vegetables, fruits and meats was soon to erase seasonal variations in the availability of many food items.

By the mid-'50s it was unusual for a Dunbar family not to have an automobile, a refrigerator, a washing machine and a record player. Sawdust furnaces were replaced with oil-burning, forced-air furnaces in most houses, and television sets were eagerly sought. Beginning in 1952, as automobile traffic increased on Vancouver streets, B.C. Electric removed the streetcar tracks and replaced its streetcars with electric and gasoline-powered buses. The net effect on Dunbar and other major streets in Vancouver was to enable greater automobile speed and manoeuvrability. People began to travel much farther from home in order to shop and engage in other activities. With an increasing variety of merchandise available, cash purchases also became more frequent.

In return for helping with the household chores, the young people of Dunbar were often given small allowances, some of which could be spent on the Saturday matinees at the Dunbar Theatre. The kids loved the cartoons preceding the main feature — they could not wait to find out what would happen each week to Bugs Bunny, Elmer Fudd, the Three Stooges, or Donald Duck, Daisy and Uncle Scrooge McDuck. Then came the main feature — usually an animal production such as *Lassie* or a comedy/adventure, perhaps starring Judy Garland and Mickey Rooney. Westerns starring such heroes as the Lone Ranger were always popular. If the kids were lucky, they might have enough money for popcorn and maybe a soft drink. The best part was that all their friends were usually there too. Theatre tickets cost about 25 cents. And if it was someone's birthday that week, that person got to see the movie for free.

AFTER-SCHOOL JOBS

Employment opportunities existed for enterprising teenagers. Many young boys earned their bicycle and movie money and helped buy some of their own clothes and school supplies by delivering newspapers door to door in the early-morning hours or after school. The *Vancouver Sun's* green-painted "paper shacks" were located on 16th Avenue half a block west of Dunbar, in the lane west of Dunbar between 27th and 28th Avenues, and on the southwest corner of Dunbar and 41st Avenue adjacent to the B.C. Hydro substation. These were the pickup points for the paper carriers. The *Province* had a similar shack in the alley behind the stores on the east side of Dunbar between 18th and 19th Avenues.

Former paperboy Ron Gowe recalls that every afternoon between 1:30 and 3:00 the newspapers would be dropped off at the 10' x 12' wooden shack. A senior boy, the "sub-manager," would oversee the count. Wooden benches were placed on each wall inside the shack for holding the large canvas bags. After school, the boys and girls counted and stuffed the papers for delivering to customers on the routes. Then they plodded off to make their rounds. Some of the boys had bicycles with large metal baskets mounted in front of their handlebars to hold their papers. Outside the shack stood a 45-gallon metal drum, where excess wrapping paper and scrap wood were sometimes burned to provide a bit of warmth in winter. Much good-natured banter and some horseplay took place around the paper shack.

Other young people worked part-time in Dunbar shops. Craig Pinder cycled to Southlands Meat Market at 5621 Dunbar as soon as school was out. The meat was already wrapped and ready for delivery. Craig pedalled his heavy red bicycle, the metal basket in front filled with meat for customers, between 33rd and 55th Avenues. Craig always enjoyed delivering meat to Eric Nicol's house and chatting with Mrs. Nicol. One day, Eric appeared at the door and said to him, "Craig, just deliver the meat!"

At Southlands Meat Market, Craig was junior to two university students who were slightly older. He earned 50 cents an hour. Mr. Beaddie was a kind employer whom Craig liked and respected very much. In fact, he had real misgivings when he finally decided to leave Southlands to work for Super Valu, a few blocks north on Dunbar, for triple his wage.

In 1957, sixteen-year-old Sharon (Eddy) Randle worked after school and on weekends at the Blue Moon Confectionary (5529 Dunbar).

> I was paid 50 cents an hour and all the pop and candy I wanted. I remember we had a big old cash register with enormous keys you pressed down. If people happened to be buying more than one item you added everything up in your head. The Youngs lived in the back of the store at that time — they had also bought the store next door. Mrs. Young always kept a bowl and beaters in the fridge in the summer, and when anyone brought back their whipping cream because it wouldn't whip she would pour it in her bowl and whip it. She said you always needed a very cold bowl and beater to whip cream in the summer. This, of course, was before everyone had an electric beater. Both Mr. and Mrs. Young always thought I was too skinny and used to make me milkshakes with whipping cream and ice cream and buy me custard tarts from the bakery.

Improved economic conditions combined with technological advances in many areas of Canadian life created a spirit of optimism and a willingness to widen one's horizons: to try new foods, to drive greater distances to shop and for vacations, to expand one's wardrobe, to purchase recorded music, and to spend more for luxuries and entertainment. More than ever, Dunbar merchants, to survive, had to adapt. And many were quite successful.

Consolidation, 1960s to the Present

The next 45-year period in the history of Dunbar's commercial development is best described as marked by gradual change. Within the district, well-constructed single-family dwellings now sat on almost all of the available lots. Dunbar's own branch of the Vancouver Public Library was opened in 1950 at 29th Avenue; and a well-designed community centre was completed in 1958 on Memorial West Park grounds near 31st and Dunbar. The community had become a quiet, stable urban neighbourhood with all the supporting infrastructure and amenities necessary to sustain a bright future — in short, a great place to live, to raise a family and ultimately to grow older, as the following story of one family shows.

In 1929, Mr. and Mrs. Peter Nicholson moved from Kingsway and Nanaimo to 3962 West 22nd Avenue. Their former neighbours referred to Dunbar Heights as "Mortgage Heights" (or "Mortgage Hill," because nearly everyone in the area had a mortgage on their home). Mrs. Nicholson shopped on Dunbar except for large grocery shopping excursions every week or two, when she went downtown to Stong's (then located at 95 West Hastings).

In 1942, the Nicholsons' older daughter, Margaret, married Jack Claridge, stationed with the RCAF in Regina. Jack's father had immigrated to Canada in 1909 and sold real estate at Dunbar and 41st Avenue between 1909 and 1911 (when building lots were offered for $250). After the war, Marg and Jack returned to Vancouver and bought a house at 3947 West 21st Avenue, one block from where Margaret had lived with her parents on 22nd Avenue.

In 2003, Margaret and Jack Claridge were in their late eighties. Margaret continued to shop at Stong's (which moved from its downtown location to Dunbar in 1955). She still enjoyed being greeted warmly by Stong's employees, as she had been for many years. Marg and Jack's sons, Lloyd and Norman, both became schoolteachers and lived in Richmond. Like many others born after the 1940s, they could not afford to buy a house and raise children in Dunbar. Karen (née Stong) and Bill Rossum's daughter, Cori Bonina, is now manager of Stong's. She lives in North Vancouver, as she finds Dunbar housing too expensive. Can we once again call Dunbar Heights "Mortgage Heights"?

From 1950 to 2000, commercial Dunbar experienced a slow decline in its absolute number of businesses, as shown below:

DATE	1930	1940	1950	1960	1970	1980	1990	2000
NO.	58	146	167	163	142	138	146	135

The raw numbers, of course, do not say much about the actual nature of the evolution that has taken place. Here are some trends that have shaped Dunbar's changing commercial scene.

The first trend, as already mentioned, was increased reliance on the private automobile since the 1940s, which made it practical for Dunbar residents to range farther afield to shop and to work. Shoppers began to think nothing of driving to downtown Vancouver and to Burnaby or Richmond for specialty items or bargains. Commuting by car to work became the norm. Dunbar has thus become closer in a time sense to the critical centres of the city — the downtown commercial district, the airport, the university, the recreational areas. There has been a steady increase in the flow of traffic along Dunbar Street itself, making it harder to locate parking spots and more difficult to cross the street.

A second trend was the gradual replacement of skilled working-class residents by middle-class professionals. This transformation was, in part, driven by the expansion of the nearby University of British Columbia, which by the 2000s was host to more than 40,000 full-time students and was one of B.C.'s biggest employers, with a payroll in 2004 of more than $700 million. Many of UBC's faculty and staff live in the Dunbar district, and thousands of students live in rented basement suites in the area.

Social change has created a third trend. Until the mid-1960s, proportionately few married women worked regularly outside the home. By the 1980s almost as large a percentage of women occupied positions in the workforce as did men. The dual-career family became the norm rather than the exception, bringing with it new shopping and spending habits, more income, paid daycare for the children, and new stresses. Leisure time

In spring 1980, Stong's Market celebrated the completion of its new, larger store at 4560 Dunbar. Three generations of the Stong family were on hand to cut the ribbon. Left to right: Cori (Rossum) Bonina, Karen (Stong) Rossum, Evelyn Stong, Ralph Stong, Bill Rossum. Courtesy of the Stong family. ▶

for working parents became more and more a premium. Together, these changes in family life have had a significant impact on the types of new stores along Dunbar and the viability of existing businesses.

Stong's Market has been very successful in keeping up with the changing lifestyles of Dunbar's inhabitants. General manager Cori Bonina, great-granddaughter of one of the founders of the family-run business, says Stong's has always placed special emphasis on customer service. Store policies include providing a wide variety of high-quality grocery and other items, locally supplied where practicable; maintaining knowledgeable, personable and well-trained staff; tailoring product lines to customer needs and tastes; and advertising locally, using multiple media.

Bonina's strategy is to recognize shifts in customer needs and preferences and fill them. Among other innovations, she has introduced ready-to-cook meals and telephone or Internet-assisted order and delivery services. The latter have a potentially high appeal to elderly customers who no longer drive or who find it inconvenient to do so. Busy dual-career families also find this service a real time-saver. And the ready-to-cook meals are increasingly popular. Stong's Express Service (started in 1993 with phone or fax ordering) was the first such service offered in Vancouver. On-line ordering was added in April 1998, and the service is expanding rapidly. As most of Stong's customers live in the Dunbar area, their shopping trips often include encounters with their friends and neighbours.

A fourth trend, experienced primarily since the mid-1980s, is partially related to the increasing desirability of Dunbar as a place to live within the Lower Mainland and partially to an increased influx of new Canadians, mainly from Hong Kong and Taiwan. Almost every block in the Dunbar area includes several families with a non-European background. The net effect has been to increase the diversity in our neighbourhoods and to increase the economic contribution to the Dunbar district. Many of the newcomers have spent large amounts of money purchasing real estate and constructing new houses or renovating existing ones.

Ruth Chang, of 3970 21st Avenue, has worked for the Taiwan Trade Centre and holds a master's degree from the University of Pennsylvania. She believes the Taiwanese and Hong Kong immigrants to Dunbar have tended to shop for foodstuffs at the IGA supermarket on 41st Avenue (Chinese owned) or in Richmond at the Yaohan Centre or at T&T. Some are now also shopping at Choices. Stong's does not yet carry a wide enough variety of Chinese-type food items, according to Chang. For clothes, new immigrants of Chinese descent go to Richmond or, for high-end items, downtown to Holt Renfrew, the Gap or various boutiques. For restaurant dining and associated nightlife they go to Richmond, where restaurants are open much later in the evening.

Dunbar's Asian community is increasingly attracted to the excellent quality and wide variety of both Canadian and imported fruits and vegetables offered by Dunbar Produce. Courtesy of Joan Tyldesley. ▸

Most of the Chinese immigrants to Dunbar are middle-class professionals who, Chang says, enjoy driving considerable distances to make their purchases and to have fun. But increasingly they do their banking and shopping in Dunbar. In March 2002, Chinese-owned Dunbar Produce opened a greengrocery at 4355 Dunbar (the former site of the Italian-Canadian Delicatessen), carrying a wide variety of domestic and imported fruits and vegetables. The product line is selected to appeal to recently arrived Asians as well as native-born Canadians.

Other recent Canadian immigrants have established thriving enterprises on Dunbar. Dunbar Greetings (3456 Dunbar) has been run by Bilkish (BJ) Jaffer since her husband, Ali, died soon after they opened their business in 1988. Now she is assisted by her cousin, Salman (Sal) Kassam. BJ and Sal entered Canada as landed immigrants from Tanzania, then qualified for Canadian citizenship. BJ rents her premises and has to work long hours, six days a week, to gross enough revenue to stay in business. She offers her customers a wide variety of services and supplies, from a fully licensed post office to a coffee bar with light, packaged snacks. BJ is well trained in the computer field and is able to advise on or perform even the most complicated office projects. BJ and Sal know most of their customers by name and their smiling, friendly attitude, along with their competence, has endeared them to the Dunbar community. Dunbar Greetings has the atmosphere of a country store — a place to meet and chat with friends and neighbours.

Envisioning the Future, 2000 and Beyond

Three commercial sections have evolved along Dunbar Street from 16th to 41st Avenue (see map on page x). At the north end of the street is an area that extends from 16th Avenue to 19th Avenue — three blocks with businesses on both sides of Dunbar. The middle section of Dunbar begins at 26th Avenue and runs south to 30th Avenue. This shopping area is the most extensive. The third commercial section, Dunbar/Southlands, starts at 38th Avenue, extends to 41st Avenue and includes the business establishments east to Collingwood. Separating the three major commercial sections of Dunbar are residences similar in size and character to those lining the other numbered avenues in the district. The three commercial zones along Dunbar are the result of zoning plans established to conform to streetcar stops fixed when the streetcar line was laid. The idea was that residents returning home by streetcar should not have to walk too far after purchasing their convenience items from Dunbar's shops.

In many ways, the essential features of commercial Dunbar are much as they were at the beginning of the 1950s. There continues to be a wide variety of goods and services available. A 1997 study of Dunbar businesses found that their customers were mainly local residents who return on a regular basis, suggesting that most of these businesses are oriented to a local market. The businesses least dependent on the Dunbar neighbourhood for their customer base are the specialty stores, for example, the silver shop or the used sporting goods outlet. These stores offer unique lines not commonly available in other shopping districts in Vancouver, hence prospective customers are willing to travel considerable distances.

The number of auto service stations has declined to only two — Dunbar Chevron at 39th Avenue and the Shell station at 41st Avenue. Technological advances in automobile design and materials and in service station automation have reduced the requirement for complex and frequent manually performed service. Yet many Dunbarites really miss the courteous and helpful personal service provided by owner-operator Bob Lovegrove and his staff of attendants and mechanics at the Chevron station at 4184 Dunbar (now closed), or by Vernon Halverson's employees at the Shell station at Dunbar and 41st Avenue (where mechanical service is no longer provided).

Overall, as a commercial district Dunbar remains in transition, with more change anticipated. Compared to some other parts of Vancouver, Dunbar has very few vacant business premises, and those spaces that become vacant do not seem to stay vacant very long. The commercial vacancy rate in September 2005 was approximately 10 percent. However, in the Dunbar/Southlands commercial area, several new residential/commercial buildings have been built or are under construction, and many of

▲ Dunbar Greetings, like many other shops on Dunbar, prides itself on friendly service. BJ Jaffer and Sal Kassam always have good advice and a joke to pass on to their customers. Courtesy of Dianne Longson.

the new retail spaces have yet to be leased or sold. Some have been vacant for at least two years. One reason may be unattractive, expensive lease demands.

Other established businesses appear to have been adversely affected by rising rental rates or property assessments and taxes. At Quick Service Hardware's new home at 5620 Dunbar Street, Grant Frame, who operates the hardware store with his brother, Mike, can look across the street and see the old location where they plied their trade for 25 years — until taxes drove them out. Frame said the old building's municipal taxes rose from about $8,000 in 1991 to $14,000 for 1999, giving the brothers two options — quit or find a cheaper shop. Their new location across the street is much smaller — about 800 square feet compared to 1,500 — and the rent much less. Frame said South Dunbar used to have a village feel, but high taxes and rents are making it more exclusive. Only businesses with large profit margins will survive. "The little guys — the hardware stores, the confectionary stores — can't pay that [such high rates]," Frame told the *Vancouver Courier* in June 2000. "They just don't have the money."

The Dunbar district has become increasingly affluent, and the professional middle class that predominates in the area seems well positioned to

The Toronto-Dominion Building, at the corner of Dunbar and 26th, is bigger than neighbouring buildings but not necessarily better for Dunbar. Courtesy of Dianne Longson. ▶

Dunbar at the Millennium

NORTH DUNBAR

16TH AVE.
3204 – Thorntree Café
3206 – Studio Gallery
3208 – Cheapskates #3
3210 – Festive Fabrics
3211 – Atheneon Travel Service
3212 – Kay's Dry Cleaners
3228 – Cheapskates Too
3251 – B.T. Shears, barber
3271 – The Well

17TH AVE.
3307 – La Notte
3308 – Gold Star Shoe Repair
3309 – Pacific Mountain Centre
3322 – Blight's Home Hardware
3323 – Jebson Imaging
3335 – Anderson, D., dentist
3336 – B.C. Bread & Pastry
3348 – Bella Pizza
3349 – SEL Engineering
3350 – Carlito's Barber Shop
3352 – ShowTime Entertaining
3354 – Mr. Build Handi-man
3364 – Dunbar Farm Market
3376 – Hollywood Floor Fashions
3394 – Germaine's Antiques
3396 – Artisan Refinishing Furniture
3398 – Centro Flamenco,
　　　　 dance studio
3399 – vacant

18TH AVE.
3420 – Oriental Wok, restaurant
3422 – Kanata Travel Service

3432 – Dunbar Barber Shop
3434 – Classy Hair Design
3444 – Western Plumbing
　　　　 & Gas Fitting
3446 – Modern Club, restaurant
3453 – B.C. Government
　　　　 Liquor Store
3456 – Dunbar Greetings
3458 – Engineer, consultant
3467 – Ohio Cleaners
3463 – Dunbar Market
3468 – Dunbar Vacuum Sales
3470 – Airfaire Travel Agency
3479 – Dexter Associates Realty
3480 – Domino's Pizza
3496 – Cheapskates

20TH AVE.
3628 – Red & White Grocery

DUNBAR HEIGHTS

25TH AVE.
4162 – Distinctive Interiors
4168 – vacant
4186 – vacant
4188 – vacant
4192 – Esther's Alterations
4196 – George's Hair Styling
4198 – Kingsday Dunbar Market

26TH AVE.
4200 – Toronto-Dominion Bank
4205 – Royal Bank of Canada
4210 – Tang, D., dentist
4219 – Dunbar Cycles

4220 – H & R Block
4229 – Newcastle Locks & Letters
4231 – Beantown Coffee Place
4235 – Dunbar Cycles
4238 – vacant
4243 – Splash Toy Shop
4245 – Pink's Garden Shop
4250 – vacant
4253 – Just Imagine, costumes
4256 – Regent Heating
4260 – Kay's Beauty Salon
4263 – The Chancery, hair studio
4264 – Dunbar Barbers
4265 – Brick Oven Pizza
4268 – Dunbar Insurance Agency
4273 – A Touch of Wool,
　　　　 knitting supplies
4275 – Champlain Design,
　　　　 ladies' wear
4288 – Kwozzi Golfworks
4290 – Omega Custom Framing
4292 – vacant
4295 – Intercon Insurance Service
4298 – Musial, A., physician

27TH AVE.
4305 – Olinda's Boutique
4306 – Canadian Imperial
　　　　 Bank of Commerce
4311 – Ashlee Gift Shop
4315 – Enmark Jewellers
4316 – Tax Check Inc.,
　　　　 Gordon MacNeil
4321 – Ideal Bakery
4326 – Shoppers Drug Mart

continue to have significant earning and spending power. The people living in Dunbar are here because they want to be here — and this promises strong stability over time. Nonetheless, there is a threat, perceived by some Dunbar residents, that an "urban tsunami" is about to bring a flood of new multi-storey, multi-unit buildings such as the Toronto-Dominion Bank building and the Penny Farthing building, located at Dunbar and 26th Avenue. Both of these feature several small commercial rental spaces at street level below four-storey residential suites, with underground parking for the occupants.

Architecturally these structures may be utilitarian, but many local residents find them visually unappealing, containing no unique or memorable characteristics to distinguish them from many other suburban buildings in the Lower Mainland. The late Fred Dalla-Lana, a well-known Dunbar architect, expressed this concern: "I'm really sad about

Dunbar at the Millennium *cont'd*

4335 – Curiosities, antiques
4336 – Terrain Analysis Inc.
4345 – Matinee Ladies' Wear
4355 – Italian-Canadian Deli
4385 – Sushi Q, restaurant
4389 – Money's Dry Cleaning
4395 – Bank of Montreal

28TH AVE.
4410 – Dunbar Laundry
        & Dry Cleaners
4414 – Asianda Food Express
4418 – Simon's Kitchen
4424 – vacant
4428 – Video Plus, rentals & sales
4432 – Moldovano's restaurant
4445 – VanCity, credit union
4446 – MacGregor Photography
4447 – Dunbar Video
4448 – Top Cut Barbers
4455 – Cosy Inn Café
4464 – Old Western Pizza
4464 – Mac's, convenience store
4465 – POL Electronics
4467 – Starbucks Coffee Co.
4474 – Billy Bargoon's Emporium
4479 – Dunbar Cleaners
4480 – Alma Tandoori
4484 – Great Clips, hair styling
4485 – Photo Station, one-hour photo
4490 – Subway Sandwiches
4495 – EP Books
4497 – Soda's Diner

29TH AVE.
4508 – McDermott's Body Shop

4515 – Vancouver Public Library,
        Dunbar Branch
4531 – Vancouver Power Tool Rentals
4535 – The Clipper's Edge, barbers
4543 – Alta Vista Animal Hospital
4555 – Dunbar Theatre
4560 – Stong's Market
4585 – Cheshire Cheese Inn
4593 – Empress Bakery
4595 – K & K Pet Foods

DUNBAR/SOUTHLANDS
39TH AVE.
5505 – Chevron service station
5520 – Mac's, convenience store
5530 – Mastertour Travel
5540 – Southlands Insurance
5567 – Dunbar Veterinary Hospital
5579 – Waldo's Printing Centre
5581 – Huang's Food Market
5585 – Steven Lemay, photographer
5587 – Limelight Curios, old furniture
5589 – Pets Beautiful

40TH AVE.
5605 – Bosley's Pet Food
5617 – Dog Smart Training System
5620 – Quick Service Hardware
5621 – vacant
5626 – Mayfair Produce
5628 – Arnold's Coiffures
5630 – The Silver Shop
5631 – new, vacant
5635 – new, vacant
5637 – new, vacant
5639 – new, vacant

5636 – MyCom Computers
5640 – Colin Hansen, MLA
5648 – Boulevard Glass
5649 – vacant
5650 – vacant
5659 – Bank of Nova Scotia

**41ST AVENUE EAST
FROM DUNBAR**
3522 – 1 Hua Bakery
3534 – Weigh to Go
3536 – Body Logic, tanning & health
3540 – Southlands Medical Group
3548 – Southland Florist
3552 – Stationery 2000
3554 – Optic Zone
3556 – Busy Bee Cleaners
3560 – Newtech Commercial
3562 – Brompton's Hair Design
3579 – Southlands Dental Group
north – IGA & parking lot
south – four-storey building,
        under construction
3584 – Shall We Dance, studio
3590 – Viratest Ltd.
3591 – Lawrence Books
3592 – Times Restaurant, Szechuan
3594 – Gentle Touch Cleaners
south – Shell service station

Even-numbered addresses are on the
east side of Dunbar, odd-numbered
addresses on the west side.

Source: Database compiled by author,
30 January 2000.

Dunbar Street. It's just horrendous how awful those new buildings are. . . . [The] only one which is half decent is the very first one that Richard Henriquez did right at the top [Dunbar House, 3621 West 26th]. After that, all of them go downhill from there. It is just anonymity of a sort. The reason that Richard's is nice is that it has some depth to it. It has some recessed balconies, you get some sculpture and void. All the new ones are just flat."

In early fall 2005, excavation and construction began for two more large, multi-use buildings on opposite sides of Dunbar at the 18th Avenue intersection. Robert Duke and Howard Bingham Hill Architects are responsible for the exterior design, featuring clear glass, brick and wood. Each building will consist of four storeys, with the first floor designed for retail commercial units or professional offices. The top three floors are planned as luxury condominiums. Dunbar residents and shop owners are hopeful that these new complexes will fit well with existing shops and with the neighbourhood.

The concern of local residents is that if the three commercial areas along Dunbar Street experience more of this type of development, there will be less of the personal special service that in the past has made this a good place not only to shop but to spend time. Arnold Sveistrup's story (Arnold's Coiffures, 5628 Dunbar) puts this concern very well:

> On the north side of 41st, prior to the demolition of stores to make way for the IGA store, there were several small shops including an appliance repair shop where you used to go in and they would fix your fridges and stoves and stuff like that. Their name was Bruce and she was a woman that you could walk in there and say that you have a 1926 stove and you need an element for it and she would say "number 5xxx" and she'd go in the back and bring it to you. Or you'd say "I lost a screw from my" — from any kind of thing, eh — and you would tell her exactly what the screw was and where it came from on your appliance. Then she would go in the back and find the screw or part and bring it to you. The Bruces' shop was in business for a long time. Mrs. Bruce really knew her field — small-appliance parts replacement and service.

A recent survey indicated that three-fourths of the full-time and half of the part-time employees in Dunbar businesses did not live in Dunbar, but commuted to work from outside the district. About two-thirds of the employees were full-time. A reason commonly given by the employees themselves for living outside Dunbar was that their earnings were not high enough to support living in the area. It is likely, however, that a large portion of the part-time employees living in Dunbar are secondary wage earners in their households. Dunbar's primary wage earners commonly commute outside of the district.

Following a community planning program begun in early 1997 in which Dunbar residents and business people participated through a series of public workshops and a questionnaire survey, Vancouver city council in September 1998 approved a *Community Vision*. This document laid out a number of general priorities and directions for planners to implement over the next 10 to 20 years in Dunbar. Here are those dealing with commercial Dunbar:

- Dunbar residents greatly value its safe, green village-like atmosphere and see this quality as what makes Dunbar special. They want to preserve this uniqueness in the face of change which is often seen as unwelcome and unneighbourly.
- Dunbar Street shopping districts should provide a community focus and a more attractive "face" for the community.
- Changes should come about with a high level of community involvement to ensure that they enhance the community and serve residents of all ages.

The Times, They Are A-Changin'

Peggy Schofield mused on how buying bread in Dunbar has changed since 1960.

I went to get bread at my favourite bakers, and Joe's bakery [B.C. Bread and Pastry, 3336 Dunbar] has closed for good! I asked at Blight's [Hardware], and they said he was in the hole every month. I think the phenomenon of a proliferation of wonderful local bakeries, at least the traditional kind, is disappearing. I remember when I first came to Canada that loaves were 19 cents each, and just wonderful bread. Having one or more of these bakeries in each neighbourhood was a given. Could it be because it's convenient to shop on the fly at Stong's or even the Chevron station and get fairly good bread now? I wonder if the bread-making machines at home have cut into the bakeries' profits? I am continually amazed at the amount of good bread being

offered everywhere, not just at independent bakeries. There will never be dark rye, a sourdough or a Caribbean heavy brown to match Joe's, though.

Photo courtesy of Joan Tyldesley.

- The variety of small shops and services at the sidewalk edge should be continued with gaps filled in.
- Pedestrian improvements should include safer crossings, benches, plantings, and a community plaza.

Continuing community involvement and close liaison with city planners will be necessary if the vision is to be successfully achieved, and there are strong initiatives now in place. The Dunbar Residents' Association is more active than ever before in monitoring the manner in which the district of Dunbar develops; it has launched a number of projects, such as the Block Watch program and a traffic control program on side streets, to help make the neighbourhood a safer and more pleasant environment.

In early 2000, a group of approximately 60 Dunbar business people formed the Dunbar Business Association (DBA). Previous associations had not achieved long-term viability. Issues of common concern to business owners and managers include improving security and eliminating graffiti, making Dunbar more attractive and pedestrian-friendly, establishing a business directory for customers and residents, and developing closer ties with the residents' association. The DBA has recently been in the forefront of a campaign to rid Dunbar of graffiti and has been instrumental in supporting the newly completed rest area and bench in front of the Dunbar branch of the Vancouver Public Library.

Of 757 Dunbar business ventures that were initiated between 1927 and 1998, slightly more than 50 percent remained in business for only five years or less. Not all of these failed. Some left the area to continue their business activity elsewhere. However, the high turnover of individual businesses presents both an opportunity (for new membership) and a challenge (loss of dedicated Dunbar business people) to the DBA. A priority of the association is, and will continue to be, to develop more teamwork and community participation.

Peggy Schofield, 2002 president of the Dunbar Residents' Association and an active member of the Dunbar Business Association, expressed a number of the association's concerns, some of which were noted earlier by individual business owners: "For many, the property taxes or rents are too high for their businesses to make money. Most business people can't afford to live in the Dunbar area, so they have to commute from long distances. As a result, they don't have time to attend Dunbar Business Association meetings and they don't identify strongly with overall needs of commercial Dunbar. They don't see a strong reason to join the DBA. It is a real struggle."

Almost a Century of Convenience

Countering the turnover in businesses between 1927 and 1998, 26 businesses have served the Dunbar district more than 40 years and, in 2006, 12 of these were still operating. Some had changed their Dunbar locations at least once over the years. These businesses are Dunbar's commercial survivors, and each has a fascinating and unique story behind it. For example, banking and financial facilities provide the ultimate convenience for residents and business owners in any community. Branches of the Royal Bank of Canada and the Canadian Imperial Bank of Commerce have been continuously serving the Dunbar district since the late 1920s, although each bank has changed its branch location once. A branch of the Royal Bank of Canada was first located on the northeast corner of 17th Avenue and Dunbar, but moved to a newly constructed and centrally located facility at 4205 Dunbar in 1993. A CIBC branch was at 4407 but moved to 4306 Dunbar in 1948. The Bank of Montreal and the Bank of Nova Scotia established branches in the 1950s. A newcomer to the district, the Toronto-Dominion Bank opened a branch in its new multi-unit commercial and residential building at Dunbar and 26th Avenue in 1998. VanCity, a credit union, opened in 1983, offering many banking and financial services. Few businesses have been affected by technological advancement as much as the banks and similar financial institutions. Because of increasingly widespread use of credit and debit cards, ATMs and electronic banking, Dunbar's bank customers need not visit their local branch except for non-routine services. The teller's role has evolved

Ideal Bakery, Dunbar's longest continuously operating store, opened in 1926 and has supplied its customers with delicious bakery goods for 80 years. Courtesy of Joan Tyldesley. ▶

from routine and repetitive customer service tasks towards more specialized and consultative services. And fewer tellers are needed.

Characteristics common to most of Dunbar's "survivors" are a strong dedication to customer service, a quality product line and willingness to stand behind it, a sense of what will sell in Dunbar (local demand), and a sound knowledge of financial fundamentals and management techniques. With the exception of the four major banks, these businesses are not branches of chains, nor are they big-box retailers. They do cover a broad spectrum of convenience stores, selling goods and services shoppers need or desire on a regular basis.

Ideal Bakery (4321 Dunbar) was founded in 1926 by Jack and Maggie Harrison as a bakery and it has been a bakery at the same site since then. In 1928 the proprietorship changed to Jack and Elizabeth (Cissey)

The Survivors

NORTH DUNBAR

ADDRESS	NAME OF SHOP	OPENED	CLOSED
3293	De'Lite Fruit Market	Before 1940	After 1975
3295	Dunbar Pharmacy	Before 1945	After 1965
3322	Blight's Hardware	Before 1945	n/a
3408–3434	Three Smart Girls	Before 1945	After 1990
3444	Point Grey Bakery	Before 1930	After 1990
3644	Heather Handy Store	Before 1930	After 1980

DUNBAR HEIGHTS

ADDRESS	NAME OF SHOP	OPENED	CLOSED
4184	Lovegrove Service Station	Before 1940	After 1990
4205	Royal Bank of Canada	Before 1930	n/a
4219 & others	Dunbar Cycles	1927	n/a
4230 & others	Dunbar Fish & Chips	Before 1940	After 1975
4255	Thompson Sales & Service	Before 1955	After 1990
4290	Dairydale Dairy Products	Before 1940	After 1990
4295	MacGregor's Dry Goods	Before 1955	After 1990
4306	CIBC	Before 1930	n/a
4321	Ideal Bakery	1926	n/a
4326–4560	Stong's	1955	n/a
4395	Bank of Montreal	Before 1960	n/a
4455	Mayfair Dairy	Before 1930	After 1965
4508	McDermott's Body Shop	Before 1955	n/a
4531	Vancouver Power Tools	Before 1940	n/a
4543	Patterson Florist	Before 1950	After 1995
4555	Dunbar Theatre	1935	n/a

DUNBAR/SOUTHLANDS

ADDRESS	NAME OF SHOP	OPENED	CLOSED
5539–5589	Ladyfair Beauty Shop	Before 1927	After 1970
5567–5659	Bank of Nova Scotia	Before 1950	n/a
5648	Bungalow Confectionary	Before 1927	After 1965
5649–5620	Quick Service Hardware	Before 1940	n/a

Source: Database compiled by author, 1 September 2006.

Heskin. Mrs. Heskin and Mrs. Harrison were sisters. By agreement, the bakery was taken over by the Heskins upon their immigration from Preston, England, to Vancouver in 1927. The Heskins operated the bakery continuously until 1946, when they sold the business to Mr. and Mrs. Martin. Mabel Pickett, the present owner, was one of the first employees of the Martins. Joy Woolfrey has vivid memories of Ideal Bakery:

> In the mid-1950s when I lived near 37th and Balaclava, I would meet up with friends who lived nearby, Patricia McLean, Dale Brown and Joan Tyldesley, and we would walk together to Lord Byng High School. After school, we would pass Ideal Bakery about the time the fresh baking came out of the ovens. We could smell the wonderful aroma a couple of blocks away, and as hungry teenagers we began to entertain the

thought of buying freshly baked bread. We would scrounge around among ourselves to see if we could come up with the 15 cents needed to buy the bread. If we were lucky, we could purchase a loaf. We would then pull apart the warm, steaming bread and eat the whole loaf. It was a very satisfying treat on the way home from school.

During the first week of January 2002, Mabel celebrated the 50th anniversary of her takeover of Ideal Bakery. Mabel's beloved cat, Mickey McGregor, helped her greet customers for nearly three decades. Mickey died at age twenty-eight in April 2005.

In addition to the convenience-oriented businesses located on Dunbar, several outstanding specialty stores have become well established. The following Dunbar outlets are typical. Dunbar Lumber, at 16th Avenue and Dunbar, supplies professional builders and private homeowners alike, and its customers are drawn from a wide radius that extends well beyond Dunbar. Cheapskates opened a used sporting goods consignment business at 3644 16th Avenue in 1987, then expanded with a second store in the former Royal Bank location at 3228 Dunbar in 1992. In 2004 Cheapskates had four locations, all within a three-block radius, offering a wide line of used (and some new) sporting equipment. Consignment prices are reduced with time, making items ever more attractive to shoppers.

Dunbar Vacuum, 3468 Dunbar, is known as one of Vancouver's best vacuum cleaner repair facilities, selling numerous new and reconditioned vacuums. Splash, 4243 Dunbar, is a children's store, carrying a wide

Cheapskates, which had four branches in 2004, is one of Dunbar's specialty shops attracting customers from across the Lower Mainland. Courtesy of Joan Tyldesley. ▶

variety of toys and games. The Silver Shop, 5630 Dunbar, features rare antique, estate and new silver items, such as cutlery, serving trays, and tea and coffee urns. McDermott's Body Shop, 4508 Dunbar, offers collision repairs for a wide variety of domestic and imported automobiles. It has sponsored local youth sports teams for many years, and maintains an attractive flower garden next to its premises. Of great benefit to the community is Point Grey Sales and Service on 16th Avenue, just off Dunbar. For many years Erika Zellman and Ernie Mako have kept people's lawn-mowers sharp and running smoothly. Weigh to Go, 3534 41st Avenue, provides bulk foods. The store's motto is "Everything from Soup to Nuts." Lawrence Books, 3591 41st Avenue, is the destination of many book collectors from throughout the Lower Mainland because of its vast selection of used and rare books.

Specialty restaurants attract diners to Dunbar as well as delighting local residents. For example, La Notte (3307 Dunbar) offers Italian cuisine, the Modern Club (3446 Dunbar) features a Japanese menu, and Masala (formerly Moldovanos), at 4432 Dunbar, specializes in Greek and Indian food. The Cheshire Cheese Inn (4585 Dunbar) is not an inn but a pub providing an interesting array of beverages and a fine pub dining experience. While a wide selection of alcoholic beverages is offered at the B.C. Liquor Control Board's bunker-like building at 3453 Dunbar, privately owned Village Wines, 3536 West 41st Avenue, has an array of excellent B.C. wines to tempt the connoisseur.

In conclusion, as one long-term Dunbar shopper put it, "Dunbar is advancing all the time towards its objective of becoming an exciting place to 'take care of business.'" Retired merchant Lena Fisher said, "Everything you need is there on Dunbar, I think. We are very blessed as a commercial area. But being in business is tough. There is a lot of competition." There is a strong sense that the atmosphere of the old corner store with its warmth and neighbourliness will be carried on by Dunbar's friendly shops such as Point Grey Sales and Service, Stong's, Splash, Dunbar Greetings, Germaine's Antiques, the Cozy Inn, Beantown, Blight's Hardware, Arnold's Coiffures and the Cheshire Cheese. Dunbar's residents and its business community have inherited an important and valuable legacy, one that can be preserved, appreciated and enjoyed in the years to come.

CHAPTER 5

Transportation in a Classic Streetcar Suburb

—◦ Angus McIntyre

Transportation plays an important role in shaping a community's development. Before Europeans came and left their mark on the land, Coast Salish people established winter villages and seasonal camps along the north arm of the Fraser River and on the beaches of Point Grey. Canoes provided access by water, and foot trails connected settlements and food-gathering sites.

When European settlers arrived in the 1860s and began clearing the land and building dikes to establish farms along the river, they relied first of all on the Fraser River's north arm for transportation. Lumber and other supplies had to be brought from New Westminster by scow or canoes. Eventually farm produce was similarly transported to market. A small local ferry, the *Faerie Queen*, stopped to pick up passengers and produce from boat landings and river barns. Each landing had a flagpole. When the flag was raised, it was a signal for the ferry to pull in.

River transportation had a serious drawback: winter freeze-ups. Pioneer descendant Betty (McCleery) McQueen related: "The early settlers felt they had to get a road in [from New Westminster] because the river froze quite often in those days." In 1863 Hugh McRoberts was awarded the contract to clear a trail from New Westminster to the Musqueam Indian Reserve. He and the McCleery brothers cleared 12 miles in 13 weeks

to create the North Arm Trail, later called River Road. It followed the same course as today's Southwest Marine Drive.

The North Arm Trail was a narrow bridle path through dense forest. Those who used it had to ford numerous streams, often at the bottom of steep ravines, for there were only rudimentary bridges. An early settler, Henry S. Rowling, described the challenges of travelling the trail: "The rider had to dismount in several places. Some of the ravines were 40 to 50 feet deep. The banks were so steep that it was necessary to make trail by angling back and forth down the steep bank and cross the wet bottom or muskeg on a narrow planked crossing of split cedar slabs, with a narrow bridge of some sort across the creeks. Then horse and man, one after the other, scrambled up the steep opposite banks." Given such conditions, it is understandable that, except during extended winter freezes, the river provided a much faster and cheaper route than the North Arm Trail.

River transport also had its own hazards. In August 1883, John Betts, who along with Henry Mole held title to the land adjacent to the Musqueam reserve, was coming down the North Arm from New Westminster on the little ferry named the *Alice*. He had tied a canoe to the ferry, intending to call on someone along the way. Instead of asking the captain to slow down so he could board the canoe, he thought he could easily climb into the canoe without the *Alice* stopping. His attempt was unsuccessful. The canoe capsized and Betts drowned.

After the sale of timber leases in Point Grey, logging roads were built. Loggers used them to haul out logs with oxen, to reach events and to visit neighbouring logging camps. Excavation work on Blenheim Street in 2002 revealed an underlying corduroy "skid road."

A New Streetcar Suburb

The first electric streetcar was already running along Vancouver's Main Street with a branch along Powell Street in 1890, but the Dunbar area was still remote and undeveloped. It would be another dozen years before residents began establishing homesteads, orchards and farms in Dunbar. Musqueam boys helped plough the land with a team of horses, and walking was still the main way to get around.

In 1908 the municipality of Point Grey was formed when West Side landowners broke away from South Vancouver over its assessment practices. In 1909 a money bill authorized the expenditure of $280,000 for roads. The plan was to build main thoroughfares a half-mile apart. Within that grid, new roads could be added later as development took place. In September of that year, Canada's governor general, Earl Grey, opened the new Granville Street Bridge, which allowed easier access to Point Grey and Dunbar. In 1911 streetcar service reached 10th Avenue and Sasamat Street via Fourth Avenue and Alma Road. The fare at this time was

◄ Snow is still visible on the North Shore mountains in early 1951 as streetcar 303, a 1912 veteran, ascends the Dunbar Diversion. Neighbourhood resident Mel Stevens snapped this view with a Brownie box camera during the last week of service. Note "Mission-style" substation above front of streetcar in Almond Park. Courtesy of Mel Stevens.

◄ Early settlers punched River Road, now Marine Drive, through virgin forest. This view of the road near the McCleery farm was taken c. 1900. City of Vancouver Archives, photograph #STR.P133.1 N91.1.

5 cents, six tickets for 25 cents and rush-hour tickets for workmen at eight for 25 cents.

With this expansion of streetcar service, Point Grey was beginning to develop in a pattern described by author Sam Warner in his book *Streetcar Suburbs*. Although Warner is writing about Boston in the late 1800s, his description refers equally to the new municipality of Point Grey in the first decades of the twentieth century:

> There existed a consensus of attitude which caused each man to build houses much like those of his neighbors and to seek to locate in a neighborhood or on a street which was popular with families of an income similar to his own. The new suburban environment emphasized the pleasures of private family life, the security of a small community setting, and the enjoyments of an increased contact with nature. Every year more and more middle class families lived in the suburbs. The streetcar and utility networks brought a steady increase of land available for settlement.

Streetcar service would provide a relatively inexpensive means to get to and from the developing "suburb" of Dunbar.

Early residents still had a lengthy walk to the nearest streetcar service. A former city alderman, C.H. Wilson, acquired an estate of five acres near the crest of Dunbar Heights, at a time when all that area was either forest or forest clearing. City archivist Major J.S. Matthews later interviewed the Wilsons and wrote: "The home was near Balaclava and King Edward at the end of a corduroy road leading down by easy grades through the forest to salt water near the English Bay Cannery on Point Grey Road (near Bayswater Street). At that time the approach to their residence was possible by horse and buggy, but not much more than possible, and a horse was by far the best means. . . ." He notes that Mrs. Wilson described how they used to walk down "the old Johnson Road [now Blenheim Street] all the way from Twenty-fifth and catch the car at Fourth."

The first streetcar service to Dunbar opened in September 1912. It ran along 41st Avenue from the B.C. Electric interurban line in Kerrisdale and provided the first transit service into southwest Vancouver, establishing Dunbar as a "streetcar suburb" for the first time. This single-track line operated a 15-minute service with one car. It featured open track adjacent to a dirt road.

On 2 June 1913, a second streetcar line started to provide a north-south service in Dunbar. With almost no housing in the area, the single-track line 2.4 miles in length started at 10th Avenue and Crown Street, ran south on Crown, east on 16th Avenue and south on Dunbar Street to 41st Avenue. A single two-man car ran a shuttle service every 30 minutes, with 20-minute service promised within one year. Early photographs show Dunbar and 29th Avenue with the single track close to the centre

The Johnson family in their horse and buggy on Blenheim Street, still a dirt road, c. 1913. Equestrian activity is still very much a way of life in present-day Southlands. Courtesy of Gayle Mitchell. ▶

of the street with a dirt road on the east side. Wood poles on both sides support the trolley wire. Would-be passengers hailed the car to stop. Marked "car stops" did not appear until later.

Over time, service on Dunbar's single-track line improved and two cars were assigned to operate on the route. A system was needed to ensure that the cars running in opposite directions on the single track passed each other safely at passing sidings. The first car to enter service on any day carried a baton, which granted permission to use that section of track. Ronald N. Gowe described this "passing block" as "a piece of wood about 2 inches square and 14 inches long. . . . As the cars passed on the two tracks on the passing siding, the motorman would lean out of the left window of the car and pass this block to the motorman of the car going in the opposite direction." Jean (McLean) Vivian related this baton episode: "My parents told me about the single-track line on Dunbar and the passing of the baton. On one occasion the oncoming car was late at the passing siding, and the motormen proceeded until both cars were nose to nose." Usually in these situations the passengers were transferred and at the end of the day the cars would return to the car barn out of sequence. At the end of the day, the last car returned the baton to the car barn.

During the 1920s three commercial strips started to develop on Dunbar: at 16th Avenue, 27th Avenue and 41st Avenue (see chapter 4). In each

The newly graded Dunbar Diversion in 1923 affords an expansive view of Kitsilano, with many newer homes visible, but land west of Alma Road is still lightly developed. The worker at bottom right is preparing to have a trolley-wire pole erected. Courtesy of B.C. Hydro Information Services. ▼

A steam shovel and two Mack trucks with solid rubber tires are shown at work with a construction gang on 22 June 1926. The double-tracking of the streetcar line had commenced in this view looking north from Dunbar and West 29th Avenue, with the community hall to the right of the steam shovel. Courtesy of B.C. Hydro Information Services. ▶

case most people could walk from their homes to these stores or alight from the streetcar and make a purchase on the way home. This is another way Dunbar fit the "streetcar suburb" definition: streetcars conveyed people and goods efficiently.

Construction of the Dunbar Diversion

The route of the Dunbar streetcar on Crown Street to its terminus at West 10th Avenue required a transfer to get downtown. This inconvenience for passengers was something that the B.C. Electric Company sought to eliminate. But it required a major improvement to Alma Road. In 1923 the *B.C. Electric Employees' Magazine* reported:

> It was found necessary to create a new street in order to avoid the steep grade of Alma Road, so a road was surveyed and property purchased. The new street, which is yet to be named, is 82 feet wide and has been graded along the side hill for two city blocks between Alma Road and Dunbar Streets and Twelfth and Fourteenth Avenues. . . . The old tracks on Sixteenth Avenue and Crown Street are to be torn up. The work was undertaken under a three-cornered agreement between the City of Vancouver, the municipality of Point Grey and the B.C. Electric.

Once the diversion opened for business on 13 November 1924, there was through service to downtown, then east on Hastings Street to Boundary Road. Eighteen-minute service was provided on the Dunbar line (at the cost of a reduction in the number of stops). On 17 November 1924, a new passing siding was installed at 33rd Avenue, which allowed a 10-minute rush-hour service along the still single-track line.

Since 16th Avenue marked the boundary between the municipalities of Vancouver and Point Grey, an extra fare was charged when you crossed the boundary. Long-time resident Ed Bowman said: "I remember my mother saying that when she went on the streetcar to go up Dunbar, she had to pay an extra fare because she was in another district. The conductor would come around with this little fare box. He would put a cap over his regular fare box and bring this little portable one for the extra bit." When the streetcar arrived at 16th Avenue, many people would get off to walk the extra few blocks rather than pay another fare. This earned the intersection of Dunbar and 16th the nickname "Scotsman's Corner." For convenience, conductors sold books of "settlers" tickets at the same price as a cash fare. Beginning 1 January 1929, when Vancouver amalgamated with the municipalities of South Vancouver and Point Grey, Dunbar residents no longer had to pay two fares to travel downtown.

The Observation Car

Warm summer weather heralded the appearance on Dunbar Street of a Vancouver institution — the observation car. This roofless streetcar featured tiered rows of seats for an unobstructed view on a two-hour tour of the city. Two of these "sightseeing" cars were built in 1909 and performed their community service as car 123 and car 124 until 1950. Ed Bowman recalled that in the 1930s "there was one car that ran in the afternoon and then one in the evening. It was quite interesting for people to take the

◀ Wood ties are ready for streetcar rails to be attached during double-tracking — from this vantage point looking south at Dunbar and 31st Avenue, June 1926. Streetcar service is maintained on temporary track shown on the east side of Dunbar Street. Close-up view shows original 1926 wood ties at Dunbar and 26th Avenue exposed during 1999 roadwork. Top left photo courtesy of B.C. Hydro Information Services. Top right photo courtesy of Angus McIntyre.

▲ The earliest known view of the streetcar line on Dunbar features three observation cars on a B.C. Electric Railway employees' picnic in September 1919. A young Teddy Lyons is standing on the road (in uniform) at the front of car 124. The second observation car was converted from a regular passenger car and later rebuilt to its original condition for badly needed capacity during World War II. Courtesy of Coast Mountain Bus Company.

evening car because the city was all lit up . . . all neon signs and everything — big white lights — and for a lot of people who came from the Prairies, this was all new to them and they enjoyed it. It was sunset and it was really a nice thing and not only that, [the conductor] had blankets, red blankets, that passengers could wrap around themselves."

A twenty-four-year-old employee named Teddy Lyons became the conductor on one of the two open cars, a job he held for almost 40 years. Lyons was described as having an "effervescent personality," and he was an immediate hit with his vaudevillian patter that included puns and jokes. Passing a new funeral home, he would say: "See that building? People are dying to get in." Dick Gardner, an accomplished magician and musician, joined the other observation car as conductor in 1925. He and Teddy Lyons travelled nearly 600,000 miles in cars 123 and 124 before retirement. In earlier years the conductors used megaphones, and later the cars were equipped with a loudspeaker system.

From the earliest days children were attracted to "the streetcar without a roof." At points along the route the observation car would stop and children would entertain the passengers. Ian McGlashan recalled the summers of 1935–36 when a group of four to eight children gathered to sing songs for the observation car at Dunbar and 22nd Avenue. He said this was done for the fun of it rather than for any coins that the passengers tossed. Jean (McLean) Vivian described another small group of children that sang songs at 33rd and Dunbar. She said five- and ten-cent coins were thrown for them. One girl took elocution lessons and recited jingles and short stories — a compulsory stop when Teddy Lyons saw her. Jane (Pyatt) Hubbard had this recollection: "From about May to September the observation car (we used to call it the funny car) went by two or three times a day. It stopped in front of our store [at 41st Avenue and Blenheim] because these kids all congregated and they sang 'God Bless America' because most of the tourists were American. Then they would do a little tap dance and people on board would throw them money."

Some performers played a different game, as evidenced in this remembrance from Mel Stevens. As young boys, he and his friends would hide in the shrubs alongside the Dunbar Diversion and wait for Lyons and the observation car:

> Well, at 14th and Dunbar, I remember quite well, he did two things. One of them we used to ruin for him, 'cause there used to be a laurel hedge on the west side of the Dunbar Diversion and he used to always talk about how *there's a laurel hedge and it's very hardy* so it's Laurel and Hardy. So we used to ruin his punchline by yelling it out as soon as we could. And the other thing was, he used to either whistle or call for a pet crow that used to fly out from somewhere and would perch on the top of the car on one of those crossbars with all the lights on it.

Lyons usually acknowledged the boys, and some people on the car thought they were part of the act.

Vic Waters said Lyons "was known as something of a freeloader — always invited himself to dinner Friday nights after a run." There was a precedent for this in that the wealthy German entrepreneur named Alvo von Alvensleben, who lived on a 20-acre estate south of 41st Avenue and Blenheim Street, often supplied meals to the conductors. Vancouver archivist Major Matthews recorded the following conversation in 1931 with B.C. Electric motorman Coiret Clampitts that includes a reference to von Alvensleben's legendary hospitality:

> I helped to build the 41st Avenue car line 20 years ago. At first we had a little "dinky" car which ran "jerkwater" from the interurban (Eburne-Vancouver) to Dunbar Street. [Jerkwater refers to a trolley line to a lightly populated area.] It was a wild kind of a place then, but those people who lived there were the kindest people I ever knew. I remember one time, it was Christmas, the folks in some house — I forget just which one — brought us out a Christmas dinner, and we, the conductor and I, ate it in the car. They had it all fixed up on a silver tray, with white napkins, silver napkin rings, silver jugs, turkey dinner, and hot mince pies. Another Christmas we had five turkey dinners in the car. I know I got 28 cigars on one day and the conductor got 25.
>
> You remember Alvo von Alvensleben, the German, friend of Kaiser Bill? Well, Taylor, he ran the night shift; he never troubled to take lunch. Every night, they never missed, Alvensleben sent him out his lunch, and [with emphasis] *a glass of wine.*

▲ Teddy Lyons stands on the left at the front platform of observation car 123 as it prepares for a 30-minute downtown farewell trip on 17 September 1950. Car 124 following had just completed its last trip from Dunbar Street. Courtesy of B.C. Hydro Information Services.

With the abandonment of the single track along 41st Avenue in 1947, the observation car started to run both north and south on Dunbar, turning around at the wye at 41st Avenue.

On Sunday, 17 September 1950, car 124 made its final trips to Dunbar, leaving Cambie and Hastings Streets at 10:00 A.M. and 2:00 P.M. Car 123 appeared fully decorated at 4:00 P.M. for a 30-minute downtown tour, followed by a reception at the home of B.C. Electric's president, Dal Grauer. Grauer honoured Teddy Lyons and Dick Gardner for their long service. In 40 years, the observation cars had carried 1.5 million sightseers. With those final trips, decades of summer entertainment with scores of Dunbar children came to an end. The observation car run had been cancelled due to lack of available track.

Childhood Pranks and Memories

Besides trying to disrupt Teddy Lyons' act, Dunbar kids got into other mischief involving the streetcars. Lionel Jinks recalled a method used to get two rides from a single streetcar ticket: "In those days the streetcar fare was four cents — if you purchased the blue tickets. And what we used to do . . . [was] to spend about a half an hour splitting the blue ticket down the middle. And if you were careful, you could split it and then you'd wet the bottom to make that part heavier. And you'd drop it in and of course it would go down with the printed half facing upwards."

Gordon Jinks remembered the use of "catnip" on streetcar tracks as a boyhood prank. "We used to go to the drugstore and we'd buy some sodium nitrate or something like that — some nitrate. And you'd mix it with charcoal and it made it into gunpowder. And we used to wrap it in a little package, put it on the streetcar tracks. Well, when the streetcar went over it, it would go BOOM!" Ronald N. Gowe recalled: "We often put pennies on the streetcar tracks to flatten them out. They would end up the size of the old-style English pennies." Marjorie (Tryon) Jones, who performed for the observation car passengers as a child, also recalled placing things on the tracks: "Another thing we used to do was put nails on the rails. . . . I remember that when the streetcars ran over the nails they were made into what we called 'scissors' because they were pressed together."

Hallowe'en was another occasion for pranks. In 1952, B.C. Electric's weekly newsletter for passengers, *The Buzzer*, published this bit of Dunbar history: "Some years ago the kids of a certain area of Point Grey used to take time out from their Hallowe'en labours — which were not inconsiderable — to grease the tracks where the old Dunbar Street cars wound up the hill. Mostly, by shooting a bit of sand, the motorman could make the grade, and all was well. Once or twice, we had to send out a track crew to clean up the mess and that led to investigations and sorrow among the youngsters responsible."

Conductors became impromptu babysitters on occasion, when a mother placed a child on the streetcar with a fare for the round trip. Mothers were of course usually in touch with one another about children's whereabouts, and traffic was very light. Other people relied on streetcar conductors to help with their household shopping, as evidenced in this anecdote from Ena Montador:

◀ The motorman appears to be eating a doughnut as he returns to car 216, running in unaltered condition since built by J.G. Brill in 1911. This mid-1940s view shows the car pointing south on Dunbar at 41st Avenue, with Nightingale Drugs in the background. Vic Sharman / Ken Hodgson collection.

Rattan seats provide comfort for passengers in this July 1926 view of the interior of a streetcar built by Canadian Car at their factory in Montreal. The conductor's station is visible at the rear of the car. Courtesy of B.C. Hydro Information Services. ▶

In 1913 my husband's parents lived on 33rd Avenue near Camosun Street and used the streetcar to obtain delivery from Mrs. Montador's favourite meat market at the other end of the run. The order was personally given to the streetcar conductor, who hopped off the car to pass the list to the shop owner. On his return trip he would take delivery of the meat, and at Dunbar and 33rd Avenue the family chow dog would meet the car. It was trained to bring the package of meat back, intact. This was possible because in those days there was so little traffic, either streetcar or automobiles, and people had more time.

On 12 October 1943, 11 women were hired as streetcar "conductorettes." Pat Cowen knew a friend whose mother was a conductorette on the 14-Dunbar car. "We'd all get on the streetcar and ride to the next stop while her mother told her what she was to get ready for dinner. Then we would walk home and Shirley would get on with making the vegetables and whatnot."

Roller skates and bicycles, in addition to their own two feet, gave Dunbar youngsters mobility in the early days. Pat Cowen recalled the skates that attached to a pair of shoes with a key:

We skated everywhere. There was so little traffic on King Edward [25th Avenue]. The road across from us on the south side had hardly any cars because they went up and down the other side. It was very safe to go from Blenheim all the way down to Balaclava. You'd go "clickety click, clickety click" over the big stone slabs. Then when you reached Balaclava, you could go down safely to Carnarvon. So we could skate on the roads, especially King Edward, because there was very little traffic. When I think of what goes up and down there today!

Elmer (Al) Tryon learned to ride his sister's bike, complete with wood wheels and spokes. Tryon also remembered an early bicycle purchase. "Fred Deeley had a [cycle] store way down on Hastings Street near Woodward's. I do not know how we got down there — must have been by streetcar. At any rate, we picked up the bike and I pedalled back on the bike all the way back to 37th Avenue. I had just learnt how to ride! There were not too many cars on the road." Tryon's bicycle required numerous repairs because of the rough skid roads on the Musqueam reserve, where he had a paper route. In 1927 Dunbar Cycles and Scooters opened for business at 26th and Dunbar; it was still in business in 2006.

Weather Delays and Heavy Fog

Saturday, 19 January 1935 went into the record books as the coldest day in 26 years: 4.5°F (−15°C). Snow started the next day and by Monday morning two feet had fallen. Wind created large drifts and soon an icy

◀ B.C. Electric maintained a fleet of "sweeper" cars to remove snow from the track area. A revolving broom of cane brushes at the front of the car pushed the snow off to the side of the rails, with stones often breaking car windows. Courtesy of B.C. Hydro Information Services.

The Effects of Fog

The Buzzer of 18 October 1946 had this to say about fog:

The season is approaching when we are apt to go out in the morning and find the atmosphere as thick as that of any well-known licensed premises. You have to accommodate yourself to it. The trouble is that your district may be entirely free while another part of the city is blanketed in the stuff. So you go out to your favorite street car stop and wait and wait and wait, not realizing that fog has tied up traffic somewhere along the line. You see, street car and bus schedules are knocked galley west when there is fog. Motorists may leave their cars at home, which overloads the system, and this delays some cars, making the service irregular.

The most difficult time is waiting in the sunshine when in another part of the city fog is tying up the traffic. We can only hope that you will suspend judgment and make allowance for matters over which we have no control.

rain began. Of nine major power circuits into Vancouver, only two remained functioning. All streetcar traffic ceased during the storm, except for the Fairview inner car line. Temperatures then rose quickly, and by Tuesday most streets were rivers of flowing water. One exception was described in the *B.C. Electric Employees' Magazine*:

> On the Dunbar Hill the driving rain had packed the snow down so tightly that the severe frost of the week previous met it at the surface and froze the snow into a solid mass of ice. It was a case of using hand labour, and picks were called into action. A streetcar with 50 men arrived at Broadway and Alma, and with the help of a "sweeper car," the men hacked at the ice, one to three inches thick, on the rails. The sweeper ground ahead foot by foot, and they got the outbound track opened to 41st Avenue. This gang worked from 9 on Monday morning to 9 the same night with practically nothing to eat. Rain was descending in torrents, and every man was soaked to the skin.

The next day gangs started in at each end, as progress had slowed the previous evening. In the meantime, a torrent of water was rushing down the hill at 16th Avenue, and men had to be stationed there all night to divert the water. Reports were received of Dunbar residents who made hot coffee and fed stranded crews, passengers and trackmen. The *B.C. Electric Employees' Magazine* related: "W.H. Dinsmore was looking after a gang of men on Dunbar Street on the first day of the storm and went into a cake shop looking for some food for the men. 'How many of these meat pies have you got?' he asked the proprietress. 'Oh, lots and lots of them.' 'Then, give me a hundred.' The lady nearly fainted, and it transpired that her stock totalled six."

In 1936, streetcar ridership increased, but again as the year drew to a close a period of three weeks of snow caused severe ice conditions. Motormen often had to operate with the front window down for proper visibility. Hills became very difficult to negotiate, and to keep lines open B.C. Electric employed seven sweepers and two salt cars.

During the '30s and '40s, sawdust and coal provided energy for industry and home heating but also contributed to air pollution. Fog and smoke created severe visibility problems for motorists, but the streetcars helped, as Frank Robertson explained:

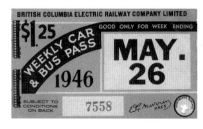

> The streetcars and the streetcar tracks were an important thing for the people with cars to come home from downtown. They would follow that streetcar and follow the tracks all the way. It would be a slow process, but it was better than abandoning your car. And when they got to where they were going to have to cut off on Dunbar, say to 15th, the kids [would help out]. We used to have "bugs" and they were made of tins, jam tins with a candle, a hole in the bottom and a candle shoved up. You'd light the candle and you'd go down and you'd say to the driver "Where are you going?" And he'd follow my bug . . . and you'd walk to his home and he'd give you 25 cents.

Residents said streetcar passengers often left a hurricane lamp on a post by their regular stop so they could see to walk home when they returned after dark.

Early Automobiles

Although automobiles started to appear on city streets around 1915, they were still considered a novelty. Jamie Malkin remembered: "Father had a car. It was a Cadillac. The model was called — if you can believe it — a Chummy Roadster. That's how we moved around. It was a local car, one of the funniest looking things you'd ever seen in your life. . . . You had to pump up the vacuum for the gasoline to get into the motor. There were a lot of things you had to know to run a car in those days. For the rest of us, we got here by streetcar."

As more people began to own cars, "jitneys" started to appear on Vancouver streets. Named after the five-cent coin that was their fare, these were private automobiles — usually rundown Model T Fords with benches carrying up to nine passengers. These jitneys competed with streetcars for passengers.

British Columbia was one of the few places in North America where drivers drove on the left side of the road. The rest of the province changed to driving on the right in July 1920, but Vancouver, Victoria and New

Remembering What's Right

When B.C. Electric changed its operation from the left side of the road to the right side in 1922, *The Buzzer* had this advice for its passengers:

"How, you may ask, am I to remember that the rule of the road has changed?" By sitting down tonight when you go home and thinking how you are going to walk or drive or board a car next Sunday or Monday; by putting some reminder on your finger, if necessary, on your front door or on your garage.

Those who have been used to carrying their parcels in the left hand and holding on by the right when alighting will need to reverse the process. Be sure not to face the rear when alighting. Especial care in boarding and alighting will be necessary in view of the fact that practically all cars in Vancouver will have no gates at first.

After you alight, always bear in mind that danger lurks around the rear of the car. At first the different direction of traffic will confuse you. Your best practice is to stand still until the car moves away, or go straight to the curb and then proceed to the regular crossing.

Westminster did not do so until 6:00 A.M. on 1 January 1922. When it happened, the switch to right-side driving was as disruptive for the streetcars as it was for motorists. B.C. Electric had to install new steps and temporary partitions on 250 streetcars, and trackwork and trolley wires had to be altered.

Looking back in 1932 on that day ten years earlier, *The Buzzer* recalled: "It was fortunate that January 1st fell on a Sunday. The average pedestrian ventured forth gingerly that day, and a goodly number of drivers left their cars at home. Thus the people had a few days to become acclimatized to the new conditions. Accidents were actually less than usual, due to the greater caution being taken. A booklet on safety was sent to every school teacher in the district. In an astonishingly short time the public became used to the new rule of the road." The Dunbar single-track line needed alterations only at passing sidings and the wye at each terminus. However, for B.C. Electric the final work of this mammoth undertaking was not completed for another year and a half.

Dean Lundy remembered some of the automobiles from the 1930s and 1940s:

The police had '36 Plymouth cars with a stick shift and no radios. They were light blue. We had a Buick in 1938 and there were Chevrolets, Fords, Cadillacs and the Lasalle by GM. There weren't as many different models back then. I remember the rumble seats in the Model A Fords were very popular. They were very reliable because they didn't have automatic transmission. (The first [automatic] was the Oldsmobile hydromatic in 1940–41.) Because of the war there were no cars from 1942 to 1945. After the war, veterans got them on priority. In 1946 we paid $1,700 for a new Dodge.

Automobile ownership was increasing, and according to *Vancouver: A Visual History*, in 1929 Vancouver had one car per six residents. While some of the early automobiles were used for commuting on a daily basis, many reposed in garages during the week and emerged for a special trip on a Sunday or holiday. The frequent streetcar service combined with a reasonable fare would continue to make public transit the popular choice for many years.

Dark, Rough Streets

Early streets in Vancouver were muddy affairs and sidewalks were made of wood. Point Grey installed wood sidewalks later than Vancouver, due to unstable ground conditions. Leslie (Adam) Harlow remembered life at 19th Avenue and Highbury Street:

> The back of us was all bush and swamp. We were there until I was four years old and I remember the wooden sidewalks and men building them. Snakes' nests were always underneath them. If you lost a penny, you didn't bother to stick your fingers down. I remember that very clearly because we had workmen out there building or repairing them and I used to hang around when they had lunch until they gave me something. My mother used to get after me and say "Don't take food from a stranger." I just kept going there and I can still smell the tea they poured out of their thermos.

Kenneth Jessiman recalled that in 1925, 21st Avenue at Collingwood was of corduroy construction. "For many years [it] did not have curbs and gutters. We did, however, have sidewalks, although I notice that there are today still no curbs along much of Collingwood." Leslie Harlow also recalled "the people who delivered the bread and milk who were in horse-drawn buggy things, and sleighs in winter when we had snow." Horses still provided transportation of goods; milk delivery by horse and wagon continued until the 1950s (see also chapter 4).

The 1929 amalgamation of Point Grey and the City of Vancouver simplified the names and numbers of streets. Point Grey bylaws in 1912 and 1914 had already changed names of north-south streets to match those of Vancouver. Johnson Road became Blenheim Street and York Road turned into Carnarvon. Dunbar Street was called Clere Road until 1912 in recognition of James E. St. Clere, a Point Grey councillor.

Numbered avenues in South Vancouver did not mesh with Point Grey until 1929. Mayfair Avenue came into being in 1930 and ended years

Once Upon a Road

Many of the numbered avenues in Dunbar once had names. The names disappeared with the amalgamation of Point Grey, South Vancouver and the City of Vancouver in 1929.

PRESENT NAME	FORMER NAME
29th Avenue	Buckland Road
30th Avenue	Bath Road
31st Avenue	Devon Road
33rd Avenue	Bodwell Road
34th Avenue	Murton Road
35th Avenue	Leonard Road
36th Avenue	Taber Road
37th Avenue	Whitehead Road
41st Avenue	Wilson Road
42nd Avenue	Manor Road
43rd Avenue	Harcourt Road
49th Avenue	Magee Road
Blenheim Street	Johnson Road

of confusion. Originally called 38th Avenue South to differentiate it from 38th Avenue, it was renamed Lower 38th Avenue in 1927 for three years. Irregular surveys and boundaries made it necessary to renumber streets in South Vancouver. The trail slashed through the bush and known for years as the North Arm Trail and then River Road was given the name Marine Drive in 1915 by the Point Grey municipality. Upon amalgamation, Vancouver named it Southwest Marine Drive.

In 1925, the new campus opening at the University of British Columbia brought improved service on both 10th Avenue and Dunbar Street. New housing in Dunbar further increased ridership, and the Dunbar line was finally double-tracked in the summer of 1926. The tracks were set in concrete, and bracket-arm incandescent street lights were installed to illuminate the cross streets. As a long-time resident of West 22nd commented later: "When they double-tracked Dunbar, we thought we were really big-time." Side streets themselves had limited street lighting until the 1950s. On 8 July 1951, the City of Vancouver brought in legislation called "Through Street Authority" that required the installation of stop signs on residential side streets intersecting with Dunbar Street and other major arterials.

The Last of the Streetcars

From early on, Vancouver's transit system faced competition from the automobile. Other challenges included labour strife and bad weather that interrupted service periodically. In 1915 an estimated 250 jitneys were operating in Vancouver. A sign in the car window indicated the route. A jitney would scoop up intending streetcar passengers at stops ahead of regular transit service. Vancouver City Council tried banning jitneys, but then the B.C. Electric Company cut fares, renovated cars and ended motormen's strikes. The improved service ultimately won back streetcar riders.

On 17 July 1921, Cleveland fare boxes replaced the original portable Coleman jug-type boxes. With a six-cent fare, the old fare boxes were too small. The Clevelands would collect fares until the end of streetcar service in Vancouver. On 1 February 1922, one-man streetcars started to operate on Dunbar. These "safety cars" had air-operated doors and a "dead man" controller. (If the motorman released the controller handle or fell onto it, the car made an emergency stop.) Dunbar went back to two-man cars, however, on 5 November 1923. In 1923 all Vancouver streetcars were designated with a route number for the first time. The number 18 was assigned to Dunbar but very soon changed to number 14. The 41st Avenue single-track line was number 7.

B.C. Electric sought to eliminate inconvenience and attract riders with the new Dunbar Diversion that opened in 1923. Early streetcar

transfers showed routes such as Dunbar, P.G. and Wilson, P.G. (for Point Grey). By 15 April 1929, cash fares were set at seven cents, with tickets at four for 25 cents throughout the City of Vancouver. On 6 October 1930, a new transit service started on Macdonald from Broadway to 41st Avenue. Although in previous years this would have been a new streetcar line, B.C. Electric indicated a change in direction by operating this new line with motorized buses. Within six months the initial 30-minute service had another bus added for 15-minute rush-hour service. A third bus was added by early 1932.

Real estate development in Mackenzie Heights and a 1927 diversion on Macdonald between 16th and 18th Avenues clearly increased bus ridership. On 16 May 1932, four two-car "trains" started morning service on Dunbar to deal with heavy patronage. The new six-lane Burrard Street Bridge opened on 1 July 1932, signalling a faster route for automobiles from downtown to the West Side. By 16 July, major cuts were implemented on all streetcar lines except Dunbar and West Point Grey. Still, the importance of the streetcar transit system during the Depression, at a time of low automobile ownership, is exemplified by an open invitation to a meeting of the Woman's Christian Temperance Union held at a private Dunbar residence. The invitation card for the "At Home" included the printed direction "Dunbar Car, 23rd Avenue" under the address of the house.

▲ Dunbar and 41st Avenue was a busy spot where, until 1951, Dunbar cars turned around by "wyeing." A southbound car first turned west onto 41st Avenue. Then, guided by the conductor, it reversed through the intersection to the east, and finally proceeded forward and turned right onto Dunbar northbound. Until 1947, 41st Avenue cars turned around in a similar manner. Photo by Jack Lindsay. City of Vancouver Archives, photograph #CVA1184-3632.

Conductors on the streetcars started a new procedure with transfers in 1935. Instead of conductors having to punch an expiry time at the bottom of the transfer, a new design allowed the transfer to be torn off at the appropriate time. This type of transfer was in use until 2001, when electronic fare boxes and magnetic encoded tickets were introduced.

Streetcars still in service after 30 years started to be rebuilt with new features in the 1930s. Old wood-slat seats were replaced with tubular metal frames with leather-covered foam seat cushions. In late 1938 B.C. Electric took delivery of a modern streamlined Presidents' Conference Committee (PCC) streetcar, and in early 1939 put it on display for the public. This lightweight, comfortable, quiet car was an immediate hit with everyone except the Street Railwaymen's Union, who viewed this one-man car as a threat to cars run by a motorman and conductor on heavier-use lines.

As the Second World War got underway, more old streetcars were modernized and three new PCC cars arrived. Blackouts darkened Vancouver at night, reducing speeds on the streetcar and bus routes. By late 1941 ridership was rising quickly due to wartime industry, and three measures were introduced to improve efficiency. The number of car stops was reduced to increase average speed, automobile parking at stops was prohibited where necessary, and staggered work hours were introduced. When gas rationing was enacted nationally on 1 April 1941, ridership rose 27 percent in one week.

B.C. Electric ordered 20 more PCC cars, but Alderman Jack Price opposed any further purchases of one-man cars, with support from a

Although streetcar service to and from Dunbar and 41st Avenue was considered reliable, it was not without problems. This backup of cars southbound on Dunbar Street at 40th Avenue might have resulted from a wyeing difficulty. Wallace Young collection. ▶

number of communities. By 1944, streetcar ridership had levelled off somewhat, but the system still suffered extreme overcrowding at rush hours. Transportation consultants were retained to advise on the future of transit in post-war Vancouver.

B.C. Electric Converts to Buses

On 1 May 1947, motor bus service commenced on 41st Avenue between East Boulevard and Dunbar Street, ending 35 years of streetcar operation. This was one of the first lines abandoned as part of B.C. Electric's modernization program. Streetcar tracks needed major renewal, and the issue of two-man cars also remained unresolved. If B.C. Electric could not run one-man streetcars, it would buy one-man trolley buses. The first trolley bus line, Fraser-Cambie, opened for revenue service on 16 August 1948, following a day of free rides.

The last streetcars ran on West 10th Avenue into Point Grey on 15 September 1949, and by the next day the Dunbar streetcar was the last line remaining west of Granville Street. It was hooked up with the Main Street line to become the Main-Dunbar. Since the number 7 was no longer in use on the 41st Avenue line, it was assigned to the Dunbar route and remains unchanged to the present. As the conversion to trolley buses continued, 48 streetcars were burned at the Kitsilano shops at the south end of the Burrard Street Bridge.

Ridership on the system (inversely related to rates of car ownership) had started to decline at the end of the war, and this drop-off continued with the end of gasoline rationing. B.C. Electric cited jammed swing-span

◄ This 1947 model Brill trolley bus is shown travelling eastbound on 41st Avenue at Dunbar, c. 1960. Note four-way traffic control light, classical incandescent street lights and the Nightingale Pharmacy. Photo by Wallace Young.

This 2002 view of 41st and Dunbar shows a Flyer trolley bus southbound on Dunbar. A Scotiabank occupies the former Safeway supermarket building. Courtesy of Angus McIntyre. ▸

bridges, fires, accidents and parades as possible contributors to delays in transit service, and a new radio system was implemented to help reroute transit vehicles. Nonetheless, 38 years of streetcar service on Dunbar Street ceased on 20 May 1951, to be replaced by trolley bus service. The free-standing post-top incandescent street lights that lined Dunbar Street were removed and "classic" incandescent lights were installed on the new steel trolley poles. These were positioned near the top of the pole and provided a very even white light over the street surface.

The introduction of trolley buses on Dunbar brought a few new procedures for both passengers and drivers. Riders had boarded the two-man streetcars at the rear door and exited by the front door. As the car stopped in the street, boarding and disembarking passengers had had to take care that motor vehicles had already stopped, as required by law. With a bus or trolley coach, passengers now waited at a designated stop as the vehicle pulled in to the curb and boarded by the front door. They exited onto the curb. The streetcar had priority in traffic and as such set the "pace" for the flow of traffic in the street. The bus, on the other hand, had to wait for a break in the traffic or a courteous motorist to be able to pull out from the curb.

Inflation after the war caused transit fares to rise frequently after decades of a nickel fare. Reddy Kilowatt, B.C. Electric's public relations cartoon mascot, related the predicament in *The Buzzer* in 1951. "Okay, we raise fares to meet rising costs, so fewer people ride, so we're still in the red and costs keep going up! So we have to go back and hike fares again and that again means less riders — oh why did I ever get into the transit business? It's a vicious circle!"

These fare hikes occurred at the same time as a massive modernization program, with $27 million spent between 1946 and 1952 on new trolley and motorized buses. The fact that B.C. Electric was a private company is obvious in an item from *The Buzzer* dated 14 February 1952: "Standing by itself — and recording substantial losses in every post-war year — the transit system obviously could never have raised a single dollar toward this modernization program. This could only be carried out because of two subsidies: one from the electric system and a larger one from the company's shareholders. In the first five post-war years, the company raised and spent over $100 million for more electric, gas and transit service. It has kept up with service demands despite the record growth of the communities and areas it serves." Although vehicle traffic was certainly increasing at this time, the Dunbar area still had no traffic signals.

The old Granville Street swing-span bridge had for years caused delays to Dunbar streetcar riders as it opened and closed for False Creek marine traffic. As the new Dunbar trolley bus service got underway in 1951 and used the swing-span bridge, construction started on a new eight-lane bridge, Canada's largest. The new Granville Street bridge finally opened to traffic in early 1954, with access at both ends by four ramps. The old bridge was demolished and then the final connections of the main roadway were made at the north and south ends.

Only four years after the last streetcar graced Dunbar Street, the final streetcars in all of Vancouver ran on Hastings East. On Sunday, 24 April 1955, an estimated 13,700 people travelled the line for free between 1:00 P.M. and 5:00 P.M. Ceremonies were held at Exhibition Park with the Vancouver Firemen's Band playing. Thirty-six streamlined PCC streetcars provided the service — some only 10 years old. At the end of the day, instead of returning to the car barn at Main and 13th Avenue, they were towed through False Creek freight trackage to the Kitsilano shops to await scrapping. B.C. Electric proudly declared in May of 1956: "Vancouver rides the nation's largest fleet of trolleys — 327 in all — and this city was the first large community in Canada to complete the change-over from rails to rubber."

Gradual Transit Improvements

One-way streets came to downtown Vancouver in 1957 and this affected transit route hookups. Dunbar trolley buses were paired with 10th Avenue trolley buses, and from Broadway and Alma both routes combined to provide service as 14 Hastings along Broadway, to downtown. This dupli-

The Musical Fare Box

B.C. Electric replaced the Cleveland fare boxes with electric-mechanical Grant money meters in 1959. Tickets were replaced with tokens, and the new machines serenaded passengers and drivers with different sounds for the various coins and tokens.

COIN OR TOKEN	SOUND
1 cent	buzz
5 cents	bong
10 cents	bong bong
25 cents	bing bing
A token—student	bing
B token—adult	brring
C token—child	no sound

Drivers were able to monitor fares paid without looking at the fare box. These fare boxes, which did not accept paper money or tickets, had started to wear out by the mid-1970s. In 1976 new Duncan fare boxes arrived that accommodated all coins, paper money and tickets.

The sweeping curve of the Dunbar Diversion at West 14th Avenue affords a panoramic view of the city and mountains as car 335 heads towards Broadway. This 1951 view was taken during the last week of streetcar operation. Photo by Jack Lindsay. City of Vancouver Archives, photograph #CVA1184-3633.

cated the route followed by Dunbar streetcars for many years. The Macdonald bus was through-routed with the Knight Road bus.

The last chance for a ride on an electric interurban was on 28 February 1958, from Steveston to Marpole. As far as passenger service was concerned, this was the final day of the "Rails to Rubber" program. Automobile ownership in Vancouver continued to rise rapidly, as Austins and Morris Minors from England joined Fords and Chryslers. In Dunbar most homes were built between 1924 and 1929 and few of them had garages, since the majority of residents did not own cars. As people acquired a car they built a carport or garage for it. A walk down a Dunbar back lane reveals quite a diversity of garages, but originals from the 1920s are few and far between.

Some Dunbar residents used rotary dial telephones in their homes for the first time in the late 1950s, and transit riders saw the number for bus information change from KErrisdale 7500 to AMherst 1-4211. As automobile traffic increased on Southwest Marine Drive, hitchhiking supplemented the transit service. Terry Slack, who lived with his family at the booming grounds three miles from the end of the bus line, recalled that people would recognize his group walking to school and wave because they walked twice a day. "People even gave us a ride once in a while,

◀ Dunbar Street in the mid-1940s was a wide thoroughfare lacking traffic and parked cars. This vintage car showed how well B.C. Electric maintained their equipment. Henry Ewert collection.

which was very nice. . . . I remember one day I got picked up on a police motorcycle and taken right to the front door of my school. The kids were absolutely astonished — on the back of a police motorcycle! Of course, there were no helmets in those days."

One commuter was known to Southlands residents as the "Howdy man," since that was his greeting as he pedalled by on his bicycle. He started out from the east side of town on the 49th Avenue bus, but then to get down to the Fraser River, he rode a bicycle that he hid in the bush at the Point Grey Golf and Country Club. At the end of the workday he rode his bike back to the hiding spot and caught the 49th Avenue bus home.

For many years, Fageol and Brill motor buses from the 1940s and 1950s served on the Macdonald route. In 1965 "new look" General Motors diesel buses started to appear. These vehicles featured slanted side windows and large glass windows at the front and rear. Weekday morning and evening riders could now take the Macdonald Express, which ran local service on Mackenzie and Macdonald, and express through Kitsilano to downtown. Brill trolley buses continued to serve Dunbar and 41st Avenue, but for the first time it was suggested they be replaced with diesel buses within a few years. An initial indication of this trend came in 1968 when the 10th-Hastings trolley service was replaced with new GM diesel buses that could provide through service to UBC without a transfer at Blanca Loop.

After many years of declining ridership, B.C. Hydro had to start improving service. Downtown office development, apartment construction

An unusual passenger service ran on Blenheim Street down to the shipyards along the Fraser River after World War II. It was known to the locals as a "crummy" and is described by Sharon Slack: "That was B.C. Packers' truck. The man who drove it we called Puff. He had a green truck with benches in the back and a tarp over it. He picked up the men at the bus stop and drove them down in the morning and took them back at the end of the day. In between times he was delivering goods and stuff to the shipyard. He didn't serve any of the residents down there. It was strictly for B.C. Packers staff."

Proactive Scheduling

When Dunbar resident Ian Graham started first year at UBC in 1966 he used the direct service along 41st Avenue and Southwest Marine Drive to the campus. Information in the form of a B.C. Hydro timetable was almost non-existent, so Graham decided to print his own time-tables and distribute them at bus stops. He even made cardboard "take one" boxes to dispense the schedules and kept them filled. This resulted in such an increase in ridership that extra buses had to be added and thereby assured continued operation of the service.

and suburban expansion had brought new passengers to the system. Advertisements inside buses compared fares in other Canadian cities: Montreal — 50 cents; Toronto — 40 cents; Vancouver — still 25 cents.

The first new bus route in the Dunbar area in many years was the Burnaby to UBC 49th Avenue service, which used 49th Avenue, Southwest Marine Drive and Dunbar Street. This started on 21 March 1975. In a short time diesel buses on 41st Avenue started to displace the trolley buses and this became a major route to UBC.

In the early 1970s B.C. Hydro purchased second-hand Brill trolley buses from Winnipeg and Saskatoon. By 1975 the company had decided to replace the oldest, smaller 1947 and 1948 Brill trolleys with 50 new Flyer units equipped with reconditioned electric motors and controls. These trolleys arrived in 1976 and made occasional trips on the Dunbar route.

Getting to UBC

Until 1949 the only bus service to the UBC campus was from the 10th Avenue and Sasamat streetcar stop. UBC service was subsequently provided from the Blanca bus loop. Mel Stevens commuted to UBC by an informal car pool. "I usually got a lift with friends who had cars, and they used to take a carful out, but usually we had to come back on the bus." Marine Drive was still two lanes from Camosun Street to UBC, and the student population was about 15,000. In 1965 a limited-stop bus service commenced along 41st Avenue to the UBC campus.

A few Dunbar residents bucked the automobile trend and commuted to work by bicycle. Professor Larry Moore rode a bicycle to his office at UBC from 21st Avenue for 30 years. "Only one or two of us were regularly cycling to work. The route I often followed took me west on 16th Avenue in front of Lord Byng High School. The teenage students seemed to have trouble understanding why an adult in a sports jacket and tie would be riding a bicycle." Moore's raingear included a yellow sou'wester, rubber rain hat and gumboots, and he used a backpack to carry things. His bicycle was equipped with lights, reflectors and fenders.

In the early '70s, more and more cyclists joined the two-wheeled parade to UBC. To cater to the increased use of the bicycle for pleasure and commuting, the City of Vancouver implemented a network of urban bicycle routes. The Midtown bike route enters the Dunbar area along 39th Avenue. Another route follows Southwest Marine Drive to UBC.

Over the years bicycle design has changed considerably from the old CCM one-speed backpedal brake, as described by Lea Holz of Dunbar Cycles: "There are still road bikes out there and then there are the hybrids, which are city bikes that people are commuting on. And we still have comfort bikes for people who are older. (They want to sit more upright as they used to in the olden days and be able to manoeuvre around the

◀ Dunbar's elevation often affords snow when the rest of the city receives rain. A woman boards a southbound Brill trolley bus on Dunbar at 21st Avenue in 1978. Courtesy of Angus McIntyre.

city.) I think cycling's just getting better and better because they're finding out what people's real needs are and they're trying to market to that."

As automobile ownership increased, traffic congestion followed and inevitably Dunbar's first traffic signal started operation on 21 January 1966, at 41st Avenue and Dunbar. Even before this time, the location had had a flashing red warning light for Dunbar and flashing amber for 41st Avenue above the centre of the intersection. Earlier, signals had been installed at 4th Avenue and Macdonald (in 1952), and at 10th Avenue and Alma (in 1959).

In 1968, traffic signals were installed at Macdonald and King Edward as well as at Dunbar Street and 16th Avenue. The basic arterial and residential grid in the area remained unchanged until 1975, when Southwest Marine Drive west of Camosun to UBC was widened from two lanes to a four-lane divided highway.

Mobility in the Modern Era

An indication of increasing traffic volume was the installation of Dunbar's first pedestrian traffic signal, activated on 31 October 1978. On residential streets the old bracket-arm incandescent street lights were gradually replaced with a bluish-white light source called mercury vapour. In some cases established trees had to be removed to accommodate the new steel poles. Now these streets are graced with modern "cobra head" fixtures that glow orange by night.

B.C. Hydro conducted a major review of the trolley bus system in 1979. Economics and the desire for pollution-free operation led to a decision to keep the existing electric bus system. In 1980 a new Crown corporation, the Urban Transit Authority, took over transit from B.C. Hydro, and Metro Transit became the new operator of the city's buses. An order for 245 new trolley buses was placed with Flyer Industries in Winnipeg in 1982 and the Province created B.C. Transit.

Vancouver's transit system had always been downtown oriented, but as the city and suburbs developed, a need for more cross-town lines became apparent. Dunbar residents travelling east by bus always had to head north to Broadway or south to 41st Avenue to find a cross-town line. On 17 December 1982, the 25–King Edward service commenced from Brentwood Mall to Blanca Loop, travelling west on King Edward, north on Dunbar and west on 16th Avenue to Blanca. Peak-hour trips ran through to UBC. When 16th Avenue was extended west of Blanca Street to Wesbrook, the 25 started to use that route to run to UBC at all times.

The year 1983 marked the arrival of most of the new Flyer trolleys and the departure of the venerable Brills, some of which had travelled more than a million miles. Some of the first Flyers arrived in an orange-and-white paint scheme, but this was soon changed to the red, white and blue of B.C. Transit. On 14 January 1984, six Brill trolley buses toured the various routes, with Dunbar Street and 41st Avenue being part of the "Farewell to Brill" tour.

As the last Brills were replaced, planning started on a new automated light rail transit system, later dubbed SkyTrain. The introduction of Sky-Train to the east end of the city left the West Side without an improvement, so it was decided to inaugurate an express service on Dunbar. In late 1990 the 32–Dunbar Express commenced service, providing a local rush-hour service on Dunbar Street, then express along 4th Avenue through Kitsilano and to downtown over the Burrard Bridge.

In the 1990s UBC-bound traffic generated enough volume and delays on major arterial streets that motorists took to residential side streets to bypass problem areas. These secondary streets did not have stop signs or other traffic controls but increasingly were expected to handle larger numbers of cars. During the 1970s a resident of Dunbar Street commented on the noise level of traffic. When asked about the streetcars in earlier days, she replied: "Well, they came by every five or ten minutes, and that was it. But now the automobile noise is almost constant."

The 50th anniversary of trolley bus operation took place on 15 August 1998, with a parade of four vehicles. A commemorative book, *Vancouver's Trolley Buses: 1948–1998*, was published. Trolley buses have served Dunbar Street for almost 60 years, continuing a tradition of electric transit service that began with streetcars 114 years ago. Although new technology such as the Ballard hydrogen fuel cell bus is being developed, a new generation of trolley buses is planned for introduction by September 2006. Vancouver will join Seattle and San Francisco in renewing their fleets of true zero-emission vehicles.

Consumers' choice of automobiles has changed in recent years from the traditional sedan to much larger vehicles such as minivans, sport utility vehicles (SUVs), vans and pickup trucks. Residential side streets in Dunbar and Mackenzie Heights that had only a few cars parked on them in the 1970s now reflect the congested parking that comes with increased automobile ownership.

Recent aids to traffic control in Dunbar, as in other Vancouver residential areas, include the introduction of traffic calming measures such as stop signs, traffic circles and speed bumps. Where only one traffic signal existed in 1966, Dunbar in 2006 had 15 such devices to monitor traffic and pedestrians. In the past, commuters tended to travel by streetcar or bus to downtown Vancouver, whereas today jobs and activities take people throughout the Lower Mainland.

Dunbar resident Jim McPherson saw his workplace move from Main and Terminal to suburban Surrey. He commented: "I followed the company out to where they relocated the work site because there was a promise for an agreement where the company might provide a transportation service to and from the nearest bus line. They did put one into effect, primarily because of the screaming of several of us who were moved out there and did not own cars. After about six months it was cancelled, and they would not renew it." McPherson was forced into buying a car to continue his employment with the company, and the transit system lost a long-time customer.

In September 2003 both UBC and Simon Fraser University introduced student "U-Pass" plans, with a $20 per month fee allowing unlimited riding in all three transit zones. This initiative increased ridership on UBC runs by 53 percent and overwhelmed existing service. Some Dunbar neighbourhoods became virtual Park-and-Rides as students avoided pay parking on campus. Other improvements in service in the region caused an overall increase in ridership of 11 percent.

Dunbar's location on the edge of Vancouver offers some advantages with regard to traffic. The major generator of traffic is UBC. Arterial and residential streets are affected as a university population of up to 50,000 commutes throughout the year. New and planned residential development at UBC will add more traffic to existing roads, while residents of Blenheim Street will see their street reclassified as a "neighbourhood collector." Four million dollars will be spent on rebuilding the street to improve safety and calm traffic. Dunbar, however, has so far been spared the chronic congestion of other areas of the Lower Mainland that must deal with bottlenecks at bridges and permit parking. Traffic volume, noise and pollution continue to increase, and the challenge for the future liveability of the neighbourhood must be a commitment to careful development and a balanced transportation plan.

CHAPTER 6

The Residential
Landscape

⸻ Shelagh Lindsey and Helen Spiegelman

The streets of Dunbar, with their rows of mature shade trees and tidy well-kept homes on narrow lots, evoke a feeling of home. Decades of successive development booms have introduced a variety of housing styles. Some were controversial at first, but over time most of the new homes have seemed to settle in with the old. Despite soaring land values towards the end of the twentieth century, Dunbar's homes retain the modest, middle-class appeal that brought buyers flocking to "Vancouver's Finest Suburb" in 1925 (Wynn 96). Dunbar's residential neighbourhood was developed and shaped in its broad outlines by a town-planning by-law that was passed in 1922. Promoted with the hyperbole of real estate developers, Dunbar's homes were constructed mostly by small, independent builders relying on standardized house plans. Together they have created a neighbourhood of serviceable homes that still give pleasure to their owners.

The Earliest Houses in Dunbar

A "fort" fifteen hundred feet in length and ninety feet in breadth: this is how the row of houses belonging to the Musqueam people appeared to explorer Simon Fraser when he reached their village on the north arm of

the Fraser River in 1808. Fraser observed that the dwellings of the Musqueam were constructed in rows, with detached outbuildings nearby. Those shed-roofed structures built with hand-split cedar planks have long since vanished without even a photographic record.

The earliest dwellings constructed by European settlers in Dunbar/Southlands were farmhouses in Southlands. These were humble but important symbols of Britain's hegemony over the newly founded colony of British Columbia. A century later, they are all gone. Hugh Magee's farmhouse, known as Spruce Grove, stood at 3250 West 48th Avenue until it was demolished in early 1959, at which time, according to historian Michael Kluckner, it was being used as the office of the Hyland Barnes nursery (Kluckner 144). Built in the 1860s, it was the oldest house in Vancouver when it was demolished. Henry Mole's farmhouse, located near Marine Drive and Blenheim, was used by the Point Grey Golf and Country Club as a clubhouse for some years, but was eventually demolished and replaced. Fitzgerald McCleery's 1873 farmhouse and heritage barn located at 6750 Macdonald Street were torn down at about the same time as the Magee farmhouse. The McCleery house was demolished by the Vancouver Park Board to make room for the 11th tee of the new public golf course named, ironically, for the McCleery family.

Larry Killam, who spent much of his childhood and youth at the McCleery farm in Southlands (by then operated by McCleery's descendant Gerry Logan), happened to be present when the Vancouver Fire Department burned down the barn as a training exercise. "They lit a match to the original barn and sat there hosing it lightly until it all burned down to nothing. I can remember coming and [finding that] it was mostly burned down by the time we got there. I was just sick about the thing. Not that anybody talked about heritage in those days, not that there was anything anybody could do. But this was the city of Vancouver — that we're the owners [of] — burning up the heritage!"

Although just a young man at the time, Larry Killam said the experience caused him to "get involved" to try to rescue the McCleery farmhouse. He phoned an alderman and even considered recruiting a couple of his Southlands pheasant-hunting companions to carry out what today would be called "direct action" to protect the old farmhouse:

I talked to my friends as to whether we would barricade [the house], whether we would get our .22s so we would make the national news. . . . We talked big. . . . Then it just sort of — it all changed. We went to university and everything and the parks board did stop for a while. They put it off for a few months, thinking about the thing. And then the conclusion was that this alderman said to me: "Well, we can't have the golf course [held up]. They need where the house is [to build the golf course]." Then they tore the thing down. . . . I mean the thing was

◄ The second McCleery farmhouse, built in 1891 at 2650 West 50th, pictured several years later. Built in the popular style known as American Carpenter Gothic, it features ornamental scrollwork on the gables and the porch post capitals. The house was later moved to 2610 Southwest Marine Drive. Courtesy of Betty McQueen.

First Fitzgerald McCleery farmhouse, built in 1873 at 6750 Macdonald Street, as it appeared in 1892. The two-storey bunkhouse addition at the rear was added in 1883. When the family built a second house in 1891, this became the farm manager's house. Courtesy of Betty McQueen.

The McCleery farm as it looked around 1900, with the 1873 farmhouse (centre of the picture) and the 1891 house on the ridge overlooking the river. Courtesy of Betty McQueen. ▼

one hundred percent original. It was like nothing [else] — it was like no other heritage building in Vancouver.

A second McCleery farmhouse, built in 1891 on a ridge overlooking the farm at 2650 West 50th Avenue, is also gone. The house was in a style called American Carpenter Gothic. A photo taken a year after the home's construction shows the paired bay windows on both storeys and ornamental scrollwork on the gables and roof overhangs.

The cedar houses in the Musqueam village and all of the nineteenth-century farmhouses from Southlands' early days are gone, along with many other structures from Dunbar's early history. Not until 1974 would the City of Vancouver have the legal authority to protect such remnants of its heritage.

Heritage Preservation in Vancouver

The historic Dunbar dwelling located at 5503 Blenheim and known as the Morrisette Farmhouse was probably never part of a working farm as were those in Southlands. It was built on a small parcel of land (10 acres, according to a city staff report to council). Farm or not, the Morrisette Farmhouse is one of Dunbar's oldest houses, built in 1914, and it is listed on Vancouver's Heritage Register.

Until the Vancouver Charter was amended in 1973, heritage preservation was the responsibility of the provincial government, and the city had no authority to create a register of heritage houses and protect their heritage value by regulating how they could be altered. In 1974, Vancouver city council received this authority and adopted two heritage protection bylaws that created the framework for an inventory of heritage sites and established a committee later known as the Vancouver Heritage Commission to provide advice on heritage preservation. In 2005 there were 22 heritage sites in Dunbar/Southlands.

Vancouver's heritage bylaws do not prohibit the destruction of designated heritage structures. Rather, they provide negotiating tools — incentives and disincentives — that the city and the property owner can use to prevent loss of heritage value. However, heritage preservation is a delicate process that requires negotiation between private property owners, the city and supportive neighbours.

The Morrisette Farmhouse is a case in point. Straddling two legal lots at 5503 Blenheim, the house is too large to relocate within either of the existing lots. The long-time property owner, Victoria Zabolotny, worked with the architect Rick Balfour to develop a proposal for subdividing the property. The proposal would allow a second house to be built on the smaller lot while the heritage farmhouse would be converted into a multi-family dwelling without destroying its heritage value. The project had strong support from the neighbours, and city council approved the plan. However, by 2006 Zabolotny had not pursued the redevelopment project.

Earlier modifications to the house to operate a rooming house did not affect its heritage value, which was described as follows in a report to council: "It is a rare example of a historic farmhouse in the Dunbar area. Surrounded by streets on three sides, it remains prominent in the land-scape and is a local neighbourhood landmark. It is a good example of the classic box-style farmhouse, featuring a generous verandah that wraps around the south and east facades and a random-cut granite ashlar foundation. A perimeter garden wall, also in granite, is a strong feature on the landscape" (McGeogh 2).

First Residential Boom, 1900–1920

The Morrisette Farmhouse is a legacy of the first of many residential development booms that occurred in the twentieth century, creating the "streetcar suburb" now known as Dunbar. These booms were driven — and braked — by economic cycles. They were also made possible by the development of civic infrastructure. The first development boom in Dunbar occurred in tandem with the development of a streetcar line from Kerrisdale along West 41st Avenue in 1909. This line was followed in 1913 by a connecting line running north on Dunbar Street to 16th Avenue and west to Crown Street.

◄ Henry Mole's home, built in 1901. Bell-cast eaves with wide overhang, filigree along the top of the house and dormer, and formal touches on the front porch and window frames distinguish this home, designed by Parr & Fee, from ordinary boxlike farmhouses of the era. After purchasing Mole's property in 1922–23, the Point Grey Golf and Country Club used this house as its clubhouse until it was demolished and a new clubhouse built. Visible behind the house is the small cottage, built in 1877, that served as the family's home for many years. Courtesy of Betty McQueen.

▲ The 1914 Morrisette Farmhouse at 5503 Blenheim not long after its construction. Courtesy of Robert Morrisette.

The latter streetcar line was paid for by local realtor Charles Trott Dunbar to enhance the value of his building lots. Land speculators such as Dunbar were buying up parcels of land and subdividing them into residential lots for resale. Dunbar distributed free calendars to promote his building lots in "Dunbar Heights." The promoter of another subdivision called Bryn Mawr (near the southeast corner of Blenheim and West 29th) assured buyers that there would be "no unsightly shacks" in their neighbourhood because sales were restricted to builders who would invest $2,500 in improvements: "This restriction is your protection and is ample assurance that your neighbourhood will be desirable" (Wynn 89).

Despite the hyperbole of the land speculators who pressured would-be buyers with warnings that lots were "selling like hotcakes" (Wynn 96), few houses were actually built in Dunbar during the period from 1910 to 1920. June Binkert, who lives in West Southlands, prepared a series of walking tours of historic houses in Dunbar as part of the neighbourhood's Salmonberry Days festival. Binkert identified a small number of Dunbar houses built between 1912 and 1914 south of West 37th Avenue. Houses of this period are even rarer up the hill in Dunbar Heights, where, according to Bruce Macdonald's *Vancouver: A Visual History*, a logging camp was still operating near 16th and Collingwood until 1920. Graeme Wynn, a UBC geographer, described how in 1918 there were only nine occupied houses, out of a total of 583 legal lots, in the area between Dunbar and Blenheim Streets from 16th Avenue south to 25th (Wynn 96).

◄ The Mount house at 3379
West 22nd Avenue during its
construction in 1912–13. The
partially completed house stands
isolated and surrounded by slash.
This modest house was one of
the oldest in Dunbar Heights.
Photos courtesy of the Mount
family.

◄ Miss Mary Mount in front
of the same house, c. 1919–20.
It was demolished during the
redevelopment boom in the 1980s.

Three girls, possibly students from Sacred Heart Convent, pose before a house at 3519 West 21st Avenue, c. 1920. City of Vancouver Archives, photograph #CVA214-10. ▶

One of these houses still stands at 3566 West 20th Avenue. Built in 1915, according to its present owner, it is designed in the "California" or "Craftsman" bungalow style. These distinctive one- or one-and-a-half-storey houses were built in cities across North America. The plans were distributed by mail order and published in "pattern books" that were used by local builders. The designs were based on principles of simple living first espoused by the English Arts and Crafts movement as a reaction against elaborate Victorian detailing and later by *Craftsman* magazine, an American publication that published house patterns and information about interior details, including furnishings. The Craftsman bungalows have wide front porches and deep roof overhangs and were typically surrounded by beautiful gardens.

The most renowned Dunbar example of a Craftsman-style house from the 1920s is the Haigler House at 3537 West 30th. This stone house on a 100-foot lot surrounded by a stone wall was listed in the "A" category of the Vancouver Heritage Register in 1991. Like the Morrisette Farmhouse, the Haigler House became a *cause célèbre* in Dunbar. Lissa Forshaw remembered that the neighbours were "the catalyst," working with the developer and city officials to find a way to preserve some of the

◄ The heritage-designated Haigler House at 3537 West 30th Avenue. Community support led to the preservation of the house and its stone wall, although a superb cottage garden and a conservatory were lost when the 100-foot lot was subdivided. Courtesy of Joan Tyldesley.

heritage value of the property when it was subdivided. The garden was lost, Forshaw said, along with the conservatory on one side of the house, but the house and its wall are still part of Dunbar's community heritage.

The Last Log House in Vancouver

Dunbar home builders would continue to rely on pattern book designs, which would change over time to suit the buyers' tastes and needs. The pleasant mix of compatible styles would come to define the "character" of Dunbar. However, the streetscape would include anomalous buildings here and there that had unique stories to tell. A simple log structure that stood at 3344 West 27th Avenue until its demolition in 1996 is thought to have been built by the gardener of a land speculator and city alderman, Charles Henry Wilson. Wilson had just purchased his Dunbar Heights estate, comprising five acres of bush near the intersection of Blenheim and King Edward. While the Wilsons were overseas in 1912, their gardener constructed his log cabin using materials at hand. The logs were harvested from the second-growth bush on the Wilson property and hauled to his homestead site. Empty kerosene tins and dynamite crates were salvaged from a portable sawmill nearby, the tins flattened to form roof shingles and the wooden dynamite boxes nailed in place to make the floor.

In 1996 the log house was sold to a developer, who applied for a permit to demolish it. Heritage-conscious neighbours convinced the new owner to allow the removal of some of the original logs. These still lie under a tarp in Helen Spiegelman's backyard, waiting to be fashioned

▲ This house was built of logs salvaged near the present Lord Kitchener Elementary School. It stood at 3344 West 27th Avenue until it was demolished in 1996. Seated on the porch in this 1918 photo is Edith Johnson. Courtesy of Gayle Mitchell.

someday into a historical marker in the schoolyard at Lord Kitchener Elementary School, where they were cut nearly one hundred years ago.

Again with permission from the owner, a Dunbar architect, Tom Grant, made measured drawings of the log house before its demolition. He conducted a structural survey, took complete plan and elevation measurements, and photographed the building and yard with both a still camera and a video camera. The demolition operator co-operated by letting Grant photograph parts of the building while it was being demolished. All of Grant's documentation has been offered to the Vancouver City Archives. After reading in the newspaper about the demolition, a former resident of the log house, who lived there as a little girl, contacted Grant, and their correspondence provided Grant with information about the house in the early 1920s.

Town Planning Shapes a Community

With the exception of the early farmhouses in Southlands, all of the houses described so far were built after the municipality of Point Grey was formed. As described in earlier chapters, Point Grey was formed when property owners west of Cambie Street, including the Dunbar area, seceded from the municipality of South Vancouver to become a separate municipality. One of their reasons for separating was a vision in the minds of civic leaders of a city created with an orderly pattern of development and public amenities that would be financed with property taxes. In 1922, Point Grey established the first zoning bylaw in Canada. This bylaw created the loom on which the fabric of Dunbar development would be woven.

The Point Grey bylaw, drafted by an esteemed American planner named Harland Bartholomew, established single-family residential districts where only single-family homes and their related outbuildings could be built. The following community uses were also permitted: churches, schools, golf courses, public museums, libraries, parks and playgrounds, farming and truck gardening, nurseries and greenhouses, and stables. The bylaw's goals were to prevent the overcrowding of land; to preserve "the amenity of residential districts"; to secure adequate provisions for light, air and reasonable access; to conserve the value of the land and the nature of its use and occupancy, the character of each district and the character of the buildings already erected and the "peculiar suitability of the district for particular uses"; and to conserve property values and the direction of building development (Bartholomew and Associates 286).

Accordingly, the height of buildings in single-family districts was not to exceed 35 feet or two and a half storeys, front yards were to be not less than 24 feet in depth, backyards not less than 25 feet in depth, side yards not less than 5 feet (or 3 feet, depending on the width of the lot), and open space had to make up at least 60 percent of the lot. Certain older houses in Dunbar, built before the 1922 bylaw was adopted, are set back farther on their lots. In 1929 Point Grey amalgamated with the City of Vancouver and became subject to the city's bylaws. Interestingly, the Vancouver bylaws included many of the same provisions as Point Grey's.

Dear Little Houses and Builders' Specials

Once the First World War was over and the Spanish flu epidemic of 1918–19 had subsided, development in Dunbar began in earnest. New settlers were arriving in Vancouver in huge numbers. The city's population grew almost one-thousand-fold between 1886 and 1936, as its boundaries expanded and settlers arrived. As land became scarce in older neighbourhoods such as the West End, new settlers looked to the "suburbs." The destination for the elite was Shaughnessy, created by the Canadian Pacific Railway, but many buyers of more modest means seized "an opportunity to secure Homesite Bargains in Vancouver's Finest Suburb," Dunbar.

Development in the 16-block section of Dunbar bounded by 16th Avenue, Blenheim, King Edward and Dunbar Street between 1918 and

Two side-by-side houses (3664 and 3678 West 21st Avenue) built by George Hargreaves, who was responsible for many handsome houses like these bearing the popular half-timbering ornamentation. The design is identical, just inverted. Courtesy of Joan Tyldesley. ▶

1930 was traced by Wynn in an essay in *Vancouver and Its Region.* The area filled out from less than 2 percent of available lots developed in 1915 to more than 80 percent in 1930, when only scattered lots were still undeveloped. The greatest amount of building occurred in the second half of the 1920s, the period when Dunbar's "character" was established.

Empty building lots in Dunbar were typically purchased by small builders who proceeded to erect homes to be offered for sale. Most of these homes were built, as Luxton diplomatically put it, "without the direct involvement of a professionally trained architect" (Luxton 16). Instead, builders continued to rely on pattern books. A builder might have several crews at work on nearby houses, virtually identical, sometimes inverting the floor plans or modifying the exterior detailing to provide some level of customization.

The horizontal, deep-eaved California bungalow style that was popular in the first decade of the century gave way to various other forms. Wynn suggests that when architect-designed Tudor Revival mansions appeared in prestigious Shaughnessy Heights, with their English look "redolent of tradition and stability" (Wynn 104), they became identified as the "ideal house" for Vancouver, and pattern books provided builders with modest versions for neighbourhoods like Dunbar: a one- or two-storey home with stucco walls, steep roofs and a suggestion of half-timbering.

One such builder in Dunbar during the 1920s was George Hargreaves, who built several houses west of Dunbar between West 18th and West 24th Avenues. Hargreaves was an Englishman and the crews building his houses were trained in England. Hargreaves was remembered as a well-dressed man who continuously smoked hand-rolled cigarettes and remained a bachelor all his life. He would frequently have lunch at his friend Peter Nicholson's house in Dunbar. Nicholson's son-in-law, Jack Claridge, said that Hargreaves would be inspecting his houses under construction in the area and then turn up for lunch.

The buyers that builders like Hargreaves were catering to, according to Wynn, were mainly young married couples. They were looking for their first home — a "dear little house" in a modest middle-class suburb. "Picture your own first home — the fondest memory of all," coaxed one advertisement. Builders were offering buyers in Dunbar and other neighbourhoods across the growing city a range of affordable and utilitarian house designs specially suited to standard city lots, measuring 33 feet or ½ chain. These homes became known as "Builders' Specials" or "Eastern Cottages" (Wynn 98). Harold J. Chisholm's family moved into such a house in 1925. His memories of the house are clear and detailed:

> The inside design of our house did most certainly matter to me. It was better designed than most houses built in 1924. I'm not sure if an architect or a house-plan was used. More than likely the latter, as it was designed with a family of six in mind; [it was] nothing fancy. [A] nice warm kitchen [with a] wood stove, later converted to oil [and then] later electric. [A] nice nook seated eight. No fridge 'til the late '40s. We had an ice box — ice delivered by Morrow. We had a cross-hall dining room, all hardwood floors, plate rail, seated ten. We had only one bathroom — to my knowledge [it] wasn't ever a problem. A small den, four bedrooms up and a closed stairway. [In] later years, a completed rumpus room in the basement. [I] forgot: yes, a living room with wood-burning fireplace.

A fashionable home design in the 1920s and 1930s was the cozy stucco bungalow pattern marketed by the English architect C.F.A. Voysey. These houses have a cottagey, close-to-the-ground look achieved with "false buttresses" pierced with curved archways, downswept gable rooflines (known as "cat slides") and rounded roof edges to imitate thatch. (In 2006, cat slides are once again appearing in new construction, as builders cater to a new generation of buyers who value traditional styling.)

Another distinctive style was the small bungalow with a turret or other feature that suggested a miniature castle. These were the specialty of a developer named Jack Wood. Wood left his mark on Dunbar and nearby Mackenzie Heights, constructing many of these small bungalows based on patterns imported from California. During the 1980s Don Watters became acquainted with Wood and did construction for him during the last years of his life.

According to Watters, Wood built his very first house near 39th and Blenheim, but he had trouble attracting buyers. "It was out in the middle of nowhere," Watters explained. "In fact it was just dirt trails. In order to

▲ George Hargreaves, one of Dunbar's most successful builders during the 1920s, photographed at the home of his friend Peter Nicholson. Courtesy of Jack Claridge.

Dozens of "castle houses" like this one at 3815 West 39th were built by Dunbar developer Jack Wood during the 1930s. Wood and his wife lived in this particular house. Courtesy of Joan Tyldesley. ▶

build [the house] he and another fellow and a horse had to drag a cement mixer from 16th and Trafalgar (down on the flats) all the way up the hill through the bush." Six months after the house was completed, Wood had still not been able to get anybody to come see it.

Watters explained how Wood handled the challenge: "He had heard of a university professor out at UBC who lived in Burnaby but wanted to get closer to the campus. So Jack found his way out to the university, sought this guy out and said to him, face to face: 'I have a deal for you that you can't refuse.' He took out a $100 note — this was back in the '30s and $100 was equal to a month's pay for this professor. He tore the bill in half, gave him one half, and [said], 'I will give you the other half when you come to see this home.'" When the professor and his wife arrived at the house, Wood handed over the other half of the bill, offered him $500 in cash for moving in, and promised to sign the house over free of charge if the professor would live in it for one year. "Jack wasn't being so silly," Watters pointed out. "All of a sudden Jack's subdivision had prestige. Within six months, he had sold one hundred lots and built over fifty homes."

One reason for Wood's commercial success might have been his thrifty nature. Watters said Wood enforced a rule that any piece of wood over 12 inches long had to be built into the building. He would make a deal with his crew supervisors that they would get a new truck every year if there was no more than a level pickup load of scrap to come out of any house. "Now, you go to work on these properties," said Watters, "and there is so much bridge blocking holding studs together! Just about any piece of wood that could fit into a slot was fitted in." Watters has a portfolio with architectural drawings of many of the homes Wood built in the Dunbar area. "These renderings and a floor plan on a 10 by 14 piece of paper was all that was required in those days for a building permit."

In Dunbar as elsewhere across the city, piecemeal development by small builders like Jack Wood and George Hargreaves produced the "diverse but not disorderly landscape" (Wynn 105) that generations of Dunbar residents have enjoyed.

Architect-Designed Houses

While the "character" of the Dunbar neighbourhood is largely defined by its pleasant mix of pattern book houses, there are also architect-designed dwellings in Dunbar. Several examples are in the West Coast style celebrated in a special exhibition at the Vancouver Art Gallery in 1997 *(The New Spirit: Modern Architecture in Vancouver, 1938–63)*. Barry Downs is a practitioner of this style. Downs grew up in Point Grey, went to Seattle to complete his architecture training, and returned to Vancouver in the late 1950s to find what he called an exciting "organic school" of architecture flourishing here. In an interview, Downs said it was the same school of West Coast architecture, borrowing heavily from Frank Lloyd Wright, that had come up the coast from California, but he found emerging in Vancouver a unique architecture in this area. "Slightly further north, [it] had more rain and more overhang, more need to harness daylight through skylights, framing views and pushing the boundaries of indoor/outdoor, plainer architecture — flat roofs were okay. It had more to do with cubism and Japaneseque — the light and thinness and detailing." Downs designed and built a house for his family in this style in 1958, located at 6275 Dunbar Street. Another noted practitioner of the West Coast style was architect Fred Dalla-Lana of Dalla-Lana, Griffen architects, who designed two houses in Dunbar in the West Coast organic style, including the one he designed as his family home.

Architect Peter Oberlander and his wife, the landscape architect Cornelia Oberlander, chose a completely different approach when they built their avant-garde modular "tic-tac-toe" house on a large sunny lot at 6029 Olympic in 1958. Cornelia explained: "Here is a house that makes us question many widely accepted principles of residential design on the West Coast, because it rose above the environment! It was a house on stilts, high above the ground." Everybody in Vancouver, Oberlander noted, lived pretty close to the ground. "This was the opposite. Now why? Because Peter says it rains so much that children should play under the overhang." Oberlander said that the house was originally designed for steel and masonry construction in 1947 and submitted as an entry in

West Coast Modern

Three contemporary architect-designed homes in Dunbar/Southlands. Descriptions by June Binkert.

Barry Downs house at 6275 Dunbar Street. "The house is designed with blank walls to the neighbours; the inner spaces open upon a natural entrance garden and a forest grove to the rear, with skylights allowing light to penetrate the interior." Courtesy of Joan Tyldesley. ▶

Fred Dalla-Lana house at 6290 Collingwood Street. "The house is a post-and-beam composition, framing a glazed living pavilion which bridges the site at the rear, thus preserving views for the neighbours to the north. On the east the house backs onto the tall trees of Point Grey Golf Club and, like other [contemporary houses] on this tour, emphasizes the horizontal rather than the vertical." Courtesy of Joan Tyldesley. ▶

The Oberlander house at 6029 Olympic Street, completed in 1958. H. Peter Oberlander and Leon G. Dirasser, architects; Cornelia Hahn Oberlander, landscape architect; and Oliver Builders Ltd., builders. Leonard Frank photo. Otto Landauer, photographer. Courtesy of Cornelia Oberlander. ▶

the small home competition organized by the *Chicago Tribune* news-paper, winning second prize. Adapting the construction to wood altered the architectural interpretation but did not change the basic design. Oberlander gave much credit to the conscientious work of the builder, Jim Oliver of Oliver Builders Ltd.

Another architect-designed Dunbar house is located at 6095 Bala-clava, designed by Arthur Erickson in the early 1960s. Like Erickson's own home in Point Grey, very little of this actual house can be seen. The reason for this, points out Barry Downs, is Erickson's distinctive land-scaping: "He scooped up all the front yard, piled up the dirt against the road for privacy (a berm), planted bamboo there, [and] set the house back." Oberlander, too, said that she prefers landscaping set away from the house, rather than against the foundation, because it can be viewed better from the house and provides screening from the street.

Wolfgang Gerson designed and built a modernist dwelling in Dun-bar in 1977, shortly after he retired from the School of Architecture at UBC. Gerson designed this house for himself and his wife, Hilde, to live in. It is set on an east-sloping 33-foot lot at 3363 West 18th Avenue and takes advantage of the slope so that light penetrates the house through-out the day, with Burrard Inlet and the mountains beyond visible to the north. The Gersons are no longer living. Their daughter Erika lives in the house now.

Expanding at the Edges

The heart of the neighbourhood was almost fully built up by the beginning of the Second World War. After the war, Dunbar's borders expanded through the authorization of several small new subdivisions on Dunbar's western edge. The first of these was in the early 1950s, when a little bedroom community of post-war bungalows was created from a parcel of city-owned land. The first residents of that community were the future parks board commissioner and city alderman May Brown and her husband Lorne.

In 1949 the Browns were newlyweds living in an apartment and expecting their first child. May Brown commented that housing was very hard to find in Vancouver, and many landlords did not allow children. Driving around looking for an area where they might like to settle, the Browns saw that the city had cleared a parcel of land extending from 29th to 31st Avenues between Crown and Camosun Streets. Brown later learned that the existing neighbours were caught by surprise: "They thought the city ended at Crown! So the people living there were quite amazed when the city came in with bulldozers and cleaned off absolutely every blade of grass and every tree right across the land."

The city created thirteen 53-foot lots on the cleared land, extending three streets (the north side of West 31st, both sides of West 30th, and the south side of West 29th), then auctioned off the lots. Many of the buyers were young couples looking for their first house. May Brown said that one buyer, who would become her neighbour, bid $1,400 on a lot and lost it, then bid $1,500 on the next lot and got it. A contractor named Mr. Neilson bid successfully on four lots, including the one where the Browns' house would be built. The developed lots, like one the Browns purchased from Mr. Neilson, were priced at $10,000 including the house, and another $500 if the purchasers wanted a garage. The Browns moved into their new house at the end of April 1949 with their newborn baby.

The new subdivision was quite isolated. Promised commercial amenities were never built. Brown recalled: "The real estate man said that there was to be a bus line along Camosun Street and that we wouldn't have to walk to Dunbar. This was one of the selling points when they were advertising the houses. There was also to be a shopping centre on Camosun. We laugh about it at this point because we wouldn't want it, but . . . when our children were all small and we were pushing them around in prams, we thought a shopping centre at the end of the block was quite attractive."

Municipal improvements that had been enjoyed in other parts of Dunbar for decades had to be achieved one by one in the new subdivision through petitions. Brown recalled: "The road was just gravel when we

The Changing Face of Dunbar

A house built in the subdivision created in the 1950s on city-owned land in the 4000 block of West 30th. Fifty-three-foot lots were sold at auction for approximately $1,500 each. Houses like this one sold for about $10,000 completed, with an extra $500 if the purchaser wanted a garage. Courtesy of Joan Tyldesley.

◄ A luxury home built in the early 2000s next door to the 1950s bungalow. Courtesy of Joan Tyldesley.

came in. It was quite difficult sometimes, having to leave our cars on the other side of Crown and walk in, so the road was soon paved. Then we decided we should get a sidewalk, and so we got that. When we had something paid for, we'd plan for the next 'local improvements': street lights, etc. We had to petition for each one."

Another new subdivision was created in 1970. It was located on a triangular piece of land owned by the Jesuits just west of St. George's senior school, which was being built at about the same time. The residential subdivision includes two connecting streets, Doncaster Street and Kevin Place, which open onto West 29th Avenue west of Camosun Street, plus a one-block stretch of King Edward Avenue separated from the rest of

These two single-family homes in the 4000 block of West 21st were built on the site where the Penta co-op planned to build a housing co-op in the 1970s. Courtesy of Joan Tyldesley. ▶

Dunbar by the B.C. Hydro substation, opening onto West 29th at the edge of Pacific Spirit Park. This little out-of-the-way corner of Dunbar is unabashedly an automobile suburb, an evolutionary step beyond the streetcar suburb that is the rest of Dunbar. Here, large ranch-style houses are tucked behind broad driveways and two-car garages.

A third new subdivision occurred in the 1970s on city-owned land near the edge of Camosun Bog. At the time the city works department was using the land for a storage yard. The first developers to show an interest in this small parcel of land were the members of the Penta housing co-operative. The co-op had been searching for a site to build a shared-housing complex. "It was the mid-1970s when alternative housing was in the air," remembered Nichola Hall in a phone interview. She and her husband Ray had friends who were members of the co-op. Hall recalled that the United Nations Habitat conference was being held in Vancouver, drawing crowds of people to Jericho Park to discuss alternative futures for cities.

When local residents learned of the co-op's plans, they organized to oppose it. They rented a vacant storefront on Dunbar Street, held meetings there, and invited Dunbar residents to register their objections to the new development. The first public meeting at City Hall had to be cancelled because there was not enough room to accommodate all the people who wanted to speak. The second public meeting, held at Queen Elizabeth Elementary School, was also standing-room-only. In the end, the opponents won by a single vote.

The Penta co-op eventually found land to build their housing development near Jericho Beach, and the city put the Dunbar land on sale as single-family lots. These were priced at $60,000 each, according to Dunbar resident Gerald DiCarmo. Today the cul-de-sacs at the western ends of West 20th and 21st Avenues are lined with large single-family homes. DiCarmo mentioned in an interview that he formerly owned two additional lots on land that would have become a westerly extension of West 22nd Avenue if the city had chosen to create a subdivision there. However, he said the city decided to set aside the land as parkland instead.

Just up the hill from the subdivision on West 21st, two houses on the south side of the street have interesting histories. Fred Albinson built the bungalow at 4018 West 21st Avenue in 1948, when the street was just a dirt road with wood planks to drive on. The house next door to Albinson's to the east, which has undergone much remodelling, started out as a care-taker's cottage on English Bay. It was the childhood home of Fred Albinson's wife, Betty. While Fred was building the new bungalow, he and Betty lived in his parents' basement. His parents were the newlyweds pictured on page ii standing on the forested site on West 29th Avenue where they would build Fred's childhood home.

Infill and Renewal

Over time the remaining vacant lots in Dunbar disappeared one by one but still people kept arriving, looking for a place to call home. The demand for houses in the city, especially on the West Side, drove up property values. Buyers who could afford to look at property in Dunbar wanted more than a "dear little house" with only one bathroom. The mullioned windows and doors in the 1920s Builders' Specials were charming, but the structures were drafty and hard to maintain and maybe a bit rundown. Even long-time Dunbar residents began to upgrade their properties.

One solution was remodelling. Many of the houses in Dunbar have been altered and expanded. An addition to the back of the house or a second storey on top provided extra bedrooms. Undeveloped basements were converted to secondary suites to rent out to UBC students or to house a nanny. Bathrooms were added and kitchens modernized. During the mid-1970s the federal government encouraged homeowners to install energy-efficient windows, and the mullioned casement windows disappeared from many 1930s Builders' Specials, replaced with double-paned aluminum sliders.

Sometimes the chosen solution was not remodelling but demolition and redevelopment. During the 1970s, 1980s and 1990s developers would purchase a property, level the existing house and garage, and build a new house to offer for sale. This fostered the emergence of an informal sub-trade of contractors who would hold weekend demolition sales before the houses were taken down. Hand-scrawled signs appeared on street corners on Friday afternoon directing builders and home renovators to the site of a "demo sale," where customers would bring their own hammers and crowbars and strip the building of windows, oak flooring, fir panelling, plumbing fixtures and other serviceable building materials. The sales were over and the temporary signs removed by Monday morning when the sign bylaw enforcement officers returned to work.

VANCOUVER SPECIALS

The first major wave of redevelopment in Vancouver occurred in the late 1960s and 1970s. On Vancouver's East Side and on smaller lots in West Side neighbourhoods such as Dunbar, small cottages and bungalows began to be replaced with a distinctive style of house that became known as "Vancouver Specials" or "1970s Builders." Like the Builders' Specials of the 1930s, Vancouver Specials were a vernacular architectural form. They were created by builders rather than architects, and they reflected the needs of ordinary people.

Vancouver Specials were inexpensive to build and provided plenty of habitable space, including the option of separate quarters on the ground level for an extended family or a secondary suite. The builders of 1970s Vancouver Specials, like the builders of the older homes they replaced, started with standardized plans and adapted or embellished them to suit their own or their buyer's taste. Thousands of these simple utilitarian houses were built across Vancouver. Today almost every block in the northern half of Dunbar has one or more of them nestled among the older homes.

More than a thousand Vancouver Specials have been documented by Keith Higgins with photographs that are published on his Web site (www.vancouverspecial.com). In an e-mail correspondence with the authors, Higgins pointed out that unlike earlier pattern book houses, the Specials are an original Vancouver expression. The Vancouver Special plans were made locally, whereas many of the earlier bungalow plans

Two of hundreds of "Vancouver Specials" built during the 1970s, designed with Vancouver's zoning regulations in mind. Courtesy of Joan Tyldesley. ▶

came from the United States. Higgins corresponded by e-mail with the son of a man who may have been the inventor of the Vancouver Special. Jack Cudney wrote to Higgins:

> My father, Larry Cudney, was a self-employed draftsman who operated a drafting business for approximately 30 years during the early '50s. He retired in 1976 or thereabouts. I remember asking my father if he drew the original plans for the Vancouver Special. He thought he might have, but he was fairly certain that the original concept came from a builder named Crawchuck who built economical houses at the time. He explained to me that the Vancouver Special was an extremely practical house to build on Vancouver's 33-foot lots (a legacy of early surveys in the city, 33' = ½ chain). The Vancouver Special is often referred to with a condescending sneer; however, its worth has been proven over the years. My father said he would not design "a big stupid house as a monument to someone's big stupid life," and he took some pride with his involvement with the Vancouver Special.

Jon Ellis, who moved to Dunbar in the early 1970s and worked as a planner for the City of Vancouver, recalled in an interview that there was a business at Broadway and Yukon Street where the house plans were sold. "There were draftsmen working there. You could buy a set of drawings for $100, except for the foundation. You would get an engineer to draw the foundation plan and then you would be ready to apply for your permit."

According to Ellis, the Vancouver Special was specifically designed to fit the city's zoning and the needs of the builder, allowing builders to save time and money by meeting all of the regulations at once in their permit application. Each of the Vancouver Special's unique features represents the solution to a problem. The exterior footprint of the house is designed precisely to fit the standard 33-foot lot and its setbacks. The shallow, "four-in-twelve" roof slope is the minimum that will still shed rainwater and uses the least wood possible. The trusses are easy to build and set up on site, and the shape also allows maximum habitable space beneath it.

Ellis further explained that the Vancouver Special's distinctive front entrance — at-grade rather than up a flight of steps — is a result of a change in the zoning regulations. When the earlier bungalows were built, the zoning regulations did not count the basement area in allowable floor space ratio (FSR), so long as the basement floor was more than one foot below the ground. As a result, those homes typically included an undeveloped basement that was actually only half underground, with the main entrance at the top of a front stoop or small porch. But the rules were changed in 1974. The new zoning rules allowed higher density (higher FSR), but the entire area of the house including basement counted as floor space. This is why the Vancouver Specials are typically two-storey houses built "slab-on-grade" with no basement. "It saved digging an expensive hole," said Ellis. Basements were necessary in earlier times to accommodate furnaces that burned sawdust or wood slabs, but today's gas and oil furnaces and water heaters can be accommodated in utility closets.

Another characteristic feature of the Vancouver Special, said Ellis, was the interior staircase leading directly from the front door to the second floor. This meant that the Vancouver Special could be changed from a single-family house into an up-and-down duplex by simply closing an inside door at the foot of the stairs.

"MONSTER HOUSES"

In an Internet blog, Keith Higgins suggested that Vancouver Specials were an evolutionary step in the development of vernacular architecture in Vancouver and that the next step in that evolution was the 1980s design that was dubbed the "monster house." Although the homely utilitarian Vancouver Specials were met with quiet disdain by long-time residents of the city, the 1980s monster houses set off a storm of protest. These houses provoked Michael Kluckner, Vancouver's most nostalgic historian, to write: "They may be no uglier than the little 1930s and 1940s stucco boxes that some of them replaced, but they are in addition big and ostentatious — a formidable combination when combined with ugliness" (Kluckner 16).

Continuing the story that began with the pattern book houses of the early part of the century, one finds that most of the monster houses were built from standard designs without an architect. Developers and builders used stock plans, choosing features that they hoped would appeal to buyers. In the 1980s, these features included symmetrical designs and pastel colours, grand entranceways with etched glass windows, double doors and two-storey entrance halls. Because of the continually rising cost of land in Vancouver, developers tried harder than ever to build the maximum FSR possible under the zoning bylaw, favouring the low-profile roof slope and slab-on-grade construction that had been introduced with the Vancouver Specials. Homes were equipped with high-end fixtures and set like mansions in spare formal gardens that contrasted starkly with the trees and colourful English gardens that had been the pride of earlier generations.

University of Washington geographer Katharyne Mitchell (2004) has written that Canadian federal government policies on immigration, finance and land control were a driver in Vancouver's 1980s development boom. In anticipation of the transfer of the administration of Hong Kong to China in 1997, Canadian immigration policies were changed to create an "investor category" of applicant who could move more quickly through the processing queue. New rules also reduced barriers to foreign investment in Canada, and Canadian banks opened offices in Hong Kong, offering investor immigrant services to help wealthy clients purchase real estate in Canada.

◀ An example of the new, much larger style of house that developed in the 1980s and '90s, and often replaced much more modest homes. Courtesy of Joan Tyldesley.

The federal government hoped that the flow of capital, culture and people from Hong Kong and Taiwan would contribute to Canadian prosperity. The flow of funds was estimated at $6 billion per year by the late 1980s and early 1990s, one-third of it to British Columbia, with most of the funds invested in property. This created a gold rush opportunity for developers in Vancouver, who bought up standard city lots, demolished the existing houses and built mansions.

During the 1980s Barbara Pettit, a planner, studied the monster house phenomenon in Vancouver. In an interview with the *Vancouver Courier* in 2004, Pettit said that the Hong Kong immigrants she spoke to told her they bought the monster homes because that was what was available. They assumed this was the latest style. "We interviewed them and they were shaking their heads. Immigrants that were coming in were educated. In many cases, they [monster houses] weren't the houses they wanted to buy, but they wanted to seem Canadian and they assumed for the longest time that it was what Canadians liked" (quoted in Carrigg).

A frequent complaint in Dunbar about monster houses was that they violated what residents felt to be the existing "scale" of the neighbourhood. Richard Archambault, a well-known architect who worked in partnership with Barry Downs, said that he enjoyed the scale of the earlier houses: "I guess there is a scale about it that I like. It's just 'Dunbarish.' I am not fond of the big monster houses, like most people." Many residents in West Side neighbourhoods put pressure on the city to do something about the monster houses, and the homeowners' association in

174 / THE STORY OF DUNBAR

Shaughnessy drafted, at its members' expense, a special zoning regulation to control the design of new homes, which was adopted by the city. For other single-family neighbourhoods including Dunbar, the city responded to public complaints by creating a new single-family zoning category called RS-5. This provided incentives for developers to consult with the neighbourhood and build houses with traditional features such as steeply sloped roofs. The benefit to builders if they met the city's design standards was extra FSR — a larger house. But the Dunbar Residents' Association (DRA) was skeptical. In February 2004, seven years after the RS-5 zoning was introduced, the DRA looked back at advice it had given the city. "The DRA spoke against the RS-5 zoning at public hearings in 1997 because we felt it contained two significant flaws. First, it completely missed dealing with Dunbar's main complaint about the newer housing being built: that they were too big and too tall. The RS-5 allows houses to be 15 percent bigger and 8 percent taller than before. Second, we felt that the 'neighbourhood context and consultation' process in the zoning was unworkable and would at best only be window dressing" (Ellis 7).

When the DRA surveyed 32 houses in 1999 that had been built in Dunbar during the first two years after RS-5 zoning was introduced, it found that many builders had forgone the extra FSR, presumably to avoid the costly design review process. It also found that new houses built without design review were beginning to fit into the neighbourhood better than in the 1980s and 1990s, perhaps because the neighbours articulated so clearly their dissatisfaction with the early monster houses. It appeared that the market was responding to consumer demand.

A NEW PLAN FOR VANCOUVER

The strong real estate market in Dunbar during the late 1980s and early 1990s drove up property values to levels where some long-time homeowners on fixed incomes found it difficult to pay their property taxes. When elderly residents moved out of their modest houses, developers tended to replace them with luxury homes. Many young people who had grown up in Dunbar could not afford to settle there to raise their own families.

One factor reducing the affordability of housing in Dunbar, argued Barbara Pettit, was exclusionary single-family zoning. At this time, the City of Vancouver was already preparing a public consultation aimed at revisiting the single-family zoning concept that had shaped development in much of Vancouver for the past half-century. Over a period of three years, from 1992 to 1995, Vancouver citizens participated in workshops to develop the first new plan for the city of Vancouver since the one Harland Bartholomew had presented to council in 1928, at the time of the amalgamation of Vancouver with Point Grey and South Vancouver.

Although the Bartholomew plan was never formally adopted, it had nevertheless left its mark on the city. It called for concentration of industry on the waterfronts, concentration of high-density apartment housing in the West End, and vast expanses of single-family housing modelled after the Point Grey vision in the remaining 70 percent of the city. Bartholomew further elaborated that, among the single-family districts, the former municipality of Point Grey would become a "desirable residential district," while the former municipality of South Vancouver and Hastings Townsite would be places where "those who gain their livelihood by manual labour could find . . . a place where they can build modest homes."

These words were quoted by Ann McAfee (1997), Vancouver's director of city planning, who oversaw the development of Vancouver's new town plan in the 1990s. McAfee wrote that citizens who participated in the planning workshops valued the neighbourhood character of single-family areas, but they also wanted "more choice of housing." The intent of the new "CityPlan," which was formally adopted by council in 1995, is to accommodate additional housing in single-family neighbourhoods, concentrating it on commercial streets that would become "neighbourhood centres." This would leave much of the existing neighbourhoods intact, while accommodating new and more diversified housing. In 1996 workshops were held in Dunbar to adapt the broad principles of CityPlan to the local level. These culminated in the *Dunbar Community Vision*, which was approved by council in 1997.

Following the adoption of these new policy directions, older buildings on Dunbar Street and West 41st Avenue began to be demolished and redeveloped in a "mixed use" pattern that is now appearing city-wide: commercial spaces on the street level and three storeys of condominium apartments upstairs.

One challenge posed to citizens participating in the CityPlan workshops was to decide how their neighbourhoods might accommodate more people. In a region expected to double its population to 3 million by 2021, every neighbourhood was told it should expect to take "its share" of the new arrivals. Dunbar had already expanded to its outer limits. The new housing would have to be built within.

Secondary suites were one option, allowing a single-family house to accommodate a second, smaller household. In the early 1990s the northernmost streets in Dunbar were included in the Secondary Suites Program, allowing them to have legal secondary suites, but it was still illegal to have a suite in the rest of Dunbar. In March 2004, council relaxed the restriction on secondary suites, making it legal for houses in all single-family districts in the city to have secondary suites. Even before the change in the bylaw, many homeowners in Dunbar had already built unauthorized suites to use as "mortgage helpers." This demonstrates a will-

▲ This "thin house," located at 3814 West King Edward, provides a single-family dwelling on a narrow lot. Courtesy of Joan Tyldesley.

ingness within Dunbar to provide affordable housing informally, but homeowners have repeatedly resisted formal proposals that would increase housing density and introduce new housing forms on their streets. The Penta co-op is just one example. Another is a development proposed by Polygon Development just off Dunbar Street near West 28th and West 29th, which also was defeated due to neighbourhood objections.

Dunbar homeowners were powerless to block two subdivision applications in 2004 and 2005, which will go ahead despite objections from neighbours. In both cases developers applied to subdivide lots that were less than the standard one-chain (66-foot) width, resulting in "orphan" lots that were, in turn, less than the standard ½ chain (33-foot) width. The city's director of development services, Rick Scobie, explained that the city had no grounds to refuse the applications. Subdivision decisions had to be based on legal precedents rather than neighbourhood concern, and many similar applications elsewhere in the city had been approved.

As the number of subdivided orphan lots grows, so will the challenge of ensuring that the new homes fit in well with the adjoining ones. Several were built in Dunbar during the 1970s and 1980s on legal lots narrower than the standard 33 feet. Such houses, dubbed Narrow Houses or Thin Houses, provoked complaints from neighbours, but they are permitted under the existing single-family zoning. In 1981 Shelagh Lindsey of the UBC School of Architecture oversaw the work of students who proposed a set of guidelines for the design of these houses to "minimize the negative impact of narrow houses, provide comfortable accommodation and be harmonious with the prevailing pattern of the block face" (Williams 2). The guidelines were accepted with some small revisions by the Vancouver Planning Department.

One of the intentions of CityPlan endorsed in the *Dunbar Community Vision* was to encourage residents to live near where they work. Dunbar architects Pat Bourque and Willi Bruegger designed their architect studio, which was approved by the city, and built it behind their house on their residential lot on West 26th Avenue. Bourque knew from experience as a Vancouver city planner that this use was permitted "outright" (without negotiation) under the single-family zoning rules in place at the time. She and Bruegger saw an opportunity to test an unconventional use of single-family land, a use that they felt might actually preserve the "character" of Dunbar. They wanted, they said, to better utilize their lot, "take the [allowed] square footage and distribute it, break up the massing, keep the scale of the established neighbourhood, and provide an alternate use." Similarly, architect Richard Archambault said in an interview that he and his associate Barry Downs did some of their early work in an "old cottage at the back [behind Downs's house in Dunbar] that the city didn't require him to take down."

A Sustainable Neighbourhood?

As the twenty-first century unfolds and the new CityPlan shapes future development, the physical face of Dunbar/Southlands will gradually change. If the past is any indication, the changes will reflect the complex interplay of social, economic and cultural forces. One of these forces will be a growing awareness of the ecological impacts of our lifestyles. The "streetcar suburb" has now become an automobile suburb, with most people driving long distances for work, recreation and shopping. Transportation accounts for half of a household's 20-tonne contribution of greenhouse gases causing global warming. The other half comes from the home itself: space heating and cooling, water heating, appliances and lighting. Building construction, including home renovations, demolition and redevelopment, accounts for nearly one-third of the solid waste produced in the Greater Vancouver region. Each summer the city and the regional water authority put restrictions on water use because population and lifestyles have outstripped the region's supply of fresh water. Each winter the rains wash contamination from our streets into the Fraser River.

In light of these facts, some innovative programs are just beginning to draw the public's attention. During Dunbar's Salmonberry Days festival in 2005, homeowners and home builders listened to a presentation about geothermal heat pumps, which are now being installed in several new homes in Dunbar. Homeowners on Crown Street hosted a tour of the innovative storm drainage system installed by the city's engineering department on their street as a demonstration project. Will lanes in Dunbar be surfaced with permeable paving that reduces storm water runoff during the winter rains? Will water metering that provides direct feedback on water use be implemented? Will home builders in Dunbar entice buyers by offering the distinction of "green design" certification? Dunbar is home to UBC professor Bill Rees, after all, who was the originator of the concept of the "ecological footprint," a methodological tool for measuring humans' demands on the natural environment. It would be only fitting if his neighbourhood became a pioneer in exploring new ways to adapt the residential landscape so that it blends more comfortably with its ecological context.

CHAPTER 7

People and Places in the Arts

—๑ Pam Chambers

There's a magic to working in the arts.
— BETTE COSAR

Dunbar has always been rich in people engaged in artistic activities, whether professionally or as skilled amateurs. Local churches and schools have encouraged music and theatre. The nearby University of British Columbia has had a great impact, both in attracting internationally respected artists and teachers and in providing educational opportunities for the enrichment of the community. The dedication of those in the arts is evident, as is their desire to share their knowledge and to "give back" to the community that has nurtured them.

This chapter just scratches the surface of the talent to be found in Dunbar. Musicians and artists have grown up here and stayed to enrich their home neighbourhood. Others have moved away and made their mark elsewhere. Still others have come to make Dunbar their home, while working both here and in the wider sphere. "But I'm not famous!" replied more than one respondent to a request for an interview. This remark reminds us that a tapestry is made up of many stitches, large and small, brilliant and more subdued. Yet all are of vital importance to the whole.

Music at Home in Early Days

In pioneer days, life at the edge was so rugged that there was not much time for leisure pursuits. Nevertheless, there was always music. Kerrisdale resident Betty (McCleery) McQueen is the descendant of two pioneer families of the Dunbar/Southlands area, the Moles and the McCleerys, who took up farming on the rich lands on the north bank of the Fraser in the 1860s. McQueen says that while the families spent their days in hard physical labour, they were spiritual people with depth to their lives. No one was left to be alone at Christmas. Extra tables would be brought in to the 30-foot-long McCleery dining room, which was filled with family and visitors. About 1890 the family brought a piano, now preserved in the Vancouver Museum, from London around the Horn, and the McCleery sisters played while everyone sang. There was also an organ in the house, used when the Wesleyan Methodist services were held there.

The Mole family also valued music. In 1893 Henry Mole bought for his daughter Annie (Betty McQueen's mother) a Williams piano, which was shipped across Canada by train. This piano is still in the family's possession. Mrs. McQueen said Henry Mole bought the first foot-pumped organ for the Wesleyan Methodist church located in the Eburne/Marpole area. Later Mole gave a pump organ to the first Knox United Church, then at 42nd Avenue and Macdonald. An excellent organist, he would play his favourite hymns "in the quiet of an early Sunday afternoon" according to the reminiscences of another granddaughter, Winnifred (Mole) Challenger.

Musicians Who Made a Difference

James (Jamie) Malkin, a long-time resident of Collingwood Street, grew up at "The Dogwoods," 3563 Marine Drive, where Glendalough Place was later built. To the east was the estate of his uncle, W.H. Malkin, and south across Marine Drive was the Mole farm. Three Malkin brothers had emigrated from Staffordshire before 1900 and prospered in the wholesale grocery business. Eldest brother W.H. (Harold) Malkin, mayor of Vancouver in 1929, built the Malkin Bowl at Stanley Park in memory of his wife, Marion Dougal Malkin. This covered stage has been home to many musical performances since its opening in 1934.

Younger brother Philip married accomplished musician Georgina Grundy, and all four children in their family had piano lessons. After the family moved to Marine Drive in the early '20s, Georgina brought to the house the two grand pianos that remain in the possession of family members. Jamie Malkin remembered internationally known performing artists such as the Hart House Quartet and Josef Szigeti, the famous Hungarian violinist, coming to their house as guests after their concerts. He said,

◄ Beverly (Barkley) Craig was a ballerina in the 1950s and '60s. In 1965 she met her husband, lawyer James Craig, who was a supporter of the Vancouver Ballet Society as well as a keen mountaineer. "He offered me a pair of climbing boots instead of an engagement ring." Courtesy of Beverly Craig.

however, that he got the most out of listening to his older sister Ursula practise. After studying in Germany, she pursued an international concert career, later performing and teaching for many years in Vancouver. On 5 October 1930, Ursula was the soloist playing Beethoven's *Piano Concerto No. 4 in G Major* at the inaugural concert of the Vancouver Symphony Orchestra upon its revival after more than a decade of dormancy. Her brother remembered, "The tension in our family was at the breaking point!"

Ursula Malkin's contribution to the cultural life of Vancouver went far beyond concert performances. She was instrumental in creating and supporting such Vancouver institutions as the Vancouver Academy of Music, the music department at UBC and the Vancouver Youth Symphony Orchestra.

During the 1930s, Eva (Twaites) Redmond was growing up in the 3500 block of West 23rd Avenue. Every Saturday she would sit with her father and listen to the Metropolitan Opera radio program. "He could never understand how I knew where to cry," she said. "I couldn't understand the words but it was the music that did it." Redmond sang from early childhood. During the Depression her parents could not afford lessons, so for the next few years she sang at school events. Then she was accepted into the Vancouver Opera chorus. For years after that, Redmond juggled her work in music and her family, eventually participating in Dunbar Musical Theatre.

The three Parker sisters could always be counted on when music was needed. Daughters of Yukoners Bert and Helen Scott Parker, they were

◄ The Mole family piano, still in use, being played in 2002 by Alison McQueen, great-great-granddaughter of Henry Mole and Fitzgerald McCleery. Courtesy of Douglas McQueen.

Ursula Malkin (1908–96) performed in recitals worldwide. Here she is pictured at a performance in Vienna during the 1920s. Courtesy of Jamie Malkin. ▶

raised on West 33rd Avenue, having moved there in 1931. According to the youngest, Elizabeth (Liz) Rowley, when they first moved to Dunbar they looked for a Sunday school. Eldest sister Jean found the gospel church that met in the old community hall at 29th and Dunbar, which they attended until joining Knox United. Liz said, "I loved going to Sunday school because of the singing and the gospel songs." She related with a chuckle the time her mother was shopping on Dunbar and looked up to see her three little girls going by in the back of an open truck. "Here's Jean and me and Pop [Pauline] driving up Dunbar singing 'Sunshine in My Soul Today' or something like this, and 'saving' everybody on Dunbar. I can still remember the songs; they were so much fun. . . . We never stop singing. Now we get captive audiences at the nursing homes." Jean (Parker) Clarke was also one of the original members of the Knox Operatic Society, singing leads and serving on the executive. Pop and Liz sang in the chorus. "Dad used to say, 'That's as close to Hollywood as you'll ever get.'"

Choirs, Operettas and Musical Performers

Those who sang at home and at church were often drawn to join larger singing groups. Melita Miller remembered the Philomel Ladies Choir formed by her friend Mildred Seymour in the 1930s. During World War

◀ Jim and Melita Miller at their piano. Music was a feature of their home, where Melita taught piano for many years. Photo by Peggy Schofield.

II, the choir gave many concerts to raise money for the war effort. Later, when Mrs. Seymour retired, many of the Philomel members joined the larger Vancouver Bach Choir.

KNOX OPERATIC SOCIETY AND DUNBAR MUSICAL THEATRE

James and Melita Miller were members of Knox United Church. Melita recalled: "Jim and another member of the choir, Bert Mills, decided one night after a slow practice that they would start a society. Church member Owen Thomas, a school superintendent who had previous experience with musical productions, was called on for help. Several other people in the choir backed up the project and the inaugural performance was *Trial by Jury* in 1942. It was known variously as the Knox Operatic Group and the Knox Operatic Society. We went on year after year, doing almost all of the Gilbert and Sullivan operettas. We did about 18 of them, which would be 18 years. During that time we had countless well-known singers."

Jim Miller (1899–2002) developed into an excellent patter singer, taking roles that required the ability to sing these fast-paced songs. At his hundredth birthday party at Brock House, accompanied by Melita on the piano, he sang all the verses of "I Am the Very Model of a Modern Major General" from *The Pirates of Penzance*. Melita was an accompanist and piano teacher who influenced many Dunbar young people.

Audrey Wills was in the Knox Operatic Society from the beginning. Her long-time friend Pat Waldron joined about 1948. By 1960, having done the Gilbert and Sullivan operettas, the group switched to other

Architect Richard Archambault played many roles with Dunbar Musical Theatre, among them the brash Harold Hill in *The Music Man*. Photo taken at Alexandra Park bandstand in 1970. Courtesy of Richard Archambault. ▶

types of shows. The church could no longer accommodate the demands placed on it by the company, which was now attracting members from far and wide. According to local historian Ted Affleck, in 1967 the group moved rehearsals to the Dunbar Community Centre and restyled themselves as Dunbar Musical Theatre.

By this time Dunbar architect Richard Archambault was also involved. Although architecture was his profession, the stage was his avocation. For years he sang in the chorus, graduating to lead roles such as Harold Hill in the 1970 production of *The Music Man*. In his semi-retirement years he continued to volunteer in the service of serious amateur theatre. Another Dunbar citizen who earned his expertise in the same way is Johnny Duncan, described as "Mr. Metro Theatre" for his devotion to that Marpole venue.

After the 1966 season, the Dunbar Musical Theatre group ran out of money. Wills remarked, "We didn't have a penny that we could put into royalties to do another production." To raise money, they organized a musical tour and did pub nights at the Billy Bishop Legion in Kitsilano. Selling "Save the Orpheum" Lotto tickets as well, they scraped together $10,000. Dunbar Musical started again in 1968 with *My Fair Lady*, which they repeated in 1969 for the reopening of the Malkin Bowl. In 1984 Pat Waldron produced *Annie* at the Gateway Theatre in Richmond, calling the company Dunbar Musical Theatre. "But it was out of sentimentality," she said. After 1985 the society, no longer active, was deregistered.

About the Dunbar Musical Theatre days, Waldron said, "We had a lot of fun, we did a lot of shows, and we made a lot of good friends. So what more could you ask for?" Said Eva Redmond, "We did it just for love. They couldn't have paid us to work as hard as we worked in those things."

DUNBAR HEIGHTS UNITED CHURCH GIRLS ENSEMBLE

Also active during the '60s was the Dunbar Heights United Church Girls Ensemble. It began in 1961 and was directed by Nancy Masson Allan, a dramatic soprano. The Allans' daughter, Betty Turner, said that while raising children and helping in the office of the family shipbuilding business, her mother pursued a busy career as a vocal soloist. Under her dynamic leadership, the Dunbar Heights United Church Girls Ensemble was active until 1978, singing at many functions throughout the city. Turner recalls: "My mother was an unofficial social worker. . . . I still get

Young people of Dunbar Heights United Church are in costume for a play performed at the Wilson house, 25th Avenue and Balaclava Street, c. 1930. Courtesy of Marion Funell. ▼

Bette Cosar, Opera Singer

Bette Cosar has combined an opera career with family life in Dunbar. Early influences were the music department at Prince of Wales School, Nancy Allan's Girls Ensemble at Dunbar Heights United Church and private voice lessons with Leslie Monk, also with the Dunbar church. In 1973, after completing an arts degree at UBC and joining the Vancouver Opera chorus, Cosar attended workshops with Dunbar resident and UBC professor French Tickner. "He was very difficult to please but an absolute genius at his craft. He taught me almost everything I know about how to move onstage. Then I was very lucky to be accepted to the Opera Centre in London, England. I remember in my résumé sending the letter and all the excerpts that I had done with French Tickner. The reply was, 'What is there we have to teach you?'"

On her return from London, Cosar continued to study and perform. She says her real passion is the song repertoire,

but she continues to be a proud member of the Vancouver Opera Association chorus.

Bette Cosar (fourth from left) sings in the Vancouver Opera Association production of The Rake's Progress *in October 1989. Courtesy of Bette Cosar.*

calls today, some 20 years later, from the girls saying things like "Your mother changed my life." I don't pretend to understand it, but it was a powerful thing. . . . There was always show business with my mother, whether it was a party, a funeral or a wedding. She even planned her own funeral. She died of cancer at the age of sixty-four. But she planned how she wanted her funeral to go. . . . So we all ended up laughing around the piano at her wake, which was how she would have liked to be remembered." Betty Turner now lives in Ladysmith, where she has started a choir in her own neighbourhood.

Music Teachers: Quiet Mentors

Aside from the organizations bringing people together to make music, there have always been private music teachers, working almost invisibly in their homes. At least a dozen of the 250 members of the Vancouver branch of the Registered Music Teachers' Association have their studios in Dunbar. Mary Tickner, UBC Professor Emerita and wife of French Tickner, has taught outstanding students both at university and privately; and for many years she has taken on the role of valued mentor to the young student teachers of the Registered Music Teachers' Association.

◄ Flutist Karen Suzanne Smithson and her late father, composer Elliot Weisgarber, were close musical collaborators for many years. Photo by Steven Lemay.

At an earlier period, about 1918, George Tedlock was an altar boy at the Convent of the Sacred Heart. In return for his services, he received an hour of piano instruction every Saturday. He said: "My teacher was a five foot chubby nun of the Sacred Heart order, Mother Eliza. She had a constant smile from ear to ear and wore black-rimmed glasses. After two years I left having a pretty good idea of musical theory and how to play and read music for simple pieces. I realized I would never be a pianist . . . but it instilled in me a love of music which I still have."

Jocelyn Pritchard is a musician and teacher who lived in Dunbar from 1975 to 1987. During her time directing the music at Knox United Church, Pritchard and Kerrisdale colleague Margo Ehling created a children's summer music school, Dunbar Summer Music. For three years, from 1980 to 1983, the church threw open its entire space to the group for classes in piano, flute and strings. The program was so popular that students came from across the Lower Mainland. In 1996, another teacher, Tara Wohlberg, created the Collage Festival of Canadian Music in conjunction with the annual Canadian Music Week. These non-competitive festival sessions have been held at Dunbar Heights United Church, attracting young performers from throughout Greater Vancouver.

Karen Suzanne Smithson is the daughter of the late composer Elliot Weisgarber. She is a flutist and teacher who teaches five days per week in her Dunbar studio; most of her students are local. Smithson began to play the flute in 1963 at the age of eight and plays regularly in the West Coast Symphony. In 1994 she completed writing and publishing her own flute teaching method. After the method became established all over the continent, she turned her attention to promoting recognition of her father's work in the United States, his country of origin.

Composers: Their Influences and Inspiration

Massachusetts-born, Elliot Weisgarber moved to Vancouver in 1960 to join the new faculty of music at UBC. Weisgarber's music has been associated with the sounds of Japan. For 20 years he spent much time in that country, becoming a master of the shakuhachi, the bamboo flute, for which he wrote many compositions. But when interviewed in January 2000, he said, "That's only one of my many, many interests. We change, develop, and move on."

Weisgarber retired from his position at the university in 1984 but never retired from music. In December 1999, when he reached his eightieth birthday, several concerts featuring his music were performed in his honour. In a *Vancouver Sun* article celebrating the occasion, Max Wyman quoted Dunbar resident Colin Miles, violist and Pacific Region director of the Canadian Music Centre, as saying: "He creates very beautiful and profound music. . . . You think you're looking at a picture and in fact you're looking through a picture window."

Stephen Chatman is another Dunbar composer associated with the University of British Columbia. After receiving his doctorate at the University of Michigan, he accepted a position at UBC in 1976. At the university, Chatman coordinates the composition division. His studies were in the late '60s, he says, "when the avant-garde was very important and influential." He has received many commissions over the years, including two pieces for the Vancouver Symphony Orchestra that premiered in January 2000, to open the first concert of the millennium.

Tara's Dream, named for Chatman's wife Tara Wohlberg, was shortlisted for the Masterprize 2001, an international award for which there were more than 1,000 entries from 62 countries. The second piece, *Fanfare for the Millennium*, was played again on 15 May 2000 by the VSO in B.C. Place Stadium with an orchestra of 6,000, mostly students, led by conductor Bramwell Tovey. This broke the world record for the largest orchestra ever assembled for a performance, earning a listing in the *Guinness Book of Records*.

Stephen Chatman was not the only Dunbar composer to be performed in that flamboyant VSO millennium concert. Frederick Schipizky's composition *Ten Minutes of Nine*, an adaptation for the student players of part of Beethoven's Ninth Symphony, was also on the program. Schipizky has received many commissions from the Vancouver Symphony and other large orchestras. *Meditation and Dance* was specially composed for young student string players at the 2001 Collage Festival of Canadian Music. In his studio on West 20th Avenue there is room for his double bass, a piano and his trusty 1986 Atari computer, on which he is able to write all the parts for an entire symphonic composition.

Artists with Vision

The record of painters active in the early years of Dunbar is scanty to non-existent. According to Betty McQueen, the McCleerys and the Moles did not have time for painting; photographs of their homes show that the pictures on the walls were mainly family photos. Once an itinerant artist came to the McCleery farm looking for work and, in return for food, painted a small watercolour, which Betty McQueen still has.

After the turn of the twentieth century, other artists stayed to share their talents here. One artist of significance was Charles Hepburn Scott (1866–1964), who immigrated to Canada in 1912 after training at the Glasgow School of Art. Following service in World War I, he returned to Canada and in 1926 became principal of the Vancouver School of Decorative and Applied Arts, which later became the Emily Carr Institute of Art and Design. He guided the education of generations of students until his retirement in 1956. A resident of 6212 Balaclava Street for many years until his death in 1964, he was also a driving force in the founding of the

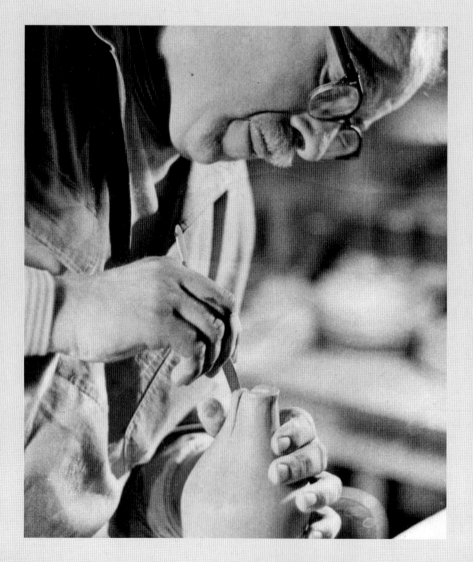

David Lambert, Potter

According to his son Jim Marlon-Lambert, David Lambert, originally from England, was inspired by the art of the Natives of the West Coast. In the 1960s he was asked by both the federal and provincial governments to record and produce their designs. This was before the renaissance of Native pride in their own heritage, and "cultural appropriation" was not the issue it became 30 years later. Lambert also produced works in many other styles and techniques. Jim has set up a prize for students of ceramics at Langara Community College in his father's memory.

Potter David Lambert (1919–85) had a store on Dunbar near 18th Avenue from 1958 to 1966 where he sold his distinctive designs, which have since become collector's items. Courtesy of Jim Marlon-Lambert.

first Vancouver Art Gallery in 1931. Distinguished artist Gordon A. Smith studied and later taught at the Vancouver School of Art after the Second World War. He and his wife Marion also lived next door to the Scotts for several years in the immediate post-war period. Smith described Scott warmly as "always very dignified, a wonderful man," who wore a French smock over his suit and tie while at work.

Peter Winchell Sager (1920–85) began his career as a precocious teenager at Lord Byng High School just before World War II. As a seventeen-year-old student of sculptor Beatrice Lennie in 1937, he became the youngest artist ever to hold a solo show at the Vancouver Art Gallery. For a short time in 1938 before leaving for further studies in London, he also showed his works independently in a makeshift store on 16th Avenue at Dunbar, using orange crates as both seating for guests and plinths for his flowing abstract sculptures. He held another solo exhibition at the gallery in 1940. His sculptures and prints are represented in American galleries and private collections.

Vern Tremewen (1913–80) was an Australian artist who lived in Vancouver from 1961 until 1976, when he moved to Hawaii. His son Charles, who still lives in Vancouver, said that his father went every possible morning to the riverbank to paint the fishing boats and the life on the Fraser River. His work is represented in the B.C. Archives as well as in private and corporate collections.

As with local musicians, the visual artists of Dunbar include those who have made their mark internationally and others who are known only closer to home. Painter Bill McLuckie has worked quietly near the corner of 16th and Dunbar for more than 30 years, painting ships and the North Shore mountains. In her home studio, Valerie Pfeiffer painted flowers that have become a familiar sight on the ferries and in other tourist venues throughout B.C. Dunbar printmaker Catherine Stewart's photo-etchings, which arise from her interest in both mathematics and art, have been shown locally and in such diverse venues as Yokohama, Warsaw, and the Isaac Newton Institute for Mathematical Studies at Cambridge, U.K.

Paul Ohannesian, who painted the cover for this history, is a watercolourist and printmaker who is also a practitioner in the architectural profession, having studied architecture at the University of Southern California at Los Angeles. His art, learned mainly through classes and workshops, reflects his interest in early settlements with their railways, urban streetcars and trolleys. From his reading of early B.C. history, he is particularly passionate about steam locomotives. Growing up in Los Angeles, Ohannesian has resided in Dunbar since 1978 with his wife, Susan, who is a church musician, and his son, Ben.

Jill Edgar is a painter who uses her art for the benefit of others. Born in Nairobi, Kenya, she trained as a nurse in Zimbabwe, and, being the

◄ Lori-Ann Latremouille was photographed at home before one of her own paintings. Courtesy of Lori-Ann Latremouille.

adventuresome one in her family, travelled and worked in many places before settling in Vancouver. In 1986 she took a year off nursing to devote herself full-time to painting, but soon found something missing. "I was spending too much time in my own little world of painting," she said. She needed to balance her artistic and her caregiving side. Since then, she has shown her works for the pleasure of the elderly residents at the intermediate-care home where she is a nurse. Edgar says, "It is amazing what art does to make people feel good." From 1992 until 1999, Edgar was the coordinator of the Dunbar/Kerrisdale area for Artists in Our Midst.

Painter Roz Marshall is a full-time artist and teacher. She was born in Wales into a Royal Air Force family, moving frequently with her father's foreign postings until coming to Vancouver at age fifteen "The Persian Gulf influenced my work," she said. "It's kind of the cornerstone, the way I express myself, the colours and patterns."

Marshall graduated with honours from the Vancouver School of Art in 1970. As a teacher, she has had a strong influence on her many students in the city, both adults and children. Marshall's own children are now grown up. Her daughter Kate followed her through art school, winning a design award in the local film industry. In 2002 Marshall moved to Hawaii, where she has recharged her vision with the warmth and brilliant colours of the islands. Her life has taken her to many parts of the world, giving her an international perspective, but, she says, "Dunbar has provided me a lot of comfort in the sense that it's a kind, comfortable sort of community."

Lori-Ann Latremouille and Angus Bungay have their studios in their home on a quiet lane in Dunbar. Latremouille grew up in Dunbar, from a very young age filling the sidewalk with large chalk designs and winning the art prize at school. After high-school graduation she did not attend art school. Instead, after viewing another artist's show at a local gallery, Latremouille decided she could do the same. She quit her job and prepared for her first show. "Looking back on it now," she commented, "it was kind of bold, and my work was quite naïve." However, as a result of that first show she was invited to be in group shows at other galleries. Then art dealer Sonia de Grandmaison introduced her to the Heffel Gallery, where she was taken on when she was just twenty years of age and had her first solo show in 1987. Since de Grandmaison introduced her art to American galleries, most of her work has been sold in the United States. Latremouille's distinctive style features black-and-white interlocking forms plus one or two brilliant colours. She works almost exclusively in charcoal for the rich, velvety black that she feels best expresses the dreamy, surrealistic atmosphere of her figurative designs.

Latremouille's husband, Angus Bungay, came to Vancouver in 1991 to join with some musicians in making videos using Playmobil toy figures. He met and married Lori-Ann and has never left. Raised in an English army family, he lived in many places in the world during his father's postings. Bungay took a degree in sculpture at Coventry Lanchester Polytechnic, but went on to work in graphics, fashion and jewellery design.

Bungay works from home, balancing his time in the animation industry with his own creative work. Regarding himself primarily as a sculptor, he said he is influenced by old medical illustrations of what he called "menacing looking contraptions." Although he and Latremouille are members of the West Coast Surrealist Group of artists with their friend

Angus Bungay seated in his studio with several of his 3-D creations. Courtesy of Lori-Ann Latremouille. ▶

Paul Binkert, Metal Sculptor

Paul Binkert (1908–95), a noted sculptor and environmentalist, was born in a small town in Germany. According to his widow, community activist June Binkert, as a young man he apprenticed as a tool and die maker. When Hitler came to power, Binkert fled on his bicycle across France and eventually escaped to England. From there he emigrated to Bogota, Colombia, then to Vancouver in 1950. At age fifty-nine, he decided to retire early and work full-time in his Dunbar studio at his sculptures, which he created of mild steel with bronze highlights. His work was exhibited during his lifetime in many group and one-man shows in Vancouver and across the country, and is held in many private collections.

Metal sculptor Paul Binkert works on a model for a sculpture of a nude figure outside his home studio in 1977. Courtesy of June Binkert.

and mentor Michael Bullock, Bungay does not consider his work to be surreal.

Toni Onley (1928–2004) was a well-known Dunbar resident who succeeded in making art the whole focus of his life. Born on the Isle of Man, he received his early training there and was influenced by the work of the great British watercolourists. He also studied architecture and land surveying. Onley came to Canada with his parents in 1948, living first in Galt, Ontario, then in Penticton, B.C., where his father had settled after leaving a Shakespearean stage career. In Ontario, Onley worked in land surveying and industrial design. Products still bearing his label designs are Aylmer soup, Swan chalk for blackboards and Nalley's pickles.

In 1955 Onley found himself a very young widower with two children to care for, so he moved to Penticton to be near his own family and where he found work as an architectural draftsman. But he also wanted to get back to his art. "So I packed up my children and we went to live in Mexico for three years," he said. He studied on scholarship at the Instituto Allende in San Miguel de Allende, then went to London, England, for further studies in watercolour painting. In 1961, he returned to Canada, settling in Vancouver.

At the invitation of the renowned modernist painter B.C. Binning, Onley taught from 1964 to 1974 in the Department of Fine Arts at UBC. He resigned as full professor because he again wanted to paint full-time, making his home in Musqueam in a quiet location surrounded by tall evergreens. His best-known works are landscapes of austere simplicity, often painted in remote areas to which he had flown in his own aircraft. Represented in galleries and museums in Canada, the United States and Britain, Onley was the recipient of many honours over his long career. In 1999 he was made an Officer of the Order of Canada, and in 2000 he was given an honorary doctorate by Okanagan University College. His most

Toni Onley was one of Canada's most distinguished artists, receiving many honours in his long career. Photo by Steven Lemay. ▶

Laszlo Jozsa, Hungarian Woodcarver

Laszlo "Les" Jozsa has become noted for what he jokingly refers to as his "Hungarian totem poles." This form of folk art is still practised in the forest villages of Transylvania. His carved gates and poles are visible in his own Dunbar garden and at several other homes on the West Side. In 2001 he carved the large Sopron Gate erected in front of the faculty of forestry at UBC to commemorate its 50th anniversary as well as the arrival of the Hungarian foresters.

Jozsa came to Vancouver in January 1957 in the aftermath of the Hungarian Revolution. An eighteen-year-old university student, he was one of a group of about 500 forestry students and professors from the University of Sopron who fled over the Austrian border as Russian tanks rumbled towards their city. Under their dean, Kalman Roller, some 200 of the group moved to Canada, staying together under the wing of the forestry department at the University of British Columbia until they graduated. Now semi-retired, Jozsa is still busy training professional foresters and woodworkers in B.C.

Wood sculptor Laszlo Jozsa is a forester in his professional life. He uses his artistic ability to do colourful illustrations and three-dimensional models of the complex inner structures of wood, "a good marriage between my hobby and my profession," he says. Courtesy of Laszlo Jozsa.

recent recognition was the set of commemorative stamps issued in 2002 by the Isle of Man, depicting scenes he painted there on a visit the year before.

Onley also became famous for a spectacularly successful run-in with the Income Tax Department in 1984. He prepared a bonfire of his works on Wreck Beach, fully intending to torch them, because the department insisted on taxing artists on the value of their inventory whether sold or not. It was a successful piece of street theatre, attended by the public and the media. Without lighting a match, it set in motion changes to income tax law benefiting all professional artists in Canada. On standing up to the power of government, he said, "That comes from being a Manxman. You back us into a corner and we come out fighting."

On Sunday, 29 February 2004, Toni Onley's plane crashed into the Fraser River near Pitt Meadows. Three months later, his body was found a few kilometres downstream near Maple Ridge. He was a high-spirited man who had lived his life with passion and pursued his interests to the end.

▲ Susan Point has a large bright studio in her home at Musqueam, where she designs and creates many of her innovative artworks based on her Coast Salish heritage. Courtesy of Susan Point.

Wool, Whorls and Wood: Musqueam Traditions

A special niche in the contemporary art world is occupied by the many artists working in their own aboriginal traditions. Musqueam is home to a vital community of artists doing fine work in printmaking, Salish weaving, basket making and carving in yellow cedar. Four large weavings by Helen Calbreath, Gina Grant, Krista Point, and Debra and Robyn Sparrow hang above the international arrivals escalator in the Vancouver airport. The revival of traditional Salish weaving on the reserve was celebrated in 2000 with an exhibition at the UBC Museum of Anthropology featuring the weavings of 18 women and one man.

During the past 20 years Susan Point has been honing her skills as a Coast Salish artist, taking the traditional designs and forms to new levels of sophistication. In 1981 she enrolled in a jewellery course offered to First Nations students at Vancouver Community College. While she was at home raising her children, her interests and abilities grew, encompassing painting, printmaking, woodcarving and working with glass. To learn more, she consulted friends skilled in various crafts.

Point is recognized as an innovator and is credited with introducing Coast Salish art to the wider world. Because much of this art has customarily been of a very private nature, many Coast Salish artists had chosen to work in the northern styles more familiar to the general public. Point's inspiration is rooted in the knowledge passed on to her by her late mother, Edna Grant-Point, who was one of the last artisans able to weave the large rush mats traditionally used to line the inside walls of family houses. She is passing on her knowledge to her daughter Kelly and her niece Lisa, employing them as apprentices in her studio. Her husband, Jeff Cannell, is her business manager and deals with the technicalities of large-scale public commissions.

Point's art ranges from delicate line drawings depicting the dragonflies that abound in the Musqueam area to monumental repeating designs covering entire sides of buildings. An "icon" of her work is the traditional Coast Salish spindle whorl, a circular motif repeated in many of her creations. Probably her best-known piece is the cedar whorl she carved in 2000, 16 feet in diameter, entitled *Flight*. It is mounted on the wall by the international arrivals escalator at the Vancouver airport. At the base of the escalator are two more of her works, house posts carved in 1996 and 1997. Point has experimented with artistic collaborations with her niece Krista Point. Krista has created weavings for the lids of Susan's carved bentwood boxes and also a large blanket, pierced by Susan's wooden spindle whorl, appropriately entitled *Collaboration*.

Another recurring theme in Point's work is that of peoples from the four corners of the world coming together in a multicultural society. Her singular vision has enabled her to see the possibilities in the use of modern materials and industrial processes, while remaining true to the spirit of traditional Coast Salish images and motifs.

Point chose early to work only in her native Coast Salish style, and according to Gary Wyatt of the Spirit Wrestler Gallery, "She viewed the limitations and restrictions not as obstacles but as possibilities and challenges that she addressed with great energy and vision, though always with respect." In celebration of her 20-year career, in 2000 the Spirit Wrestler Gallery hosted an exhibition for which Point created 45 works over a period of two and a half years, during which time she also completed several monumental commissions. She said, "I would love to do a show again, but not as massive as that. . . . It's good to be busy but I don't like to be pressured. . . . I just take my time and make sure the quality is there and it's perfect. I'm a perfectionist."

In 2004 two honours for her work came to Susan in the form of high-profile commissions. In July, one of her designs in collaboration with her daughter Kelly Cannell was a winner in the City of Vancouver's competition for its new decorative manhole covers. The city chose only two designs from the 643 submissions. In September, Point won a com-

Douglas Campbell Baker, Carver

Doug Baker bridges the worlds of the reserve and the city by taking his art to local community centres and teaching a mix of locals and immigrants not only how to carve, but also something about the meaning of his culture and its symbols. Baker worked at various labouring jobs before realizing his true calling as a cedar carver in the 1980s.

"When I get new students, I tell them they have to give their first piece away. That's how I was taught when I first started." When Baker was showing his early carvings, his aunt asked him which one he had done first. When he pointed to it, she said: "This one is mine." At this point his uncle sat him down and said, "You've got to give your first one away." Baker replied, "I didn't give it, she took it!"

Baker's works are in private and gallery collections in Vancouver and Seattle.

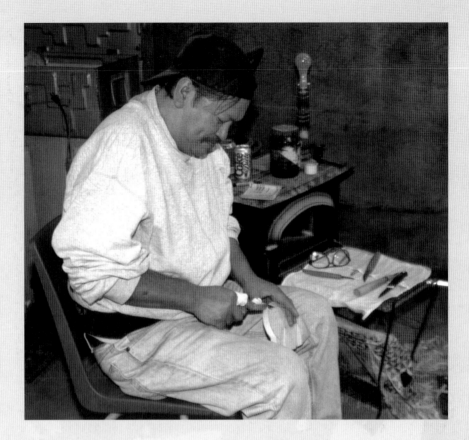

Doug Baker is a wood carver and teacher. When he is not teaching, he works at a Musqueam carving shed owned by Jack Stogan and shared by several other carvers. Photo by Joan Tyldesley.

mission by the Canadian government's Department of Foreign Affairs for a sculpture to be donated to the new National Museum of the American Indian at the Smithsonian Institution in Washington, D.C. *The Beaver and the Mink*, a two-foot-high carving, is based on both the West Coast canoe and Point's iconic motif, the Salish spindle whorl. It will permanently occupy a prominent place in the Great Hall of the newest Smithsonian building.

Debra Sparrow has become well known as a weaver in the distinctive Salish technique. She is also highly articulate, expressing with eloquence the effects of the collision of aboriginal and European cultures. Sparrow grew up in Musqueam in a large family influenced by her mother's Norwegian-Scottish background and by her Musqueam paternal grandparents, who lived nearby. Debra and her older sister Wendy (now Wendy Grant-John) as young adults began asking themselves what was special about Musqueam culture and visually reflective of the people.

They asked their grandmother Rose Sparrow to tell them more about the old-time Salish weaving. Their grandmother brought a weaving down

◄ Debra Sparrow's grandfather Edward is wrapped in the Salish blanket hand-woven in 1995–96 by Debra and her sister Robyn for the international arrivals area of the Vancouver airport. Courtesy of Debra Sparrow.

from the attic, saying, "I'm not supposed to show anybody this but it's Daddy's." The weaving belonged to their grandfather, Edward Sparrow. It was a ceremonial blanket woven from mountain goat hair, made especially for his naming celebration when he was about five years old. Because they were interested, their grandmother took them to Chilliwack to visit the Coqualeetza weavers who had revived the traditional craft.

When the Vancouver Indian Centre offered a class in Salish weaving, Debra joined the second group, learning the whole process of dyeing, spinning and weaving. "What was exciting was that it was the foundation of the people. It was a reflection of their life; it interwove into every part of the community." Although often described as an artist, Sparrow says, "I've never really thought of myself as that, because the gift that I have is not about art, it's about life." She said that these artistic skills were once regarded as integral to life in most aboriginal communities, but then things changed. Cloth could be made by machines, and with the industrial changes the hand weaving was lost for 85 years.

Debra had a special relationship with her grandfather, Edward Sparrow, a much-respected elder who lived into his hundredth year, passing away in the spring of 2000. As the years went by, everything that Debra made she brought to show him. "The one that we made for the Vancouver International Airport [1995–96] really was the success of all successes. Those 16-foot weavings are there with their message, saying 'We have always been here. We are an intelligent functioning society who welcome you . . . because of the people that we are.'"

Before taking the finished commission to the airport, Debra brought it to her grandfather and unrolled it in his living room. He walked up and down, looking at it, and said, "You girls never cease to amaze me now." She draped the blanket around his shoulders and took his picture, calling him by his family nickname, "King Edward," the king of the family. Debra said, "He was so proud. And it hangs at the airport now, reflective of him and his people."

Debra and her younger sister Robyn began weaving together, sharing every commission and large project. Important commissions on which they have collaborated are a blanket of mountain goat wool for the Museum of Civilization in Ottawa and one for the Smithsonian Institution. Both women also work as cultural teachers, presenting school programs from elementary to university level, celebrating the story of the Musqueam people as a vital part of Vancouver's history. In recent years, both Susan Point and the Sparrow sisters have designed blankets to be manufactured by commercial machines, bringing blanket history full circle.

From Hollywood Stars to Ballet Barres

In the "Dirty Thirties," entertainment reflected the urge to escape the grim realities of the times, at least for those able to pay the dime required for admission to the movies, with their fanciful plots and costumes. In the age of Shirley Temple movies, Hollywood was a mecca for talented youngsters hoping to be chosen for careers down south when it seemed impossible to advance in one's own hometown.

Two Dunbar girls who travelled to Hollywood were the daughters of businessman Alexander Borrowman, who moved his family to 3538 Dunbar Street in 1927. His daughters, Sheila and Nora (Polson), showed talent from an early age, and when Mrs. Borrowman developed asthma, the doctor recommended a warmer climate. Mr. Borrowman remained in Vancouver, working in the family business while his wife took the girls with her to California.

◀ Nora (Borrowman) Polson was a child singer and actress in Hollywood when only six years old and still has her American Equity card. Courtesy of Nora Polson.

Nora and her sister were accepted as students with the most out-standing vocal teachers. "I joined the Screen Actors Guild at six and still have my card. I did bit parts in movies," Nora said. Despite the lonely times away from their father, the sisters have many happy reminiscences about their days in Hollywood and stars such as Shirley Temple, Jane Withers and "Uncle Victor" McLaglen whom they met during their five years there. "We really didn't realize what an unusual and interesting childhood we'd had until returning to Vancouver."

When their mother's health improved, they came back to Vancouver during the war and pursued careers in community theatre and music. At age fifteen, Nora joined the Theatre Under The Stars company. After school graduation, she worked for the Vancouver Symphony and later married violinist Arthur Polson (1934–2003). The couple spent 20 years in Winnipeg, returning to Vancouver in 1986, when Arthur became the concertmaster of the CBC Chamber Orchestra and also conductor of

George Walker and the Tiny Tutus

Dance classes were offered at the Dunbar Community Centre from the time it opened in 1958. One teacher who had a great effect on the community was the late George Walker, whose early career was as a soloist with the Royal Winnipeg Ballet and other dance companies. Later he began teaching while continuing with a busy performance career in Vancouver. He performed with the Dunbar Musical Theatre in the 1970s and was involved in Dunbar Summer Music in the 1980s.

Gary Lum, community recreation coordinator at the Dunbar Community Centre for many years until 1981, remembered George Walker as a charismatic person. His classes were "Tiny Tutus for Twos" all the way up through the age groups to older adults. Lum says that one day after a new dance class was registered Walker said to him, "It's happened! I think I've got my first offspring of a mother who took my Tiny Tutus herself!"

George Walker is shown here at a Dunbar Musical Theatre rehearsal, c. 1970. Courtesy of Pat Waldron.

the Vancouver Youth Symphony Orchestra. "I can't say my life has been boring. In music, you're always creating something."

Kaye Connor was another talented child singer and violinist who, while still in elementary school, left Dunbar in the '30s with her mother. In Hollywood she continued to develop her voice and had a successful career in the heyday of operettas and musicals. Never again residing in Vancouver, she returned to her hometown several times to perform in early Theatre Under The Stars productions. She is described in the 1947 program for *Waltz in Old Vienna* as starring on the London stage, in New York musicals and in featured roles in Hollywood movies. (See also chapter 12; Kaye Connor is the daughter of C.F. Connor, the "bee man.")

In the same period, Vancouver dance teacher June Roper became known as "North America's greatest star-maker." Her well-trained students were accepted in many professional dance companies. In 1938 Patricia Meyers at age fifteen was accepted as a member of the de Basil Ballet Russe, described as "a hybrid of up and coming young dancers and leftovers from Diaghilev's troupe." As was the custom of the times, she had to accept a Russian name and became "Alexandra Denisova." According to Nora Polson, who knew her in Hollywood, Meyers later went into acting and took many parts in Hollywood movies, as did Peggy Middleton, who became known as Yvonne de Carlo.

Patricia Meyers' older sister Sheila became a member of Sally Rand's dance troupe, famous for its leader's provocative (for those days) performances, wearing only a pair of dextrously wielded giant ostrich-feather fans. Patricia and Sheila were the daughters of Grace Meyers, who during the 1930s taught dance in her home at 3762 West 24th as well as at the community hall at the corner of 29th and Dunbar

Twenty years later Beverly Barkley was another child of Dunbar who dreamed of becoming a dancer. She remembered going with her sister to watch for Teddy Lyons' observation car and dance for the passengers. She began acrobatic lessons at Margaret Johnson's Dunbar School of Dancing at 3624 West 24th Avenue. At age fourteen, Barkley started ballet with teacher Mara McBirney. Near the end of high school she had a chance to go to the ballet festival in Toronto. Both the counsellor and the principal at Lord Byng refused her permission to take the time off school. However, her policeman father, who had always been supportive of her aspirations, gave her his blessing to attend. As a result, she was discovered in Toronto by ballet greats Betty Farrelly and Gweneth Lloyd, the founders of the Royal Winnipeg Ballet. And so began her professional career.

Barkley stayed with the Royal Winnipeg Ballet for more than 14 years, with the exception of 1954 when she performed in *Bamboula*, one of the earliest TV shows produced in Vancouver. At Theatre Under The Stars she became the first recipient of the E.V. Young Memorial Scholarship, enabling her to study at the Sadler's Wells ballet school in London. After her marriage in 1966 she continued for a short time to dance with the Royal Winnipeg Ballet. Since retiring, Barkley has volunteered for various arts organizations. "You can give up your time and give back so that someone else can have the same opportunity that you did," she said.

Flamenco teacher Rosario Ancer and guitarist Victor Kolstee ran a successful dance studio at the corner of 18th Avenue and Dunbar Street from 1989 to 2005, attracting students from all over Greater Vancouver. Ancer was born and raised in Mexico. At a very young age she fell in love with flamenco. "It's an art form that includes the music, singing and dance of the people of Andalusia, in the south of Spain," she said. To understand the real flamenco culture better, in 1979 she moved to Spain, where she lived for six years.

While there, she met her husband, Kolstee, who had also come from Vancouver to study flamenco guitar. Born in Holland, he immigrated with his family to Vancouver at the age of ten. "People ask me how I decided on flamenco. Well, it was more a question of flamenco choosing me." Ancer and Kolstee were married in Spain, and even after their daughter, Alejandra, was born in 1983, they lived a Gypsy lifestyle, following seasonal performing work. One year they circumnavigated the globe, flying between performances in Moscow, India, Thailand, Hong Kong,

Rosario Ancer and Victor Kolstee project the fiery rhythms of the flamenco dance. Photo by Steven Lemay. ▶

Vancouver, Toronto and back to Spain. When their son Antonio was about to be born, they decided it was time to settle down.

In 1989 they returned to Vancouver, this time to stay. They took over the studio that was built and maintained for many years by the late "Pete" Peterson, an award-winning teacher of competitive ballroom dancing, naming it Centro Flamenco. However, after 16 years, they were forced to leave the studio where they had felt comfortable and secure because the building was slated to be demolished for redevelopment. They reluctantly left the neighbourhood for new quarters at 4th and Alma after searching in vain for another location in Dunbar.

Jamie Zagoudakis has integrated dance into his life while pursuing another career as the head teacher in the English department at Sir Charles Tupper Senior Secondary School. This is a long way from his beginnings as a fourteen-year-old immigrant, sent alone by his father from Athens in 1958 to make his way in the New World. Although he was expected to return home once he became prosperous, Zagoudakis came to like Vancouver. After he had worked a few years, his English was good enough for him to go to night classes for his high-school and university education. He was also interested in music and dance, and after dance studies with Norbert Vesak, he gradually developed into a full-fledged performer. "My first production was at the Queen Elizabeth Theatre, with a full symphony and a full dance company. I was smitten."

He started his own company and dance school, Prism Dance Theatre. He has choreographed for the Vancouver Opera Association and for the Metropolitan Opera Company in New York, where he decided that he did not like being away from his wife and children. In 1988 he went back to university for his teaching qualifications and has worked for the Vancouver School Board ever since. Zagoudakis has commented, "Energy is the greatest force in my life. Working with some great people inspired me to move forward and be the best that I can be."

In his teaching career he tries to inspire his students by bringing English literature alive. He also continues to work as a choreographer, bringing his energy to the Vancouver Figure Skaters' Association as well as to theatre and operatic groups. Like that of so many of Dunbar's artists and performers, his interest is focused on giving back to the community rather than being onstage himself.

Dreams and Memories: Dunbar's Silver Screen

Since 1935, the Dunbar Theatre at 30th and Dunbar has been a landmark in the community. It is one of the few Art Deco buildings in Dunbar, although somewhere along the way the distinctive curved parallel lines have been stripped from the detailing of its facade. It was built by film pioneer J. Howard Boothe, who previously had managed theatres in Winnipeg and knew Charlie Chaplin. Soon after moving to Vancouver in 1918 he began producing travelogues and other short films. He ran the theatre with his son Frank until 1941, when the Odeon interests bought it and made the Dunbar Theatre the first of a nationwide chain. After Boothe was promoted to become an Odeon executive, Mrs. A. Thompson became the first woman theatre manager in Vancouver.

Raymond Poulter, who has lived across the lane from the theatre since childhood, watched the parade of cement-filled wheelbarrows as the walls slowly went up. He says the theatre became a good place for the young people of the neighbourhood to find employment. Poulter remembered

Members of the staff of the Dunbar Theatre in November 1958. Left to right: Cathy Duncan, cashier; Bud McKenzie, doorman; Weslyn (McBride) Morrison, usherette; Bill MacDonald, manager; Leslie (Walker) Deeth, candy girl. Kneeling in front is usherette Ray Gjelstad. Usherettes carried trays with popcorn, ice cream bars and soft drinks down the aisles during intermission at double bill showings. Courtesy of Leslie Deeth. ▶

the Saturday-morning matinees sponsored by various businesses. Children could go to a 10:30 A.M. show, bringing the required number of cardboard milk bottle caps or candy wrappers in lieu of the regular price of 10 cents. As was the custom of the times, the theatre was never open on a Sunday.

By the 1960s the price of admission was no longer a dime. Elaine Schretlen remembered: "On Saturday we'd get our quarter for the movies and we'd go to the penny candy store first. We would take our little brown bag and then we'd pay our 15 cents at the theatre. Saturdays they would have birthday parties. So, if it was your birthday that day or week, you'd get to go up on stage and be given a cupcake with a candle on it. The whole audience would sing 'Happy Birthday' to the birthday children."

According to Haakon "Yogi" Feilum, relief manager in the '70s, Odeon closed the theatre in 1987–88. By his time, theatre admission was two dollars or more. Famous Players took over for about 10 years under manager Don Barnes, who went on to help found the Vancouver International Film Festival. Then the theatre closed again, apparently to be demolished and replaced with a block of stores and condominiums. According to current business owner Ken Charko, the theatre "did not fall into the desired business model, a destination type of theatre like Silver City [in Richmond], which is like ten Dunbars run by one person so that its economy suits a large corporation."

The redevelopment plans, however, were met by a community outcry, in the midst of which three students approached the building's owners in February 1998 for permission to operate the theatre as a summer project. The three, among them Ken Charko, had worked for Cineplex. Charko intended to work at the Dunbar part-time and return to university. Eight years later, with university still on hold, he was also running the Varsity Theatre, until its closure in January 2006. Charko puts in long days, not only for economic reasons, but also because he has a passion for the movie business and strong beliefs as to what a local theatre means to its community.

As in the past, the theatre's show times suit students' schedules. All staff positions today involve customer service, for the projectionist's job is obsolete. Charko said, "I equate the projectionist to the people who used to stand out at the airports and turn the propellers to start the airplanes. It was a very important job once, but now it's just not needed."

The cinema is not all about business, however. The Dunbar Theatre is, Charko explains, where many people, including himself, received their first kiss. An older lady who now comes to the theatre alone tells of having met her husband when he was an usher. Another woman, an ush-erette in the '40s, saved the same seat every week for a handsome young man, and not long after, they were married. Many times a couple will come in and mention they are going to sit in the balcony because that's where they met 20 or 30 years ago. Charko says he will keep the theatre going as long as he enjoys going to work and as long as he feels that people are glad he is there.

A Legacy of Children's Theatre

Joy Coghill is a name instantly recognizable in the Canadian theatre world. Coghill studied social work at UBC, where she also took every theatre course possible from the much-loved and -respected Dorothy Somerset. Realizing that it would be feasible to follow a career in theatre, she went on to take her master's degree in children's theatre at the Art Institute of Chicago, where she was inspired by Charlotte Chorpenning, a leader in children's theatre. In 1953 she received an offer from Dorothy Somerset to do children's theatre in the old Frederic Wood Theatre in the army huts at UBC. She recalled: "That's how Canada got its first professional children's theatre, professional meaning that you use the very, very best actors, the best designer, the very best musicians, everything. . . .

Joy Coghill (right) is depicted in a Holiday Theatre presentation of *Flibberty Gibbet* during the 1950s. Coghill plays Nanny and Dan MacDonald is Flibberty Gibbet. Rehearsals took place in the store near 18th and Dunbar. Courtesy of Joy Coghill. ▶

So I came back to UBC to start what turned out to be the Holiday Theatre. I got married to John Thorne and we moved into a house just off Dunbar at 3550 West 17th. The people who owned the house also had a store for rent at 3480 Dunbar, near 18th, so for Holiday Theatre we rented the store."

At the theatre's beginning, six founders each put in $20 to get the project started. They called their creation Holiday Theatre because, as Coghill said in an early brochure, "Every day becomes a holiday when you go to a play." For the dedicated founders, however, it was unremitting work, and for meagre pay. But they believed in what they were doing; the small store, with its sputtering stove that was always too hot or too cold, was their classroom, their rehearsal space and their booking office. Everything was done there to prepare for those first performances in the Freddy Wood Theatre. Soon their vision expanded and they began taking their plays to children outside Vancouver. A map of their tours, planned by Jack Thorne, reveals a connect-the-dots pattern radiating outwards from the Dunbar Street address to encompass almost the whole province. Coghill was the artistic director from 1953 to 1967.

After the group started teaching at the shop, the demand was so great that the classes could no longer be accommodated in such a makeshift space, so they moved to the Dunbar Community Centre. This growth echoes the theme already familiar from the Knox Operatic Society of the 1940s. Exciting developments in the 1960s were the Summer School for Theatre created especially for teenagers, plus participation plays for the younger children. "That community nourished us," Coghill commented. "People got used to coming there and to it being the centre for children."

By 1967 they were touring Canada with original works written especially for Holiday Theatre by Betty Lambert and Eric Nicol. In 1979 Holiday Theatre amalgamated with the Vancouver Playhouse, becoming Holiday Playhouse.

In 1994 Coghill started the first professional seniors' theatre, Western Gold. "There was a generation being set aside simply because they were old, yet they were pioneers at the height of their powers both in wisdom and imagination. When I looked around the world, there was no such company anywhere." For giving her life to the ideal of human communication through live dramatic performances, starting with the children's theatre in the store on Dunbar Street, Coghill was named a Member of the Order of Canada in 1991 and in 2002 received a Governor General's Performing Arts Award for lifetime achievement.

Another person who has contributed to the cultural life of the neighbourhood and of the city is Margaret Clark, always known as Peg. Clark graduated in 1948 from the University of Aberdeen with a fine arts degree in painting and theatre. After graduation she studied speech therapy with Catherine Hollingworth, who started the first children's theatre in Britain.

◄ Neighbourhood puppeteer Peg Clark is shown with one of her small puppet characters that she uses to help tell stories to children. Photo by Steven Lemay.

There she learned to do glove puppetry, an excellent therapy for stutterers. After settling in Dunbar with her Canadian husband in 1962, Clark joined the Vancouver Guild of Puppetry in 1967. With Eve Alexander and Shirley Embra she performed at the Vancouver East Cultural Centre opening and also at one of the first shows of the Children's Festival in Vanier Park. "I'm a glove puppeteer primarily because of my speech therapy background," Clark said. "Children put on a glove puppet, get behind a screen, and the stammer or stutter, if it's only an emotional thing, just disappears when they can't be seen. They talk through the puppet."

For 12 years Clark was a docent in the ethnology department of the Vancouver Museum, making all her own puppets and performing West Coast Native stories for visiting schoolchildren. She created and performed with puppets for the Frederic Wood Theatre at UBC, and also for a seniors centre where she was coordinator for five years. But her main interest remains working with children. "I love storytelling and I love kids. To work with them, that's my big love."

Film and Video Making: Holding a Mirror to Life

Dunbar residents have been in the forefront of the bustling scene of film and video, developing what has become a feature of Vancouver life. The late Peter Jones was director of the Pacific regional studio of the National Film Board from its inception in 1965 until his retirement in 1982. He and his wife Marion had joined the film board in Ottawa in 1945. After several years in Montreal, Peter was sent to open an office in Vancouver. According to their daughter Gwynneth Jones, in 1965 the West Coast city was considered by easterners a "distant and remote place." "Montreal was at its peak as a city; it was a wonderful cosmopolitan international city. But my parents were ready to take the opportunity to leave Montreal. Around the time we left, the FLQ were blowing up mailboxes in our neighbourhood. Frankly, they felt that no matter how bilingual I became, there just wasn't going to be a place in Quebec for a girl with the last name Jones."

The family settled in Dunbar on West 32nd Avenue, where Peter and Marion lived for the rest of their lives. Said Gwynneth: "I think it's hard to imagine now, but when he first came out here there wasn't really anybody in Vancouver that had a lot of experience in film. There were no people that had been trained as technicians; there were no university programs to train filmmakers. There were a lot of people doing a lot of creative and artistic things, but nobody had had experience in film before."

Peter travelled around the countryside to see what stories British Columbians had to tell. "He would then bring people in and give them access to film, to technical expertise, and teach them the business in his

◄ Peter Jones (left) confers with Evelyn Cherry and Grant McLean at the National Film Board before opening the Vancouver office. Courtesy of Gwynneth Jones.

own sort of way. He would commission his own film scores. He would never use music out of a can for a film. . . . So he gave the opportunity for composers like Elliot Weisgarber and Peter Bering and Michael Conway Baker to write film music."

As a producer, Peter Jones won many prizes at international festivals and was twice nominated for Academy Awards. His daughter said: "I think that probably his major contribution is as a mentor and as a person who created an environment for people to come and learn film. I think his legacy is the film industry that we see out here now in Vancouver, which really started with that Pacific regional studio."

Robert Chesterman, a resident of Dunbar since 1966, has been an independent video maker since leaving the CBC in 1988. Raised in England, Chesterman came to Canada in his mid-twenties for the adventure. He found a public relations job with the B.C. Telephone Company, travelling throughout the province and writing stories for the company. "It was an incredible introduction to Canada and this province." Hired by CBC Radio in 1959, Chesterman was soon producing programs ranging from classical music to jazz, drama and religion. "The CBC became my university and I learned everything from this corporation of ours.

I am a passionate believer in public broadcasting and everything that it represents in the country."

By the late '80s, when the CBC was wracked with budget cuts and dissension, Chesterman decided to accept early retirement. Unready just to play golf, he decided to pursue a new career as an independent video maker focusing on cultural themes. Having already done a radio documentary about gifted musical children in Vancouver, he now produced *Which Way to Carnegie Hall?*, which was narrated by Vancouver concert pianist Jon Kimura Parker. The film followed six talented Vancouver children and posed the question: what will their future careers be? Nine years later, he did a follow-up on the same children and found all but one were engaged in active concert careers.

A career highlight is his documentary of Ernest Ansermet, the legendary conductor of L'Orchestre de la Suisse Romande. As a conductor for more than 50 years, Ansermet had worked with virtually all the innovative composers of the twentieth century. Chesterman commented, "When you have the opportunity to speak with such people . . . it will open up a whole musical world."

Linda Ohama and her husband Jack Darcus are filmmakers living in Dunbar. Ohama works at home, completing her film editing and narration there, which is now possible because of digital computer technology. For more than 10 years she has drawn on her experience as a third-generation Japanese Canadian, raised in Alberta, where her family was forcibly relocated during the Second World War. In 2001 she completed *Obaachan's Garden*, about the remarkable life of her then 102-year-old grandmother, Asayo Murakami, who came to Canada from Japan in 1924 as a "picture bride." The film is Linda's fifth, a feature piece done

Filmmaker Linda Ohama with expert cinematographer Kirk Tougas filming in Japan. Tougas grew up in Dunbar. Courtesy of Linda Ohama. ▶

with the National Film Board. It earned the Most Popular Canadian Film Award at the 2001 Vancouver International Film Festival, provoking a highly emotional response from its audiences. Ohama said that she was very close to her grandmother (Obaachan), who died in 2003 at age 104. Darcus explained that the desire of Japanese returnees to tell their story for the public record is very strong. "It's been very fulfilling for her to do that. I'm very proud of her."

Darcus said his own life for the past 30 years has segued back and forth between painting, filmmaking and writing. Since 1969 he has written and directed eight feature films and has had many shows of his paintings at major galleries. His first film was a drama about the life of a woman whose portrait he had been commissioned to paint. Darcus has taught film directing and writing, as well as painting, through various school programs and his own workshops. He said, "Filmmaking as a language is a wonderful form of expression, especially if you're coming out of painting, because paintings hold time still. They freeze events or moments, whereas films liberate you, and now you're freezing a change, or you're freezing something in transition."

According to Darcus, his paintings address different subjects from those in his writing. They are principally figurative and landscape paintings in the luminous colours of the egg tempera medium. His favourite painting places in Dunbar are Pacific Spirit Park and the banks of the Fraser River. "There's a haunting quality to that area," he said. "Whenever I'm there I see paintings and find things to do. Telling stories and painting pictures . . . I've been very fortunate to be able to play in both fields, and it's made for a very rich life."

Writers and Publishers: From the Humorous to the Surreal

Eric Nicol and John McLachlan Gray are two Dunbar writers of different generations who have each made their mark with great versatility, their output ranging from newspaper columns to plays to novels.

Eric Nicol grew up at 16th and Crown. His parents bought their home just after Point Grey became part of Vancouver. Nicol and a friend would ride their bikes along 16th Avenue to the trail through the woods to the agriculture barns on the UBC campus, splashing through the mud puddles to feed the cows. A renowned humorist, Nicol began his writing career with the Lord Byng school newspaper, *Scarlet and Grey*. He continued with the *Ubyssey*, writing columns under the pen name of "Jabez." His literary career has spanned more than 60 years, his first collection of humour appearing in 1943. Three times he received the Stephen Leacock Medal for Humour, and in 2001 he was named a Member of the Order of Canada. He maintained a career as a syndicated columnist from 1951

Eric Nicol is one of Canada's most distinguished writers and the recipient of many awards, particularly for humour. He has lived in Paris and London, but is certain that Dunbar is the best place to live. Photo by Steven Lemay. ▶

to 1986 for the *Province*, writing more than 5,000 columns. During this time he also published numerous books and wrote many stage plays, including children's plays for the Holiday Theatre. Nicol feels that living in Dunbar has enhanced his ability to write. "I think the natural environment of woods and the forest itself is . . . well, you're not stressed out as I was in London by the urban environment, which sort of makes you a bit neurotic and you might write a different thing. . . . This atmosphere that we have here in Dunbar with all our richness of parks is really favoured. I have my office upstairs and it has a view over the whole area here. I can see right over to the Olympic Mountains."

After wartime service with the RCAF, Nicol returned to UBC from 1945 to 1948 to finish his M.A. He then went to the Sorbonne to obtain his doctorate in French. All the while he was still writing for the *Province*, sending home columns about Paris life and his student adventures. He also began writing for the now defunct Vancouver morning paper the *News Herald*, in his words, "fifteen bucks here, fifteen bucks there."

While Nicol was in Paris, a Vancouver couple, Barbara Kelly and Bernard Braden, arrived in London. Kelly was from Dunbar and Braden from Kerrisdale. They were stars in Canadian radio, with a variety show on the CBC called *Stag Party* for which Nicol had contributed material. However, the Bradens had decided, said Nicol, that they were going to "crack the really big time," the BBC.

> Bernie phoned me in Paris and said, "Can you come over to London and write a trial script for us?" So I hustled over to London and was introduced to BBC Variety, and I wrote the first of a series of shows called *Leave Your Name and Number*, which was about a Canadian couple arriving in London and trying to get into showbiz. The whole show had a very Canadian flavour. . . . It took off like a shot because they were new voices; there was no class distinction. The money was rolling in, which was rather interesting. The only trouble was that I hadn't had time to find a place to live.

Nicol spent his whole time in London living in a closetlike room with no window and just enough space for a desk and a typewriter. It was intense, strenuous writing. He wrote many shows for the Bradens, until they launched into the new field of television. "I decided I didn't want to live the rest of my life in Britain, so came back to Canada. England's great. London's great. But once you've lived next to the University Endowment Lands, Hyde Park doesn't do it for you."

Award-winning writer John McLachlan Gray came to Vancouver to study for his M.A., after which he founded, with Larry Lillo, Tamahnous Theatre, which he directed from 1971 to 1974. He left to tour with musical and theatre performances until 1982, when he met his wife, Beverlee. They settled down on West 37th Avenue in a 1920s Craftsman-style house surrounded by greenery. Gray loves the way the trees in the neighbourhood arch overhead. "It's magical," he said.

Gray has written and composed seven musicals, of which the best known is *Billy Bishop Goes to War*. He has written articles, newspaper columns, screenplays and books, both fiction and non-fiction. After three years writing a column for the *Vancouver Sun*, he moved to the *Globe and Mail* for a time. "So, a different audience, and rather than trying to explain Canada to the West, I try and explain the West to Canada." In 2000 he completed a novel, a thriller entitled *A Gift for the Little Master*, and in 2003, *The Fiend in Human*, which were well received. His many awards include the Governor General's Award, festival awards, and honorary doctorates from Mount Allison and Dalhousie universities. He became an Officer of the Order of Canada in 2000.

In 1968 Michael Bullock, a poet and translator, was invited to come as writer-in-residence to UBC from England and stayed to teach in the creative writing department at UBC until his retirement. He is also a

John McLachlan Gray writes newspaper columns, plays and novels from his tiny office in his home on one of Dunbar's tree-lined streets. Photo by Steven Lemay. ▶

painter and does many of the illustrations for his own books, much of it surrealist poetry, fiction and drama. Now in his eighties, Bullock publishes a new book of poetry almost every year. He has translated close to 200 books. His own works in English have been translated into many other languages, and he is working on a bilingual project, *Moons and Mirrors*, to be published in both English and Chinese. The Chinese translator for this book is Dunbar resident Jenny Tse.

As a very young fabric arts student in 1936, Bullock attended the exhibition introducing the surreal art of Salvador Dali and others to London. He says he was "absolutely bowled over by it." After his arrival in Vancouver he helped found the West Coast Surrealist Group. Artist Gregg Simpson, another founder, who formerly had his studio in the 3600 block of West 16th, said the group is a loosely knit organization created in the mid-'70s. It maintains a Web site to promote surrealist art and writing.

W.M. Seivewright, Cartoonist

William "Miki" Seivewright was a New Zealander who settled in Vancouver with his young family in 1924, moving to Dunbar in 1931. After leaving a career at sea he established himself as a newspaper writer and cartoonist, working with the *Vancouver Sun* and later the *Province* on labour, marine and sports commentary (see cartoon, page 235). Often working at home, he would wrap his stories and cartoons in a folder he created out of several thicknesses of newspaper, then take them down to the office near Victory Square on the streetcar. Modern journalists such as John McLachlan Gray can submit their productions electronically.

W.M. Seivewright, c. 1956.
Courtesy of Pam Chambers.

RONSDALE PRESS

Ronald Hatch's family came from Fort William, Ontario, to settle in Vancouver about 1947. He was raised in Dunbar and except for a few years working for cuso in India and teaching in Germany and France, he has lived in Dunbar.

A professor of English at UBC, Hatch and his wife Veronica operate Ronsdale Press from their home office. "We do fiction and poetry, books of ideas, history and some biography. Normally each year we have one or two writers for whom it would be a first book, although we also have authors who have published quite a bit. . . . One of the reasons for starting it, I think, was I had been teaching Canadian literature at UBC for many years and I felt I knew something about it, and that I might be of help in editing manuscripts by Canadian writers."

Ronsdale Press has done translations of works by Quebec authors Michel Tremblay and Marie-Claire Blais and is planning to do more. One of their translators is Dunbar writer and poet Michael Bullock. Hatch has collaborated with local artists such as Lori-Ann Latremouille in the creation of cover art for the press. Designers Cecilia Jang and Alvin Jang designed nearly all of Ronsdale Press's first book covers. Hatch has also used the work of another Dunbar artist, Susan Madsen, for two book jackets. Veronica Hatch is responsible for the children's section of the press, recently issuing three books by poet W.H. New, illustrated by Dunbar artist Vivian Bevis. A recent title on Canada's military history is *Brave Soldiers, Proud Regiments*. Written by Dunbar resident and retired history teacher Allen Andrews, it starts with Wolfe and relates stories of bravery by both Native warriors and by regimental soldiers, up to the present day. Such collaboration among locals seems to be a hallmark of Dunbar's cultural scene and has made Hatch the natural publisher for this volume.

Books for a Reading Community

Many long-time residents of Dunbar speak of the neighbourhood lending libraries with great affection. They were usually located in gift shops, renting books to their customers for five or ten cents per week, at a time when there was no public library branch in Dunbar but only the distant Andrew Carnegie Library at Main and Hastings. On Dunbar Street in the 1940s there were three lending libraries: the Ridgewell at 3494, the Dunbar Lending Library and Gift Shop at 4311, and the Point Grey Lending Library at 5557.

DUNBAR LENDING LIBRARY AND GIFT SHOP

On the guest list of the official opening of the Dunbar branch of the Vancouver Public Library in 1950 were the names of Mr. and Mrs. N.R. German. Kathleen and her late husband, Norval "Peter" German, operated the Dunbar Lending Library and Gift Shop for a period of about seven years in the 1940s and '50s, making their home on 33rd Avenue near Blenheim. They developed a successful business selling fine china and gifts, but considered the library an important part of their enterprise.

In choosing her books Kathleen relied on the advice of the book wholesalers as well as her own instincts, stocking mainly fiction. Somerset Maugham was a favourite author at the time. She said that "our best customers were also our worst," as they were the ones who read so fast that the Germans had trouble keeping enough new books in stock for them. They found they were also often called upon to order books and stationery for the teachers at St. George's School nearby.

The library part of the business came to an end with the opening of the Dunbar branch of the VPL. The couple had no idea that the public library was being planned and were left with a stock of 3,000 books that were no longer in demand. They stored them in their basement for

several years until they were able to ship them to a new library being opened in a northern mining town. "That was a break for them and a break for us," said Kathleen.

When Norval German passed away at age ninety-six in November 2001, Kathleen received a letter of condolence from a former customer. The writer was a man now in his sixties who as a young boy had come into the store daily after school while his parents were at work. He would sit on the stool in front of the children's books and read until it was time to go home. The couple, who had no children of their own, were happy to let him read in peace.

DUNBAR PUBLIC LIBRARY

The Dunbar branch of the Vancouver Public Library, a modular post-and-beam structure designed by architect Douglas Shadbolt, was opened officially on 28 November 1950 by the education minister of the day, W.T. Straith. The ceremony was attended by 200 invited guests and members of the public. Betty Thornton, the first librarian, said that the branch was stocked with 7,000 books and was so heavily used from the very first day that she and her staff soon had to place a severe limit on the number of borrowings allowed per library card.

By 1960 it was the busiest branch in the city after Kerrisdale. Re-modelled in 1955, the library required another addition by 1967. It was closed for only two days while the collection was reshelved. The largest renovation came in 1990, forcing the branch to close for five months. It reopened 9 February 1991 with 45,000 books and items to circulate. By 2000, Dunbar patrons were requesting material in all the new electronic formats. The branch collection now stands at 60,000 items.

Catherine Connell was head librarian from 1996 to 2002. "I can't imagine a better job," she said. Discussing the many changes that have taken place at the branch since the beginning of her career there in 1969, she said that in the "old days" all the items were checked out by hand. The library catalogue was on cards housed in large polished oak cabinets of drawers. In 1990 the catalogue was converted to a computer database. Occasionally the computer goes down and the staff gets a taste of those old days when books must again be checked out manually.

The Dunbar branch presents all the programs common to the whole Vancouver library system, from telling stories for children and families to presenting authors in person. The branch's annual reports characterize the Dunbar community as stable and prosperous, with a high literacy rate. The staff regards as very important their work with children, who make up 37 percent of the branch's users. Reading is not in jeopardy here. Audio and CD are popular formats, but books are still far ahead. According to Connell, users come to the library for social reasons as well as for the books. "It is the living room of the community," she said.

The branch likes to promote Canadian authors, and a significant number live in Dunbar. In addition to Nicol and Gray they include Laurence Gough, who writes award-winning murder mysteries; Avis Harley; Pat Wastell Norris; Norma Hawkins; and young people's writers Mary Razzell and Linda Bailey. Two other writers are known for books on their educational specialty: Meg Hickling, who writes about sex education for young people; and the late Sheila Egoff, world-renowned for her work promoting children's literature. Egoff's lifelong commitment to books for children had an enormous impact on the growth of library services and the publication of books for children in Canada. An Officer of the Order of Canada, she died 22 May 2005 in her eighty-eighth year. Another Dunbar writer is Shar Levine, known as "The Science Lady," who has concentrated on writing children's books since closing Einstein's, her science-oriented toy store. In 2006 she was busy writing her 45th book.

In November 2000 the library celebrated its 50th anniversary with a series of events, including the planting of an Eddie's White Wonder dogwood tree in the new garden at the corner (see page 79).

LAWRENCE BOOKS

Over the years Dunbar booksellers have come and gone. The store that has stayed the longest is Lawrence Books at Dunbar and 41st. Anne Lawrence, who runs the store since her mother Joan died, says it was started in 1983 by her father, the late Joseph C. Lawrence, a retired UBC history professor, and moved to its present location in 1989. It has become a destination for those interested in its specialties, such as militaria and Canadiana, stacked floor to ceiling in narrow canyons of shelves punctuated by tall ladders. Dunbar resident Margaret Moore reminisced about inquiring for a book at the store.

> One day I phoned to ask if they had a copy of a little-known book which had been published more than 50 years ago. Mr. Lawrence answered the phone and within seconds informed me that they did indeed have the book. Delighted with this news, I went to the store immediately and complimented the owner on his ability to keep track of his huge inventory. "You must have it all on a computer," I commented. "The only computer I have is on her shoulders," he responded, nodding towards his wife, a petite woman who had already headed down the aisle and was now climbing a ladder to retrieve my book from among the 50,000 other books advertised in their store.

The dedication of the Lawrence family has made the store an institution far beyond the immediate neighbourhood. Part of its success has been attributed to the proximity of the university and other schools, but another reason comes into play as well. Commenting in 1989 on having a large grocery market as neighbour to his new store, Joe is quoted as saying, "The grocer offers food for the table, but I offer sustenance for the mind and heart."

Other Cultural Venues

The only "official" cultural institution in the neighbourhood is the Dunbar branch of the Vancouver Public Library. However, people will always make their own institutions, whether official or not, and some businesses have achieved status as cultural icons because of the way they are run by dedicated owners. Other Dunbar residents have also brought their passion for the arts to the community.

THE OLD "CHURCH HOUSE"

The house at the southwest corner of 39th and Dunbar was built as a residence about 1929. In 1945–46 the church hall was added, and it became the Southlands Chapel and later the Bible Holiness Mission (see chapter 10). After the last congregation moved away, Prudence Leach, a clay sculptor who was represented in several Vancouver exhibitions in the early 1970s, lived there with her family until moving to California.

In 1977 the multi-talented dancer and sculptor Morley Wiseman moved in, running the house as a commune of dancers. He has pursued

▲ Dancer and artist Morley Wiseman on the dance floor with his drums at the old "church house" in the early 1980s. In the background under the tarpaulin is one of his sculptures in progress. Courtesy of Morley Wiseman.

a career in dance since 1957, taking leading roles with several ballet companies in Canada and abroad. In 1973, while ballet master at the Staatstheater in Darmstadt, he developed the Wiseman Body Technique, a teaching method to promote strength and flexibility in his students.

Seeking a space where he could combine his sculpting and his dance teaching under one roof, Wiseman gathered together at 39th and Dunbar the group of dancers who became during the 1980s the Wiseman Choreographic Community. He designed what he called their "paraliturgical" robes — comfortable denim garments based on the habit of the Benedictine monks with whom he had resided for two years in Mission, B.C. "All the neighbours thought we were the latest cult," he said with a chuckle. Wiseman, today known by his spiritual name "Padam," left the house in 1985. Now in his seventies he is lithe and vigorous, with a career at Vancouver's skating clubs, training young competitive skaters in the Wiseman Body Technique.

Drummer David Jones moved into the commune in 1979, making it his home ever since. The hall with its excellent fir floor is in constant use as a dance studio. Jones's wife Kim Pechet is a dancer who left what she calls the "real world" of business to teach belly dancing, both at the home studio and elsewhere. Jones works as a music producer, engineer and writer. The couple maintain the house as a home and private studio, raising their son Zack and sharing the space with several other artists. "The house," Jones comments, "has had a tremendous degree of talent coming through for years and years."

The couple feel very protective of this arts space, and with their commitment to all the arts, had hoped to keep it going for many more years. That dream came to an end in February 2006 as the house and adjoining property were sold for redevelopment as an apartment. Boldly, Pechet asked the developer whether the couple could have the building, which would otherwise be torn down. It was given to them, but they face many hurdles before they can find an affordable lot to move it to in their months remaining at the corner of 39th and Dunbar.

OMEGA CUSTOM FRAMING AND GALLERY

Tien Ching immigrated to Vancouver from Beijing in 1983 (see also page 74). She has been with Omega Custom Framing and Gallery since 1986, first on Dunbar near 41st Avenue and since 1989 in the 4200 block. Since 1991 Tien has operated it on her own, showing the work of local and other artists in addition to framing pictures. She says that over the years she has seen a real shift in the community's interests — from commercial prints to original works of art. "It is more than just a store," said Dunbar poet and artist Michael Bullock. "Ching is really trying to make things happen for art in this neighbourhood."

◀ Tien Ching and Roz Marshall in Omega Gallery at a showing of Marshall's colourful paintings. Courtesy of Tien Ching.

Because of her strong belief in the value of original art, Tien has since the mid-1990s encouraged the showing of children's art. Realizing how much her own children enjoyed having their art framed, she wanted to encourage other parents to preserve their children's artwork. After receiving many favourable comments, she has made the children's show an annual event. "To me it is very inspiring and satisfying," she said.

The people whose lives have been sketched in this chapter are by no means the only artists working in this community. There is a sense that there is not so much an "arts scene" in the neighbourhood as a quiet underground river. Visual artists and writers by their very nature tend not to act together in a coordinated way. Although many express a desire to "give back to the community," they do this on their own terms, quietly, within their own field of interest. They are a collection of passionate individuals rather than a collective. Group action has come through the performing arts, such as choirs, other musical groups and the Holiday Theatre for young people. All were so successful that they soon overflowed the neighbourhood boundaries and outgrew available premises, going on to enrich the life of the entire city.

CHAPTER 8

Sports and Recreation

⁓ Margaret Moore

Playgrounds adjacent to ancient bogs and streams, parks overlooking a city skyline, trails through extensive forests, golf courses bordering a busy river, tennis courts ringed by tall trees, a lively community centre — these amenities would have been far beyond the wildest dreams of Dunbar's earliest residents.

Children have always invented their own forms of recreation, and Dunbar offered an ideal setting. Open fields and dirt roads near 27th Avenue and Dunbar were George Tedlock's playground during World War I. "We filled empty Campbell's soup cans with dirt and took positions 50 or 75 feet away. Hiding behind stumps, trees or high grass, we lobbed them at each other, like hand grenades." It would be at least another decade before playing fields appeared in Dunbar parks.

World War I had just ended when Stan Cornish's parents paid $960 in 1919 for a house without plumbing at 3983 West 33rd Avenue. The area was mostly bush, with only scattered houses. As a young boy, Stan and his friends played in the wet ditches on either side of 33rd and built forts around the huge stumps that remained after the forest was logged.

In the 1920s and '30s when new houses were appearing on every street, children played in the houses under construction once the workmen went home. When it snowed, 33rd Avenue was closed between Blenheim and Balaclava Streets so children could sleigh ride on the road.

They also congregated at 21st Avenue and Crown Street to coast down the steep hill that ends near Camosun Bog. Many winters the lily pond at Camosun Bog froze over. Fred Albinson played ice hockey there in the early 1930s. "I traded an old baseball bat for some single-blade ice skates. People traded because they had no money. The skates were too big so I'd wear a couple pairs of thick woolly socks. We'd use some rocks for the goal posts. When we got cold we'd build a fire from some sticks and maybe an old tire. We didn't have a huge fire — just enough to keep warm. Nobody bothered us."

Girls played tag, skating over the frozen network of trails that spread out from the lily pond like a spider's web. They skated on the pond when hockey games were not in progress and imitated famous figure skaters such as Sonja Henie. At home, little girls treasured Shirley Temple dolls, and boys made box scooters by nailing an upright wooden apple box with two handles on top to a two-by-four. Roller skates pulled apart were used for wheels and feet provided propulsion. One shoe always wore out before the other. Cowboys and Indians as well as cops and robbers were played in vacant lots on every street.

Safety never seemed a concern. Mothers would say "Go outside and play," often adding "Be home in time for dinner." Bicycles were a big item in children's lives, giving them the freedom to explore and a sense of independence and adventure. In the summer of 1944, eleven-year-old Helen Wolrige and Margaret Campbell would cycle out to UBC to watch the cows being milked and to see the new litters of pigs in the agricultural barns. Sometimes they went to Wreck Beach. Their parents knew where they were and did not worry.

In the 1950s the focal point for recreation in the Southlands area was the frog pond, which was about 200 metres west of Southlands Elementary School. Boys and girls carried home bottles of tadpoles and frogs. If a bottle was not handy, a gumboot would do. Sheila Smyth recalled other "recreational" activities at the frog pond in the 1950s. "We would smoke cigarettes at a fort in the swampy area. Our next-door neighbour's daughter had umpteen brands of cigarettes in a blue-striped zippered bag. We would experiment puffing on cigarettes through plastic peashooters full of filters. It was almost impossible to get any air, smoky or otherwise, through these contraptions." Smyth said she and her friends sat on old logs beneath the cedars among the skunk cabbages and felt delightfully naughty.

A rapidly growing metropolis on the east, a forest on the west and farmland bordering a river on the south all contributed to the unique combination of organized recreational opportunities that developed in Dunbar. Horseback riding started in the late 1920s because logging skid roads through the woods were easily transformed into riding trails. Golf gained a good foothold because tracts of farmland along the Fraser River

◄ Derek Sankey, #35 for UBC, playing against Simon Fraser University in the 1967/68 season. Sankey was inducted into the Canadian Basketball Hall of Fame in 1995 as both an athlete and a builder of the sport, one of only two former UBC players to be given this honour as of 2005. Courtesy of Derek Sankey.

▲ The Gowe children and their friends on a bobsled at 38th Avenue and Balaclava Street in 1935. Cardboard, tin trays and homemade wooden sleds were good substitutes when money was scarce. Many winter activities required no equipment — making snow forts, snow angels and snow men; having snow fights; and playing fox and geese. Courtesy of Doug Gowe.

◄ Where's the puck? John Young recalled the month-long cold spell in 1950: "We flooded two front yards at 39th and Crown by banking the edges of the lawns with dirt and turning on the hoses. The kids would play hockey there after school and the parents would skate at night. Don Nelson attached speakers to a radio or gramophone and we'd skate to music. Don flooded it late every night so we'd have a new surface each day." Courtesy of John Young.

were being sold as farmers could no longer make their operations profitable in the face of rapidly rising property taxes.

Beginning in the late 1920s organized sports began to appear, coordinated at first by the churches. A church with a gym and a sports program had an advantage in attracting children and their parents to its congregation. In the 1930s schools began to play a role, followed in the 1940s by the community. In 1958 the new Dunbar Community Centre provided a nucleus for the wide range of sports and recreational opportunities by then available to Dunbar residents. Sports and recreation also benefited from two other combinations found in Dunbar: a growing population that had "arrived" with plans to stay, and an abundance of parkland that had been accumulated before 1929 by the municipality of Point Grey. This chapter introduces each sport at the time it gained prominence.

Sports at Musqueam

"Canoe racing was a great part of the life of Musqueam young men. It started way back when — before contact," elder Rose Point explained. Down through the years many racing canoes were built, but the most famous within recent memory was the *7 Sisters*, carved by Dominic Point, George Roberts and other band members from a Stanley Park tree blown down during Typhoon Frieda in 1962. The name referred to the cluster of trees that grew in the park.

Rose Point noted that the training for canoe racing was very rigorous and the competition keen. "Young men would train for a race before and after work. In the morning they'd run along the shoreline to the lookout

Musqueam men in the *7 Sisters* canoe on the Fraser River about 1956. Front to back on left: Lyle Sparrow, Gordie Point, Willard Sparrow, Cagney Point and, from Tsawwassen, Harold Williams. Courtesy of Rose Point. ▶

◂ A Musqueam lacrosse team, c. 1930. The photo was taken at a park in New Westminster, B.C. Standing, left to right: Abraham Point (spare), Paddy (Casimir) Johnny, Gabriel Joe (goalie), Herman Guerin, Edward Sparrow, Sam Grant, Andrew Charles, Johnny Point. Front row, left to right: Alec Peters, Aloysius Peters, Joe Peters, Henry Louis, James Point. No helmets or face guards were required, and padding was minimal. The Musqueam had their own field for lacrosse on the reserve. Courtesy of UBC Museum of Anthropology.

and back, which is about five miles. After work they'd go and pull on the canoe for about an hour and a half. During training period they weren't allowed to drink liquor, smoke or go out with girls. They'd compete all over — Cowichan, Cultus Lake, Chehalis, Harrison Mills, Lummi. There would be about 20 canoes in one race." Native canoe racing was still going on in 2006 but Musqueam no longer had a team.

In addition to canoe racing, members of the Musqueam Band have a long history of achievement in lacrosse. The game started as field lacrosse. By 1933, lacrosse boxes had been built at Locarno, in North Vancouver and at Brighouse in Richmond, and the game was referred to as "box lacrosse." Musqueam men and boys were some of the best stick handlers around and could shoot equally well right- or left-handed. Their teams became feeder teams for the Senior A and B lacrosse leagues in the Lower Mainland. Victor Guerin played for the North Shore Indians from 1939 to 1945 except for three years when he was serving in World War II. He played 65 games and scored 32 goals. In recent years, soccer and basketball have been the sports of choice for Musqueam youth.

The Early 1900s: Hunting and Fishing

An excerpt from the 1978 article "Vancouver's Old Streams" paints a picture of the city before it was developed. "A little over 100 years ago, the site of Vancouver was a wilderness. . . . Here lived cougars, deer, eagles, bears and myriads of other wild creatures. There were great swamps, too, that harboured ducks, geese, fish, frogs, insects." All these creatures could be found in Dunbar's forests.

In the early 1900s a simple hunting lodge was built at 3993 West 35th Avenue in what was then the municipality of Point Grey. The house was

▲ The opening of the Dunbar Community Centre in 1958 provided a permanent room for the monthly meetings of the Dunbar Rod and Gun Club. Speakers, slide shows and field trips attracted outdoor enthusiasts. Courtesy of Rollie Wakeman.

like a camp — people kept adding to it. Narrow steps led up from the main floor to a front bedroom and to a smaller bedroom at the back over the kitchen. The owners came out to the Dunbar area from Vancouver to enjoy the excellent bird hunting. Flocks of mallards congregated in the swampy area near 33rd and Highbury in what would later become Memorial West Park, pheasants hid in low bushes where logging had opened the forest, and migrating birds flocked to the wetlands that stretched south from Marine Drive to the Fraser River.

Hunting rifles and shotguns kept in pristine condition could be found in many a Dunbar basement. In some basements in hunting season — and out of season too — a brace of pheasants or a string of ducks would hang from a nail on a basement beam waiting to be plucked and roasted for dinner.

In 1926 Benjamin Craig, an expert marksman, and his wife retired to Dunbar and built a house at 3593 West 39th Avenue. Craig had made his money in Dawson City grubstaking prospectors. Many youngsters, including four of the Gowe children — Ronald, Douglas, Eileen and Grace — learned about rifles from Craig. Ronald Gowe recalled the early 1940s: "Ben constructed an indoor range, complete with targets and 'butts,' in the sawdust bin in the basement of his house. He trained many children in the safe and proper way to handle rifles, provided they were courteous and paid attention. Using .22 cal short ammo, he would give instruction and practice until most of us became quite proficient in handling, cleaning and firing these small-bore rifles." The Craigs, who had no children of their own, also built a two-storey playhouse with furniture in their front yard. Children were welcome — as long as they were well behaved.

Jack Kermode, a keen sportsman, took his cocker spaniel hunting in the University Endowment Lands from 1937 to 1942. Ducks and a few snow geese could be found along the north arm of the Fraser River, pheasants and ruffed grouse lived in the forested areas, and on one rare occasion in 1940, he saw a solitary deer walking in the forest.

Charlie Bunker of 3920 West 20th Avenue was one of Canada's top field trainers for golden retrievers in the 1940s and '50s. He kept ducks in a pen in his backyard for training his dogs. With ducks and dogs he would go to the University Endowment Lands to practise commands. The ducks became tame and were quite accustomed to being placed in the tall grass, where they would wait with their heads tucked under their wings for the dogs to retrieve them. One of the retrievers trained by Bunker won the Retriever Field Trial Championship — a top North American award.

In the early 1900s fish could be found in abundance in the numerous streams flowing south through Dunbar into the Fraser River. Thousands of coho spawned in the gravel beds of the stream where the Dunbar Theatre now stands, and cutthroat trout could be found in ponds in

◄ Charles Bunker training golden retriever "Rockhaven Raynard of Fo-Go-Ta" from Samuel Magoffin's Rockhaven Kennel in North Vancouver. Bunker initially owned and trained "Oakcreek's Van Cleve" (1946–61), who went on to win almost every top award in Canada and the U.S. in field trial championships. From *The Complete Book of Golden Retriever*, Howell Book House Inc.

Memorial West Park and as far north as the Chaldecott marsh. An article in the *Daily News Advertiser* with the placeline Point Grey, dated 1 December 1912, described one scene: "Steelheads meandered up a crooked brook which passes under Marine Drive. The fish have ranged from five pounds to fifteen pounds, and the tackle with which they have been landed would fill a large museum. Pitchforks, stove pokers, hoes, shovels, to say nothing of humble clubs, have all been used with results. The steelheads are still running up the brook." About 1915, culverts were installed under Southwest Marine Drive near Blenheim Street, which ended access for the salmon to their spawning grounds upstream.

The 1920s: Organized Recreation Begins

From 1922 to January 1929 recreational activity exploded in Dunbar. Besides seeding new lawns and planting gardens, many residents were ready to start participating in a variety of sports, including golf, lawn bowling, horseback riding, track, tennis and badminton. The municipality of Point Grey — which at this time included the Dunbar area — was fiscally sound, and newly formed church congregations were looking to the future. A gymnasium to accommodate a variety of sports for young people and to double as a church hall was often the first building to be erected.

GOLF

The Dunbar/Southlands area is often referred to as a golf enthusiast's dream for its two private courses and two public courses all bordering the Fraser River. A group of Vancouver businessmen who had served overseas in World War I and played golf in England and Scotland formed a company, sold shares and in 1922 purchased the Mole family farm for their new venture — the private Point Grey Golf and Country Club at 3350 Southwest Marine Drive. The club's golf professional, Dunc Sutherland, and club member Roscoe Brown acquired many unique trees for the perimeter of the course.

Ian Fraser caddied at the course from 1931 to 1936 when he was a high-school student. He was paid 75 cents for the three-hour round — considerably more than the 15 cents per hour he made working at Woodward's during his Christmas holidays. Caddying was a healthy way to earn money, he recalled, and many men did it during the Depression when it was the only work they could get.

Map 4: Golf Courses, Dunbar/Southlands. One of Vancouver's last wild salmon streams — Cutthroat Creek — meanders through the Musqueam Golf and Learning Academy, providing a water hazard on four holes. Map by Ron Simpson. ▼

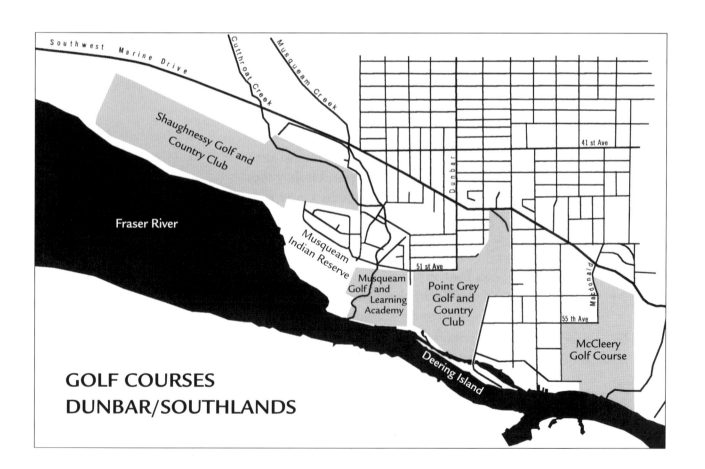

GOLF COURSES DUNBAR/SOUTHLANDS

Jack Pomfret, "Greatest Athlete"

Retired UBC football coach Frank Smith referred to Jack Pomfret as "the greatest athlete to come out of B.C." It is hard to find a sport in which he did not excel. In 1939 he broke the world record in the 50-yard breaststroke. After graduating from Lord Byng High School in 1940, he accepted a scholarship to the University of Washington. There he captained the basketball team, played football, and swam on the medley relay team that equalled the world record. He won all his fights in boxing by a knockout or TKO; he played on coast league lacrosse and soccer teams — the list goes on and on.

Pomfret was offered a baseball contract with the New York Yankees and an ice hockey contract with the New York Rangers. He went on to an outstanding career in teaching, coaching and administration at UBC, where he was head coach of UBC varsity teams for a record 35 years.

All-around athlete Jack Pomfret in 1941 in practice session to defend his world record for breaststroke. Courtesy of Marilyn (Russell) Pomfret.

Seventy percent of the Point Grey golf course is below sea level and thus dependent on the diking along the Fraser River. In the early years, irrigating was done at night, when the floodgates on the Fraser River would be opened to let the water in to cover the greens.

In 1957 the Vancouver Park Board began developing McCleery Golf Course at 7188 Macdonald Street on land that had been homesteaded by pioneer farmers Fitzgerald and Mary McCleery. Close to the 11th tee is a cairn built of stones from the foundation and stairs of the original farmhouse. The 18-hole public golf course was officially opened in July 1959. A major renovation in 1996 included new water hazards, a new clubhouse and the reseeding of greens.

Shaughnessy Golf and Country Club moved to its present site at 4300 Southwest Marine Drive in November 1960. The private club's lease of 162 acres from the Musqueam Band expires in 2033. The original fairways were located on both sides of Oak Street between 33rd and 37th Avenues, on 67 acres of land leased from the Canadian Pacific Railway on 26 April 1911. In 1960, golf greens gave way to lawns and flower beds when VanDusen Gardens took over a large portion of the original golf course.

In 1965 businessman Jack Ellis obtained a 75-year lease of 60 acres along the Fraser River from the Musqueam Band. A driving range opened in 1967, and the nine-hole public Musqueam Golf Centre opened in

▲ About 1928 Vancouver artist W.M. Seivewright drew this cartoon depicting some of the more picturesque members of Point Grey Golf and Country Club. The original water wheel used on the Mole farm is the emblem of the private club. Courtesy of Pam (Seivewright) Chambers.

1968 at 3904 West 51st Avenue with Bill Wright as the professional. The course later expanded to 18 holes with an 80-stall, two-level driving range. A foursome including Willie Nelson and Waylon Jennings was once quietly hosted at the golf course after the group was turned away from a private course because of dress code. The lease was purchased by Eaglequest Holdings in the 1990s. In May 2003 it was bought by the Musqueam Band and Gino Odjick, a former NHL player from the Algonquin Nation. Eaglequest Golf Centre became the Musqueam Golf and Learning Academy in January 2004.

Two of Dunbar/Southlands' four golf courses are among the five in B.C. that have recently qualified for the prestigious Audubon Cooperative Sanctuary certification, which recognizes courses that meet the highest standards for encouraging wildlife. Point Grey Golf and Country Club qualified in 1993 and McCleery Golf Course in 2004. At McCleery, a wide range of mammals and 77 species of birds have been identified. Water birds, in particular, are attracted to McCleery's 15 ponds.

LAWN BOWLING

The Dunbar Lawn Bowling Club, the oldest public club in continuous existence in Dunbar, celebrated its 75th anniversary in 2001. The clubhouse and greens are located in Memorial West Park near 31st Avenue and Highbury Street.

In 1926 "Dunbar Heights Lawn Bowling Club" signed a lease with the Point Grey Park Board, setting the rent at $1 per year. The greens were seeded and ready for play the following year. In his history of the club, Blake Campbell noted the many awards received by club members. Ross Moir and Arlie Hoar were Canadian champions in 1963 and went on to the Australian Commonwealth Games in 1964. Dunbar bowler Ab McBride was elected president of the Canadian Lawn Bowling Council in 1975.

The minutes of the club over the years provide some historical insights. In 1942 Sunday bowling was defeated by motion, but two months later the vote was reversed. In 1946 membership fees were $10; in 2000 they were $100. In the 1950s the men held a weekly cribbage tournament in the clubhouse. In 1953 the motion to include women in the cribbage tournament was defeated unanimously. Humour abounded on the notice board, as witnessed by the following message in 1964: "Members are respectfully reminded that only coroners and surgeons are entitled to hold inquests and post-mortems. All players please note."

The Dunbar Heights Lawn Bowling Trophy has also had an interesting history. It was first awarded in 1928. John Berry won it in 1960. A few months later the trophy disappeared from the clubhouse, never to reappear. That is, not until a mysterious phone call in 1985. A couple from

West Vancouver phoned to say they had bought a bowling trophy at a garage sale and — noting the name engraved on the trophy — had called to inquire whether the club still had any interest in it. The couple obligingly drove to Dunbar and presented the trophy to the club 25 years after it had vanished.

The club has had many long-time members over the years, but perhaps the record went to Heather Kellaway, who was active from 1929 until 1999. Many of the 80 playing members and 17 associate members in the club in 2005 were in their senior years, and members have made a concerted effort to recruit new members.

HORSEBACK RIDING

Dunbar/Southlands has long been a natural centre for horseback riding. In 1927 a group of prominent Vancouver businessmen who were avid horsemen obtained a 21-year lease on logged-off areas in the University Endowment Lands south of 16th Avenue. In charge of the project was Charlie Clinton, who had been General Arthur Currie's personal groom in the Canadian Expeditionary Force in World War 1. Clinton built stables for the Point Grey Riding Club in the forest at the western end of 33rd Avenue. He used the former logging skid roads as bridle paths and he also built Clinton, Top and Malkin Trail, now called Salish Trail. He, his wife Hannah, and their son Alfred lived above the livery stables for 20 years. Club members referred to the stables as the Point Grey Riding Club; in the neighbourhood they were often referred to as Clinton stables. The meadow where the stables once stood is called Clinton Meadow on the 2005 official trail map for Pacific Spirit Park.

Between 1932 and 1934 the B.C. Hussars regiment made weekly trips from Clinton stables to the Bessborough Armoury at 2025 West 11th Avenue, where the dirt parade floor was used for practising equestrian drills. Major R.N. Keen recalled that 12 troopers were taken over to the stables, whereupon each rode a horse back to the armoury while leading a second. At the end of parade, they returned the 24 horses. At other times Colonel Graham Blyth, then a corporal, would be detailed to ride one horse and lead a string of horses back to the stables. He then walked four blocks east to Dunbar Street and caught a streetcar, using the B.C. Electric streetcar ticket given to him by the unit.

Clinton had a steady stream of eager workers over the years. In 1935 he saw a group of fourteen-year-old boys hanging around under the street lamp at 33rd and Camosun. "What's the matter with you kids? Don't you have jobs? I'll give you work to do." He showed Gordon Jinks and his friends how to saddle and ride the horses and how to cut trails. They rode the horses down to Marine Drive cutting the overhead brush. Then off they galloped along Marine Drive to the "lookout," where they dismounted, dropped the reins so the horses could graze, and slithered

Charlie Clinton, an expert horseman and equestrian, at Point Grey Riding Club. Courtesy of Sally (Anders) Clinton. ▶

Stable Memories

Almost five decades later, Sheila Smyth vividly recalled the many hours she spent at Clinton stables. "I will always be thankful for the great good fortune of a skinny little horse-crazy girl of twelve who arrived from England in 1956 to find herself living a few minutes' walk from 'The Stables.' I remember Corky, Calico, Golden Wind, Butterfly and Flint, the pretty little dapple-grey pony. Once the gentle palomino, Butterfly, took a misstep and I went flying into the mud. The other time, naughty Calico screeched to a stop from a brisk canter and I was airborne again. . . . I remember the smell, that indefinable mix of hay, oats, manure and horse, and the pungency of the molasses in the horse feed. Mostly I remember just hanging out, sitting around on bales of straw, mucking out, grooming and tacking up for the paying riders."

Corky in Clinton stables, May 1960.
Courtesy of Sheila Smyth.

down over the bank for a skinny dip, then headed back to the stables to report for more work. The trails are now part of Pacific Spirit Park.

In 1954, young Alfred Clinton brought his bride, Sally, to the suite he remodelled above the stables, where they lived for the next two years. Sally remembers one day very vividly. This was "when the horses got out of the stables and walked down Camosun Street eating the flowers in all the gardens! Calico, I'm certain, was the instigator." In 1962, Clinton did not renew the lease because the University Endowment Lands' manager, Mr. F. M. Ferguson, expected the area to be developed for housing at any time. For more than three decades it had been a special treat for children to come to the stables to pat the horses and a delight for residents to catch sight of horses and riders on the streets and back lanes of Dunbar. The empty stable was destroyed by fire in 1968. A picnic table now stands on the site of the Point Grey Riding Club. The plaque reads: "To Charlie and Hannah Clinton, Remembering happy days at Point Grey Stables."

In 1943 a group of horseback riders formed the Southlands Riding Club. Their first clubhouse was an abandoned Japanese fisherman's net storage hut on Deering Island that they dismantled and carried piece by piece across a narrow footbridge to property at 55th Avenue and Blenheim Street. In 1949 the club purchased 16 acres of the McCleery farm for $7,500 and built a clubhouse at 7025 Macdonald Street that was still in use in 2006.

In the 1950s and '60s polo was very popular, with summer matches taking place on the beach at Spanish Banks and at the Southlands Riding Club grounds. On one memorable occasion a dashing East Indian polo team arrived in colourful turbans and bushy black beards. Only after the game finished was it revealed that these were actually club members cleverly disguised.

Volunteers from the club have helped build and maintain many kilometres of trail along the Fraser River and through Pacific Spirit Park. Thanks to members of the Southlands Riding Club and to others who love the rural atmosphere of the "Flats," cars still give way to horses and their riders in this pastoral area near the river.

TRACK AND FIELD

Dunbar has been a popular training ground for runners since the 1920s. Access to trails in and around Pacific Spirit Park, relatively flat terrain, grass boulevards and numerous parks have encouraged residents to enjoy walking, cycling and running. In 1922 the Corporation of Point Grey commissioned a design for the layout of Dunbar Heights Park, renamed Memorial West Park in 1929. An oval cinder track was built in the southeast quarter of the park near Dunbar and 33rd Avenue.

Louise Cornish, who was sixteen years old in 1928, recalled going to the park every morning that spring to train for the 100-yard dash at the Vancouver high-school track meet at Brockton Point. "There were big old trees near the track and it seemed very lonely there early in the morning. I wore the new kind of running shoes with spikes on them. One morning I fell and some of the cinders got into my knee. For years after, I had a scar like a blue pencil mark on my knee to remind me of the cinder track and the early-morning practice sessions."

A few years before Cornish was training, Harry Samuel Johnston moved to the Dunbar area, and it was not long before he was bringing home trophies for track. Later as a high-school teacher and a school principal he continued his interest in the sport. When he retired in 1969 he was honoured for his contribution to track at the 58th and final Vancouver and District Inter-High School Track Meet on 22 May 1969 by being appointed "Honorary Referee." The following appeared in the track program on that occasion: "In 1922, Harry Johnston ran for UBC in the Washington Relay Carnival. In 1923 the records show that one Harry Johnston helped his class win the Normal School Track Meet and was individual champion of the meet with firsts in the 440, 880, one mile; seconds in the 220 and hurdles; and thirds in the 100 and long jump. The records do not state why he did not also compete in the pole vault, javelin, discus and shot put — probably lazy!" Normal School for Johnston also included rugby and basketball, and his interest in basketball

◄ Track and field star Harry Johnston in 1930 beside some of his many awards. Courtesy of Norma (Johnston) Landstrom.

continued with 16 years on the executive of the B.C. Amateur Basketball Association, of which he was an honorary life member.

In early 2004 Dunbar's ninety-two-year-old Ivy Granstrom was not only a world record runner in Masters track meets at home and abroad, she was also "Queen of the Polar Bear Swim" at English Bay, having completed 76 consecutive swims. Granstrom, who was blind, received the B.C. Master Athlete of the Year Award in 1982 and the Eugene Reimer Award for excellence and leadership in sports for athletes with a disability in B.C. in 2000. In 2001 she was inducted into the Terry Fox Hall of Fame in Toronto. Her favourite award was her Order of Canada medal, which she received in 1989 from Governor General Jeanne Sauvé.

Granstrom's career in track started out by "accident" in more ways than one. As Bob Mackin wrote in his 2000 article entitled "Blind Octogenarian Still Setting Running Records":

Ivy nearly ended up in a wheelchair after a freak accident in 1976 when an out-of-control taxicab struck her. "When they told me I'd be in a wheelchair the rest of my life, I told them to forget it," Granstrom said. "I wanted to run around the block and I ended up doing all this."

"All this" is her window-sill collection of trophies and medals accumulated since the mid-1970s, in bowling, curling and swimming, but mostly for running. She can't see them, but the world can.

Ivy Granstrom, Hero to Many

Beginning in 1979, Ivy Granstrom entered both blind sports and Masters track and field competitions — attached by an elastic strap to her long-time pacer and constant companion Paul Hoeberigs. Hoeberigs and Granstrom met in 1979 when he offered to be her running guide. Granstrom's obituary in the *Vancouver Sun* on 19 April 2004 referred to her "twelve unchallenged world records and many people inspired by her positive outlook, bold competitiveness, beguiling charm and winning smile." It continued: "She was cheered and feted across Canada and the United States — South Africa, Australia, Italy, Japan and many more. The awards and accolades fill volumes."

Ivy was a familiar figure in Dunbar as she practised for local track meets and competitions around the world. Photo courtesy of Katherine Pettit.

On 1 January 2004, with her constant companion and running guide seventy-six-year-old Paul Hoeberigs at her side, Granstrom announced her retirement from the Polar Bear Swim to an appreciative crowd at English Bay. Granstrom died 14 April 2004.

Eldo Neufeld remembered Dunbar Community Centre's popular 5-kilometre Fun Run that started and ended at Memorial West Park. He still had his ribbons to prove that he won in the "60 and Over" category during the mid-'80s. The year 2004 marked the run's 20th anniversary, but the number of participants had dropped to 200, and the Fun Run ended in 2005.

Vancouver's Pacific Spirit Triathlon Club, with more than 200 members, was formed in November 1996 and took its name from Pacific Spirit Park, adjacent to the club training base at St. George's School. Athletes, including many from Dunbar, train with experienced coaches and compete in triathlons that combine swimming, cycling and running. Keith Iwasaki, Debbie Butt and Jim Miller are three Dunbar athletes who have completed the Ironman Canada Triathlon race held each summer at Penticton. The race involves a 3.84-kilometre swim, a 180.2-kilometre cycle and a 42.2-kilometre run. In 2005, 42-year-old Gerard Charlton had the

Lynda Adams, Olympian

"Canada's greatest woman diver" and "Queen of the Athletes" were phrases used to describe Lynda Adams in the 1938 Lord Byng annual, for she was not only an Olympic diver but also a star in grass hockey and basketball. In 1934 Adams competed in the British Empire Games in England. Two years later she was a member of the Canadian Olympic team in Berlin. In 1938 she sailed to Australia for the British Empire Games, where she placed second in both the tower and the springboard events.

Jack Pomfret recalled being one of a group of Lord Byng students who "helped" Adams learn the required dives for her world competitions. While Adams balanced on the edge of the diving board at Kitsilano Pool, a group of Byng students sat in the bleachers and — reading from the official Olympic text — called out the requirements as Adams listened intently and then practised each dive over and over again.

Photo from the Lord Byng High School annual, 1938.

fastest time of the 26 entrants in the Ultra Man competition in Penticton, which involves a 10-kilometre swim, a 418-kilometre bike ride and a double marathon over a three-day period.

TENNIS AND BADMINTON

Starting in the late 1920s, tennis became very popular in Dunbar. In 1929, St. Philip's Church built two courts where the church now stands, at 3737 West 27th Avenue, and the parks board built six courts in Memorial West Park east of the lawn bowling green. In the 1930s some Dunbar residents purchased two adjacent lots — one where they built their house and the one beside it where they built their tennis court. For many decades, balls could be heard bouncing on the tennis court next to the Lane family home at 3859 West 22nd Avenue.

At St. Philip's Church a tennis club was formed on 25 January 1929. Annual fees were $2.50. The highlight of the year was the "flannel dance," with music supplied by the popular Rhythmic Serenaders. Tickets cost 25 cents per person. Tennis and flannel dances ended at St. Philip's in 1941 when the new church was erected on the site of the tennis courts.

The Bardsleys — Jim and Jean and their sons Tony and Bob — have often been referred to as "the first family of B.C. tennis." UBC athletics historian Fred Hume had high praise for all four. "Jim and Jean Bardsley were terrific athletes. During the 1930s and '40s, Jim was one of B.C.'s, if not Canada's, best basketball players and tennis players. He led UBC and Vancouver Senior A basketball teams to several Canadian men's championships, starting in 1937 with the UBC Thunderbirds team. Jean was an outstanding tennis player, winning many tournaments at UBC and later, at the Masters level. She also coached tennis extensively and played basketball at UBC." Hume added that the Bardsleys' sons carved out tennis careers "as illustrious as their parents'."

In the 1940s and '50s free tennis lessons were offered at selected city parks. At Memorial West Park, Jim Bardsley taught hundreds of Dunbar children to play tennis. In 1945 Lionel Davenport brought ten-year-old Lee to the park for lessons. When she was only fifteen, Bardsley encouraged her to enter a competition at Stanley Park. She won her matches to become top B.C. Junior under 18 in 1950.

In 2006, the Dunbar Community Centre continued to manage six courts. In a stable community like Dunbar it is not unusual to find players who have used the courts for many decades. Art McKay played here for more than five decades and encouraged young and old to enjoy the sport. Another long-time enthusiast, Bernice McDonough, noted that over the years these courts have occasionally provided partners for marriage as well as for tennis.

Badminton was a popular sport at St. Philip's Anglican Church hall as early as October 1929. In 1931, a junior club was started and players were charged five cents each night they played. Badminton was also popular with members of Dunbar Heights United Church and Knox United, where they had enthusiastic turnouts for many decades.

"Keep your eye on the ball!" Jim Bardsley introduces his two-year-old son, Tony, to the finer points of the sport at the tennis courts in Memorial West Park in 1947. Courtesy of Tony Bardsley. ▶

Jean Bardsley was very active in badminton as both player and coach. Throughout the 1940s and '50s Bardsley and Daryl Thompson each won seven Canadian singles, doubles and mixed competitions.

Twelve-year-old Heather Ostrom registered for the beginners badminton class at the Dunbar Community Centre in 1981. By the age of fourteen she was Canadian Junior Ladies Singles Champion in the under 19 category. She went on to play in competitions in Europe, Japan and Mexico. Of her many awards, the one that pleased her parents most was the Badminton Canada "Fair Play Award," which was presented to Heather in 1987 in recognition of her sportsmanship.

Badminton classes and clubs, from beginners to experts, keep Dunbar Community Centre's gym busy 12 months of the year. Tuesday evenings are reserved "since the planet began" — as one member put it — for the Dunbar Badminton Club. Jim Kelly mentioned the dedication of the members: "It's one of the best community clubs around for high-level competition. A few in the core group have been here at least 15 years and many play 12 months of the year. Some play at three other community centres on other nights of the week." Members frequently discuss the finer points of the game over refreshments at the Cheshire Cheese Inn on Dunbar Street.

The 1930s: Team Sports Take Off

Team sports gained prominence in the 1930s as gymnasiums, playing fields and other facilities became available. Lord Byng High School produced winning teams in various sports, and teams from Dunbar churches competed in city-wide church leagues. Character building was often considered more important than competition. Beginning in the '30s some outstanding multi-sport athletes emerged.

Lord Byng High School's interest in rugby started early in the history of the school. A paragraph in the school annual in 1937 attests to this fact: "The outlook for the Senior Rugby team last fall was far from promising, for Mr. Morrow, who has coached many a Byng team to the New Zealand Shield, decided that he would have to relinquish his coaching duties. . . . Fortunately, one of our new teachers, Mr. Dodd, turned out to be a New Zealander and a rugby enthusiast (the two really go together) and he kindly agreed to fill the breach." For nine years in a row, from 1938 to 1946, the Lord Byng team won the New Zealand Shield, the top rugby award in Vancouver high schools, donated by the touring New Zealand All-Blacks in 1925.

Like other sports in Dunbar, rugby produced some outstanding players. Douglas "Buzz" Moore began his rugby career at Lord Byng. He played rugby for the Meralomas for 28 years (1938 to 1966), and from 1948 through 1964 he played in every international match in which B.C.

Ted Hunt, All-Round All-Star

One of B.C.'s best athletes in the 1950s and '60s, Ted Hunt played rugby at Lord Byng, captained UBC's Thunderbird rugby team for four years and later played fly-half for the Vancouver Kats, which won 12 consecutive provincial championships. The high point of Hunt's international rugby career was in 1968 when, with an 85-yard run, he initiated a try scored by Byng graduate Peter Grantham that led the B.C. Reps to an 11–3 victory over the famed British Lions. Hunt's lacrosse career with the Vancouver Burrards (1954–64) included three Mann Cup championships. A three-year professional football stint with the B.C. Lions earned him the Western Canada Rookie of the Year award in 1957 and Most Valuable Canadian in 1958.

▲ Keith Iwasaki of the Pacific Spirit Triathlon Club on the Ironman Canada Triathlon course near Penticton on 24 August 2002. Iwasaki completed the Ironman in 14 hours 38 minutes 35 seconds. Courtesy of Keith Iwasaki.

▲ Lord Byng's Senior A English rugby team, coached by Arthur Dodd, once again won the highly prized New Zealand Shield in 1939–40. Front row, left to right: Dick Elvin, Sammy Caros, Bob McLaren, Jack Pomfret (captain), Boyd Crosby, Ed Green, Jack Kennedy. Back row, left to right: Bob Bennie, Bill Poupore, Gordon Ling, Bob Bartlett, Tick Payne, Bud Spiers, Arthur Dodd (coach). Courtesy of Lord Byng Secondary School.

participated. In 1962 Moore was the first Canadian to be named an honorary Barbarian by the legendary British rugby club, conferring on him "world all-star status" in rugby. Moore has devoted decades to volunteer work for rugby and for sports in general, especially at UBC.

Doug Mowatt, a member of the legislative assembly for West Point Grey, played rugby for Lord Byng in the 1940s. After an accident (not a rugby accident) left him a paraplegic, he became an active participant in the Paralympics. In 1974 Spence McTavish started teaching at Lord Byng and since then has been a mainstay of the rugby program. For many years he played on Canada's national team, after a stellar career at UBC. In 2004 he divided his teaching time between Lord Byng and UBC. "The neat thing about the game is that there's a lot of camaraderie. Rugby builds good character and there's room for people of all sizes, which is pretty important in high school."

In 1999 Byng's rugby team once again won the B.C. championship and brought home the provincial shield after an absence of 38 years. During the 1990s Byng's teams toured New Zealand, Australia and Fiji. In 2003 they played in Hawaii, New Zealand and Australia.

Say the word "hockey" anywhere else but in Canada and they will know you are talking about field hockey or grass hockey. After soccer, it is the second-largest participation sport in the world. In the 1930s the

Lord Byng girls' grass hockey teams carried off many high-school championships, ably coached by teachers such as Miss Lawrence and Mr. Putnam. Grass hockey continued to be a popular sport with girls at Byng until the late '70s, and many trophies were won by teams at all levels. Gradually girls' grass hockey faded from West Side schools. Meanwhile, it was being played by men and boys in community clubs, where it was referred to as "field hockey" or simply "hockey."

In 1977 two Vancouver clubs merged to become the Vancouver Hawks Field Hockey Club. It is the largest hockey club in North America. In 2004, 523 girls and 284 boys were registered in Vancouver as well as six women's teams and six men's teams. The biggest turnout for registration was at the Dunbar Community Centre.

Hockey in B.C. has benefited from the fact that the game was played throughout the Commonwealth. Brian Seymour arrived from England in the early 1970s and has been a driving force behind the club and the junior program ever since. John McBryde, captain of the Australian Olympic team in 1964, left Australia to study at UBC and was soon coaching teams at St. George's School. When student Alan Hobkirk went to England in 1974 on a Rhodes scholarship he became captain of the Oxford team. He played nine years on Canada's national team, participating in nearly 100 international matches. Fellow student Jon Wade became captain of the award-winning Nova Scotia team when he went east to study.

Don Paterson arrived from Scotland in 1971 to take a position at UBC and has been active with the junior girls' club since its start in 1986.

▲ Lord Byng High School junior grass hockey team, 19 October 1935. Left to right: Mary Boyd, Molly Gray, Peggy Cairns, Mary Woodworth, Jean Nicholson, Muriel Wilson, Dorothy Henderson, Margaret Gray, Betty Sharp, Leslie Adam, Bay Logie, Norma Allen. Courtesy of Lord Byng Secondary School.

▲ Jack Rush recalled surprising his colleagues at Lord Byng in 1949 by setting up a cricket practice area behind the school. With some old posts and some reject netting obtained from a fisherman on the Fraser River, he soon had serviceable practice nets. The appearance of these nets and other strange equipment like a flat-sided bat, leather balls, knee padding and gloves aroused many puzzled looks from staff and students. Courtesy of Lord Byng Secondary School.

He noted that the hockey season for boys and girls ages eight to eighteen starts when soccer ends, so many Dunbar players move from soccer right into hockey — field hockey, that is.

A new sport emerged at Lord Byng in 1937. The first table tennis tournament was held in the study hall before a crowd of 100 excited fans. Future humorist and writer Eric Nicol battled to the finish and became the first singles champion. Starting in the 1940s, a house that boasted a ping pong table in the basement could be guaranteed a steady stream of visitors for singles, doubles or round-the-table ping pong. Since 1958 table tennis has had a faithful following at the Dunbar Community Centre of both beginners and experts in recreational and competitive clubs.

The 1940s and 1950s: Sports and Recreation Hit Their Stride

During the 1940s, Dunbar's streets were often busier with sporting activities and roller skating than with cars. Barrie Lindsay described his street in the 1940s: "Olympic Street was our playground. Softball, football and soccer were regular activities on the street. Naturally we were told to 'watch out for cars' but, in reality, it was the cars who were patient with us. For the most part, the neighbours were tolerant of stray balls in their flower gardens. A few people were extremely intolerant, however, and it took some ingenuity and courage to retrieve errant balls." Bolo bats, yoyos, marbles, lacrosse balls and hopscotch signalled the arrival of spring on the school grounds each year. In summer, children played kick-the-can or run-sheep-run in unpaved back lanes. Sometimes they quickly and quietly scaled a picket fence to raid a neighbour's cherry tree or strawberry patch.

After World War II, more time and money were available for recreational hobbies. Founded in the early 1940s, the Dunbar Merchants Bowling League has been active for almost 60 years. Initially the league consisted of 10 teams of 5 bowlers each. When it started, many Dunbar stores sponsored their own teams — Dunbar Meats, Pulham and Blight Hardware, Dunbar Barber Shop and Heather (later Heather's) Handy Store.

Beginning at 9:00 P.M. on Monday evenings, the 10-lane Alma Bowling Centre at 3617 West Broadway was the scene of many lively bowling tournaments as Dunbar's mixed teams engaged in friendly competition. Using its more skilled bowlers, the Dunbar Merchants formed special teams to compete in a city-wide league. When the Alma Bowling Centre closed, the league moved to Varsity Recreation at 4346 West 10th Avenue; when Varsity Recreation closed, the league moved to Ken Hayden's Varsity-Ridge 5-Pin Bowling Centre at 15th and Arbutus, where a few of the originals, now in their eighties, still bowled in 2006.

Helen Stewart, Freestyle Medallist

Helen Stewart (later Hunt), a Lord Byng graduate, began swimming at the Crystal Pool in 1945 when she was seven years old. The pool was located at 1490 Beach Avenue on Vancouver's English Bay. Later she trained under coaches Percy Norman and Howard Firby. In 1954 she won a silver medal in the 440-yard freestyle relay at the British Empire and Commonwealth Games in Vancouver and two silvers for relays at the Pan-American Games in Mexico City. Stewart broke the world record for the 100-yard freestyle in 1956 before competing in the Melbourne Olympics. She was named B.C. Athlete of the Year in 1955. She played on 11 Canadian championship volleyball teams from 1966 to 1973. On 22 May 1958, Helen Stewart married Ted Hunt (see page 244).

Stewart doing the crawl at UBC's outdoor Empire Pool in 1954. Photo by Bill Cunningham. Courtesy of Helen (Stewart) Hunt.

In 1949 two five-pin bowling alleys were built in the basement of St. Philip's Church. Mixed teams bowled almost every evening and on Saturdays. On 20 September 1949, Archie Phelps organized a group of church members from the Men's Club to bowl every Tuesday evening. By 1975 three charter members were still bowling. Four of the bowlers were over eighty, and one was over ninety. In 2006 the bowling alleys were still there but the teams were long gone.

In 1849 a captain of the Royal Navy introduced the game of cricket to Victoria. One hundred years later, in 1949, Jack Rush introduced cricket to students at Lord Byng High School. Rush taught at Lord Byng from 1947 to 1968. The first team entered the school league with St. George's School and three other private schools. By 1968 three teams were entered in the league. When Lord Byng held its 75th anniversary celebrations in the year 2000, Jack Rush was there. "I was approached by an elderly grad about fifty years of age who said with a smile, 'Mr. Rush, you taught me cricket at Byng!' He sounded as if this had been an important event in his life," recalled Jack Rush with a smile.

Dancing became popular in Dunbar in the early 1940s. As teenagers during these years, Lionel and Gordon Jinks looked forward to Saturday-night dances at the Alma Academy at 3679 West Broadway. The girls would stay on one side of the hall and the boys would have to go across to ask a girl to dance. Dances featured live music in the '30s, with Vancouver legend Dal Richards in one of the bands. In the '40s Mr. Lane, who owned Lane Music at 16th and Dunbar, spun records for the dancers. Between 1938 and 1941 Gordon Jinks was a member of the four-piece band the Rocky Mountain Ramblers, which played on some of the "booze cruise" trips to Bowen Island.

The Alma Academy was also a popular hangout for the Alma Dukes, many of whom came from Dunbar. Recognized by their zoot suit stride pants, which were wide at the knee and narrow at the ankle, and by the long chain that looped from the pocket of their pants down to their knees, they stood out on the dance floor with their distinctive hairstyles referred to as duck cuts.

On Friday nights in the 1940s, Queen Elizabeth Elementary School auditorium was *the* place to be for Dunbar's younger and less sophisticated teenagers. "Teen Town" took over at that time and the walls of the auditorium reverberated to the 78s of Frankie Lane, the Mills Brothers and Mel Tormé and to a sea of teenagers dancing up a storm.

The "Dunbar Grads" including, top left to right, Guy Heather, Gerie Richardson, Doug Gordon, and bottom, Clista Heather and Marge Gordon. On Wednesday mornings in 2005, eighty-seven-year-old Clista Heather, whose husband Guy was one of the first presidents of the Dunbar Merchants Bowling League, was sure to be bowling with her friends Marge Gordon, Gerie Richardson and other teammates under their new (since 1992) name, the Dunbar Grads, rolling with the best of them. Courtesy of Clista (Davis) Heather. ▶

Master Model Ship Builder

Recreational hobbies gained new significance
following World War II. After four years in the
Canadian Air Force, Jack Claridge, with his wife,
Margaret, bought a house in Dunbar and Jack
found time to pursue his childhood hobby of
building model ships. From the age of eight to
the age of eighty when his eyesight failed, he built
models of CPR and local ships ⅛" to the foot.
One year an escaped pet hamster built a nest for
itself in the hull of a model under construction.
Jack continued his meticulous work on the model
while the hamster continued its occupation of
the hull. In all he devoted over 20,000 hours to
constructing his models, and his skill as a master
model builder is admired by visitors from around
the world when they visit the Claridge Gallery at
the Vancouver Maritime Museum.

*Jack Claridge beside some of the models he was working
on in 1969. Courtesy of Lloyd Claridge.*

Radio announcer Jack Cullen was the popular DJ. Spot dances, lady's
choice, tag dances, elimination dances and loud music kept the room hot
and the dancers moving. The strains of "Goodnight Irene" always ushered
in the home waltz, the signal for fellows to rush across the floor to dance
with the girl they hoped to "walk home."

Couples enjoyed a different type of dancing at Dunbar Heights
United Church. A square-dance group called the See Saws started in 1954.
Avis Schutz remembered that at times there were as many as 12 squares
for a total of 96 dancers. In 1963 the See Saws moved to the gym at the
Dunbar Community Centre, where they paid $15 a couple for the season.

Ruth and Norm Hutton were invited to watch the dancing one
evening. "You'll never get me in those fancy clothes!" said Norm. Before
long he was wearing a wide belt with an elaborate silver buckle, slim
trousers, square-dance boots with pointed toes and a tie made from the
material in his wife's full skirt! Ruth recalled the wonderful floor for
dancing and the work done by caretaker Russ Hunter and his wife, Joan,
to see that it was in perfect condition on Friday nights, especially for the
big "Thank Goodness It's Spring" dance, where callers Jim Murray, Ron
Docherty and later Jim and Marg MacPherson kept the dancers swinging their partners. On Saturday nights Scottish country dancers filled the
hall and kilts swayed to strathspeys, reels and jigs.

BASKETBALL

In the 1950s basketball started to gain widespread popularity, although a few enterprising individuals had started laying the foundations for the sport in the late 1930s. The 1938 Lord Byng annual reported: "Another evidence of Byng's enterprise is shown by a group of basketball enthusiasts who organized a basketball team in the face of many odds. With no gymnasium at the school, they held two workouts at the Western Sports Centre gym. Aided by the wisdom of Coach 'Tony' Osborne, these pioneers played three exhibition games. Thus ended the first basketball season at Byng, but a precedent has been set." There was good news for Lord Byng's basketball teams in 1939. Queen Elizabeth Elementary School opened and offered its brand-new gymnasium to them for practice sessions and games.

In the 1940s a homemade court was set up near the Chinese market gardens on property belonging to the Mercer family at 3876 Southwest Marine Drive. Barrie Lindsay recalled: "Hundreds of hours of labour went into hand-digging the hay field, and then levelling it and rolling it with a big neighbourhood lawn roller. The hoop itself was very high-tech for those days, with support posts set three feet behind a fan-shaped backboard. The hoop even had a net! The key was properly marked in with some of Dad's lime. A lot of hours were spent on that court."

In the mid-'40s another homemade court was set up amongst the trees at Memorial West Park adjacent to Wallace Street. Underbrush was

Howard Kelsey conversing with U.S. players Devin Durrant and Charles Barkley (right) after he received a gold medal for men's basketball at the World University Games in Edmonton, Alberta, in 1983. It was the first time Canada had won gold in men's basketball. Yugoslavia came second in the tournament, USA third. Courtesy of Howard Kelsey. ▶

Mary Stewart, Record Holder

Helen Stewart's younger sister, Mary Stewart (later McIlwaine), born in 1945, trained with coach Howard Firby. During her career she won gold, silver and bronze medals for freestyle, butterfly and relay races at swimming meets all over the world, from the Pan-American Games to the British Empire Games to the Olympics (Rome in 1960 and Tokyo in 1964). She established and broke her own world records in 1961 and 1962 for the 100 metres and 110-yard butterfly stroke. Stewart was recognized as Female Athlete of the Year for 1961 and 1962 by the Canadian Press news agency. Besides being a swimmer, she was an accomplished dancer and acrobat, performing from 1956 to 1963 as "Little Leo," the B.C. Lions mascot.

Seventeen-year-old Stewart on 20 April 1962, in Sacramento, California, when she established a new American record for the 110-yard butterfly stroke with a time of 59.2 seconds. Courtesy of Helen (Stewart) Hunt.

cleared, a backboard was nailed to a tree, and everyone in the neighbourhood was invited to play. The "spark plug" was Sonny Kent, one of the 14 children in the Chow Kent family who lived opposite the park at 31st Avenue and Wallace Street. Glen Drummond recalls that the seven brothers were real assets to the community and taught basketball, tennis and baseball to the neighbourhood children. The quality of basketball there was very high, led by the likes of Sonny and Bunny Kent and Glen and Barry Drummond. Barry had a fine basketball career at UBC.

In the late 1940s two enterprising brothers from Lord Byng, Sam and Barry "Moose" Stewart, put together a neighbourhood girls' team. The Vancouver School Board let them rent the gym at Queen Elizabeth Elementary School for very little money, the principal gave them a key to the school, and practices were underway. Commercial league games were played at night in the King Edward school gym at 12th and Oak. Night basketball was the big thing in the 1940s and '50s.

Derek Sankey has had a profound impact on basketball as a player, coach and sport administrator. He gave the following account of basketball in Dunbar:

> The history of basketball in Dunbar traces its point of explosion to two individuals in the 1950s: Bill Norton, the long-time coach at Lord Byng High School, and Dr. Peter Mullins, coach of the UBC varsity basketball. These two individuals provided not only the support but also the environment in which the sport could flourish in Dunbar. Others picked up this passion and have carried it forward to the present day.

Bob Hamelin, Queen Elizabeth School elementary teacher in the late 1950s, provided an intramural venue for young boys to play basketball, many of whom went on to star at Lord Byng. Lord Byng was the focus of basketball in Dunbar, whether it was the outside asphalt courts crowded with players every weekend or the competitive nature of the school teams, but the magic of the sport and its influence was self-evident.

Lord Byng qualified for the provincial tourney 13 times and won the provincial championship in 1958 under Bill Norton. In the 1960s the best Lord Byng teams were coached by Peter Merson. These teams qualified for the provincial championships and were led by Derek Sankey and Don Sweet. Sweet later starred in the Canadian Football League as a kicking specialist with the Montreal Alouettes. Sankey has continued to contribute to every aspect of the sport on the civic, provincial and national level.

Howard Kelsey's interest in basketball was kindled in 1969 at the age of twelve when he began playing at St. Philip's Church. His passion for the game was contagious in the Kelsey family, and soon younger siblings Doug and Cheryl were winning awards too. Howard and Doug led their Point Grey High School team to a first-place victory in Vancouver in 1975, scoring 80 points between them. Howard was a member of Canada's Olympic team in 1980 and 1984. In 1998, when Vancouver *Province* sportswriter Howard Tsumura selected his high-school five-person dream team for the past 50 years, Howard Kelsey was on it.

Howard and Doug Kelsey are co-founders of the HSBC Metro Vancouver Basketball Tournament, which had 130 teams competing in 2006. It is one of the largest high-school basketball tournaments in North America, with up to $120,000 in basketball scholarships awarded annually to players. The hoop game has come a long way since its pioneer days at Lord Byng in 1938.

SOCCER

The Dunbar Soccer Association (DSA) was founded in 1957. Ron Winkleman gave the following account to the *Courier* newspaper in 1972: "Bill Coleman, then secretary-treasurer of the Vancouver & District League, a post he held for over 25 years, looked at Chaldecott Park and saw there wasn't much going on for boys there. He decided it was time to start soccer in the Dunbar area. He went to the schools with notices telling all the boys that soccer would be starting Saturday morning at Chaldecott. Over 100 boys turned out, many of whom had never seen a soccer ball before." Four of the fathers who turned up with their sons — John Gibson, Brian Creer, Joffre Joyce and Jim Hodge — ended up being the first coaches in the league; and from that time on, no one could look at the parks in Dunbar and say there wasn't much going on there for boys — and for girls too.

▲ "Ludere Causa Ludendi" — to play for the sake of playing the game. True to its motto, Dunbar Soccer Association has always tried to ensure that all boys and girls have a chance to play at a level suited to their individual abilities. Badge courtesy of Rollie Wakeman.

Dunbar's teams have excelled in soccer ever since. By the year 2005 the DSA had grown to be the largest and one of the most successful community clubs in the city of Vancouver, with 1,648 players registered. The number of girls continues to increase and they now make up 50 percent of divisional membership. But soccer started in Dunbar before 1957. For many years, St. Philip's Church sponsored boys' soccer teams. During the 1930s the church had a championship team coached by Bert Rush. From 1951 to 1967, Reverend "Cap" Cummings often did double duty as rector of the church and coach of St. Philip's entry in the Sunday School Soccer League. Many fine young players were developed through these teams.

When the DSA was formed, fees were $2 per player, and the association had an annual budget of $2,000. In the year 2000, fees and budgets were 50 times that amount. Back in 1957 the teams played on Memorial West Park and shared Chaldecott Park with St. George's School. In 2004, the DSA used more than 12 fields, two with lights paid for by money raised by the organization.

The DSA has produced a number of provincial and national champions, an admirable accomplishment for a small community-based association. DSA players who have played professionally for the Whitecaps and the 86ers include Ivano Belfiore, Ralston Dunlop, Steve Nesin and Carl Shearer. One particularly outstanding team during the 1970s was

An outstanding team — Dunbar Stong's soccer team, 1977–78. Standing, left to right: Paul Stolk, Doug Elton, Ralston Dunlop, Rob Irving, Carl Shearer, Ivano Belfiore, Mark Henderson, Pat Brown. Front row, left to right: Rob McGinley, Jim Armstrong, Bruce Bates, Steve Smith, Steve Nesin, Craig Hibbert, Warren Pow. Courtesy of Steve Nesin. ▼

Dunbar Stong's. Donald Dunlop and Ron Shearer described this team in the foreword of their 1980 book *Don't Make Mistakes! Play Perfectly!* as "Hodge's Stong's," to distinguish it from other Dunbar Stong's teams. "There can be few youth teams which practised as often or as long, and played so many games — league, cup and exhibition. They consistently sought out the highest class of competition to test their own mettle. . . . The team was a credit to all associated with it but especially to [coach] Spud Hodge, the driving force behind the team through all nine years [1969–78]." In eight years the team played 138 league games, winning 131, tying 5 and losing 2. In the 1977/78 season they won the Canadian championship in Montreal by a score of 4 to 1. On one occasion the parents of the opposing team were overheard reporting that the Dunbar team had a coach for every player, that the boys were on a special diet and that they were not allowed to play any other sport!

Dunbar has produced not only great players but also great coaches: Spud Hodge, Geoff Smith, Ron Winkleman, John Docherty, Mike Mason and Ron Shearer. The generous sponsorship of Ralph Stong and Bill Rossum of Stong's Market was important to the success of soccer teams over the years. As former DSA president Ron Shearer pointed out: "Any discussion of organized sports in Dunbar has to pay special tribute

A Summer Stunt

This photo was taken on a bright summer day, c. 1954, on the lawn between Kitsilano Pool and Cornwall Street. Ted Hunt was asked to perform, having just come back from Europe and the world championships in Sweden that February. As he related: "Vancouver had several of these trestle jumping events, built by keen skiers during the long cold winter spell of 1951. There was one built on West 8th Avenue where Point Grey Academy now resides. Ten thousand people came to watch. The Kitsilano jump was on crushed ice with preservative chemicals and was very slippery, as you can see by my imbalance during my first jump. I was also acrophobic and did not like that skinny little ramp so high off the ground. I was practising for the show that night when I was to hold two flaming torches as I flew through the air in the dark — terrified that I might miss the narrow landing hill and that the flames might burn my arms. No, I was not paid. And no, I wouldn't do it again if I was."

Photo courtesy of Helen (Stewart) Hunt.

to Stong's. They played a major role in supporting youth soccer; they also played a major role in baseball. Bill Rossum has been a jewel ornamenting the community." Many other Dunbar merchants have also supported the DSA. A list of some 1968 sponsors included Arnold Coiffures, Copp the Shoe Man, Creerys, Dunbar Meats, Eldridge Drugs, Esso, Fisher's Pharmacy, Good Service, Halversons, Morton & Gale, Nightingale Pharmacy, Roberts' Jeweller, Royalite Service Station and Schicks as well as private individuals such as Dick Ott.

In the 1980s and '90s, Joan and Russ Hunter, night security and caretaker, respectively, at the Dunbar Community Centre, supported a girls' and a boys' soccer team in Dunbar by going out to every practice and every game. As Joan said in 2000, "We couldn't afford the uniforms, but we'd provide a big lunch at McDonald's. Eventually we were able to buy them a trophy. The boys' team petered out; but the 'Green Beans' — the girls' team — is still going strong."

Over the years, both parents and former players have pitched in to coach, referee, line field, look after uniforms and do numerous other jobs. Graham Laxton, president of Dunbar Soccer Association at the beginning of the twenty-first century, stated that "DSA is as vibrant as the community that we serve and has been the catalyst for many long-lasting friendships."

BASEBALL

California prospectors brought baseball to B.C. during the 1858 gold rush. During the 1930s Ralph Stong of Stong's Grocery on West Hastings played on the semi-pro circuit. Throughout the 1940s and '50s, scrub baseball was played on almost every street in Dunbar. Boulevard trees became bases. Few cars were parked on the streets, as many families did not own a car and those who did parked in their single-car garage. The street served as a playground.

In 1958, George Fisher, Ralph Stong, Dan Potvin, Ralph White, Con Conlin and Joffre Joyce got together with others and planned a six-team Little League for boys. Forty years later David Joyce, Joffre's son, recalled sitting at the top of the basement stairs while the coaches and managers met below in the recreation room. "I listened quietly while my friends' names were drawn and assigned to a team. The next morning I would go to school smug with the secret knowledge and not saying a word, just smiling, knowing that Bill was with Stong's while Big Al was playing for the Fisher team."

After the Little League, Joffre Joyce also started the Babe Ruth League for boys thirteen to sixteen years of age. Dunbar Little League grew and expanded throughout the 1960s; by 2004 it was one of the strongest and most respected leagues in B.C. In 1998, to celebrate 40 years of Little League baseball in the district, Dunbar Little League hosted the provincial tournament in Memorial West Park. David Joyce, a player in the original league, chaired the tournament committee.

Some of the original members from the Stong's/Shop-Easy Dunbar Little League baseball team. Taken in 1962, the photo appeared on the cover of the 1998 booklet celebrating the 40th anniversary of the Dunbar Little League (1958 to 1998). Stong's was honoured as the Anniversary Sponsor. Courtesy of the family of Joffre Joyce. ▶

On 1 August 1998, Gordon Weatherill — president of the Dunbar Little League Association — summed up the incredible amount of planning, organization, money and hard work that had gone into putting the tournament together and preparing the site at Memorial West Park. "Our field was completely rebuilt. New bleachers, a beautiful concession stand and a scoring booth were constructed. This great new facility is thanks to the dedication and commitment of not only parents and volunteers but also the Dunbar and Vancouver business communities as a whole. It is amazing what can be accomplished with the kind of community spirit we are fortunate to have in the Dunbar area." On 16 May 2003 two teams from Dunbar Little League hosted six Lower Mainland teams at Memorial West Park for the first annual Ralph Stong Memorial Tournament.

DUNBAR COMMUNITY CENTRE

In November 1958 the Dunbar Community Centre (DCC) opened at 31st and Dunbar. It has been a hub of activity ever since. A $1.4-million expansion in 1982 added an up-to-date fitness centre, a whirlpool and sauna as well as two squash courts and a racquetball court. The fitness centre is a far cry from the original one that was tucked into a dark corner of the basement behind the leather archery curtain. In 1998 the racquetball court was transformed into a weight room, replacing the original weight room — a small room in the basement that was designed for a dumb waiter in case kitchen catering would be required on the main floor above. The fitness centre is in constant use from 6 A.M. to 10 P.M.

Dunbar resident Erroll Jang has been using the fitness centre and weight room for 17 years and speaks enthusiastically of its spirit of camaraderie and co-operation. People of all ages work out together — not only young people but also older people such as eighty-four-year-old Kay Plumbley, who was part of a regular exercise group working to fend off osteoporosis.

The 1960s and 1970s: Innovative Activities

Creative play continued in spite of the increasing popularity of television in the 1960s. Early in the decade the Hughes children — Gordon, Jane, Neil and Paul — gathered discarded fishing nets and heavy ropes from the Celtic net loft on the Fraser River and hauled them to their backyard at 48th and Dunbar. Together with other neighbourhood children, they built tree forts and set up elaborate systems of ladders, aerial ropes and pulleys in a grove of birch trees. One of the fishing nets became a huge hammock that could accommodate up to 16 children at one time. Skateboarding, a new type of transportation, appeared on Dunbar streets in the early 1960s.

▲ A bouquet for Dunbar's May Queen from a Little League player in the early 1960s as Joffre Joyce, one of the founders of the Little League, looks on. Photographer Bill Cunningham captures the moment once again at Memorial West Park. Courtesy of the family of Joffre Joyce.

An old washtub suspended on ropes and a pulley provided seven-year-old Paul Hughes of 3646 West 48th Avenue with a quick descent from the tree fort to the ground in 1960. Higher authorities removed the washtub after it flipped following too rapid a descent, chipping one of Paul's front teeth. Courtesy of Paul Hughes. ▶

Brian Creer introduced kayaking to Dunbar. In the book *Paddle Quest: Canada's Best Canoe Routes*, Creer is referred to as "B.C.'s Teacher Extraordinaire." He was eleven years old in 1926 when his parents moved to Dunbar. To reach the 33-foot lot they had purchased at 4098 West 17th Avenue, they had to cut a trail through the bush from 16th and Camosun. From 1965 to 1979, Creer taught physical education at Lord Byng High School. In 1970 a parks board pool was added to the school, and Creer took advantage of the facility to provide programs in swimming, scuba diving, canoeing and kayaking. In addition to courses at the pool, students practised canoeing and kayaking in the fall at Locarno Beach and on the Fraser River. In winter they took courses in scuba diving; then in spring they had 10 weeks of kayaking on the Seymour, Capilano and Chilliwack Rivers. Creer described part of his course:

> The outdoor class in the morning was from 8 to 10 A.M. and the afternoon class was from 2 to 5 P.M. After the first week the students discovered that there was not enough time to do all the things that had to be done. They persuaded me to start earlier and stay out later. This process continued until we were starting the morning class at 5 A.M. and ending the afternoon class at 9 P.M.
>
> The kids had to pay close attention to all the instructions I gave because they didn't want to find themselves hanging upside down in the water from a capsized kayak and not know what to do.

He added with a straight face: "I'd rescue any kid who hadn't been listening. I never let any of them drown."

Pam Withers taught kayaking skills at Lord Byng pool for six years until 2003. Then she switched to writing novels for teenagers involving

◄ The thrill of skateboarding —
Robin Forshaw enjoying his new
board in the early 1960s on West
22nd Avenue. Dunbar Street can
be seen in the background.
Courtesy of Lissa Forshaw.

extreme sports such as kayaking, skiing and skateboarding. The first five
of a six-book series had been published by 2005. Her son Jeremy Withers
placed second in the Canadian National Championships in the 14 and
under category in whitewater slalom kayaking at Mudawaska River near
Ottawa in August 2002, carrying on the tradition of kayaking at Lord
Byng started by Brian Creer in 1970.

A new sport, Ultimate, was introduced to Dunbar in the mid-1970s.
The game is played with a plastic disc and resembles non-tackle football.
It is a self-refereed sport enjoyed by people who want to have both exercise and good-natured fun. Charlotte Stenberg explained the game: "It is
a co-ed game played with seven people per team on the field at a time.
There have to be at least three girls per team. The object is to score by
catching the disc in the opposite end zone from which you started. A big
part of Ultimate is the spirit aspect. At the end of the game the final score
is entered as well as a 'spirit' score — how sportsmanlike the team is." By
the 1990s Ultimate was one of the most rapidly growing sports in the
Lower Mainland. In the summer of 2004 almost 5,000 participants were
registered and there were 232 teams in the Vancouver Ultimate League.
Dunbar had its share of participants at all levels.

The 1980s and Beyond: Fresh Pursuits and New Horizons

Since the 1980s women have been knocking down barriers in the world of sport, and the future looks bright for even greater participation in widening fields of endeavour. Running marathons, paddling dragon boats, playing rugby and ringette — these were some of the new activities that attracted women in Dunbar.

Pauline Kot was fifty when she ran her first marathon during Expo year, 1986. She had become interested in running in the late 1970s. "At first I couldn't even run for five minutes. I went to Balaclava Park after dark so no one could see me, and I wore $9 running shoes from the Army and Navy store." Mary Ann Carter was fifty-seven when she started running marathons. Her interest in long-distance running was kindled by training for the 10-kilometre Vancouver Sun Run in 1997. In 2000 Carter ran the Portland Marathon in four hours six minutes. In April 2002 she ran her 10th marathon — the Boston Marathon — and came 13th in the 60–69 age category.

Midge Oke took up dragon boat racing in 1997 after she heard about a team for breast cancer survivors. She explained why she paddles dragon boats. "Ages range from thirty-one to seventy-nine, and we come in all shapes and sizes — the only prerequisite is to have had breast cancer. Our first captain and founding president was Dunbar resident Brenda Ho-chachka. Being a member of Abreast in a Boat is a remarkable experience — it is exhilarating to be out on the water of False Creek on an early

Old-fashioned fun in the new millennium. A pony and trap on 21st Avenue near Crown Street provided some Dunbar youngsters with an unusual outing at a birthday party in 2001. To old-timers the outing brought back memories of the horses at Clinton stables that were once a common sight in Dunbar and on the trails in the University Endowment Lands. Courtesy of Margaret (Campbell) Moore. ▶

summer evening in a boat with 21 other very diverse women, all of whom have shared similar life-threatening situations, all working together to be as strong as we can be, paddling our hearts out, sharing jokes and stories during our breaks." In June 2005 the Vancouver members hosted a "10 Year Abreast Regatta," and more than 50 breast cancer teams from around the world came to help celebrate the anniversary.

Rugby and ringette both became popular among girls in the 1990s. Ringette, a no-contact ice hockey game involving teamwork and co-operation, originated in Ontario in the 1960s. In the '90s it took off in Vancouver thanks to the active part played by Elliott and Bonnie Burnell and their three children.

An unusually quiet recreational activity gained popularity in Dunbar in the 1980s. It was the pursuit of birding. A Vancouver *Courier* article referred to Jude (Fuller) Grass and her husband Al as "Vancouver's First Couple" when it came to birding. "People like the Grasses have made bird watching the second most popular hobby in North America, after golf." The Grasses returned to live in Jude's childhood home on Dunbar Street in 2002, where Jude identified at least 30 species of birds in her backyard. She commented that Camosun Bog was her second home when she was growing up in Dunbar.

T.K. Ho moved to Dunbar in 1994 and quickly realized that his new neighbourhood was ideal for walking. Soon he had walked every trail in Pacific Spirit Park. Ho helped organize a walking group, many of them new Canadians, which meets at the Dunbar Community Centre every Thursday morning. In 2002 they decided to combine walking with bird-watching and invited Brian Self to be their guide. Self noted, "Few places can match Dunbar and its surroundings for variety of terrain and abundance of bird species."

In future, team sports will continue to flourish in Dunbar, with the number of teams limited only by the availability of existing facilities. By 2006 the installation of night lighting had considerably increased the hours that some parks and school grounds were available for practice sessions. The Dunbar Community Centre continues to widen the scope of its programs, catering to all ages and to more ethnic groups, the number of programs constrained only by space limitations. As people become increasingly aware of the health benefits of physical and recreational activity, and as the city continues to densify, the pressure on Dunbar's parks and its community centre will increase. Dunbar residents will reap countless benefits from the legacy of time, energy and planning passed down to them from the previous century.

Percy Norman, Swim Coach Extraordinaire

Considered by many to be Canada's top swimming and diving coach, Percy Norman was head coach for the Vancouver Amateur Swim Club at the Crystal Pool from 1931 to 1955. He trained many of Canada's top swimmers, divers and coaches as well as thousands of young swimmers during the years he lived at 3805 West 35th Avenue. He led the Canadian swim team at the 1932 Los Angeles and 1936 Berlin Olympics. Percy Norman Pool near Queen Elizabeth Park is named for him.

CHAPTER 9

School Days

⁓ Peggy Schofield and Joan Tyldesley

The earliest education in the Dunbar area was non-institutional, informal instruction largely unfettered by clocks, desks or schoolrooms. This was the case for both the Native community and the early white settlers. The Musqueam taught their children skills, values and traditions according to their culture, with all members of the community sharing the responsibility of educating their young people. Settlers "home schooled" their children, the first classroom being the kitchen of the McCleery farmhouse. According to Betty (McCleery) McQueen, "The McCleerys hired a lady to come and tutor their two daughters and a niece who was with them at the time. The Magee family came later and had their two girls there as well."

As more families settled on both sides of the north arm of the Fraser River, a formal school system slowly took shape. At this time, Sea Island had the larger population of the two areas and was the site of the first schoolhouse for the area. Children from the flats on the north side had to row across the arm of the Fraser River to attend school. The arrangement caused much concern among the families.

Finally the cabin 12 x 14 feet that the McCleery brothers had built as their first residence became available around 1881. This building, dubbed "St. Patrick's Cathedral" because it was used on occasion as a church, was the first schoolhouse on the Point Grey peninsula. In the beginning,

about 12 students attended, ending the wet and dangerous boat rides for the McCleery, Magee and Mole children.

First on the Block

The population in the South Vancouver/Point Grey municipalities increased dramatically between 1900 and 1910, creating the need for new schools. Kerrisdale school led the procession. It was followed before the end of the century by many more schools, both public and private. Their history is traced here with the help of both those who attended and those who worked in these institutions. Dusty cardboard boxes were located in out-of-the-way places, thanks to the assistance of school personnel. They often yielded valuable information that helped in piecing together the stories of each school. Recurrent themes of discipline, influential teachers, learning tools, subject matter and just plain fun emerged.

KERRISDALE ELEMENTARY SCHOOL

In 1908 the provincial government granted the municipality of Point Grey a nine-acre site for a school west of Carnarvon Street and north of 41st Avenue. Although not within the Dunbar/Southlands area, it was the school that Dunbar children first attended. A two-room, wood-frame building served 12 students from age six to fifteen, under the tutelage of one teacher. This became the first class at Kerrisdale school. In the beginning, several of these young people were from out of the area but lived with relatives to make up the required number of students.

Although the school had electricity, there was no indoor plumbing. Students were required to trek to an outhouse when the need arose and to visit the well with dipper in hand for a drink of water. By 1911 the school boasted a registration of 43 pupils and a new four-room building, complete with indoor plumbing. In 1913 an annex was built near 39th Avenue; it was still in use in 2006. The larger brick building was added in 1924 and has been listed on the City of Vancouver Heritage Register.

Mary Gillard, who attended Kerrisdale school from 1936 until 1939, gave the following account of her time at Kerrisdale, relating details that were typical of schools at this time:

> I still recall the smell of the oiled wooden floors in the classroom and can picture the high transom windows which, if you were lucky, you got to open using a long pole. Individual desks were nailed to the floor, each complete with an inkwell. At the end of the school day the teacher refilled these using a long-spouted copper ink can. No such thing as a ballpoint pen! Instead we had a wooden pen holder with a removable steel nib. When the nib became scratchy, a new one was issued. This had to be sucked before using, rather like the reed of a clarinet.

◀ The annual Lord Byng Christmas Cheer drive, 1950. Members of the Girls' Executive, Pat McFeely, Julie Mond and Maureen Sankey, help prepare hampers. Courtesy of Lord Byng Secondary School.

Gillard also remembered that the library was housed in a regular class-room with bookshelves running along the walls. After giving instruction, the librarian would often read to the class from books such as *Silver Chief: Dog of the North* and tell stories about Grey Owl.

Sheila (Fitzpatrick) McGivern, who attended Kerrisdale from 1947 until 1954, recalled the iodine pills that were dispensed once a week to prevent goitre, which afflicted a small percentage of Vancouver pupils. She remembered the pills as being "big brown chewable ones." Mc-Givern liked them, but Joan Tyldesley had another opinion:

> I hated the taste of those iodine pills, so my seven-year-old mind con-ceived a way of getting out of taking them. My last name was difficult to pronounce and my teacher, Miss Wright, invariably stumbled when saying it. So when she mispronounced my name, I reasoned that she didn't really mean me so I didn't bother going to the front of the room to claim my pill. I noticed that she didn't keep track of who got a pill or not, because I watched her slide the extras back in the bottle. Perhaps others employed similar tricks.

Traditionally the Friday before the May 24 weekend was designated as sports day. The large expanse of playing field on three different levels provided a backdrop for a grand spectacle. The event began with each class in turn marching out the school's front door along 39th Avenue

▲ Manual arts training class, c. 1924, Kerrisdale school. While girls learned sewing, boys in this class typically worked on simple woodworking projects such as pencil boxes, plant stands and decorative wall brackets, which the boys on the right are showing. Photo by Rowland Towers. Courtesy of Kerrisdale Elementary School.

onto the field. Music from a gramophone perched on the sill of an open window accompanied the marchers. Decorated bicycles, wagons and scooters were sometimes part of the festivities. McGivern described her impression of sports day:

> The Grade 6 girls did the maypole dance while the boys put on a gymnastic display. One year we did a dance called the Lambeth Walk under the tutelage of Mr. McCrae. Square dancing was a popular choice as well. The year that Prince Charles was born [1948], the whole school massed on the field to form the letters BPC for Bonnie Prince Charles. After all the grades had finished performing we'd rush into the school and change into shorts and gym shirts for the sports events that took place next. Relay races, potato races, sack races, three-legged races, dashes, etc. all followed, and most kids got at least one ribbon. Hot dogs, doughnuts, pop and popsicles were sold by the PTA.

As a tradition, the annual sports day has endured, although its form has somewhat changed. In particular the maypole dance has disappeared and students no longer put on performances. The emphasis today tends to be on team participation rather than events for individuals.

Boys' gymnastic display, c. 1940, in preparation for sports day at Kerrisdale school. Every class put on some kind of a performance, often in costume, on the hard dirt upper field that acted as a stage for the events. Courtesy of Kerrisdale Elementary School. ▶

◄ Grade 6 students at Kerrisdale school in the early 1950s were taught square dancing by teacher Stuart McCrae and other teachers. The students also learned social skills in preparation for high-school dances and other social activities. Courtesy of Kerrisdale Elementary School.

During its first 47 years, Kerrisdale school had only three principals: Miss Park, Mr. MacDonald and Mr. Houston. Mr. MacDonald is remembered for standing in front of a bulldozer, stopping it from destroying a stand of trees in the southeast corner. The trees still thrive today as a result of his action. Mr. Houston was a particular favourite, with his gentle manner and his distinctive white hair. During an era of firm discipline and formal ways, he could be seen surrounded by clusters of primary children as he walked around the playground during recess. Every Friday afternoon he showed movies to the students, who sat on the floor of the auditorium, while the Grade 6 students had the privilege of sitting in the balcony. The films were mostly documentaries from the National Film Board about such topics as mining, logging and the building of dams. Occasionally Mr. Houston would run part of a film backwards, much to the delight of the young audience.

During the 1970s, Kerrisdale school was the largest elementary school in Vancouver, with more than a thousand students. Enrollment in later years began to drop and in 2006 was down to 520. A strong sports and athletic program remains an important feature of the school. The arts have also been emphasized, especially the music program, featuring band, choir, and recorder and ukulele ensembles.

LORD KITCHENER ELEMENTARY SCHOOL

Built in 1914 on King Edward Avenue between Blenheim and Colling-wood Streets, Lord Kitchener school was named after Lord Horatio Kitchener, the British secretary of war at the outbreak of World War 1. The construction of the wooden building meant that the children in this vicinity no longer had to make the trek to Queen Mary or Kerrisdale schools. Many of the new residents in the area lived in tents or log cabins. Stan Cornish, who began attending Lord Kitchener in 1923, walked from 33rd Avenue and Crown Street. "When I went to school that was really something. . . . Had to be all dressed up. Anyway, I went with my sisters. We went through the trails. They weren't much — just a path through the bush."

When Marion (Tulloch) Funell started as a Grade 1 pupil in 1919, Mr. Feast was principal. One of his duties was to ring a large cowbell to sig-nal the end of recess and lunchtime. He also passed on messages to students from their parents when they telephoned the school. Funell said the messages usually involved some sort of an errand for the child to do on the way home from school, such as "Tell Johnny to bring home a plug of tobacco."

Although the school playing field was noted for being very muddy, recess games and activities flourished. Funell remembered playing jacks most of the time. "There was a raised square cover over some pipes beside

Grade 1 class at Lord Kitchener with teacher Miss Monroe, May 1948. The desks were nailed to runners, creating very straight rows. Photo by Dubarry Studio. Courtesy of Eunice Liversidge. ▼

◄ Sports day at Lord Kitchener, 1949, featuring the Grade 2 girls' book race. The race originates from a time when students were required to walk with a book on their head to develop good posture. Courtesy of Leslie Deeth.

◄ The old and the new at Lord Kitchener Elementary School. The original frame building, constructed in 1914, is listed on the Vancouver heritage building register. The playground was completed in 2002 with the help of parent-organized fundraising. Courtesy of Joan Tyldesley.

the school that was a prized area to play jacks on. When it was recess time we would dash out and try to be the first ones to claim it." Cornish enjoyed games of marbles and playing with milk tops and cards. "You'd flick them up towards the wall and see who could get closest to the wall. Recess wasn't long enough."

Dunbar Heights was becoming even more popular in the 1920s as people bought the many lots that were for sale. Two portable classrooms had to be brought in, and in 1924 a new brick building was constructed as enrollment reached 300 students. By 1929 the population had doubled to 600 students and a south wing was added to the main building. Later that year the Grade 7 and 8 students were sent to Point Grey Junior High School, and only Grades 1 to 6 remained.

Memories that are not so happy are also part of the school experience. Betty (McGlashan) Abbot, a Grade 1 student in 1936, remembered "quivering in [her] shoes" as she was threatened with the strap for talking during class. Vic Stevenson, who attended Kitchener in the '40s, recalled an incident with Miss Mould, the art and music teacher. "I guess she didn't think I was doing very well one time. She handed me the strap and she sent me out of the room and said, 'I'll see you later.' I was sure I was going to get it, but anyway the thing was that I think just holding the strap was worse than getting it! In the end she didn't strap me. I didn't mind her. The strap never bothered me. People said you were marked for life but it was never a problem." The use of the strap disappeared for good on 14 February 1973, eliminating fear in some students. However, it was reported that some teachers still kept a strap in their top drawer as a reminder of what had been.

Pat Cowen, a student at Lord Kitchener in the early '40s, described her experience concerning teachers. "In Grade 1 I had Mrs. Bradbury and I thought I was going to have Mrs. Bradbury forever. Nobody told me that we would change teachers. When I got to Grade 2, I came home crying my eyes out. 'Mrs. Bradbury's not there and I got this cranky old lady called Miss Murphy!' She was a red-headed Irish woman. My mother went to see her once and she said, 'Patsy was a little bit upset because you were shouting.' 'Well,' said Miss Murphy, 'I don't have this red hair for nothing. But I don't shout at Patsy!'"

The final addition to the school, a north wing attached to the main building, was opened in 1962. It included a lunchroom, an activity room and a kindergarten area. Various programs were added to the school curriculum, such as a strings program for young musicians, a computer lab, a peer helper program and a program for gifted students.

Sheila Herman taught the enrichment program at Lord Kitchener. Believing that "parents are your best resource," she started a mentorship program where parents would volunteer time in a specialty area such as math, astronomy or sewing. This was extended to include UBC students, who received credit for their time with Kitchener students. According to Herman, "It was an incredible experience. We had students who had been in medicine, who had been in science, who had been trained in opera, who were pilots, who had all this different expertise and were willing." The Vancouver School Board decided to make the situation more equitable in the 1980s and provide this service for students throughout the school district, which meant fewer Kitchener children could be included.

John Bolton, a filmmaker and Dunbar resident who went through the program in the 1980s, had this to say at Herman's retirement party in 2001:

> When I look back to the Learning Enrichment Centre, I find my memories have blurred into one long session spent with my friends around a table, challenging and inspiring and daring each other, making each other laugh and, occasionally, cry, and drawing up recklessly ambitious plans that more often than not were actually carried out. This is exactly how I most productively spend my time to this day. When I got to high school and later university, I realized that I already knew what it was like to discuss ideas in seminars, listen to guest lecturers and enroll in directed studies. I'd been doing it all through elementary school.

In 2006 the enrollment at Lord Kitchener Elementary School was 534 students, and in spite of its size, the entire student body is involved, every second year, in a musical written by two teachers, Colleen Coulter and Gerry Kent.

Private Schools, 1911 to 1942

The private schools in Dunbar were started either by groups seeking to have Roman Catholic views emphasized in education or by British immigrant groups wishing to have their traditional values supported by the educational system. The Convent of the Sacred Heart and Immaculate Conception schools both subscribed to the belief that the Jesuit ideas of education, as part of Catholic teachings, were important. St. George's School, Crofton House School and Athlone School (1940–73; see sidebar) were based on the British model and were established to perpetuate British traditions and social structure. Each of these private schools in Dunbar is rooted in its own unique history.

CONVENT OF THE SACRED HEART

In 1911, people were coming into Vancouver from Britain, from across Canada and from Europe in increasing numbers. Archbishop Neil McNeil appealed for sisters of the Jesuit order of the Sacred Heart to come from Montreal to establish a school in the city. Six nuns responded to the call and first taught in two downtown locations until the convent on West

Athlone School for Boys

A much smaller private school, Athlone School for Boys was founded by Mrs. Violet Alice Dryvynsyde, who decided to fulfill her husband's dream of starting his own school when she became a widow with a son to support. Her husband had been a master at St. George's School before he died. In 1944 neighbours tried to prevent Athlone school from obtaining a licence but were ultimately unsuccessful. Although there were difficulties with St. George's at the beginning, over time the two schools co-operated and Athlone, which had both day students and boarders, became a feeder school for St. George's.

Yvonne (Goddard) Wheatley lived in the area. She said, "I remember going down 39th on my way to Kerrisdale school and seeing the boys happily working in the front yard." However, outward appearances may have been deceiving. Apparently Athlone school was feared by its students because physical punishment was readily meted out for relatively minor offences such as crying. Many of these students were part of a large number of boys who had lost fathers in World War II and were put into private schools. Some evacuees from Britain, separated from their families, also attended the school.

Enrollment increased and earlier problems subsided. In 1973, Athlone school was forced to close due to financial difficulties. It was no longer a profitable venture.

Athlone School for Boys was founded at 6550 Granville Street in 1940. It moved to this house at 3231 West 39th Avenue in 1944. Courtesy of Ross Hill.

29th Avenue, in what was then called Point Grey, was completed in 1913. The sisters' devotion to teaching and nurturing children from all segments of society enabled the convent to have a strong impact on the community. Airlie Ogilvie, a student at the convent in 1965, said: "It was like walking into an enormous castle in which you were welcomed. You were made to feel it was not just a castle, but it was your home and that you were part of a family. It was very clear. We were called children of the Sacred Heart."

Jacqueline (Chevalier) Cowley attended the convent in 1923. Her parents, both French, had home-schooled her the first few years, but then moved to Dunbar to escape the pollution from downtown sawmills. Cowley rode her bicycle from the family home near Collingwood and 37th Avenue. "There were woods, but they were not deep woods, because all that had been cleared, and it was second growth. They were the loveliest woods, especially in the fall. We'd have an early-morning frost, and you'd have the Oregon grape, the salal, with the little edging of diamonds

▲ The Convent of the Sacred Heart under construction but nearing completion, c. 1911. Wallace Street can be seen crossing 29th Avenue (Buckland Road). A farmhouse and farming area are visible in the background. City of Vancouver Archives, photograph #STR. P.17, N.323.

on it with the frost, and there were a lot of roots, and I would be riding my bicycle so enthralled with my fairyland that I would forget there was a root and find myself over the handlebars." Cowley said their small class of only six students finished the curriculum early in the year and went on to learn many other things. "I think I skipped about two grades."

The convent grounds were ideal for celebrating grand events such as the procession of the Blessed Sacrament for the Feast of Corpus Christi. There was a grotto on the grounds and trails through the woods, ensuring solitude for devout nuns. At recess pupils would play in the gazebo at the end of Pine Alley. The convent also had an orchard of fruit trees surrounded by conifers. Maddy (Shaw) Schmelcher remembered: "The convent used to have a large property for farming beyond it. Wallace Street — that was the property that they farmed on." Doug Edwards remembered seeing the nuns working on the grounds in the 1960s. "We'd walk around the convent, and the sisters would be out. In those days they all wore the full habits. You'd see these poor sisters out and they'd be trimming the grass the other side of the stone wall with short garden shears. They'd be bent over trimming, and their rosary beads would be getting in the way."

For the students, the grounds were a special delight, as Lissa Forshaw described. "Pine Alley was a favourite place for all of us to play. In those days there were many more trees and a gate that opened onto the east side of the Immaculate Conception parish hall. Pine Alley connected up to the old caretaker's cottage on the northeast portion of the property. . . . Of course, the old cottage was just that — an old wooden structure that seemed quite at home surrounded by trees." The outside surroundings of the school were as important as the inside of the building to many students. Here, in the narrow alleyway shrouded by trees, students could play their games without too much adult interference.

Although academic subjects were the major focus of the curriculum, tennis, horseback riding, dancing, theatre and music were also offered. The school even had its own printing press, used to publish the yearbook and other literature. Ogilvie described how the nuns provided a sound academic foundation:

> We all took French lessons from the time we got there, which would have been Grade 1, but we didn't do conversational. I was sad about that in a sense, but I guess it wasn't part of the B.C. curriculum. We had Latin and in the higher grades, we had mythology, which very few of my other friends had ever heard of. . . . We of course had to take the government exams, regardless of our qualifications in our own school. A lot of us did tremendously well. We had fine teachers. They definitely were there to teach. There was no monkey business. At the same time there was lots of love, too. Of course, there were no boys in the way.

One of the convent school's policies was to accept students from various religious and ethnic backgrounds. In 1956 the convent welcomed refugee children from Hungary. Although most of the students were from white, upper-class families, the sisters held cultural nights to encourage those of differing backgrounds to express their own heritage. Ogilvie remembered the girls who came from Mexico — often seen shopping in Dunbar village. "In the '50s or '60s a number of Mexican girls came to study at the convent to learn English, and they sometimes stayed two or three years.

The Minim Study Hall at the Convent of the Sacred Heart could also be a play area, according to Airlie Ogilvie. "My darlingest nun whom I just adored . . . was Sister Diane Dupré. She and my sister, who was about a year younger than I, would go down to the Minim Study Hall. She would turn out the lights and say, 'I'm coming to get you!' and we would play this wonderful hide-and-seek kind of game in the dark." Courtesy of Marcelle O'Reilly. ▶

They were just adorable. Of course, they had bucketloads of money, so they always had the fancy private rooms along the top of the building."

Since not all the students were Roman Catholic, sometimes the nuns made concessions that further endeared the teachers to their students. Lissa Forshaw provided this example: "I think my knees will never be the same after kneeling on the cold concrete floor of the gym for daily Mass from Grades 1 to 4. However, in Grade 5, I befriended a new student, Kim, and this turned out to be a blessing. Given the fact that she was Jewish, somehow Kim managed to convince the nuns that she shouldn't have to attend daily Mass, and that weekly should suffice. Well, weren't my Anglican knees happy. The same deal was struck for me." Nuns clothed in their black habits were often perceived to be sterner than they really were. Usually the sisters were understanding and reasonable, as this incident points out.

Eventually it became clear that the order could not provide enough sisters to keep the convent school viable, and in 1979 the building, considered unsafe, was slated for demolition. Many people felt strongly that the building should be preserved. Among them was Forshaw, who organized a successful public campaign to save the historic structure. Alan Brown, headmaster of St. George's, saw a way to alleviate the overcrowding at his own school and arranged for the purchase and upgrading of the convent, thereby preserving the heritage building. When moving day arrived, it was St. George's students who helped with the move. Each year the alumnae of the convent return for a reunion in the old building.

▲ Shelagh O'Dwyer in her convent uniform, 1928. According to Lissa Forshaw, "The nuns were very particular as to how their students dressed and conducted themselves off the school grounds." Courtesy of Shelagh O'Dwyer.

IMMACULATE CONCEPTION SCHOOL

The school that was part of the Jesuit Immaculate Conception parish in Dunbar was established in the basement of the church in 1925 at the western end of 28th Avenue. The first principal was Mother Daly, who presided over 41 pupils in five grades. In 1932 an addition was built and two more grades were added. After Mother Daly resigned in 1948, a lay staff member took on her responsibilities. The Sisters of St. Ann took charge six years later, and in 1958 a new school building was constructed across the street. It served 310 students.

Jennifer Sweeney remembered the nuns before and after the reforms of Vatican II. "When I started Grade 1 in 1966, there were still nuns teaching in full habit. Sometime around Grade 2, after Vatican II, the nuns stopped wearing their habits and went back to their given names. Sister Mary John became Sister Janet Faulds. It was at that time that I realized that they were actually women, since I wasn't sure what their shape was under those habits. The year I graduated from Grade 7 in 1972, there were 20 kids in the class: 13 boys and 7 girls. This ratio was pretty consistent all the way from Grade 1."

Sweeney said there were several kids in her class from the Musqueam reserve. "I used to envy them because they got to ride the cool school bus to school and eat lunch in the lunchroom. I don't remember any racial tension at the school. I considered many of the kids from Musqueam as my friends." Her father, she said, was a big supporter of the school. "He donated barrel tables and stools that were assembled at Sweeney Cooperage for each classroom. He also had two large wooden signs made for the front of the school on 28th and the back on 27th."

Cathy Varsek, who attended the school until 1972, appreciated her teachers and the small class sizes. She remembered a fun class outing. "Mrs. Locke was a cool-looking sporty lady who once invited our class to her West End apartment at night to listen to the Beatles on her record player. Or was it the Rolling Stones? I felt so grown-up that evening. Also she had the coolest coloured beads hanging from the ceiling. They are now back in fashion."

The religious part of the curriculum means special attention is paid to Christmas and Easter. There is prayer three times a day, and Masses are held at the church on special occasions about once a month. However, many non-Catholic children attend. Linda (Chan) Fong explained her reasons for choosing the school for her sons. "I like the uniforms and the whole structure and discipline of the school. Besides the high academic standards, I also appreciate the parent participation program. There is a sense of community. You feel so welcome the minute you walk into the school. The teachers are very helpful and really make you feel that you are part of the teaching that goes on there." The demographics of the school, like those of the neighbourhood, have changed over time. Now 20 to 30 percent of the students are of Asian origin. Some students come by special bus from Richmond.

In September 2005, the new Immaculate Conception parish hall opened with a full gymnasium, so students no longer need to walk to the gym at the Dunbar Community Centre. The population of the school in 2006 was approximately 200 students.

ST. GEORGE'S SCHOOL

The original St. George's School was located in a large house at 3954 West 29th Avenue, between Wallace and Highbury. The founder and first headmaster was Captain Danby Hunter. The school opened in 1931 with 35 students and a teaching staff of six. In the first decade, a new wing was built with five classrooms, a chapel and a gymnasium. The students wore pith helmets, primarily because Danby Hunter had served in Mandalay.

Five acres of playing fields next to the University Endowment Lands, known as "Topside" (the future site of the senior school), were leased from the Jesuits. There the desirable pursuits of track and cricket were

◄ The interior of Hunter House, St. George's School, with house parents Audrey and Norman Folland and a visitor, c. 1953. Audrey described her duties: "Most of my boys were extremely polite and really no trouble at all. My duties were just to see that they behaved, and kept themselves and their clothes (especially uniforms) clean and tidy. One or two were homesick, and I did my best to comfort them, knowing only too well what they were feeling!" Courtesy of Norman Folland.

carried on. Soccer and baseball, the sports most common in the public schools, were not considered suitable for the elite, although rugby was played.

In the 1940s, the school purchased homes nearby to accommodate teachers and boarders. Norman and Audrey Folland from England described their life as house parents for student boarders beginning in 1953. Norman observed:

> The main building was built of timber and I must say was a little disappointing. We met Mr. Harker [then the headmaster], known to his friends as Johnny, with his lovely old dog. He was older than either of us expected — very much the product of the English public school! We soon discovered that St. George's emulated it in every way possible. There was a hidden agenda behind this. It appealed to families who wanted what they thought was the best for their sons — a strong, traditional, middle-class foundation, encouraging an elite society. To a large extent, I think the school succeeded in this end.

This narrow focus has widened as St. George's has become more multicultural.

In 1965, the new senior school was built on Topside, featuring 12 classrooms, a science block, a full-sized gym and a prayer hall used also for hot meals. Alan Brown became the youngest headmaster in 1971 and the

Schoolboys on caretaker Axel Mortonson's old Ford truck, behind the first St. George's School, 1955. Left to right: Christopher Fox, Jake Eckardt, John Black. Courtesy of Brian Wood. ▸

first old boy to assume this role. As has been mentioned, in 1979 he oversaw the purchase of the Convent of the Sacred Heart and the nine acres of property adjacent to it to house the Junior School and boarders' residence. This necessitated the sale of the 60 properties within the former site on 29th Avenue between Crown and Wallace. At that time Headmaster Brown thought that the enrollment figure, then 600, should be capped for good.

St. George's has always encouraged all aspects of a student's development. When Hitoshi Ujimoto became head of the senior dormitory in the old convent in 1994, he provided a variety of activities for the boarders' out-of-school time, such as canoe and rafting trips. These were designed to bring the kids together and "break the ice."

Ujimoto said that the teachers are expected to share their expertise in their spare time. An example is the bandleader, who must manage tours not only within B.C., but also to Washington and Europe. Ujimoto talked about a special teacher, Mr. Bowen, who in the 1980s brought an automobile engine into the school for dismantling and reassembling. "He was a talented man. He could build houses and he could build cars. He studied genetics at UBC. He was a master of everything, and he had all these other interests, and he could work with the kids. It's individual teachers bringing something of their personal experience to the school." The extracurricular activities and non-traditional events are often best remembered by students. Those students who had the good fortune of having a multi-talented teacher especially benefited.

Over time, some families chose to buy homes in Dunbar because of the presence of the school, while others were content with a long commute from as far away as North Vancouver or Richmond. The demographics have changed, according to Ujimoto. "Back in '74, . . . I would guess 90 percent B.C. and just a handful of offshore students. But today the numbers have turned the other way, so it would be higher than 90 percent from offshore." In 2006, the school population consisted of 1,100 students, 180 of them boarding at Harker Hall Residence.

CROFTON HOUSE SCHOOL FOR GIRLS

Crofton House School for Girls is the oldest private school of its kind west of Ontario. It was established in 1898 by Jessie Gordon and her sisters Edith and Mary in the Gordon home on Georgia Street in downtown Vancouver. Five students were enrolled. In 1901 the school moved to its own building on Jervis Street with 30 day students and five boarders.

During the late '30s, the West End of Vancouver was becoming a less satisfactory location for the school, and since many of the families had moved to the new Shaughnessy area and were attending schools there, enrollment was down. Funds were obtained to finance a move in 1942 to the southeast corner of 41st Avenue and Blenheim Street, where the 10-acre estate of the late Robert J. Cromie had been purchased from his widow for $15,000. The site had previously been owned at various times by Hugh Magee, Francis M. Chaldecott, Richard Byron Johnson and Alvo von Alvensleben.

The board of governors also bought the large Hambling House, a heritage building on West 41st Avenue, where Crofton Manor now stands, to handle the increased number of girls coming from Britain and across Canada during World War II. In the new location at Blenheim and 41st Avenue, classrooms were built, as well as a gym, a science lab and a "guide room." The latter later served as an assembly room for the entire school and as choir rehearsal space for the senior school. In the 1970s, Mr. Findlater, a well-known choral conductor and the last of a series of part-time music teachers, had difficulty keeping the nearly 200 girls in line. Deborah Jennings remembered being very naughty while rehearsing in the crowded room. She and her friends amused themselves by putting raisins on Mr. Findlater's shoes as they sat in front of him on the floor.

▲ Crofton House students and faculty outside their school in the West End, 1905. Courtesy of Beryl March.

Although non-denominational, the school has honoured Anglican traditions since its beginning. The annual Christmas Carol Service is still held. It began in St. Paul's Church then moved to Christ Church Cathedral in 1959. It is presently held in St. Andrew's Wesley Church to accommodate the entire school, alumnae, families and friends. By all accounts this is an impressive event, with the girls dressed in white berets and long white dresses that were worn on special occasions in the early '70s. As a student at this time, Jennings loved being a part of the event, from the rehearsals that began in September to the special day itself. Diana (Livingston) Filer of the class of 1950 commented about the daily prayers and hymn-singing: "Every morning we assembled in the gym for prayers and hymns. A very serious part of the day. We all stood. For the hymn, one of us played the piano, sometimes with trembling fingers. It was not seen as the eventual asset it would become of being able to make presentations to a large group of people." The daily rituals that were prevalent in the early years often had a lasting effect, as illustrated by this event.

Celebrations of the school's birthday are always held around March 1. Early in Crofton's history, this event was a celebration of Jessie Gordon's birthday in May. Since then it has been a chance for alumnae to assemble. The celebrations include a play or a musical and tours of the buildings.

Starting in the '80s, when the winds of freedom were blowing, staff found it increasingly difficult to accept responsibility for the boarders while day students were not so strictly supervised during off-school hours. As a result, the board of governors and the headmistress, Miss Addison (1970–90), decided to close the boarding component in 1990. That same year, the board embarked on an ambitious ongoing building program.

Throughout the school's history, maintaining high academic standards has remained important. As Jennings observed, "The best thing they did for me was to teach me how to learn, and when I got to university, I was miles ahead of everybody, because I knew the steps."

By 2006, enrollment stood at approximately 650 students. The old traditions have survived, but the school has been able to adjust to the times with a new curriculum and with continuing updating of the buildings and grounds.

The Growth Spurt, 1920s to 1950s

In 1922 better streetcar service helped attract more people to the Dunbar area. Dirt roads gave way to paved avenues, and bush-covered lots were replaced by newly constructed houses. At the same time, the city was experiencing an increase in the birth rate following World War I (and later World War II) that proved to be even greater than expected. The paint had hardly dried on one school before another was badly needed. In the Dunbar area six schools were built in this time period.

LANGARA ELEMENTARY SCHOOL

In 1921 the annex belonging to Lord Kitchener school at 14th Avenue and Highbury Street was moved to the northwest corner of 14th and Wallace Street. Lord Kitchener had been constructed to accommodate the increasing number of school-age children in the area. The new location soon proved inadequate. Faced with a large number of school-age children, Miss Hambly, Miss Allen and Miss Walker taught Grades 1 and 2 in a swing-shift arrangement so that one classroom could be shared by two classes.

A brick building constructed between 14th and 15th Avenues on Crown Street officially opened in mid-November 1926. Langara school, now with 11 classrooms, a library and an auditorium, was able to meet the needs of the elementary-school students in the area. The staff included a teaching principal, Mr. Shearman, seven full-time teachers and a part-time teacher shared with Lord Byng. Two downstairs classrooms were used by Lord Byng for manual training and home economics.

The auditorium with its raised stage and two dressing rooms was a notable feature of Langara, as few elementary schools possessed an auditorium at the time. By all accounts it was well used. Concerts were held every year to raise funds for extra items such as a piano and supplementary readers. The concerts were so heavily supported that often two nights were required to accommodate the large number of patrons. A music specialist was added to the staff in 1928, resulting in an emphasis on musical training, the staging of operettas and regular entries to the annual Kiwanis music festival. Although the auditorium has since been converted to a gym, the original fir floor was still in use 80 years after it was installed.

The new Langara Elementary School attracted some young, dedicated teachers. An example was Mildred Osterhout (later Farney), who taught from 1926 to 1930. Marion (Tulloch) Funell remarked that Miss Osterhout was a favourite teacher of her younger sister, Connie (Tulloch) Sluggett. "Miss Osterhout kept animals in the classroom, some canaries and white mice, and would let various members of the class bring them home for the weekend. My sister loved animals."

Osterhout eventually left teaching to pursue studies in political science and to work and travel in developing countries. During her lifetime as a social reformer and peace activist, she studied and worked with the likes of Mahatma Gandhi and Martin Luther King. No doubt some of her ideals had been passed on to her students at Langara.

Daryl (Muir) Rankine attended Langara from 1937 until 1940. After viewing her Grade 1 class photo and reflecting on her school days at Lan-

▲ Page from the MacLean Method of Writing compendium used by students from the 1920s to the 1960s. Good penmanship was stressed during this time. Courtesy of Nancy Johnson.

Nakajima Shogakko

A wholly different school was the Nakajima Shogakko, which Japanese families created shortly after their arrival in the late nineteenth century. The children who attended Nakajima Shogakko prior to 1911 were educated similarly to students in Japan, for many Japanese immigrants viewed their presence in this country as temporary. As they became more comfortable in their new country, they began to establish permanent residency and sent their children to public schools.

The teachers at Nakajima Shogakko during the 1920s then took on the important role of teaching the Japanese language. Each day after attending classes at Kerrisdale school, the Japanese-Canadian students walked home and attended Japanese-language class for two hours. An average monthly fee of $1.50 was charged for each student.

A building on the Celtic Cannery site was designated as a second Japanese-language school for the children of the Japanese-Canadian cannery workers in 1925. By 1940

about 35 families of Japanese descent made their homes in Blenheim Flats, mostly on the Celtic Cannery site and along the waterfront. They were interned and forced to leave in 1942, after the War Measures Act was invoked.

The Nakajima Shogakko (Middle Island Community School) on Deering Island in Southlands, c. 1915. Courtesy of Satoru Azakawa.

gara, Rankine commented on the lack of visible ethnic groups. "Sure, there was a Jewish family and a Greek family but that was about it. Even the children who went to Catholic schools were separate in the neighbourhood, and basically played with each other. It was a narrow focus." Rankine remembered how the effects of war, in the form of rationing and air raid drills, could be felt in her own school and neighbourhood, remote from any war zone. A Japanese family in the area "just disappeared."

In 1940, Langara students moved to the new Queen Elizabeth school (see page 288), while junior high students from Lord Byng moved into their former building. In 1978, in response to the government's interest in making Canada more bilingual, Langara was made home to Lord Byng French immersion. When the school was named Jules Quesnel, two long-time residents of the area, Margaret Cook and Marion Funell, wrote to the Vancouver School Board requesting that the name Langara be kept for historical reasons. The reply was to the effect that a French school should have a French name. However, even though the wooden sign over the entranceway to the school states "Ecole Jules Quesnel," underneath, engraved in stone, is the name "Langara."

LORD BYNG SECONDARY SCHOOL

In the early 1920s, students in the Dunbar area attended either Prince of Wales high school (on King Edward Avenue between Marguerite and Alexandra Streets) or Magee high school (on Maple Street between 45th and 49th Avenues). However, these schools soon became overcrowded and it became apparent that a new high school was needed.

In 1923, the Department of Education granted the Point Grey School Board 10 acres of uncleared land between Wallace and Crown Streets on 16th Avenue. On this site, on 28 July 1924, Lord Julian Byng, the governor general of Canada, laid the cornerstone for the new building. Previously, a contest had been held among the students to select a name for the new high school. The names of the eight students who chose "Lord Byng" were sealed in the cornerstone.

Since the school was not ready in September 1924, the students attended classes in a temporary building on the grounds of Lord Kitchener Elementary. On 12 March 1925, Lord Byng was officially opened by John Oliver, the premier of British Columbia, who also declared the day a holiday for the 122 students enrolled. The 12-room brick and concrete structure was completed for $90,000. The cost of equipment and furnishings was $9,600.

The first five staff members at Lord Byng were men, providing a contrast to the predominantly female elementary-school teachers. William Morrow was the principal and remained at Lord Byng until 1951. Teachers at this time tended to stay for many years, providing a measure of stabil-

◄ Governor General Lord Byng was presented with a silver trowel and rosewood mallet in the ceremony of the laying of the cornerstone at Lord Byng school on 28 July 1924. His speech began, "Nationhood is built on education and its surroundings." Courtesy of Lord Byng Secondary School.

The chalkboard shows Greek text including declensions:

G. πατρός
D. πατρί
A. πατέρα
V. πάτερ
D.N.A.V. πατέρε
G.D. πατέροιν
P. N.V. πατέρες
G. πατέρων
D. πατράσι
A. πατέρας

1. ὁ ἄρχων τοῖς Ἕλλησιν ἡγεμόνα ἔπεμπεν.
2. τοῦτον τὸν ἄνδρα ὠφέλει ἵνα φίλον ἔχοι.
3. ἀγῶνα δὲ ἐποιήσαντο οἱ Ἕλληνες.
4. ταύτῃ ... μεθ᾽ ἡγεμόνος ἐπορεύοντο,
5. ἡ δὲ ... ον ἀποπέμπει πάλιν ἐπὶ τὴν ἀρχήν·

▲ Lord Byng teacher Marion Lawrence, 1929, in her classroom where she taught Greek. She also taught Latin, coached grass hockey and was the girls' counsellor during her long career at Byng. Courtesy of Lord Byng Secondary School.

ity. Walter Putnam was one such teacher, whom Shirley (Yeo) Church remembered as being appreciated by his students. "He was a marvellous teacher, a wonderful teacher. In 1942 when I was in Grade 12, the school annual was dedicated to Mr. Putnam. He wasn't retiring, there was nothing special; it was just that the Grade 12 students thought he was pretty special. And he was very, very moved. He got a copy of the annual, and he looked at that, and left the classroom in a big hurry! It was very interesting." In a time when teachers were basically aloof from their students, Mr. Putnam managed to bridge this gap and gain the trust and admiration of his students. He was aptly rewarded for this.

Miss Lawrence, who taught at Lord Byng for 39 years until her retirement in 1966, was an avid supporter of girls' activities. She organized a group called the Girls' Executive that sponsored many social and service activities, such as Poppy Day, the Christmas Cheer drive and the spring tea, providing girls with leadership opportunities.

In the early 1930s reforms and revisions were implemented in the B.C. high-school system to make courses more relevant to the needs of the students and to decrease the dropout rate. The staff of Lord Byng responded with some innovative ideas that were to be in effect for many decades. In 1936 the students had individual timetables, instead of being grouped into classes, allowing them to select courses based on their interests and future goals. Promotion was by subject and not by grade, as it had been in the past.

Another progressive idea was an annual vocational conference. People in various professions and jobs were invited to the school to provide students with information and an opportunity to ask questions about their work. Helen (Hurlston) Thom credits this experience in the early '50s with fostering her interest in social work, which she eventually followed as a career.

The population of Lord Byng increased rapidly. By 1936 there were 841 students. A new wing was built that year to accommodate the extra students. However, the space soon became inadequate, for more than 1,000 students were enrolled in 1940. In this same year Lord Byng moved into the Langara building to start a junior high school, while Langara students moved to Queen Elizabeth school.

The social side of school life was an important aspect. Sheila Smyth, who arrived from England in 1956, gave her impressions of the social scene at Lord Byng:

> There I was, fresh to Canada from London, England, wearing navy serge shorts, from which protruded my knobby knees, faced with a crowd of buxom 13-year-olds in poodle skirts and white bucks. I had never heard of rock 'n' roll and was not interested in boys or baseball. It was culture shock but, so innocent was I, I didn't even know it. The different social groups in the school were so exotic to me, I didn't mind being one of the "out" kids — or even really knew what that meant. I gazed in awe at the kids in angora sweaters and carefully applied make-

▲ Members of the Lord Byng string orchestra with teacher Sherie Wilson, 1995. The school has had a reputation for its excellent fine arts, drama and music program. Courtesy of Lord Byng Secondary School.

up. The "hoods" in black leather with their girlfriends in skirts so tight they could barely sit down seemed to be something out of a movie.

Another important part of high-school life was the various clubs that allowed students to follow or develop interests. However, club activities have decreased in recent years. Claire Wensveen, class of 2003, offered some reasons for this change. "Kids these days have more to do outside of school, like taking different classes and such. I would say about a half of my class have part-time jobs. At lunchtime most of us have cars or friends with cars so we go out for lunch or to someone's house." Former clubs, such as photography and drama, are now offered as part of the coursework.

Sports, on the other hand, have remained a large part of life at Lord Byng. The school is noted for fielding strong rugby, basketball, soccer and field hockey teams. Being a member of a team can promote lifelong bonds, as evidenced by the 1958 senior boys basketball team. They have stayed in touch and for the past 35 years have enjoyed a yearly get-together at Yellow Point Lodge on Vancouver Island.

In 2006 there were approximately 1,230 students enrolled at Lord Byng. A second gymnasium was completed in 2002. An addition was completed in 2003, designed to provide space for the thriving arts program. Lord Byng Pool, under the auspices of the Vancouver Park Board, was added in 1974.

QUEEN ELIZABETH ELEMENTARY SCHOOL

In 1940 the Vancouver School Board, faced with a rapidly increasing enrollment, decided that an additional elementary school was needed. A site at Camosun and 16th Avenue was selected for the building of an elementary school, Queen Elizabeth, named after the current queen at the time, wife of King George VI.

The chosen site posed some concerns for the school administration. Since the land was part of the University Endowment Lands, a 99-year lease had to be obtained from the provincial government. Another obstacle was that the site was part of a huge swamp. However, truckloads of earth were brought in and workers on relief were employed to fill in the swampy sections, allowing construction to proceed. The total cost of this project was $88,000, funded by a loan from the federal government, an amazing financial accomplishment considering that it was wartime and Canada was still feeling the effects of the Depression.

The design of Queen Elizabeth school was a radical departure from the usual three-storey brick school building. The plan was the result of a visit to Great Britain by the superintendent of schools, Mr. H.N. Mac-Corkindale, and was based on the cottage type of school. Former student Frank Robertson states, "It blended in with the community, with lawns and gardens and a nice roofline." Many flower beds featuring colourful blooms, particularly roses, and exotic evergreens were part of the exterior design. On a least seven different occasions, Queen Elizabeth school won the Kiwanis garden contest held each year in the Point Grey area.

◄ The cottage-style design of Queen Elizabeth school was chosen so the building would blend in with the rest of the neighbourhood. Courtesy of Joan Tyldesley.

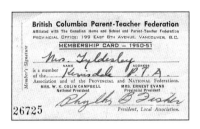

▲ Since 1917, parent-teacher associations in Vancouver have spent many hours on behalf of children. The establishment by the Ministry of Education of school planning councils in each school in 2002 formally acknowledged the importance of parental involvement. Courtesy of Joan Tyldesley.

The new school consisted of 10 classrooms, a library, an art room, a regulation gymnasium and a separate auditorium complete with stage and dressing rooms. Some of the classrooms were designated for science and manual training and were equipped with tables and chairs instead of desks. Two primary rooms with a common small library and separate washrooms were another innovation. This deviation from the traditional design reflected a change in school philosophy, where students moved around throughout the day to receive specialized teaching in various subjects.

Although Queen Elizabeth school was not officially opened until 5 April 1940, on 21 March, Langara students walked the three blocks to their newly assigned rooms at Queen Elizabeth, carrying their textbooks and school supplies. Barbara (Allan) Forbes, a Grade 1 student at Langara, made the trek and remembered her introduction to her new school:

> It had dark-brown siding on its lower half and sparkling white stucco on the upper part, new and clean, light-brown wooden shingles and large shiny windows. There was a huge playground fenced in by green two-by-fours, the top one placed at an angle (we thought to prevent people from sitting on it). . . . We were all very excited. We noticed very few people around. One gentleman I do recall. He had on a grey suit and smiled to us as we walked in. He turned out to be our principal, Mr. Shearman. We loved the smell of the newly oiled floors and the feel of the shiny new wooden seats when we sat down. The blackboards and new brushes and the long white sticks of chalk were almost too much for some of us to handle. There was even coloured chalk!

To mark this auspicious occasion Barbara and her classmates, under the direction of their teacher, Miss Hambly, made butter by shaking jars of cream that they later spread on crumbly crackers as part of their first activity in their new classroom.

Since a great deal of equipment had been left at Langara, the school population faced the immediate challenge of raising money for new equipment. The parent-teacher association, with a membership of 376 (making it the largest PTA in the province), played a major role in this endeavour. So popular was the Queen Elizabeth PTA that many of the original members continued to hold executive positions well after their children had left the school and they themselves had become grandmothers. A motion was passed in 1949 restricting executive positions to parents whose children were currently enrolled. Involvement with the PTA during the '40s and '50s was an outlet for women to develop and use leadership and organizational skills.

The PTA, by organizing whist drives and working with teachers to stage concerts and operettas, collected enough money over six years to purchase equipment that included one of the first public address systems in a Vancouver school. In 1945, in keeping with the trend of the times to a

more progressive school philosophy, coloured prints of the world's art masterpieces were hung in the hallways to foster an appreciation of art. Two of these prints still hang in the school today, albeit behind a closed door leading to the boiler room.

Queen Elizabeth's enrollment continued to grow. An addition built in 1957 greatly reduced the then available playground area, but a spacious area to the west was developed as a playground. In 1964 enrollment reached 760 pupils. This increase was largely due to the retention of Grade 7 students, a policy common to all elementary schools. Even though the annex located near 25th Avenue and Crown Street was opened in 1964, two portable classrooms were still necessary to accommodate all the students.

An open-area classroom was established at Queen Elizabeth for Grade 6 and 7 students in the 1980s. Two teachers were in charge of one large classroom consisting of about 60 students. John Richmond, one of the open-area teachers at the school, said this idea was in response to one group of Grade 7 students who displayed disruptive behaviour and were not functioning well as a group. He explained that through "lots of parent participation, . . . counselling techniques and community involvement, the students eventually learned that it was possible to work and learn together." The program was deemed a success and remains a feature of the school, although standard Grade 6 and 7 classes are also an

▲ Year-end performance, c. 1944, at Queen Elizabeth school that raised $350, of which $150 was donated to the Red Cross. One of the aims of the PTA was "to foster high ideals of true citizenship and patriotism." Courtesy of Margaret Moore.

option. Although many aspects of Queen Elizabeth school life have changed with the times, innovative responses to various situations and active parent participation have remained the school's cornerstones.

KERRISDALE/SOUTHLANDS ANNEX

The first school to open in Dunbar's south slope area was originally known as Kerrisdale Annex. Built in 1939 at 38th and Crown, it was a wood-frame building with four classrooms and administration rooms built around a central indoor courtyard. In the final year of the Great Depression, Henry Clyde Redmond, a Dunbar builder who had not had a job for 10 years, was awarded the contract. The annex had the feeling of a rural school, because 38th Avenue was a dirt road and there were few houses in the vicinity. Since the school had no telephone, the closest neighbours took the calls. Later, the staff had to go outdoors from the meeting room to enter the office when the newly connected phone was ringing. Eventually a hole was cut in the wall. Miss Grace Robb was the first head teacher and was later joined by women who became well known, including Mary Pack, who worked to found the Arthritis Society of B.C.

In 1952, when Southlands Elementary School was built nearby to house Grades 3 to 6, Kerrisdale Annex was renamed Southlands Annex. At this time Musqueam children were still attending residential school. However, former band chief Gertrude Guerin lobbied to have her two children accepted into the regular public school system. The authorities in the Department of Indian Affairs wanted to send them to a residential school, but Mrs. Guerin would not hear of it and appealed to Miss Robb. Finally she received permission from the school board to enroll Diane and Janet at the Southlands Annex. "Gertie," as she was called, went on to become a member on the executive board of the Southlands PTA, president of the Point Grey Secondary PTA and a member of the PTA council.

Janet Tomkins attended Southlands Annex in the early '60s. She remembered that one kindergarten class had a sandbox and hers did not, but apart from that inequity, kindergarten was a pleasant experience. One of her Grade 1 memories was not so positive. A boy in her class was humiliated in front of the class because he couldn't read the word "valentine," a scenario that would appall teachers today. The strap was a constant threat during the '60s, as Muriel (Schofield) Pacheco recalled. "The most dominant memory of that time was of Miss Barker getting angry and pulling out a black leather strap and whipping the desk in front of me with it, as well as the times when she took out boys from the class to strap them."

Point Grey resident Ehleen (Bohn) Hinze was a Grade 1 student at the annex. She remembered walking to school from her home on Chaldecott Street with her friends. Hinze had the perfect idea for a gift for her

teacher, Miss Rose. She brought a big jar with holes punched in the lid and placed in it several yellow flowers from the school's rock garden, along with about 20 ladybugs, which seemed to like living on the flowers. Unfortunately the holes were too big and all the ladybugs escaped onto Miss Rose's desk, causing the teacher to become quite distressed.

In 1970, to recognize the fact that there were several children at the school from the Musqueam reserve, one of the elders, Dominic Point, was asked to carve a totem pole for the school. It was installed in the adventure playground designed by resident Cornelia Oberlander and constructed by parents over two weekends. After someone thought it would be fun to try to remove it, the pole was moved inside. When the school was demolished in 1982 because of declining enrollment, the pole was returned to the Musqueam Band.

SOUTHLANDS ELEMENTARY SCHOOL

Laura de Jong, who had moved with her family to Dunbar near Camosun and 38th after the war, saw the need for an elementary school so that the pupils from Kerrisdale Annex could attend one closer to home. The school board was not listening to appeals by parents of children attending the annex. By chance de Jong discovered how Queen Elizabeth school had been built on land leased from the University Endowment Lands, and she organized the local parents in a campaign to establish the school on leased land at the south end of Camosun. A widely circulated petition convinced the school board, and Southlands Elementary opened in the fall of 1952.

Ehleen (Bohn) Hinze remembered Mr. Cameron, the Grade 6/7 teacher, who was a square dance caller. He organized a square dance group

The Miniature Market set up at Southlands Annex in the 1950s was both a practical and fun method for students to learn how to handle money. Courtesy of Vancouver School Board. ▶

that met at 8:00 A.M. once a week. He also began a tradition during the holiday season of reading Dickens' *Christmas Carol* at lunchtime, rattling a chain and climbing up and down the gym's wooden steps to represent Marley's ghost. In later years, the principal Mr. Wark carried on the tradition, captivating another generation.

Janet Tomkins, an unwilling observer to the bias of one of her teachers, witnessed the following incident concerning a Musqueam student at Southlands:

> I remember an incident in Grade 5 or 6 when we were switching rooms with another class. A Native boy in the other class made some kind of smart-alecky comment when told to let the girls go first. In response, the male teacher stood the boy in front of our class after asking him to get a paddle out of the closet — I believe that it was, in fact, an artifact of Native culture that this boy's own brother had given the teacher as a gift a year or two previously. The boy was then made to bend over and was whacked with appalling force.

Tomkins said she recalled the incident vividly and feels sure, in retrospect, that this abuse would not have been perpetrated on a white child. She had high praise for her Grade 7 teacher, Mr. Butchart. "He was not popular in the usual sense, and was tough and demanding, but he took teaching very seriously and treated us with respect."

In the late '60s it was still common for the boys to have use of the soccer field at recess, while the girls were relegated to a small corner of the playground. Dresses or skirts for the girls were the required dress, but finally on a particularly cold winter's day, the principal solemnly announced that girls would be allowed to wear slacks while the cold spell lasted.

In 1985 Valerie Jerome, a track star and lover of nature, came to Southlands to teach. Jerome, like her famous brother Harry Jerome, was interested in running, but perhaps her greatest influence was assisting the students to address community issues and to implement change. Jerome took the students into the adjacent Endowment Lands and showed them how important it was to save the forest from being built over by developers and the university. To show the children how a sculpture was created, she took the class to the Jack Harmon Foundry on Alexander Street to see the casting of the commemorative statue of her late brother, a champion sprinter, which was erected near the Stanley Park seawall.

As part of that exercise, the children became involved in trying to save the foundry from demolition. Unfortunately they were not as successful as they had been in helping to save the University Endowment Lands

◄ Southlands teacher Valerie Jerome and members of her class on a field trip in the University Endowment Lands, 1987. Her students became engaged in a campaign to save the lands in their natural state. Seated (left to right): David Harakal, Wendy Fukushima, Patrick Corney, Wade Grant. Standing (left to right): Miles Galbraith, Valerie Jerome, Kristina Cockle. Courtesy of Valerie Jerome.

from development. The class had actively solicited the support of the mayor and city council in that fight. Their efforts were recognized in 1989 when Pacific Spirit Park was created, and the members of the class were invited to the legislature buildings in Victoria. Unfortunately the class members did not attend as they were dispersed in different secondary schools and classes by this time. Reflecting on her short time at Southlands, Jerome said she felt that parents at Southlands were very supportive of everything she did.

In 1997, the school completed a project that greatly enhanced the look of the school's front. Marilyn Morrow, one of those who worked on the landscaping, commented on the project: "We got started when a representative from one of those 'greening' organizations came by the school to speak to the parents advisory council. Their timing must have been right, because the idea just took off." Now planters, trees, a native plant garden and seating areas create a more welcome look. The city collaborated by planting more trees near the street.

In April 2003, the parents, staff and students of Southlands staged a large event to celebrate the 50th anniversary of the school. In spite of rain the school was alive with enthusiastic alumni and other visitors. Almost all the former principals assembled for a group photo to commemorate the occasion.

Little Houses in the Woods, 1960s

Queen Elizabeth Annex and Kerrisdale Annex were built to alleviate overcrowding at the main schools when Grade 7 students became part of the elementary school system in 1964. Although attending kindergarten was not mandatory, parents appreciated the advantages, and during the late 1960s it became more the rule than the exception to enroll five-year-olds in public school kindergartens, resulting in a greater number of elementary students.

Both annexes are in parklike settings. Queen Elizabeth Annex is situated at the edge of Pacific Spirit Park, and Kerrisdale Annex overlooks Malkin Park. Architecturally, they were designed to blend in with their surroundings. Each offers a small, protective environment that many feel is a good pedagogical setting for primary-age students.

QUEEN ELIZABETH ANNEX

Parlez-vous français? This question may get a positive response at Queen Elizabeth Annex, located on Crown Street across from Chaldecott Park. This one-storey school of approximately 130 students was officially opened on 18 November 1964. A choice of either French immersion or English was offered in the mid-'70s.

◄ The playground equipment at Queen Elizabeth Annex in its woodland setting encouraged dramatic and imaginative play. Photo c. 1970s. Courtesy of Vancouver School Board.

A distinctive physical feature of the annex is its wooden playground equipment interspersed among the tall trees, blending in with the natural environment. Charlotte Stenberg, who attended Queen Elizabeth Annex in the 1980s, remembered the playground as having the feeling of being in the woods. "We thought it was pretty adventurous." She also remembered a favourite lunchtime activity. "Chicken fighting is when there is a log down, and you have two people standing across the log, and you go towards the middle and try to throw the other person off. There were a bunch of logs in the back and we used to do that. There were also monkey bars that you could climb across."

Stenberg, who was in the French immersion program, remembered speaking French all the time in school, but when the students played together after school they spoke English only. She also recalled caring teachers and the warm, friendly atmosphere of the annex.

Another former student, Jeremy McDaniels, who attended the annex in the 1990s, recalled the annex as having a "fantastic" educational climate. "To me the annex is what all elementary schools should be like. Some days I regretted leaving that school at the end of the day. It was like I was leaving a relative's home." He described a favourite teacher: "I still regard Ms. Stock as one of the coolest teachers. Throughout my Grade 3 year, I learned a lot from Ms. Stock, not just the curriculum. For example, even now I try as hard as I can not to use the word 'nice.' Ms. Stock hated the word and had a chart of other words to use in its place on her wall." McDaniels said the class did a number of "amazing" projects, some of the highlights being an attempt at a philosophy paper and a project on electric guitars.

Present-day students have an opportunity to be involved in such extra-curricular activities as jazz dance, chess, theatre sports and choir, which are offered in the school by the Dunbar Community Centre for a nominal fee. The nurturing and stimulating environment of this school as well as the choice of French immersion have made Queen Elizabeth Annex popular with both students and parents.

KERRISDALE ANNEX

Nestled between Malkin Park and Crofton House School, Kerrisdale Annex, with the same name as the annex built at 38th Avenue and Crown, was built in 1965 for kindergarten to Grade 3 students. At times, Grade 4 students have also been included. The California-style facility features six classrooms, a library resource centre and an office area, all constructed around two open courtyards. A gymnasium/lunchroom on the lower level has served as an extra classroom during times of increased enrollment.

Kerrisdale Annex has always had active parent involvement due to the openness of the architectural design and to the school's small size, which helps to create a family-like setting. Rea MacNeil, who was the head teacher from 1973 until 1979, elaborated: "During the early 1970s it was decided that it was in the best interests of the school to hire teachers who shared a similar educational philosophy. This resulted in a more cohesively operated school. The parents, who were typically well-educated professionals or business people, were very knowledgeable and knew what they

Kerrisdale Annex, c. 1970. Underground streams make for a muddy playing field, and students were encouraged to change into indoor shoes to help keep the school clean. Courtesy of Joyce Bromley. ▶

wanted: innovation and state-of-the-art education for their children in a safe and caring environment. They trusted us and we delivered!"

Sherry Abramson, a teacher at Kerrisdale Annex in the early 1980s, said: "The parents were really an integral part of the program. For example, one was the head of anatomy at UBC. He brought in all his stuff — brains in a bottle, etc. — so kids could ask questions. Almost every parent contributed." Abramson gave another example of how parents enriched the curriculum and supported teachers. "One time when we were studying the Inuit, Janis Podmore, who was very active at the annex, brought some caribou and muskox meat to the classroom, which she cooked so that everyone got to try it. There was always something. It was fabulous, the best school I've ever taught in, just because of the strong support and how everyone shared things all the time." Parents today have continued to take an active role in the parents advisory council, a safe arrival program, and as parent crossing-guards, volunteer drivers, classroom assistants and library volunteers.

New Learning Environments, 1970s into the Twenty-first Century

Although there have always been innovative and talented teachers, it took some time for the educational system at large to become more challenging and student-oriented. *The Putman-Weir Report*, published in 1925, proposed a shift from the formal educational practices then current to more progressive methods where students would not be subjected to "intellectual apathy." This change was gradually implemented, and today's students are more likely to experience projects and field trips instead of long lectures and exhaustive note-taking, informal desk arrangements instead of straight rows, talking through problems instead of harsh disciplinary tactics, the use of technology, and a variety of materials instead of just paper and pen in an austere classroom.

Specialized programs are now available where students can tap into their particular learning style, needs and interests. Many Dunbar secondary students go outside their area to attend schools that host special programs, such as the Point Grey Mini School, Prince of Wales Secondary School, or Winston Churchill with its French immersion and baccalaureate program.

JULES QUESNEL FRENCH IMMERSION SCHOOL

In 1963, the federal government began to promote bilingualism and urged the provinces to follow suit. At this time, the only French program in the Dunbar area was a privately run French-only kindergarten. In the mid-'70s Queen Elizabeth Annex began a bilingual program that went to

Even before kindergartens were part of the school system, young children had the opportunity to attend preschools in Dunbar. Hilda Catherall, a former teacher raising her family in Dunbar just after World War II, was asked by neighbourhood friends to start a kindergarten. "I had 10 children in the sunroom in my kitchen. First we had to get a licence from the city. They came and inspected my house as to lavatories, how many I had and tidiness and cleanliness. My husband, who was an industrial arts teacher, built a lot of furniture and play equipment. He made puzzles and toys because these things weren't available after the war."

Grade 3. Then in 1978 a French immersion program was started for intermediate students. Classes were held in part of the old Langara school that had been used by Lord Byng school. At that time two kindergarten classes were taught by Yolande Levasseur. In 1981 the annex began to send its graduating Grade 3 students to what was called the Lord Byng French immersion program. In 1985 parents and students chose the name of Jules Quesnel for the school, to honour the explorer who had been on Simon Fraser's expedition in 1808.

The school had no secretary for the first couple of years and there was no photocopier. Materials in French were not readily available, and the teachers had to create many of their own classroom materials. Nevertheless, right from the beginning the staff were enthusiastic and created an exciting learning environment for the children. One parent, Dell Whelan, said she and her husband took French for parents so they could understand their daughters. They were enthusiastic supporters of French immersion all the way through high school at Kitsilano secondary.

In 2006 the school had 400 students registered, indicating a strong interest in French immersion. Parents and students alike report that the students with French find jobs easily after graduation, some leading to employment or advanced study in Quebec, England and France.

Educating for the Future

As inkwells have given way to computers, educational attitudes and practices have also changed. Today's schools place a greater emphasis on empowering children and preparing them for the challenges of the future. The humanizing approach recognizes and values the rights of students. Experiences such as that of Leslie (Adam) Harlow, who on her first day in Grade 1 had to stand in the corner because she was humming, are a thing of the past. The days of corporal punishment have also happily disappeared.

Another major change is the increased ethnic and racial diversity of the student population in the Dunbar area. Until the 1980s, little evidence of multiculturalism existed. An incident told by Eunice (Wilson) Liversidge can be viewed as history that is unlikely to be repeated. "I had just arrived from Scotland and on my first day as a Grade 1 student in 1948 at Lord Kitchener, I was taken to the other classrooms in the school so the children could hear my Scottish accent." Such differences are much better accepted in the twenty-first century.

The main focus of early Dunbar schools was to give students a thorough grounding in the three R's. As the job market in the post-war years demanded more diverse skills, the schools responded by offering specialized courses. During the 1960s and 1970s the emphasis was on treating the student as an individual. Students were often grouped according to their learning abilities. Learning assistance was created for those with learning difficulties, and enrichment programs were offered for those who were gifted. Innovative educational strategies such as Cuisinaire rods for learning arithmetic, whole-language programs and literature-based reading programs were introduced. During the 1980s and 1990s some of these strategies were either modified or discarded. At the beginning of the twenty-first century a wide assortment of programs are available to Dunbar students, ranging from French immersion to outdoor educational experiences to special fine arts courses.

The most serious problem facing schools today stems from budget cutbacks, which have affected programs and services as well as physical infrastructure. Resource people such as librarians, counsellors, psychologists and specialists in English as a second language and special needs have had both their resources and their time limited due to funding restrictions. The composition of classes, involving the number of special needs students, and class size are issues of ongoing public dialogue.

Some of the Dunbar schools, such as Kerrisdale school, have undergone much-needed seismic upgrading, but there is still more modernization and maintenance to be done. This updating can be especially challenging when a choice has to be made between preserving heritage features at more cost or simply improving the situation at a lesser cost. Private schools in the area have fared better in this regard. The challenge in the twenty-first century is to provide schools that are safe, well equipped and have sufficient well-trained teachers and resource people to help students confidently face the future.

The role of parents in the schools has also evolved. The parent-teacher associations of the early institutions were mainly concerned with raising money for the school through hot dog sales and concerts. Parent advisory councils since the 1970s have had a greater say in school matters. Tracey Dafoe, a school board liaison member for eight West Side schools, explained: "Parents today are quite a bit more demanding. They have high standards and expect things to be better. They have quite a bit of voice on the administration of the school."

Through the decades the schools of Dunbar have tried to keep pace with the changes in society and in their community. Although educational practices and student demographics may have changed, many traditions have continued. Private school students can still be seen in uniforms. Individual school colours, logos and mottoes still play a part in encouraging school spirit. Events such as sports days, concerts and assemblies have kept their place on school calendars. Students maintain a close relationship with their peers and teachers and, when they graduate, take with them enduring memories of their Dunbar school days.

CHAPTER 10

Neighbourhood Churches

⁓ Vivien Clarke

For many people, churches are places for spiritual and social fellow-ship. For others, they are primarily unique buildings and facilities that provide community services. No matter how they are regarded, churches are a significant part of a neighbourhood's historical landscape. They also reflect changing social demographics and values. Dunbar's places of worship are no exception. Of the seven churches that have sur-vived into the twenty-first century, some have celebrated their 50th anni-versary, others their 75th. All are re-evaluating their place in society and contemplating the role of spirituality in both an increasingly complex global world and a changed neighbourhood.

This chapter focuses on nine churches, all founded in the twentieth century by members of mainstream Christian denominations. This is un-derstandable when one considers that apart from the First Nations, the population in Dunbar/Southlands up to 1950 was almost entirely of northern European descent. The area's increasingly multicultural profile has had an impact on local church attendance and survival. Recent immi-grants, especially those of Asian descent, often go outside the neighbour-hood to find religious services in their native languages.

Churches were once an integral part of community life. Now they are regarded by many as peripheral. The founders of Dunbar's churches were not only interested in building places of worship, but also in

◄ Going to church at Marineview Chapel, West 41st Avenue at Crown Street, 1 December 1974. Photo by Gordon Croucher, *Vancouver Province* newspaper. Courtesy of Marineview Chapel.

providing Sunday schools for children who would hopefully carry on the religious traditions of their parents. Today many young people are growing up with little if any formal religious or spiritual instruction. Several Dunbar churches, such as Marineview Chapel, have young people and families attending, but these may be transient, moving on once the adults have completed their studies at UBC. For some of the smaller churches, such as Dunbar Evangelical Lutheran Church, it is a struggle to replenish the dwindling number of aging parishioners with younger members. And small congregations provide less money for maintenance or improvements.

Although all of Dunbar's churches were planned to provide or house community as well as church-oriented activities, nowadays the Dunbar Community Centre, local schools and social service agencies have taken over many of the churches' outreach functions. As a result, many residents never set foot in a church facility, unless it has become a voting station or a venue for a community event, such as Artists in Our Midst. Despite the challenges of aging congregations and a lack of funds, many of those who attend or support Dunbar's churches are determined to carry on, to make churches more relevant, to build upon the legacy of church founders. Dunbar's churches have deep roots that will help them to weather the challenges of the twenty-first century.

Knox United Church

In the early summer of 1910, David Gray, a student minister delegated to establish a missionary branch, held the first Presbyterian service in the area. Twenty-five people attended the service, held on the veranda of the home of Mr. and Mrs. William Ross, just west of Yew Street and 41st Avenue (then known as Wilson Road). These home services continued for several weeks, until permission was obtained from the municipal council to use a room in the Wilson Road Public School, on the current site of Kerrisdale Elementary School, free of charge until a more permanent facility could be constructed. According to a chronology of the church's Women's Auxiliary written by Mrs. R.B. MacIntosh in 1935, "The women met together and devised many ways of raising money for the Building Fund, to which their husbands had already contributed. They gave concerts, Teas and Dinners."

This new congregation assembled under the name of Kerrisdale Presbyterian Church. A few years later the name was changed to Knox Presbyterian to honour the Scottish religious reformer John Knox. A frame building with a seating capacity of 250, a full basement and a Sunday school was constructed on the southeast corner of West 42nd Avenue and Macdonald Street in 1911, on land offered by Frank Bowser. This served the practical needs of the congregation for many years.

◀ Knox United Church in 1999.
Courtesy of Vic Stevenson.

By 1914, missionary work had become especially important. The annual report of the church's Ladies Aid Society submitted by Agnes M. Stewart in 1914 confirms this focus. It also reflects the effect of war on everyday life. "At the time that our society was organized we made a rule that there should be only bread and butter or biscuit and one kind of cake served. This has not always been adhered to and we would like to emphasize this rule at this time when economy is so much needed. At our thankoffering meeting we were very pleased to have the Rev. Mr. Scott who sailed the following week to Korea, the first foreign missionary to go from Westminster Hall [the Presbyterian Theological Seminary situated in the West End of Vancouver]."

In 1925 the majority of the congregation became part of the new United Church of Canada. Those who wished to remain Presbyterian resolved to erect their own building on Trafalgar Street and call their congregation by its original name, Kerrisdale Presbyterian. The remaining congregation chose the name Knox United Church, and then in 1927–28 decided to build farther west, owing to the fact that Ryerson United was located nearby. Initially, a large Sunday school and gymnasium were built in the 5600 block Balaclava Street at 39th Avenue to accommodate the growing congregation. Although more like an auditorium, this building was constantly in use for meetings, dances, socials and basketball games during the week, and for church services on Sundays. In the 1940s and '50s, it echoed to the sounds of the church's operatic society performing Gilbert and Sullivan operettas (see page 184). Money raised went towards

Catering to Couples and Families

Before World War II, a Couples Club or Topics Club, an idea that originated at Grandview United Church, began at Knox. "Primarily professional men and their wives met at the home of a church member," wrote Thelma Lower, who participated with her husband, Arthur. "The men were required to present a well-researched topic usually associated with their own expertise. . . . Sometimes the wives also gave a talk." Mrs. Lower added that another club that involved families also met in homes for discussion and held outings with children. The clubs kept a fairly constant membership of about 16, but after the war they began to dwindle. Mrs. Lower thought it became difficult to hold evening gatherings in homes following the bombing of Pearl Harbor on 7 December 1941, when the order was given to black out windows.

the purchase of a communion table, a new organ and the chancel glass window, titled *The Resurrection*, for the church building proper. This was finally erected in 1948 adjacent to the Sunday school and gymnasium.

The hall, which had been the site of so much enthusiastic activity and devotion, burned down in March 1975. The *Province* newspaper reported on the three-alarm fire. "'The three-storey, frame building was fully in flame by the time firemen were called to the scene,' said Vancouver Fire Chief Armand Konig. No one was injured. The blaze drew an estimated 2,000 people who crowded streets and the grounds of Kerrisdale School adjacent to the burning building. 'This is the best crowd we've had all year,' a young church worker said ruefully."

The 1948 church building survived, however, and although a modest building on the outside, it houses a most eye-pleasing and serene interior. The wall panels are of native cedar. The impressive beams of the vaulted ceiling are of fir encased in cedar. Music making is a joy, thanks to the renowned chancel, and the Early Music Society has held many concerts here. The pews and chancel furniture and fixtures are primarily of oak, and some are delicately carved. The small chapel next to the chancel is still used for memorial services, weddings and a weekly evening community service. In 1984, the church replaced some of its simple narrow windows with stained-glass creations by David Miller, son of church pioneers Jimmy and Melita Miller. Both the Millers were very active in the Knox Operatic Society, which performed until the late 1960s.

Historical memorabilia in the chapel include bronze memorials bearing the names of 30 Knox members who lost their lives in the world wars. In 1943 Russell Oliver, the session clerk at the time, sent a message from the congregation to those serving overseas. It began with a vivid description of fall in Dunbar that must have made every recipient of the letter homesick. Oliver also wrote: "Mr. Harrison got a coat of paint on the wall panels this summer which previously bore the scars of basketball games, which some of you may have been responsible for. If so we forgive you. On each side of the choir loft our two flags hang, a promise and pledge of our part with you in the Great Crusade."

Over the years a sense of shared burdens and hopes has motivated the direction and evolution of Knox United. During the Depression a small Session Committee distributed food, clothing and fuel to needy members and other neighbourhood residents. In the more optimistic 1950s the church was bursting at its seams with about 300 churchgoers, 200 Sunday school students and 40 choir members. Rev. H.A. Watts attracted members and made music an important part of worship services. Members assisted in church maintenance projects, and social evenings and dances were held for the adults, with dinners for between 200 and 300 in the original hall.

Canadian Girls in Training

Knox United played host to various youth groups. Joan Tyldesley recalled fondly her involvement in Explorers, CGIT and HiC at Knox during the late 1940s and 1950s. She remembered making candles in the church kitchen to sell at a bazaar and being banned from ever doing so again after having to spend hours scraping wax from the counters, floor, stove and ceiling. The young people engaged in more serious activities as well, making sandwiches at a Downtown Eastside mission on Sunday evenings. "I can remember cutting the mould off the cheese that had outlived its shelf life and was donated by local merchants. We then spread mayonnaise and ketchup on stale bread and added the slices of cheese. I didn't think the sandwiches were too appetizing but when we served them to the men . . . I was surprised at how quickly they were gobbled up."

CGIT members (left to right) Ruth Berry, Cynthia Cowan, Muriel "Jolly" Kirk, Joyce Kelly and Joan Tyldesley enjoy helping out at Knox United Church's Christmas bazaar in 1958 by making and selling pancakes. Courtesy of Joan Tyldesley.

At that time most Knox United members lived in the neighbourhood and volunteered by joining church committees. Now many live outside the Dunbar area and volunteer their talents and skills outside the church as well. Knox professes a philosophical desire to look for new ways to answer community needs that may not be met by other agencies or facilities. A long-range planning group maintains a good dialogue with other neighbourhood churches.

This strong commitment to spiritual and social responsibility manifested itself physically in 1970 in the construction of the Knox Fellowship Centre just south of the church, a multi-purpose facility still in constant use. Its construction followed many years of planning, with the total cost of the building being about $160,000. It has served and continues to serve everyone well: it is home to the Little People's Pre-school, educational classes, Cub Scouts and Beavers, badminton, seniors' activities, Alcoholics Anonymous meetings, choirs and a youth group. During the 1970s when the Fellowship Centre was still new, Gordon Howe, the senior minister at that time, was involved in the World Council of Churches, providing a valuable global perspective that reinforced Knox's outward vision. Reverend Howe's assistant, Jean Angus, was the first female minister at

Dunbar Heights United Church

1914–22 · Union Sunday school established, 3800 block of West 21st Avenue (multi-denominational, under auspices of Presbyterian denomination)

1922 · Preaching services started

1923 · Building moved to 3500 block of West 21st Avenue and enlarged

1925 · Union church became Dunbar Heights United Church

1926 · Building on 24th Avenue near Collingwood built with gym (present Christian Education Building)

1950–51 · Church built

1980 · Fire damaged both buildings

1981 · Buildings repaired and renovated

Knox and began a tradition that continued from the 1980s into the twenty-first century.

A quiet green space between the church and Knox Fellowship Centre is worth a special mention. In this Memorial Garden the ashes of members and friends of Knox United Church can be buried. Although there are no identifying plaques in the garden, a Memorial Garden Book records names and dates. In September 1998 Knox United celebrated its 50th anniversary with a tree-planting ceremony, symbolic of growth and renewal. Jimmy and Melita Miller were in attendance. As a young boy, Jim attended the first church services on his neighbour's veranda. Knox United Church is a landmark with deep community roots that it continues to value as it adapts to a new century.

Dunbar Heights United Church

The church now located at Collingwood Street and West 24th Avenue began as a Sunday school. It was established at the suggestion of Reverend Gordon Tanner, a Methodist minister in south Kitsilano, and with the co-operation of Baptist, Anglican and Methodist parents who wanted religious training for their children. According to a historical summary written by parishioners in the late 1960s titled *Our Yesterdays, 1914–1968*, a school was originally constructed in the 3800 block of 21st Avenue on land belonging to W.A. Gallagher with donated money, lumber and labour. A "Historical Sketch" written about 1949 states: "The little Sunday school building helped to focus community interest when houses were very few and scattered. In war-time, people's hearts were comforted and their endeavours unified."

By January 1922, the land on which the Sunday school stood had reverted to the Crown and been purchased by a Mr. J. Gibson. Although the school had lost legal right to the land, Mr. Gibson allowed the school trustees to remain in possession of the building with the understanding that it would be moved. On 19 February 1922, the trustees formally handed the building over to the control and ownership of Dunbar Heights Union Church, and it became imperative to find another lot. More than 15 choices were considered. Finally, two lots east of Dunbar Street in the middle of the 3500 block of 21st Avenue were purchased for $600. The school building was moved across the electric streetcar line to its new location on 11 November 1923, after which it was enlarged and a basement was added.

Another issue required attention at this time. By the end of 1921, the Sunday school was flourishing and concerns about its future arose — should it remain interdenominational or be turned over to one denomination? Adults were expressing interest in having worship services. Which denomination should take on this cause? The Presbyterian church played a key role by arranging for retired Reverend John Robertson Munro, a kindly, sympathetic man, to begin preaching services in February 1922. At first, these services were held on Sunday evenings because the Sunday school required the facility in the mornings. Following the renovation of the school building, morning services were offered in 1924 for those who could not attend in the evening.

In 1922, moreover, Knox Presbyterian, then located on 42nd Avenue and Macdonald Street, was appointed by the Presbytery of Westminster to assist the Dunbar Heights church in its formal organization. According to the minutes of an annual meeting, "As the church is now fully organized, the management should be in the hands of men only." The motion was carried. Prior to the meeting, supper for 70 had been prepared and served by the women. The church history reports: "The sequel to this was that, at the next annual meeting, at which no dinner was served, this motion was rescinded, and women declared eligible for office. One wonders just what the women said to the men during the period between these motions."

On 10 June 1925, the United Church legally came into being, after much debate in Parliament and the passing of a bill sponsored by Robert Forke, the leader of the Progressive Party. This was to have a major effect on two Dunbar churches. Knox Presbyterian became Knox United, as the result of the union of Methodists, Presbyterians and Congregationalists. The Dunbar Heights congregation had already adopted the name Dunbar Heights United a year earlier in 1924.

About 250 families lived in Dunbar Heights by this time, a large portion of these young married couples with children. Membership at Dunbar Heights was about 66. These pioneers were dedicated. Reverend Munro continued on until health issues required him to pass on his duties to his assistant, Reverend Rae, in 1926. The Reverend Hugh McConnell Rae, born in Scotland, had studied arts at UBC and theology at Westminster Hall. He was in his thirties when he came to Dunbar Heights.

One of the first things Reverend Rae had to deal with was to find accommodation for the ever-increasing number of Sunday school students. Six vacant lots were purchased for $2,600. Richard T. Perry, an experienced church architect, drew up the plans to build a two-storey community church school centre including a main auditorium, suitable for physical and social activities during the week and worship services on Sundays. The Home Mission Board assisted by contributing $10,000 towards the $30,300 price. The building's appearance was utilitarian. The construction of a more traditional church building would have to wait. As *Our Yesterdays* chronicles: "On 31 October 1926, the church school building was ready for dedication. When we vacated the old building the

▲ Performance of *Enchanted Isle* at Dunbar Heights United Church in 1939, with C.L. Stevens as conductor, just one example of the church's musical productions. Courtesy of Dunbar Heights United Church.

Anglicans requested temporary accommodation on 21st Avenue and our Board heartily agreed. Thus, a happy interdenominational relationship continued. Later, when an Anglican clergyman came to take charge of their work, our minister was present to take part in the laying of the corner stone and through the years this spirit of neighbourliness has continued."

Around 1926 the first Young People's Association was formed. Young men and women continued to meet in separate groups until after World War II, when joint meetings became more popular. Some of their get-togethers included youth from Knox United and St. Philip's Anglican. There was a healthy rivalry among the churches in drama and sports.

In March 1928, the congregation became self-sufficient. Its commitment to outreach was already evident in its support for such things as research into alcoholism, jail visits, a refugee fund and overseas relief, radio ministry and hospital visits to senior citizens. Women played a key role in many of these projects. Through the Women's Association they began making children's garments, sweaters and socks at home for distribution through the Red Cross. During World War II, they organized a War Time Service Unit, which remained active until 1948. Mrs. Jamieson, the church's archivist, recalled that "at one time in our church over here, you could hear five or six sewing-machines running on an afternoon and people pressing, and people cutting, putting on buttons and everybody worked, probably 16 or 18 ladies all working in a sort of rhythm."

Reverend Rae, who became known for his scholarly preaching, served at Dunbar Heights United through the socially and economically challenging years of the 1930s and World War II. By the time he left in 1948 to undertake a ministry in Ottawa, debts had been paid off and money saved for a church building.

Reverend Harold S. Clugston became his successor. With record attendance on Sundays, the auditorium's seating capacity of 300 had long been inadequate. Membership as of April 1946 was already over 700, with more than 600 Sunday school students. When it became clear that a manse was needed, the women contributed a great deal of time and talent to the project, which resulted in a $10,000 home being built on church property. Reverend Clugston became the manse's first occupant.

The architect for the new church was Twizell & Twizell, the contractor, Chester Neff. On Sunday afternoon, 18 June 1950, the cornerstone was laid while hundreds looked on from the church lots as well as the porches of neighbouring houses. The inside of the church was built according to the cruciform shape of early Christian churches. Its seating capacity was 500. The cost for building and furnishings came to $97,000. Nine months later, on Sunday, 18 March 1951, the new church was dedicated. The sermon topic was "We will build on love." Numerous gifts and memorials from individual members helped to furnish both the church and the manse.

◄ Three church women pose for a "mock wedding" in 1940, displaying a playful side to church social life. Courtesy of Dunbar Heights United Church.

▲ Easter Sunday, 17 April 1949. Mrs. Dalyrymple, Mrs. Cullon and Mrs. J.O. Smith turn the sod in symbolic preparation for the building of the Dunbar Heights United Church manse. Courtesy of Dunbar Heights United Church.

The Rev. A.L. Anderson, who had grown up in the Collingwood area and studied at UBC, came to Dunbar Heights in 1957. He was often referred to as "a minister's minister" because of his theological approach to preaching. He was a good counsellor. During his stay, the Dunbar neighbourhood was reflecting a national trend towards mobility, with one in five persons moving annually. Despite this, or perhaps even because of it, Dunbar Heights maintained a progressive spirit.

Dr. George Struthers succeeded Reverend Anderson in 1965. His preaching showed an awareness of the complex social and philosophical issues of the 1960s and '70s and their challenges to religious thought and institutions. His enlightened outlook helped to maintain stability in the congregation during a period of little growth. Among the challenges met by the parishioners and leaders of Dunbar Heights United was one that threatened to destroy decades of work and history. On Sunday, 16 November 1980, a fire caused severe damage to the Christian Education Building and some to the church. Nevertheless, not one Sunday service was cancelled, and by January 1981 most repairs were complete. The congregation had turned a setback into an advantage by seizing the opportunity to modernize and upgrade their facilities.

Since its inception, Dunbar Heights United has had many competent, responsible ministers who have understood and met the needs of their congregation. Lay participation has been another key factor in the church's survival. During one of its "lows" at the turn of the twenty-first century, Dunbar Heights United considered merging with Knox United, but as of 2006 it had decided to remain independent and optimistic about its future and to continue its commitment to the neighbourhood.

Immaculate Conception Parish

In 1625 the Jesuits (the Society of Jesus) came from France to Eastern Canada. It took 300 years for their influence to reach the West Coast, and more specifically the district of Dunbar, part of Point Grey, or "the boonies" in the 1920s. In May 1922 Father Milway-Filion, Provincial of the Jesuits, arrived in Vancouver and surveyed 10 acres of B.C. university lands that had been granted to the Jesuits by the government on condition that it be used to build a college. In November 1923, T. Casey, archbishop of Vancouver, wrote a letter to Father John Knox, S.J., chaplain to the Convent of the Sacred Heart (now the site of St. George's Junior School), asking him to inform Father Milway-Filion that he would like him to establish a parish near the convent as well as a college. Acting as liaison, Father Knox assisted in the transactions that brought about the canonical establishment of Immaculate Conception Parish. The convent chapel became its first home, Marine Heights its first mailing address, and Father Knox its first unofficial priest. He served the first High Mass on 2 March 1924 and gave a sermon titled "Faith, Hope and Charity."

One of his successors, Father Dunn, in 1925 appointed a parishioner, Bill Kitchener, to build a church and school just beyond the eastern boundary of convent land, with initial funding provided by the Jesuit order. The church faced north onto 28th Avenue, which came to a dead end at the convent property. Completed in 1926, the building was basic. Wrote Fr. J.A. Leahy in a 60th-anniversary history: "Those were the pioneering days. The church, like many of the homes, was heated by sawdust furnaces. There were no pews in the church. Chairs were used. A raised platform at the back of the church was the choir loft." The rectory was a small room with a fireplace; Father Dunn ate his meals at the convent.

The church's basement was divided into four rooms, which would comprise the first classrooms of Immaculate Conception School, referred to upon its opening in September 1926 as the Basement School. Its first students (around 40) were taught by the Sisters of the Sacred Heart Convent (see chapter 9). In order to accommodate these semi-cloistered nuns, the school and church were built adjacent to the convent property instead of on Dunbar Street, even though that would have been more

▲ Participation in a peace march in downtown Vancouver during the 1980s demonstrates the history of concern for global issues at Dunbar Heights United Church. Courtesy of Dunbar Heights United Church.

A Christmas Tradition

In 1927 Immaculate Conception Parish celebrated its first Christmas. John Schretlen directed the choir and donated a nativity scene from his family's personal collection brought originally from Winnipeg. Over the years the statues were replaced by plaster figurines from Italy and a more lifelike Christ child from Germany. The figures range in size from six inches to two feet. According to Elaine Schretlen, a granddaughter who carries on the tradition, "Parish children used to leave alms — pennies, nickels and dimes and sometimes quarters — in offering to the baby Jesus. These would be found in the grass mat and gathered up and donated to the missions. For unknown reasons this tradition has ceased since the early 1980s." After Christmas, the figurines are lovingly rewrapped, many in the original old newspapers, which are historical treasures in themselves.

Erecting the special nativity scene at Immaculate Conception Parish church has become a tradition for the Schretlen family. Kevin and Reid Schretlen are the grandsons of John Schretlen, who donated the nativity figures in 1927. Courtesy of Peggy Schofield.

Immaculate Conception Parish

1924 · Canonical establishment of parish, Marine Heights address; convent chapel used

1925 · Church built at 2776 West 28th Avenue

1932 · Extension built (Scouts Hall)

2003 · Construction of new facilities between 28th and 29th Avenues at the eastern boundary of St. George's Junior School (formerly Sacred Heart Convent School)

accessible. Even so, the nuns had to obtain permission from Rome to cross over from the convent to the school.

The first priest to remain for an extended time (1926–41) was Father John Keenan. Long-serving Father Leahy, who kept a written chronicle of the parish's Jesuit years, described Father Keenan as a colourful character who, when asked why he was so well liked, answered, "I'm humble and I'm proud of my humility." If Father Keenan saw Jane Swencisky shopping on Dunbar and was sure she had not seen him, he would go by her house and leave a note saying, "Sorry I missed you!" Once, when Father Keenan visited Mrs. Kaufman, who was ill, he mistakenly waved about his fountain pen in an attempt to sprinkle holy water around her room, leaving behind an inky trail.

Father Raymond Kennedy, who succeeded Father Keenan in 1941, was a quiet contrast to his predecessor, but was just as good at getting things accomplished. Once a week he went over to the North Shore to hear the confessions of the Sisters there. This was an onerous trip considering he had to rely on streetcars and ferries and pay for the travel himself. Thanks to some persistent canvassing by certain parishioners and the generosity of a Mr. X, a car was eventually acquired for Father Kennedy to make his day trip a little easier. When Mr. X was called and thanked

Spirituality among the Musqueam

legislation, spirit dancing was a winter function. It had very strong religious connotations. The mask dancing usually was celebrating the spring, summer, fall and [held] out-of-doors when there was good weather." Some Musqueam are Shakers. The first Shaker church on the mainland was built on Musqueam land in the early 1900s, but private homes are now meeting places for those who follow the beliefs of John Slocam, an Indian from Washington State who died in 1882, and allegedly came back to life to teach Native people to be good so they could go to heaven. H.G. Barnett has noted that Slocam was given "the promise of some new kind of 'medicine' to heal the sick. . . . His wife had been crying over his dead body for so long that her head and arms began to tremble uncontrollably." This "shaking" is considered to be the promised medicine.

Many Musqueam are Catholic, but they are not necessarily practising Catholics, and often combine Christianity with Native spirituality. When Father Leahy and the Jesuits from Immaculate Conception Parish taught catechism to band members in the 1950s, those Musqueam living in the eastern end of the reserve refused to have anything to do with the priests and continued their tradition of dancing instead. According to Andrew Charles, an elder, "Before prohibitive

A row of houses stands across from St. Michael's the Archangel, the first Catholic church built on Musqueam land, 1902. This lovely wooden structure with its two spires was destroyed by arsonists in 1963. Courtesy of Betty McQueen.

by a representative of the parish, he apparently said, "Thank me for what? What car? Never heard of it!"

During the 1940s, Junior Catholic Youth Organization classes were organized. Father Monaghan helped to reorganize the Senior CYO and inspired everyone with his musical ability. But this was an unsettled time, with World War II in progress and 89 of the parish's young members serving overseas. Seven never returned.

At the end of the war Father Adelbert Leahy arrived to provide continuity in the parish until his departure in 1984. Not only did he become a well-loved and respected assistant priest, known affectionately to some as Father "Bert," but a parish historian. He kept journals of names and events that provide an account of the Jesuit years in Dunbar. Harold Chisholm, who attended the parish with his family, wrote, "Father Leahy, S.J., was perhaps the most dynamic priest that I ever had. He headed the Catholic Doctors' Guild for some 30 years [and] worked with alcoholics. Much loved over the years, [he] married, baptized and buried all the old-timers," including Mr. Chisholm's own parents and their friends.

One of the highlights of Father Leahy's early years at the parish was its 25th anniversary, in 1949. On 6 November, 225 people attended a Silver Jubilee Banquet held in the parish hall. To celebrate further the

▲ In 1951, after the church tower became unsafe, the church bell from St. Michael's the Archangel was placed in its frame on the ground. Courtesy of Pam Chambers.

▲ St. Michael's altar in 1951. Courtesy of Pam Chambers.

parish's growth, an $18,000 project was undertaken to expand the church and attached sacristy. The Devine family donated new oak pews; the striking metal Stations of the Cross, which line the east and west walls, arrived from Montreal.

The 1950s were a decade of interesting changes. In 1954 the Sisters of St. Ann moved into the brown house south of the church and began teaching at the new Immaculate Conception School, which had been built across from the church on the north side of 28th Avenue (see chapter 9). At the request of Archbishop Johnson, Father Leahy and other Jesuits took over the priestly duties at Musqueam in 1957. The Oblates had been ministering to the Native people there since 1860. According to Kay Cronin, author of *Cross in the Wilderness*, the legendary Father Leon Fouquet "recorded his first baptisms among the Indians of the Musqueam village (Point Grey) at which time it may be assumed he celebrated the first Mass ever to be offered up in the future city of Vancouver."

Almost 100 years later, on 29 March 1959, Father Leahy celebrated the first Jesuit High Mass among the Musqueam at St. Michael's the Archangel, the first Catholic church building on Musqueam land. Unfortunately, this historical wooden structure with its two spires was burned down in August 1963 by two young arsonists. All that remains is an empty overgrown lot. A new church was completed by 1965 on a different lot. This church was an ecumenical first, since Chief Willard Sparrow had been granted permission to build one that could also be used for the occasional non-Catholic celebration or service. During the 1990s the interior of the church was redone with reproductions of Byzantine icons that resemble West Coast Native art. This was accomplished with the encouragement of Father John Horgan, who was then mission priest to the Musqueam.

In the mid-1950s the parish experienced some special internal challenges. The Catholic Youth Organization that had flourished in the early 1950s suddenly dwindled to almost nothing. There were fewer in attendance at Sunday Mass. People were confronted by the global changes occurring in the Catholic Church during the time of Pope John XXIII.

The 1960s saw a positive response to these challenges. Social activities were organized to bring people together again. When English replaced Latin as the vernacular at the parish on 21 September 1967, lay people were permitted to become readers and altar servers. For about a year, Masses were performed on Sunday evenings in especially devout parishioners' homes, to which a small group of participants were invited. Guitar masses were begun in 1969. When the altar was turned around in 1965 to allow the pastor to face his congregation, another step was taken towards greater inclusivity. In 1961 the first Mayfair fundraiser was held on the school grounds. It went on to become a successful annual event spreading out onto 28th Avenue with fun for the whole neighbourhood.

The Catholic Women's League celebrated its 25th anniversary in 1967. During World War II they had received recognition for their sewing for the Red Cross. Mrs. Joseph Archambault, who was director of the parish Red Cross, continued to invite parish women to her home after the war to stitch beadwork on felt creations, which could be sold to raise money for various charitable causes. Her husband was a pioneer parishioner, instrumental in starting the St. Vincent de Paul Society's Shelter project. When he died in 1969, an era died with him.

The 1970s continued the ecumenical focus, encouraged in part by Father Seasons, who, according to Father Leahy, knew every minister in

◄ Immaculate Conception Church celebrates its annual fair, May 2001, still using the old Catholic Youth Organization building and Scouts Hall, which have since been demolished to make room for a new parish facility. Courtesy of Vivien Clarke.

Father Leahy Remembered

A picture of Father Leahy hangs in the hallway of the original rectory at Immaculate Conception. It seems he jokingly told children that they had to genuflect whenever they passed his picture. His warmth still permeates the building and the memories of those who met him. Colleen Butchart, whose mother Leona Dundee frequently invited the parish priests to dinner, recalled that Father Leahy, a distant cousin, was her favourite. "He always smelled a little musty, looking disheveled in his old black sweater under his scruffy black suit. He had the habit of loosening his clerical collar and letting it hang askew. Being a diabetic, he allowed himself one shot of Scotch with water and ice. . . . He was a kind and wise man, well respected and much liked."

Photo of Father Leahy by Don MacGregor. Courtesy of Vivien Clarke, Richard Archambault and Immaculate Conception Parish.

Vancouver by his first name. There was a youth dance co-sponsored by Immaculate Conception, St. Philip's Anglican and Dunbar Heights United Church. In March 1974 the parish celebrated its 50th anniversary. But major changes were again on the horizon. The Jesuit founders of the parish had to withdraw their services for lack of new recruits. In his farewell message on the occasion of the parish's 60th anniversary in 1984, Father Leahy shared the following observations: "We are in a very different world from the world of 60 years ago. It is a world of rationalization and not of faith. It is a world of pleasure and material goods. It is a world of individuals, not community. It is a ME world." He did believe, however, that there was a gradual reversal occurring in some of the trends that had challenged the parish since the late 1950s. He saw signs of hope as young people seemed to be rediscovering the basic spiritual values with which they had grown up.

On 31 July 1984, Father Leahy was the last Jesuit to leave, but his legacy and that of his predecessors lives on. Since 1984 four diocesan priests have served as priest at Immaculate Conception Parish. In 1999 the parish celebrated its 75th anniversary with Father Paul Than Bui as priest. The 10-month celebration featured a wide range of activities that emphasized the parish's rich spiritual and social life. Its needs are ever growing and changing, however, as are those of its school. Seventy-five years is a long time for a "temporary" structure to try to accommodate such needs. Plans have been drawn up to give the parish a new look: both the old brown-shingled residence and the CYO and Scouts Hall have been demolished to make room for a parish facility stretching from 28th to 29th Avenue. Whether the 1925 church building remains in its present form or is eventually reborn as an improved permanent structure, no doubt there will always be a place for Father Leahy's picture to remind everyone of the parish's rich history.

St. Philip's Anglican Church

On 26 February 1925, a meeting was held at 3343 West 29th Avenue, the home of Mr. and Mrs. F. W. Taylor, from which was born the Parish of St. Philip's, the first Anglican parish in Dunbar. The nearest Anglican parish churches, located in West Point Grey, Kerrisdale and Kitsilano, were not convenient to attend, given the limited transportation available.

Adrian Joseph Moyls recorded the minutes at that first meeting. A man of determination and drive, he was a major force in the formation of the new parish. Space was rented from the Point Grey School Board for $5 per month in the original one-storey, two-room annex to Lord Kitchener Elementary School. Sunday school classes began in May with 24 students and 7 teachers. Moyls became an inspirational superintendent. By December 1929, there were more than 250 pupils and 22 teachers.

The first service was conducted in the annex on 6 September 1925. At this time the congregation called itself the Dunbar Heights Church of England Mission and had the rector of St. Mary's in Kerrisdale, the Rev. C.S. McGaffin, as its sponsor. The name of St. Philip's Anglican Church, after one of the 12 apostles of Christ, was officially adopted a year later. The Reverend Cecil B. Price, Mr. McGaffin's assistant, became its first rector on St. Philip's Day, 1 May 1927.

At the first congregational meeting on 26 October 1925, discussion centred on the need for a larger and more permanent site for the growing congregation. A complicating factor was that the school board would soon need the annex for its own educational purposes. Since a new church would not be finished for some time, the search began for another temporary site.

On the north side of 21st Avenue between Dunbar and Collingwood Streets stood a little hall once home to Dunbar United Church, which had just completed its own new building at 24th Avenue and Collingwood Street. This hall became St. Philip's second home, from 1926 to 1929. In March 1927, the congregation purchased property on the northwest corner of Dunbar Street and 26th Avenue for $2,100. This lot was sold in December 1927 in favour of the present site on 27th between Dunbar and Highbury Streets that seemed better in size and location, purchased for $1,900 in the same month.

In 1925, when the parish was established, much of Dunbar was still undeveloped bushland. By the time St. Philip's began construction in 1929, Dunbar was on the move towards development. To clear the land, the growing congregation formed industrious and enthusiastic work

St. Philip's Anglican Church in 2003. Courtesy of Joan Tyldesley.

St. Philip's Anglican Church

1925 · Private home services at 3343 West 29th Avenue (F.W. Taylor residence); move to annex at Lord Kitchener Elementary School

1926–29 · Move to small hall belonging to Mr. Stevens (north side of 21st Avenue between Dunbar and Collingwood Streets)

1929 · New hall completed on 27th Avenue

1941 · Church constructed at 3737 West 27th

1948 · Fireside Wing completed

crews. Bonfire parties with marshmallow and potato roasts offered a welcome break from the building of brush piles. According to *Retrospect*, a parish history of St. Philip's from 1925 to 1975, the final clearing of the church lot may have been performed by "a colourful character with a team of work horses by the name of Charlie Yeamen. He was apparently an inveterate tobacco chewer who gave the appearance of living and sleeping with his horses, and who launched missiles of spent tobacco juice through a gap in his front teeth with a high degree of accuracy and a range rumoured to be in excess of twenty feet."

Yeaman certainly levelled the ground for the tennis courts originally built on the present site of the church and may have done the same for the lawn in front of the hall. Thomas Jakeway, a long-time Dunbar resident who was involved at St. Philip's, helped to build the tennis court and said that when the hall was built, "the young people undertook the finishing of the caretaker's quarters at the east end of the building upstairs."

Mr. S.W. Tannar, also a member, was the architect and took charge of the construction, contracted out to the firm of A.H. Kennett. The turning of the sod was celebrated in March 1929, and on Sunday, 19 May 1929, 293 parishioners celebrated their first service in their new church building with the Rev. C.B. Price presiding. It was a shingle-faced, multi-purpose, practical building. Four hundred people could be accommodated in the hall and 100 children in a separate Sunday school room. An altar and pulpit situated at one end of the 147 x 47 foot room could be hidden by folding doors when the hall was needed for activities other than church services.

Even though attempts had been made to keep costs down, the land and hall had cost the parish $11,500, a steep sum during the Depression. The final payment was made in 1939, but with the needs of the congregation ever growing, a new building fund was required to finance the construction of a rector's house on land east of the hall in September 1938 ($5,753) as well as a new church building with chapel (about $24,000), which was dedicated on 18 December 1941 with 520 in attendance. The congregation had debated whether to postpone construction until after the war, when building regulations would be less stringent and supplies more plentiful, but the determination to proceed outweighed these concerns.

During World War II, approximately 100 men and women from the parish joined the forces. A Soldier Comfort Committee was established to send them parcels of food and knitted items. One soldier, Art Salt, who had served on the executive of the Anglican Young People's Association during the 1930s, was listed as "missing in action" over Crete. A plaque and flower vases were dedicated in his memory and are still on display.

The Women's Auxiliary was very active during the war. According to their 1942 annual report, much time was spent at meetings, knitting and sewing for outreach projects. Dorothy Piercy recorded, "During 1942 the following articles were completed: two knitted layettes, approximately

◄ Maypole dancing in St. Philip's gymnasium, 1944, with the May Queen, Joy Cook, and her entourage looking on. Courtesy of the Archives of the Anglican Diocese of New Westminster, Vancouver Theological College, UBC.

Joy Cook was chosen by the Sunday school staff and her peers to be the first May Queen at St. Philip's May Festival in 1944. Courtesy of the Archives of the Anglican Diocese of New Westminster, Vancouver Theological College, UBC. ▶

twelve pairs of hospital slippers, and one cotton quilt. Part of an outfit for a patient at St. Michael's preventorium has been started, as well as twelve babies' nightgowns, strong scrapbooks for hospitals, and children's knitted caps and mittens. Christmas gifts for the Columbia Coast Mission were made up." The Sunday school and bible classes were also flourishing. At that time it was possible to receive high-school credit for a course in bible study. The Rev. H.J. Greig and his wife initiated the May Queen festival, which was an annual hit for years. Boys and girls participated in a maypole dance and, at the end of the day, a May Queen was crowned. The candidate had to be a regular Sunday school attendee and be respected by both staff and students.

After the war, St. Philip's found a new focus. The Reverend Greig inspired the parish with his dream of an extension that would offer facilities and activities to help returning service personnel to reconnect with their church and community. Thomas Jakeway remembered the following about him: "I think he ran a hardware store in Duncan before going into the ministry. He used to say he had no hesitation in asking for money for the work of the church. He chaired a meeting more efficiently than anyone I've met." The Fireside Wing was born out of this inspired determination. In a statement to the congregation, Greig reassured his parishioners: "We have nowhere lost sight of the vital point that our task is essentially that of the Church's spiritual development. . . . We do not consider that the provision of recreation for recreation's sake is a sufficient end in itself."

The expensive renovation of the original hall/church and construction of the new wing began in 1947 and was completed in 1948. Edith Bernard, a long-time parishioner, had a special connection with the new wing:

> Archdeacon Greig was the minister when I was married in 1949 and gave the toast to the bride. His wife decorated the church with flowers. My father was rector's warden at the time and arrived home from a church committee meeting to inform me that the wedding reception was to be in the brand-new Fireside Wing. We were to be the first! Initially, I wasn't sure this is what I wanted. It turned out wonderfully well, of course. It was a pouring wet night and so convenient for the guests to just walk over to the new room, which then as now had a lovely cozy feel to it.

Another post-war development was the creation of the St. Philip's Operatic Society in 1945, which was open to participation by non-church members. *H.M.S. Pinafore* was the first production to hit the rather inadequate stage in April 1946. When it was a success, the St. Philip's Drama Club was formed in the fall. Jack Rush, who was part of the *Pinafore* cast, went on to contribute his baritone-bass voice to many more productions and the choir. He also wrote lyrics, jokes and scenes for special events. His sister Violet Rush often provided piano accompaniment to songs they would perform in church. According to Jack, "She was very talented. She could sit down and play anything. During the war she used to play the piano down at the Jericho army barracks. The guys used to sing like crazy." St. Philip's has been home to many such talented and vibrant personalities.

In the 1930s, '40s and '50s, St. Philip's was a spiritual and social centre for Anglicans and non-Anglicans, young and old alike. But as facilities such as the Dunbar Community Centre (1955) and local schools began to offer more recreational opportunities and neighbourhood services, they took over much of the community work that St. Philip's had provided. Nevertheless, the parish was determined to remain relevant to the community by filling the gaps left by others. It was active well into the 1960s providing fellowship opportunities and filling the church to overflowing.

Towards the end of that decade, changing social values as well as an increasingly diverse Dunbar community coincided with a decline in Anglicans in the general population and created a pivotal challenge to religious certainty. The church needed to be more responsive to these changes. When it celebrated its 50th anniversary in 1975, St. Philip's was a parish of about 600 families. It had paid off its debts and faced increasing secularism and multiculturalism by balancing the best of its traditions with an openness to new ideas. In 1975, moreover, the Anglican Church

The Jones Girls

An integral part of St. Philip's vitality during all its changes has been a group of women who chose the name the Jones Girls because it did not reflect their leader's name or have to be changed when that person stepped down. Joan Ashley said the forerunner of this fellowship group was formed in 1945 at the suggestion of Reverend Greig, to provide support to returning servicemen trying to settle into peacetime occupations. Lillian Simpson recalled one memorable event. "I shall always remember the year I convened the bazaar and the lights all went out. We had to have most of the supper cooked by members where there was still electricity. We ate in candlelight and everyone was so wonderful turning out to help. All said it was one of the best dinners yet!" The Jones Girls are especially appreciated for the funeral or memorial teas they coordinate after services.

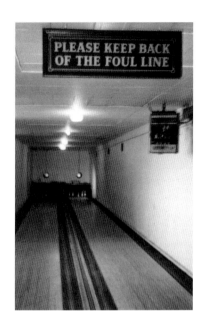

Bowling in the Basement

In 1955 St. Philip's conducted
a census of residents to determine
religious affiliations and community needs. In response to the
latter, the two five-pin bowling
alleys originally built in the
northeast corner of the hall's
basement in 1949 were offered
for community use. Edith Bernard's
father had been instrumental in
acquiring the alleys. Al Williams,
who played sports for the church,
said the lanes were built by his
father and Mr. Baxter, a neighbour
who was a carpenter by trade.
Rules established in 1948
governing the use of the lanes
probably helped to preserve them
for those parishioners and outside
groups, such as the Cubs, who
were enjoying the alleys in 2006.

*Photo of St. Philip's bowling lanes
courtesy of Vivien Clarke.*

of Canada approved the ordination of women priests. Since 1976, the
resident clergy at St. Philip's has included a woman almost every year,
with Helen Hill being the first formally appointed female priest.

A lasting reminder of the 50th-anniversary celebrations and their significance is the memorial garden built at the northeast corner of the
church. It was dedicated on 9 March 1975, having transformed a junk-
yard into a serene final resting place for the ashes of parishioners and
their families. The Centennial Garden in the front courtyard of the
church contains several benches and is open to the community for rest
and meditation. Volunteers lovingly tend both gardens.

Local and global involvement in peace and justice issues continued
to be a focus throughout the 1980s. During this time, St. Philip's also re-
defined itself as "A Church Family" rather than the more traditional
"family church" — not just in a new sign for the church, but in its commitment to inviting more lay participation in the planning of its future.
That future was to be "people focused" and involved many dedicated,
energetic volunteers, a stable clerical leadership and talented, generous
parish members.

Two interesting developments from that time are still in effect today.
Prior to 1982, baptism occurred at the rear of the church with the congregation turned about in their pews to face the font. Here a child would
receive symbolic entrance and welcome into the body of the church.
After 1982, the child and sponsors were invited to stand at a font in the
sacristy at the front of the church, thus inviting the congregation to feel
more included in the ceremony. The second change involved moving the
altars in the church and chapel closer to the congregation, to allow the
clergy to face parishioners.

In 2001, St. Philip's celebrated its 75th anniversary. Robin Inglis, a
parishioner, wrote an insightful historical essay for the occasion. He
described St. Philip's as a "jewel in the Diocese of New Westminster" due
to the "quality of the worship experiences, the pastoral care, the teaching, the generosity and apparent financial stability." St. Philip's continues
to face the challenge shared by every church in the neighbourhood: how
to remain relevant and hence alive and well in the new millennium.
Inglis suggested that the success of St. Philip's, as the embodiment of the
"middle way" between liberal and conservative beliefs and practices, "will
involve both hanging on to the traditions we cherish and being prepared
to be innovative about ministry and embracing change."

Dunbar Heights Baptist Church

The history of the church that now stands at 3996 West 17th Avenue dates
back to 1932. According to news items in the *British Columbia Baptist*
and records of the B.C. Baptist Missionary Council, however, a home

mission was first begun on this site in 1926. As with other Dunbar churches, the initial drive was to establish a Sunday school.

The northwest corner of West 17th Avenue and Crown Street was chosen as a good site because it was only a block south of the streetcar line that ran from 10th Avenue along Crown Street, then east down 16th Avenue to Dunbar Street. A two-storey shingled brown building was erected close to the lane. In 2004, Dr. Frank Anderson and his wife Janet, both of whom had been leaders in the church for over 40 years, offered the following in their "Historical Recollections of the Dunbar Heights Regular Baptist Church":

> It was the initial design that the building be two stories, the lower floor the church hall and the upper floor the sanctuary. The lower floor was about 4 feet below grade and there were outside stairs down into the building. The building was not completed when the Depression came and there were inadequate funds to finish the building. It was necessary to simply put a roof on the structure. This meant that the lower floor was to become the sanctuary and the upper floor the hall. The funds were so limited that a full ceiling was not possible. Thus the ceiling height in the centre was 8 feet, but on both sides the ceiling sloped down to 4 feet. The areas along both sides became the area for the Sunday School classes with tables and small chairs placed in the area. Adults had to stoop to walk and the teachers had to sit!

Despite these inconveniences, a Sunday school flourished and evening services were a success due in great part to the leadership of the first pastor, E.L. Leeman, and later Mr. S.P. Miller, an evangelical Presbyterian

Sticky Walls and Cold Toes

In their "Historical Recollections," long-time parishioners Frank and Janet Anderson describe the original Dunbar Heights Baptist Church building as it was in 1926: "The lower floor had thin wooden board paneling extending half the way up. . . . Due to being below grade, or due to poor quality varnish, the wood was 'sticky' and as kids we would press our hands against the wall to feel them stick. . . . The church was initially heated by a coal stove located at the front, to the left of the pulpit. It had to be filled and started Saturday night if there was to be heat on Sunday, and if someone forgot there was a cold service on Sunday!"

◄ Dunbar Heights Baptist Church. Courtesy of Joan Tyldesley.

Dunbar Heights Baptist Church

1926 · Home mission established; two-storey shingled brown building constructed

1929 · Closure of mission

1931 · Building redecorated, reopened by Rev. A.F. Baker

1948 · Extensive renovations; tower built to provide new entrance

1961 · New church completed

and father of the well-known missionary author Isobel Kuhn. During Mr. Miller's stay, the Sunday school of Dunbar Heights Mission was more of an interdenominational "Community Sunday School." There was also no real attempt as yet to establish a Baptist church. But this was all about to change.

The church suffered a serious setback when the streetcar line was discontinued. This, along with financial difficulties, resulted in the closure of the mission in early 1929. Unable to sell the property, the executive council commented in a report, "Brethren? We have made a mistake in this Dunbar affair, and let us cry earnestly to the forgiving Lord for deliverance."

Deliverance appeared in the form of the determined Rev. A.F. Baker, a veteran leader, "retired" minister, and recently appointed pastor-at-large. He believed that a Baptist church in Dunbar Heights was a viable vision, despite the economic problems of the Depression. He was instrumental in having the building redecorated and reopened for evening services in late 1931. By January 1932, a morning Sunday school was once again welcoming students, and attendance grew to more than 125 within the year. This growth necessitated further improvements to the building. In 1932 a first-grade edge-grain floor was laid in the Primary Department for $46. This was quite a sum considering that regular bills included $2 a month for electricity and $18 a year for fuel.

Pastor Baker believed that a full-time pastor was also required. The Rev. W. J. Thomson, an Irishman, arrived from Kamloops in 1933 to answer the call and served the congregation until he retired in 1946. These were hard times economically: first there was the Depression and, soon after, World War II. Attempts to relocate the church closer to Dunbar Street in the hope that improved visibility and accessibility might result in greater attendance were unsuccessful. Nevertheless, Reverend Thomson, with the help of his wife, led the church through these trying times. Theirs was one of the significant ministries of Dunbar Heights Baptist. They introduced a full schedule of services, with children's ministries being their particular strength. According to the Andersons: "During the 1930s the Sunday School reached an attendance of 150 scholars, all crammed into the church building. A Friday night children's meeting, the Twilight Hour, was likewise successful with over 100 children attending. There was singing, lantern slides, and stories told by Mrs. Thomson." A highlight for the whole congregation was a special service on 30 May 1935 that officially recognized the congregation as a Regular Baptist Church.

Upon Reverend Thomson's retirement, John Richards served as student pastor for several years. He was ordained in June 1953 and continued at the church until 1959, when he returned to Northwest Baptist Theological College, this time as a faculty member. During his ministry, Reverend Richards remained a bachelor, dedicating all his energy to the church, particularly to the youth. One example of his successful youth ministry was the establishment of the first Vacation Bible School at the church in July 1947. It continued as an annual event, with more than 120 children attending. For university and college students there was the College and Career Program. The average attendance was 50. The Andersons report that "they met Sunday night but also had weekday events such as skating parties, bowling parties, and other social events. Many, many students from out of town found a home in the Dunbar church."

The year 1948 was another turning point for the congregation. The decision was finally made to keep the church at its present location and to embark on extensive renovations. Reverend Richards designed a new church and, although it was not under construction until 1960, a tower was added in 1948 to provide a new entrance to the church with access to both floors. The tower's second storey became the pastor's study.

In 1951 pews were purchased. The Andersons remembered how Reverend Richards did his part. "Pastor Richards was a perfectionist! He did a lot of physical work around the church and built a new pulpit, built tables for the Sunday school, built benches for seats, and cupboards for storage. Often as a youth Frank [Anderson] helped him, sometimes into the wee hours of the morning." At this time the church had two musical instruments, a piano and a pump organ. Mary Martin played the piano and Rose Knight the organ. The piano was replaced in 1955 with a Heintzman for $200, and the organ in 1956 with a small spinette Conn electric organ worth $1,700. The church paid for Mrs. Knight's 10 lessons on the new organ. Frank Anderson, who eventually obtained his music degree, became one of the main organists.

Outside the church building there were changes too. In 1957 the property adjacent to the east became available and was purchased by the church for $11,500. This would eventually provide space for the projected major building expansion and for the parking lot. This expansion took place during the ministry of Reverend Richards' successor, the Reverend Don Reed. The Andersons wrote: "Rev. Reed had a family of three children. He was very organized and energetic. During his time the college and career work flourished as did the young couples. He produced the *Dunbar Visitor*, a monthly publication distributed throughout the community. Children's meetings were held annually with an attendance so large that one year the fire marshal came and made us clear the aisles." The new building was constructed by Mr. Karsgaard with Mr. Rapske as architect and was completed on 5 March 1961. Reverend Richards' design became a reality, with the men of the church contributing much time and effort to its completion. Frank Hills assisted with the wiring and Gerald Anderson's firm, Barr and Anderson, did all the plumbing and heating. Almost the first service to be celebrated in the new church was the wedding of Joyce Anderson and Al Pomeroy.

The older part of the church was rebuilt too, but not until the Reverend Jack Graham was pastor in the early 1970s. He had come from London, England, to take over from Reverend Reed. He was apparently such an "inspiring speaker that people from all over Vancouver attended the church to hear him, to the point that chairs had to be placed in the aisles and along the back."

Many others have left their stamp upon the church and its community. There was Pastor Jim Turner (1978–90), whose interest in young couples brought in more than 50 couples for monthly educational meetings and social activities. Dan Meyer, pastoral intern in the early 1990s, was instrumental in establishing the Crown Street Kids Club, a program still in operation. During Reverend Brick Sanderson's ministry (1994–97), the popular Alpha course was offered for the first time to members of the community. This involved meeting Friday nights for a meal, video and a discussion about the basics of the Christian faith. Pastor Darcy Van Horn, who served as a student assistant pastor to Jim Turner before becoming pastor at Dunbar Height Baptist (1997–2002), established a partnership with a Cantonese-speaking congregation (Vancouver Christian Logos Church), who were seeking a building to worship in until their numbers and financial situation allowed them to develop their own facility.

The year 2001 was the 75th anniversary of the original church building's construction. Dunbar Heights Baptist has gone through many face-lifts. And how will it face the future? Perhaps the Andersons' summary of their church's vision is an appropriate response:

> As needs in the community become apparent, and resources are available, the Dunbar Church hopes to meet the needs. Future ministries may include a senior's ministry, a single parent's ministry, an expanded ethnic ministry, further College and Career ministry, and possibly a ministry to persons with addictions. The Dunbar Heights Baptist church is a small church and cannot do all things. Yet it hopes to involve every member in meaningful ministry and to reach out to meet the spiritual needs of the community. Our world is changing but the inner needs of men and women remain the same. Different methods of ministry may be required in our information age but the message of God's love for mankind remains the same.

Hunter Presbyterian Church

Nothing remains of the little hall that once stood at 3670 West 27th Avenue, now the site of a residence. Only a few neighbours still remember it and the activities that once took place there. Even fewer recall its life as Hunter Presbyterian Church. Unfortunately, there are no records of the church in the Vancouver Archives of the Presbyterian Church in Canada. It is mentioned, however, in the 1937 *Act and Proceedings of the Presbytery of Canada*, which lists it as a mission field church rather than as a self-sustaining congregation.

Mr. W. J. McConnell is one previous Dunbar resident who had a special connection with the church. From 1934 to 1935 he helped his grandfather Samuel Henderson and a Mr. Hunter while they were renovating a building to make it suitable as a church hall. Mr. McConnell was then a boy of seven and thinks his helping probably consisted of holding the nails. Unfortunately, his grandfather enjoyed the fruits of his labour only for a short time. He died in 1937 at the age of seventy-nine.

The McConnells lived at 3642 West 27th Avenue, two doors down from the church. McConnell's grandmother, Hortense Henderson, used to have "tea" ready by about 3:00 P.M., just in time for his sister Kathleen to take it to the "carpenters" after school. McConnell also recalled that it became his job to "polish Sunday best shoes for seven McConnell children to attend Sunday school. I usually did this on Saturday evening

◀ Mr. and Mrs. Samuel Henderson were founding members of Hunter Presbyterian Church in the mid-1930s. Mr. Henderson and a Mr. Hunter converted a house on West 27th Avenue just southeast of St. Philip's Anglican Church into a meeting hall for a Presbyterian mission congregation. Courtesy of Bill McConnell.

Hunter Presbyterian Church

1935 · The house at 3670 West 27th Avenue is renovated as a hall by Mr. Hunter and Mr. Henderson

1936 · Listed as a mission field church

LATE 1950s · Closed

1965 · Sold to the Sweeney family, who attended Immaculate Conception Parish

1970s · Demolished and replaced by a residence, now 3688 West 27th Avenue

while my mother was pressing shirts, skirts, etc. for my siblings and me. It was a chore that I volunteered to do, I enjoyed it, and I'm still probably the best shoe polisher in the Vancouver area."

The little church hall built of donated materials and volunteer labour was simple in design, almost austere. McConnell conjectured that it was named after Mr. Hunter because he was higher up in the church hierarchy. Betty (McGlashan) Abbot believed it was because the Hunters, who lived nearby, had given the money to buy the building that became the church. Abbot, who attended Sunday school there for a short time, described it as "just a big hall with a little room on the side. . . . I think it was a house they gutted. They just had wooden chairs to sit on inside and this little platform up at the front that was about a foot high. The piano was over on the right-hand side and my mother [Mary Mc-Glashan] played the piano and we sat in the front row. My dad, I guess, was ushering or something like that."

Raymond Poulter, a Dunbar resident who attended Sunday school there about 1940, remembered the building this way: "It was more of a 'community hall' design with no markings or religious figures used anywhere. The building was ground level with only one step up into a small hallway. The seating was ordinary chairs (moveable) on a hardwood floor. It would hold approximately 60 to 70 people. The heating was done by a wood-burning heater in the back corner." The congregation consisted primarily of people with Scottish roots. The ministers were mostly temporary placements, students or guest ministers.

Activities at the church focused on the needs of the congregation. The young people helped to organize and present concerts at special times of the year, such as Christmas and Easter, but everything had to be done on a small scale. This was a challenging time to start and maintain a church with a small number of members. According to Poulter, "As it was wartime it was sometimes hard to get help or older volunteers. So I along with a couple of the other teenage boys would take turns doing the janitor work and cutting and raking the front lawn and in the fall/winter time, going in early Sunday morning to light and start the furnace that burned wood and sometimes coal."

The church closed in the late 1950s when its remaining members went to St. Andrew's Hall at UBC. Poulter surmises that the church came to an end because there were not enough young people to continue the work begun by the older members. "It was a church that had very few marriages or funerals conducted there. It was more of a meeting place on Sunday mornings and closed the other six days and nights with no extra activities conducted." Mr. McConnell's younger sister, Mary McConnell (now McGowan), was probably one of the last to be married there, in 1957.

After its church days were over, the building was put up for sale and purchased by the Sweeney family, who lived next door at 3692 West 27th

Avenue, with the proceeds going to St. Andrew's Hall at UBC. The Sweeneys rented out the building to the Knights of Columbus Point Grey Council #4615 for about one and a half years. After that it had many different tenants.

The hall is best remembered today for the fun had by those who participated in the concerts and plays that Maureen Sweeney organized in the 1960s. "I used to put them all to work at putting on a Christmas concert. They were called the neighbourhood players and the concert was always presented in the 'old church hall' and what fun we had. Each year it got bigger and kids from as far away as four or five blocks would knock on my door to see if they could be in the concert. It was also a great place for the neighbourhood New Year's Eve Gala."

In the 1970s the building was demolished and replaced with a new house (3688 West 27th Avenue). In Sweeney's words, "I don't think the neighbourhood is quite the same without the old church hall on 27th."

Southlands Chapel

On the northwest corner of 39th Avenue and Dunbar Street is a unique-looking building of "primitive English" architecture reminiscent of a house, a church and a community hall. It is a residence now, but its history is among the most interesting of any building in Dunbar. It began its life in 1929 as a house built with wood salvaged from Wreck Beach. In the early 1940s the residence and double lot were purchased by the Reverend Byron Welch, who had moved from Winnipeg to pastor several Baptist churches in Vancouver. He had already established an independent congregation in Dunbar on 18 September 1940, which met in a store near the Dunbar Theatre. He wanted to design and build a church to house his fledgling congregation, and his vision became a reality when he built an extension onto the house at 5475 Dunbar Street.

An article titled "Southlands Pastor Erects Chapel Singlehanded" from a local newspaper dated 10 September 1949 described the new church: "It is of cement block construction and will seat 150. All money received for construction came in without solicitation." The sermon of the first evening service in the new church was "The Inside Story of the Building of Southlands Chapel." Unfortunately a copy of this sermon has not been located and details are sparse. We do know that the new edifice had a spire to which, at a later date, a hand pointing to heaven was attached. During the hurricane that hit Vancouver during the 1960s, lightning struck and split the spire, knocking down the hand. When Reverend Welch applied to the city to build a different spire, the city refused the request and allowed him to rebuild only according to the old design. The city was not too keen on the hand either, it seems, and so it was not returned to the roof.

Southlands Chapel

Reverend Welch's nephew and namesake, Byron Welch, said Southlands Chapel had another unique feature. Apparently there used to be a rock garden with flowers in front of the chapel. The rocks were painted white and arranged to read "Christ Died for Our Sins." Some kids, however, decided to have a little fun one day and changed the rocks to read "Christ Died for Our Skins." Realizing that the stones were an invitation to practical jokers, the minister had them removed.

His nephew remembered Reverend Welch as being a man with a true streak of Cornish independence. He had come to Canada from Cornwall, England, in 1927. He worked on the Prairies for a few years, during which time he contracted and battled tuberculosis. He then went to Toronto Baptist Seminary and became an ordained Baptist minister. After meeting and marrying his first wife, Grace Walker, in Kamloops, he travelled with her to Winnipeg to work as a Baptist minister. Finally, they moved to Vancouver. According to Byron Welch: "Grace worked very hard to promote the chapel in its early beginnings. Often she would go from door to door in the area inviting people to the chapel services. She was the driving force behind the early growth of the congregation and the establishment of a large Sunday school." Unfortunately, Grace died of a heart problem a year before the completion of the chapel. Her son Byron ("Barry") was only two years old. Six years later, Reverend Welch married Anna Kelly. She lent him money to put the finishing touches on the chapel.

Nephew Byron Welch came to stay with his uncle in 1957, after arriving from Jersey in the Channel Islands in the company of his father, the Reverend John Welch. Byron worked as youth director and Sunday school teacher at Southlands Chapel from 1957 to 1963. His method of drawing to illustrate his lessons proved popular with the students. Creativity seemed to run in the family. According to Byron:

> My uncle was very ingenious with old wood and logs he used to drag from the beach. He made a whole playground full of rides for the kids to play on at the chapel. The rides became very popular with the locals, who would knock on his door every day to ask whether they could play on the rides. When he retired to White Rock he did the same thing for his grandchildren. The rides became so popular that people (including the Mayor!) used to drop their kids off to play. My uncle and aunt would give the kids a short Sunday school–style talk every day and then they could play as long as they liked on the rides.

By 1960, however, the church was in decline. When Marineview Chapel opened in 1961 on the corner of 41st Avenue and Crown Street, many young people left to attend there. Although nephew Byron had considered going into the ministry, he decided to study at UBC and SFU to become an educator. Reverend Welch continued on at Southlands Chapel

until about 1969. The last wedding he performed at the chapel was between his own son Barry and Marilyn Sostad. When he retired, his congregation dispersed.

For a short time, Southlands Chapel continued to be used for religious services, first by another group of Baptists, then by a group headed by a female minister, Mildred Wakefield, that renamed the chapel Bible Holiness. Eventually, Reverend Welch decided to sell the building. The money from the sale went to pay off debts incurred by the chapel and some probably went to Anna, to repay her for her loan. Reverend Welch enjoyed several years of retirement before he succumbed to throat cancer in 1985.

Prudence Leach, an artist and sculptor of clay, bought the building and worked in it for about two years, after which she sold it again and moved to Santa Barbara. Following her departure, during the early 1970s, the building was used as a preschool for one or two years. In the mid-1970s, however, it housed another religious group, called the Emissaries of Divine Light, a communal group founded by Lloyd Meeker in 1945 in Colorado. Before dying in a plane crash in 1954, Meeker converted Lord Martin Cecil, who founded the Canadian commune at 100 Mile House.

"Bishop" Martin Cecil was the director of the Emissaries from 1954 until his death in 1984, when his son Michael Exeter took over. In the mid-1970s the group moved from 100 Mile House to Vancouver and stayed in Dunbar for about two years. Since their departure, artists, sculptors, painters, dancers and musicians (see chapter 7) have occupied the house/chapel.

A little piece of history was lost when artist Morley Wiseman found the old printer's plates used by Reverend Welch for his church newsletter in the building's basement and transformed them into metal armatures

▲ The words "Repent and Turn to the Lord" are still visible on a tree in Pacific Spirit Park after 50 years of weathering. Such messages were probably written on various trees by Rev. Byron Welch, who was often seen during the 1950s entering and leaving the park (then the UBC Endowment Lands) with his paintbrush and small bucket of paint. Courtesy of Pam Chambers.

for his clay sculptures. Yet this adaptation is symbolic of the building itself, which stands as a reminder of Reverend Welch's work, despite the fact that it has undergone many changes to accommodate a diverse group of tenants and owners.

Dunbar Evangelical Lutheran Church

During World War II, several Norwegian fishermen left Prince Rupert and settled with their families in the Dunbar area. They were Lutheran, and their common interest in establishing a church in their new neighbourhood was soon shared by other Lutheran parents living in Dunbar, who were keen to have a Sunday school for their children close to home. Robert Garvin canvassed the neighbourhood for pupils, and in December 1942, classes were held for the first seven students in the Richter Iverson home at 3578 West 30th Avenue. Garvin became the Sunday school's first superintendent, and his wife assisted with the music.

Pastor Anders Aasen of First Lutheran offered to take on the task of establishing church services for parents of the Sunday school children as a personal home mission project. He rented a "hamburger joint" at 5640 Dunbar Street, near 41st Avenue, for $30 per month, which Mr. Iverson and Mrs. Garvin cleaned and transformed into a chapel. The original plain white altar and pulpit built by Mr. Garvin now reside in the basement of the present church. The building that once housed them was again an eatery in 1968, when the church celebrated its 25th anniversary. It was called the Cathay Cafe and its proprietor was known as Gus. In 2006 the old building was MLA Colin Hansen's constituency office.

The chapel was attractive enough but poorly ventilated and was heated only by a corner wood stove. Aage Pedersen, who later became council president, had a special memory of these aspects of the chapel, as quoted in a 25th-anniversary booklet. "I can remember so clearly our son, Ernest, leaving the house early every Sunday that first winter to light a fire in the old coal and wood heater. The heater was lit only on Sundays. No more than a few lucky people who were near the heater kept warm during the sermon in that cold winter." Initially there was no organized congregation and only volunteer pastors. About a dozen families attended services regularly, the nucleus being fishing families and former members of St. Paul's Lutheran Church in Prince Rupert. Chris Moan, a pioneer member, described these early days in a 50th-anniversary booklet: "Asbjurg and I came from Prince Rupert in 1943. We started attending Dunbar Evangelical Lutheran Church, which was then a Chapel with meetings held at a 'hamburger joint' on Dunbar St., close to 41st Avenue. The meetings were conducted by a layman pastor, Fred Hoyme, and about 20 people attended. Church services were held, along with a Sunday School, Ladies Aid group and a string band."

Fred Hoyme or Oscar Lokken (when Hoyme was on duty with the active Air Force) were the first to provide regular Sunday sermons. There were 38 children and eight teachers in the Sunday school. Most significantly, there was a sincere desire to expand the facility and become an official church. On 3 October 1943, a special meeting was held in the chapel, and a motion was passed to form a Lutheran congregation for the Point Grey area, to be called Dunbar Evangelical Lutheran Congregation. The church was registered as a legal entity in Victoria on 25 April 1944, under the leadership of the first elected council members.

That summer Dunbar Lutheran welcomed its first resident pastor, Arnold F. Anderson, who later wrote: "I arrived in Vancouver on July 10, 1944. . . . I first conducted a service in the little 'chapel.' . . . About 35 people were present. This response was, frankly, rather deflating to this fledgling pastor who had been given quite a different picture of the prospects for this new mission." Indeed, Pastor Anderson had received a letter that described the Dunbar mission as the most promising in the Norwegian Lutheran Church of America (renamed the Evangelical Lutheran Church after 1946). It soon became apparent that if this congregation were to grow it needed to build a church of its own. The challenge was to find a building site that was central to the Lutherans living in the area.

For the Norwegian members especially, it was important to find a site that reminded them of the hilltop churches back home. Pastor Aasen offered to assist once again and made the needs of the young congregation known to a widow who owned four lots at 31st and Collingwood,

◄ The first meeting place for the founders of Dunbar Evangelical Lutheran Church as it appeared in 1968, as an eatery at 5640 Dunbar. Courtesy of Dunbar Evangelical Lutheran Church.

Dunbar Evangelical Lutheran Church

1942 · Sunday school classes at Richter Iverson home

1942–43 · 5640 Dunbar Street "hamburger joint" transformed into chapel; first worship service

1944 · Dunbar Evangelical Lutheran Church congregation registered

1947 · Church building completed at present address, 3491 West 31st Avenue

situated at a point of elevation. He asked if she would be willing to sell one corner lot. At first she refused, but after a third request, she amazingly agreed to sell all four lots. These were purchased in 1944 with some financial help from headquarters in Minneapolis and contributions gained from canvassing.

The design for the church was drawn up by Lang and Raugland, architects from Minneapolis. A Swedish contractor, George Diffner, received the building contract. He gave the church council a good deal and they did him a favour in return — he could show the Swedish community he was capable of building a beautiful church. Because of severe building restrictions during World War II, construction did not begin until 1946.

Pastor Anderson acted as treasurer and contact person for the builders and suppliers. Members of the congregation volunteered their talents to help finish the interior. According to Chris Moan, "Robert Garvin did all the woodwork in the church, and together with a fellow manual arts teacher, Mr. Donaldson, carved the altar, the baptismal font and the pulpit. Both did the work for free. Anfelt Antonsen and I paid for the materials. In 1960, Hans Antonsen left $3,800 to the Church in his will and part of the money went to the making of the stained glass window in the front of the Church. Aage Pedersen ordered it from England, with the inscription 'The Word alone, Grace alone, Faith alone and Lo, I am with you always.'"

By Christmas 1946, the basement was available for use, and by February 1947, the whole building was ready for services and functions. Pastor Aasen attended the festive dedication on Palm Sunday. Although the church had cost almost $30,000, since the congregation had declared itself no longer a mission church but a self-supporting one just prior to the dedication, it was determined to pay off the building loan from the Church Extension Fund as soon as possible.

With a new building, the congregation experienced a boost in attendance, financial growth, and an increase in activities and programs. In Chris Moan's words, "We were a small church with big dreams." By 1951 the membership was 134, and by 1959 it was 381. On a Sunday in 1955, a record 60 people became pledged members. Pastor H. Curtis Satre described this momentous occasion in the church's 25th-anniversary booklet: "The group was so large that it was not quite possible for them to have standing room in the spacious chancel area of the church. . . . How hard it was for me to share the feelings of the lady across the street who protested Monday morning about the crowded parking conditions around the church. Understand her dilemma, yes. Share her complaints? Hardly."

As Dunbar Lutheran evolved into a thriving congregation, it never forgot its origins. The First Fishermen's Festival was held in April 1953.

The nearest bishop came from Seattle to bless the fishing boats, as they headed out for another fishing season. The special service was held at Trinity Lutheran on River Road in Annieville (now Delta), and Pastor H.A. Strand, of Dunbar Lutheran, participated. Following the service, everyone gathered for a salmon supper that became a highlight for all, not least the bishop (who apparently considered this a welcome change from the macaroni and cheese dishes he usually ate at church functions back home). In fact, fish was the main course at many a church event, with fishermen cleaning their catch in the church kitchen.

The fishermen and their families continued to be an integral part of the congregation at Dunbar Lutheran. Pastor Satre remarked that during his first year there, shortly after the First Fishermen's Festival, two men, Fred Palmer and Nathan Walters, "were perhaps the only two men from the congregation who could be present to act as ushers during the fishing season." It was especially tragic, therefore, when boats were lost at sea with church members on board. In December 1963, two Antonsens went missing. In April 1965, Olaf Sayer was lost at sea from the vessel *Combat*. And in February 1966, Roy Eilertsen drowned when the *Ocean Star* capsized. Perhaps it is a tribute to them that even after 25 years, Dunbar Evangelical Lutheran was still known by many as "The Fisherman's Church."

As an ancient Christian symbol, the fish was used as the name for a special interdenominational outreach project. Betty Gjertsen, a long-time active church member, recalled that "the 'Fish' program was an excellent effort of churches working together to meet the needs of the community. I remember working with the United Church, and Catholic Church members and others to do such things as help people who were handicapped with correspondence, provide rides to appointments, etc."

Dunbar Lutheran's involvement in "Fish" occurred primarily during the years of Pastor Bent J. Damkar (1963–77). He encouraged a charismatic movement that brought many diverse groups of people to Dunbar Lutheran. Edna Sparshu, whose family joined the church in 1967, reminisced: "I especially have many great memories from the times Pastor Damkar and his wife Eleanor were there. They were so involved in everything. She did a lot of counselling, and also was very on top of everything going on. She had us all taking meals to anyone that needed help. I must say she was probably the one lady that got us helping others. . . . It really got us knowing what Christianity is all about."

Madeleine Hawkes was the Sunday school superintendent during this special time. According to Betty Gjertsen, under Hawkes' leadership, "we had so many students that we used the kitchen, the balcony of the church, the church nave, Damkars' kitchen nook, living room and basement bedroom and recreation room (in the next-door parsonage) besides dividing the downstairs of the church into several classrooms using dividers. . . . Madeleine was a public-school teacher, loved teaching and

A Spirit of Togetherness

Two women painted vivid pictures of activities at Dunbar Lutheran in a booklet of tributes to the church's 50th anniversary. Christine Moan recalled: "Every year before Easter, there was an organized cleaning at the Church. The ladies were high and low on ladders and kneeling pads, with soap and water, with scrub brushes and lots of elbow grease, plus furniture wax and endless polishing. . . . It was then time to invite friends to a Tea at the church. . . . Those were the days when all the ladies wore hats and gloves." Tamara Karise remembered how Eleanor Damkar, the pastor's wife, helped with the making of quilts and baby layettes. "For a while, she even had her sewing machine in the basement of the church and sewed the pieces together. . . . As far as I can remember the most quilts and layettes we made in a year were fifty."

An Organ Heaven-Sent

For many years, Dunbar Lutheran used an electric organ donated in April 1951 to replace a little "hand organ." According to Eleanor Damkar, some church members were attending a retreat at Westminster Abbey in Mission, B.C., when the abbey's organist, Father Basil, told them about a pipe organ for sale in Shaughnessy. Although a new organ was not a priority, a committee went to see the organ. It was definitely suitable—and at a reasonable price. The one catch was that every pipe had to be connected to the organ keys. David Unsworth and Bud Hendrickson spent all Saturday night wiring and splicing to prepare for the Sunday service.

Jeanette Mende, David Unsworth's sister, retired in 2003 after many years as an organist at Dunbar Evangelical Lutheran Church. Courtesy of Vivien Clarke.

children, excelled at flannelgraph stories and was an excellent puppeteer." Jeanette Mende, who began her teaching career under Madeleine, recalled that the Sunday school grew to more than 100 children. When Mende joined the church as an adult after having witnessed the laying of its cornerstone years earlier, she observed: "There were adults and children of all ages. The church was family oriented and we knew the children, parents, grandparents, etc., of almost everyone. That made the church feel like home to us. It was enjoyable to talk to friends after the service. Instead of the coffee times we now have, the entire congregation would spread out over the front steps of the church and the sidewalk just enjoying talking to one another."

It is this "family atmosphere" that is most often referred to in reminiscences about Dunbar Lutheran. In his contribution to the 50th anniversary history, Pastor Satre wrote, "Dunbar [Lutheran] has not grown to be a large congregation, but it stands tall in its demonstration of love and caring for others." In his contribution to the history, Karl Erdman, a previous church member, added that "Dunbar has always been blessed with people who have been faithful to keep a neat house. It is truly a pretty church set on a hill."

In 1966 Dunbar Lutheran became loan free. Pastor A.O. Aasen, then ninety-three, was a guest of honour at a specially organized celebration. Since the late 1970s, however, Dunbar Lutheran has faced real challenges, one of which is a decline in numbers. In 2000 Alma Lawrence wrote: "Yes, our church has changed, our young people grew up, married, and moved out of town where they could afford to buy a home and work, so our numbers started to decrease; others moved to other churches for various reasons, and some have passed on. And also the time we are living in, people don't feel the need to attend church." In the early years, people who attended were not just Norwegian but also of Danish, Latvian or Estonian descent, many being from the Prairies. This was a distinct cultural mix of people, one no longer representative of Dunbar's residents in the twenty-first century.

When Dunbar Lutheran celebrated its 25th anniversary in 1968, it had plans to expand. On the last page of the anniversary booklet, Aage Pedersen wrote: "We must look ahead. My hope is still, that before too long an educational unit or wing will be standing where the parsonage is now situated. The future for Dunbar is with the youth and we must not allow ourselves to settle down and be satisfied with what we've done. The congregation has to grow and we must be prepared to have a much greater outreach." The educational wing was never built. The lot on which the parsonage stood was sold in 2002 to meet financial needs. The parsonage was torn down and replaced in 2004 by a new home. But the spirit and determination that built the church still exists in its remaining members, and there is hope that a new chapter is about to be written.

In April 2002, Pastor Ken Grambo transferred his Norwegian and Prairie roots to Dunbar Lutheran. The self-styled "Singing Pastor," who is also a recording artist, brings along his guitar or banjo every Sunday and inspires his congregation with a song — usually an original composition. He schedules public concerts at the church and presents music and anecdotes seasoned with a sense of humour and based on the highs and lows of his life. He and his wife, Noreen, are working hard to make the church once more a "light on the hill" for the community in which it stands. Dunbar Lutheran celebrated its 60th anniversary in 2004.

▲ Pastor Ken Grambo and parishioner Stacey Zabolotney inspire the congregation of Dunbar Lutheran with their music at Sunday morning services and special concerts. Courtesy of Vivien Clarke.

Marineview Community Church

Marineview Community Church, located at 4000 41st Avenue, is unique in both its architecture and its organization. Unlike other congregations in the neighbourhood, where the major responsibility for spiritual leadership is provided by a priest, rector or pastor, Marineview is a "lay" church with a group of elders who oversee all the church's ministries. A hired staff person acts as an administrator and coordinator, but does not deliver sermons every Sunday. This duty is shared with other members of the congregation and invited guest speakers. The church has been described by Ralph Bagshaw, one of its senior members, as a "bus-stop fellowship," since many UBC students and teachers and their families attend until studies or jobs necessitate their moving on.

Marineview Community Church

1960–61 · Land purchased and church built at 4000 West 41st Avenue; Will Wilding founder and architect; mostly lay leadership

1970s · Immense growth; many university and college students and young families

1971 · George Malone became first paid pastor

1980s · Congregation became so large it decided to split into three groups, two of which built fellowships at the University Chapel and in Kitsilano

The building that houses this distinctive community is the most modern of the church buildings in Dunbar. It was built for $40,000 in 1960 according to the design of one of its founders, Will Wilding, an architect. Wilding, his wife Shelagh and two other couples, Ed and Stevie Barter and Bill and Jean McAllister, who all attended Kitsilano Chapel, purchased the property at 41st Avenue and Crown Street for $10,000 in 1960 in pursuit of their vision to establish an independent community church in Dunbar.

In September 1961, Marineview Chapel opened its doors with its eye on a changing world and its roots in the Open or Christian Brethren. Even then, there was no pastor. Instead, church elders conducted the services. But in 1971, a time of spiritual and social turmoil, a call for additional leadership was answered by George and Bonnie Malone. George was a young seminary student from Texas, and his ability to teach and reach people, particularly youth, inspired an amazing growth in numbers. By the mid-1970s the church had between 500 and 600 members, far more than the seating capacity of about 175 could accommodate. According to Bruce Anthony, who became involved in Marineview as a teenager in 1978, "Marineview had three services and was so full each Sunday morning that if you didn't arrive early you would sit at the back and have a tough time seeing the front." (In tune with the times, the carpet was apparently purple and the interior painted orange.)

The solution was to offer three services: at 8:30 and 10:00 on Sunday morning and at 7:00 in the evening. With about 200 attending each service, it was still standing room only. The congregation even then included many university and college students and young families. As a result, a wide variety of programs for children, youth and adults was developed. Ralph Bagshaw remembered that the church, when he and his family joined in 1979, was "very much alive, especially youthful, crowded, enthusiastic, [and] drew folk from all walks of life."

Four other leaders came to Marineview in the 1970s and contributed immensely to its growth: Paul Stevens, former pastor at Point Grey Baptist Church; Michael Nicols, an understudy of Stevens and student at Regent College, UBC; Dan Williams; and Jan Porcino.

While the men did most of the public speaking, teaching and preaching at the Sunday services, Bagshaw recalled that "both men and women shared in leading 'House Group Fellowships,' which were a vitally integral part of the teaching and informal counselling of the church. Women had a major role with Sunday school work. Men and women co-led youth ministry. Some women leaders commenced Community Home Bible Study groups. They were well attended by neighbours and others for years. Men and women with an interest or gift in 'marriage counselling' did this in their own homes with neighbours or work colleagues."

◄ The founding fathers of
Marineview Chapel in the 1960s:
Eugene Cameron, Ed Baxter, John
Shannon, Will Wilding (architect)
and Bill McAllister. Courtesy of
Marineview Chapel.

During this time Marilyn Bagshaw founded the preschool for three- to
four-year-olds that is still in operation at Marineview.

Although this was a time of tremendous vitality, the needs of the
congregation were becoming increasingly difficult to meet and led to reorganization in the early 1980s. Bruce Anthony believed that Marineview
lost two of its most popular teachers and staff in this reorganization,
namely Paul Stevens (he always started his sermons with Herman cartoons) and George Malone, who apparently "spoke with a heavy Texas
drawl." Stevens volunteered to establish a new church called Dayspring
in the Kitsilano area and took some members with him. (This was a
short-lived venture, and Stevens later became a professor at Regent College.) George Malone moved on to minister at Emmanuel Community
Church in Richmond, B.C. Other leaders who left were Michael Nicols,
who went on to Capilano Christian Church on the North Shore, and
John Nolland and Carl Armeding. They of course took their young families with them. In addition, about 12 elders, who represented most of the
church's leadership, went to the University Chapel.

Another factor was to have an impact on Marineview. The young people who had been such an integral part of the church's life were growing
up, getting married and moving away. By May 1985, the size of Marineview's congregation had decreased to somewhere between 100 and 125
people. Of this group many more left within the year to go to jobs and
homes outside Vancouver. Many couples with young families who
wanted more space for Sunday school and youth activities also went elsewhere. This left a core group of about 75, which remained undaunted
and determined to regroup and rebuild.

The elders appointed Paul Meyers as pastor. He served for three challenging years. In 1989 Alistair Rees-Thomas, a practising lawyer, succeeded him. When he and his wife Nancy were joined in the early 1990s by Paul Beckingham, a visiting student from England studying at Regent College, and his wife Mary, new life and vision returned to Marineview. The youth who had remained during the 1980s and 1990s continued to be a dynamic part of the church. And despite the restructuring, Marineview was still well known for its music, outstanding preaching and powerful worship services. In 1994 Rees-Thomas went back to practising law and the Beckinghams went to Kenya as missionaries.

In 1998 a new pastoral team, Mark and Petra Anderson, also graduates of Regent College, arrived to carry on Marineview's purpose: to serve the community. Bruce Anthony described some of the challenges the church faces today: "As the church closest to the Endowment Lands [Pacific Spirit Park], we have had many men come out of the woods when they get too cold or wet. We have always tried to be caring but careful in the way we have helped them. The church has been generous with food and clothing and even medical attention. . . . It is frustrating to not see these people's lives transformed. . . . However, Marineview has never been so much about us changing people as it is giving people the opportunity to change as they learn more about God."

Anthony maintained, however, that there are others on whom Marineview has had a more long-term effect. "Perhaps it isn't the lives of Dunbar residents that have been affected the most by the congregation at Marineview; it is instead people who have lived among us for a short time while students, and then went back home, or off to a mission at places throughout the world. I have been told by dozens of people how they appreciated their time at Marineview, before they went off to places like Australia, South Africa, Pakistan, Nepal, Uganda, Indonesia, Liberia, Congo and Nagaland."

But for those Dunbar residents for whom Marineview is a spiritual home, there is much work that remains. They provide everyday practical help to seniors, new Canadians and international students. About 15 musicians take turns participating at the Sunday services, including pianists, drummers and guitar players. Daybreak Point Bible Camp on Anvil Island near Bowen Island still offers youth a wonderful summer experience. An open-door ministry provides support for single moms and their young children on Vancouver's Downtown Eastside. The legacy of Marineview's founders and the church's strong lay and pastoral leadership are integral to Marineview's survival and success.

Each church building in Dunbar presents an interesting history in itself, yet it is the stories and experiences of those who have participated in the social and spiritual functions of the churches that are most fascinating. As noted in the chapter's introduction, many congregations began as Sunday schools, and all felt the need for a place to practise their various faiths closer to home, in their own, emerging Dunbar neighbourhood. All have experienced some re-evaluation and transformation from generation to generation in response to social change, demographics and cultural diversity. Churches are only effective if their people and pastors are not only sincere in their beliefs but atuned to the needs of their community. In the foreword to *Retrospect: The Story of St. Philip's Anglican Church, Vancouver, 1925–1975*, there is mention of Mother Teresa, who worked among the poor in Calcutta. She is quoted as saying that "people do not expect from the church a stream of great statements. They expect love, concern and caring." As long as this remains true among the churches of Dunbar, and important for the neighbourhood in general, then Dunbar's churches will exist as more than historically interesting buildings.

CHAPTER 11

Parks, Gardens and Boulevards

↝ Margaret Moore

One of the reasons Dunbar is such a desirable place to live is that it is extremely well endowed with parkland. For every 1,000 residents there are 1.83 hectares of neighbourhood parkland, significantly above the city-wide average of 1.12 hectares. As the population of Dunbar increases and densifies, however, so does the pressure on its parks. Up until the late 1940s children played not only in parks, but also in the streets, in back lanes and in vacant lots. Children also played in bogs, marshes, ponds and streams. These natural features helped determine the location of many of the parks in Dunbar today.

For instance, the former Lake-at-the-Head Creek, which began its journey near Camosun Park and finally flowed into the Fraser River at the foot of Blenheim Street near Deering Island Park, was closely linked to some of Dunbar's largest parks. It meandered through Camosun Park, Camosun Bog in Pacific Spirit Park, Chaldecott Park and Memorial West Park on its way to the Fraser River. Without it, the residents of Dunbar might have inherited far fewer parks, for the stream created wet areas that were unsuitable sites for housing, especially given the engineering capabilities in the 1920s. In the twenty-first century these wet areas continue to present problems for the parks board. Tons of sand are applied annually to the playing fields at Chaldecott, Memorial West and Musqueam Parks, and surface water continues to rise in other parks.

Only at Camosun Bog is the legacy of Lake-at-the-Head Creek appreciated today, and work is underway to restore the volume of water required to maintain the bog.

A Natural Legacy

The reason that Dunbar has almost twice the parkland of other Vancouver neighbourhoods is rooted in civic politics. From 1908 to 1928, Dunbar was not part of the City of Vancouver but rather the southern part of the independent Corporation of Point Grey. During these years six standing committees carried out the responsibilities of the corporation, with the Subdivision Plans and Parks Committee being responsible for the acquisition and maintenance of municipal parks. As early as 1927, the park committees from the independent districts of Point Grey and South Vancouver began dedicating as much land as possible for park sites. In fact, they were urged to do so by the Vancouver Park Board (established in 1888), which saw the forthcoming amalgamation of these districts with Vancouver as a historic opportunity to gain considerable parkland without interference from Vancouver City Council. When the amalgamation of Point Grey and South Vancouver with the City of Vancouver took place in 1929, Vancouver's parkland doubled in one year. One of the major benefactors, of course, was the district of Dunbar, which had set aside as parkland an abundance of wet land unsuitable for housing. It had been important to do this before the deadline of 1 January 1929, after which future decisions on additional parkland could be vetoed by Vancouver City Council.

Before amalgamation, Harland Bartholomew, a prominent city planner from Chicago, created Vancouver's first comprehensive plan. His visits in 1927 and 1928 reinforced the views of the Vancouver Park Board, and in 1928 the Bartholomew Report for park areas in Point Grey was approved. Bartholomew felt that Vancouver, with its unique geographical setting, should use its waterfront for "water-related businesses or public enjoyment." His emphasis on waterfront access for recreational activities greatly benefited the citizens of Dunbar, who now have public access not only to beaches and waterfront on Burrard Inlet but also to much of the foreshore of the Fraser River.

The sudden acquisition of so much parkland on the eve of the Great Depression also brought the city problems. The newly acquired parks in Dunbar needed to be developed and maintained, and Vancouver City Council was sorely pressed for funding. Yet the Depression, which had an adverse effect almost everywhere else, had a positive effect on the parks in Dunbar. During the early '30s, the federal government began to provide funds to help relieve the hardships caused by unemployment. Men who received these funds were referred to as "relief workers" or "relief

◄ Margaret Campbell with daughter Margaret surrounded by flowers in her Dunbar garden in 1938. Courtesy of Margaret (Campbell) Moore.

labour." In the Dunbar area, they were hired by the City of Vancouver to work on Chaldecott, Balaclava and Memorial West Parks. The parks in Dunbar have also benefited from untold hours of volunteer labour and from generous financial support by citizens.

Unfortunately, the minutes of the parks committee of Point Grey have not survived and the chronological order of acquisition of parkland before 1929 remains unknown. The parks are described here in geographic order from Dunbar's northern boundary of 16th Avenue to the southern boundary of the Fraser River. Three administrative bodies oversee Dunbar's parks: the GVRD for Pacific Spirit Park, the Vancouver School Board for Camosun Park, and the Vancouver Board of Parks and Recreation for eight additional parks.

Camosun Park

South of 16th Avenue between Queen Elizabeth Elementary School and Imperial Street, Camosun Park was the site of the headwaters for Kh'aht-

◀ An aerial view of Camosun Park taken in February 1962. Lake-at-the-Head Creek began near 16th Avenue, north of the forest, and Discovery Street, wound its way in a southeasterly direction towards Chaldecott Park and finally emptied into the Fraser River. A darker line of trees can be seen where the creek once flowed. Centre right is Queen Elizabeth Elementary School, 16th and Camosun. To its left is Camosun Park, which would later be extended west to Imperial Street. South are the University Endowment Lands (now Pacific Spirit Park). To the east is Camosun Bog and a cleared area, the former site of the Vancouver city works supply yard. Bottom right are the playing fields of Chaldecott Park. Photo by George Allen Aerial Photos Ltd. Courtesy of the Vancouver Board of Parks and Recreation.

sulek, or Lake-at-the-Head Creek, the major stream draining the Dunbar area. Several small streams began north of 16th and Imperial, then crossed diagonally the present site of Camosun Park, where there was a swamp — or *mukwaam*. From there they continued southeast through Camosun Bog and drained out near the junction of Crown Street and King Edward Avenue into a cattail marsh covering most of the western section of Chaldecott Park. Many small drainage streams from the west fed into them along the way.

Lake-at-the-Head Creek emerged out of the marsh around Chaldecott Street between 28th and 29th. The stream continued to gather other Dunbar drainage from the east and eventually entered the Fraser River near Blenheim Street.

In the early 1940s, when Queen Elizabeth was a brand-new school, Camosun Park was still bush and bog. In 1944, the school's science teacher, Mr. McKierahan, taught a unit on the use of natural materials in building shelters. He divided the students into small groups and gave them two weeks in which to plan and build a shelter in the bush to the west of the school. They worked on the project after school and on weekends, and two weeks later about eight shelters had been constructed, which were then inspected and praised by Mr. McKierahan.

In June 1956, four new parks in Vancouver received names, among them Camosun Park. The bushes, bog, trees and ponds have long gone, replaced by a cinder track, a playing field and an adventure playground. Softball, rugby and soccer teams practise late in the evenings under the powerful lights that have been installed to prolong the hours the park can be utilized.

Quadra Park

Dunbar contains the city's smallest park, Quadra Park, which is only 0.13 hectares. It is hard to find, for it lies between the lanes on 17th and 18th Avenues in the 3400 block, east of Collingwood Street and west of Quadra Street. The little park and the short street at the south end of the park were both named for a Spanish naval officer — Juan Francisco de la Bodega y Quadra. Quadra Park was officially named in June 1958.

In the 1930s vine maples and the remains of stumps from logged-off trees dominated the area. Don Wilson and his friends Bill and Ernie Cooper and the Wallace boys would climb on the stumps, grab onto the vine maples, and yodel like Tarzan as they swung out in true African-jungle style. The park's grassy slope now offers a panoramic view over the city. Neighbours have discovered that it offers a good location from which to see the fireworks exploding over English Bay on a summer's evening. Curbs and lighting were a welcome addition to the park in the year 2000.

Valdez Park

Another Dunbar park also takes its name from the days of Spanish exploration of the coast. Cayetano y de Flores Valdes commanded the ship *Mexicana* and met Captain George Vancouver off Point Grey in 1792. Valdez Park, Dunbar's second smallest, occupies 0.77 hectares between 22nd and 23rd Avenues to the west of Balaclava Street. The western half of the block consists of houses and the eastern half is a grassy slope. Valdez Park was originally a park in the Corporation of Point Grey and was officially assigned its name in December 1930.

At the end of World War 1, Ernest Paul camped in the area that later became Valdez Park while he was building a house at 3256 West 22nd Avenue for himself and his wife, Nellie. They were moving west from Coburn, Ontario. In later years, Paul told his neighbours about sharing the area with a black bear who came to devour the blackberries and about the salmon fingerlings he saw in a nearby stream.

For several decades the park was left in its natural state. Pat Cowen recalled playing among the clumps of vine maples and larger trees growing there in the 1930s and '40s. Later the slope was grassed over. A hedge of orange-blossom bushes bordered the western boundary at one time, and neighbours Alan and Bernice Shaw kept the hedge trimmed for many years. Because of the sloping terrain, the park was not used for team sports, but since 1998 the upper part has been used for T-ball games.

Chaldecott Park

Francis Millar Chaldecott arrived in Vancouver from England in May 1890 and immediately became an active participant in the social and athletic activities of the young city. He lived at 1174 West Hastings and had his law office nearby at 626 West Hastings Street until September 1944, when he retired at the age of eighty-one. The 3.44-hectare park named for him is bordered by Crown and Wallace Streets and by West King Edward and 27th Avenues.

Chaldecott was a man of prodigious energy. Besides practising law, he worked on legislation for the protection of game birds and animals from 1891 to 1918, was on the Cricket Eleven from 1890 to 1900, played on the rugby football team, was a founding member of the Royal Vancouver Yacht Club, played golf at the Jericho Country Club and was a member of the Vancouver Club from its opening in 1893.

W. H. Lembke, a former alderman of Vancouver, is reported to have said: "When I was Reeve of Point Grey, Mr. Chaldecott lost twelve acres for non-payment of taxes, so we set it aside for park purposes, and then, afterwards, we named it Chaldecott Park in his honour."

Like other parcels of land that eventually became parks in Dunbar, Chaldecott's property was boggy and therefore unsuitable for houses. Perhaps Chaldecott simply "relinquished" the property for the purpose of a park. He owned considerable land throughout the city, including 43 hectares in South Vancouver and a half interest in 97 hectares in Point Grey. Chaldecott himself simply stated, "Chaldecott Road [later King Edward Avenue] was named for me by the South Vancouver Council and Chaldecott Park by the Point Grey Council." The only street that bears his name now is south of Chaldecott Park between 27th and 29th Avenues.

The 1926 annual report for the Corporation of Point Grey shows that $1,348.40 was spent on clearing and grading Chaldecott. In 1927 toilet installation cost a total of $574.77. The next year, $429.70 was spent on swings and $1,569.42 on a wading pool.

The results of the Great Depression were evident in 1930 as the Vancouver Park Board took over responsibility for the park. The seeding of the cleared areas was completed by relief labour at the cost of $108.71. Insurance was purchased for $2.83. A sum of $1,540.30 was allotted to Chaldecott Park in 1930 to cover payroll, tools and supplies. In the same year, "Earwig Eradication" throughout the city of Vancouver cost a grand

Left to right: Dorene Scott, Louise Hammarstrom and Joan McGirr on the south boundary of Chaldecott Park in 1937. Twenty-seventh Avenue later replaced the water-filled marsh and fence behind the three girls. Courtesy of Maddy (Shaw) Schmelcher. ▶

total of $12,733.35. In December 1932, the parks board received 27 bids to build a new field house, with the winning bid being $1,485.

Patsy (McQueen) Damms recalled Chaldecott Park in the 1930s and '40s, when she lived at 3840 West King Edward. "I can remember with absolute clarity the swings, teeters, pool, sandbox, trapeze and clubhouse over which we played 'Eidy-Eidy-I-over,' the trees we would climb, the scrub baseball games played after supper on the rustic diamond and the fern forts we would build on the edge of the bush. We knew exactly where every huckleberry bush was and would gorge ourselves each summer!" Damms said that at Christmas her whole family would go into the bush of the adjacent University Endowment Lands to find their Christmas tree. "I never could get used to buying a tree on a lot."

Maddy (Shaw) Schmelcher recalled the sounds of laughter and shouts of joy in the 1930s from children playing and splashing in the wading pool. She and her friends had a unique way of drying their wet bathing suits and warming themselves. They would lie on the warm asphalt of Wallace Street, which had been heated by the sun. Schmelcher also re-called peat bog fires occasionally erupting at the western edge of the park. There would be a "rush with honour" to break the fire alarm glass at 25th and Highbury to summon the fire trucks.

In the early years, King Edward Avenue was a single-lane dirt road. To the north of the road was a farm where dairy cows grazed in the fenced-in pasture. Betty McLean (later Albinson) or one of her siblings walked from their house on 21st Avenue to the farm every day after school in the early 1930s to have a bucket filled with fresh milk. In season they bought freshly picked greengage plums and other fruit and vegetables.

Very few of those who were children in the '30s, '40s and '50s remem-bered using the picnic area in the park. Instead, they recalled playing in the Chaldecott swamp, balancing on logs, climbing trees, eating blackber-ries and huckleberries, playing hide-and-go-seek in the bush and building forts. Before the days of organized athletic teams, a natural habitat was much more highly prized by children than a well-drained playing area.

Diane (Harper) Smith played in the park in the late 1930s. She re-members her father walking with her to Chaldecott Park from their house at 3884 West 21st Avenue. When they arrived, he would draw a circle with a piece of chalk on the cement adjacent to the wading pool. A line would radiate out from the centre and bisect the circle. "When the shade from that big tree hits this line," he would tell Diane, "then it's time for you to come home for dinner." Diane would run to play in the sandbox and on the swings and in the wading pool — but she would keep running back to the circle to check the location of the shadow on the sundial.

In 1995, the wading pool was replaced after nearly 65 years by a pop-ular water park, which has a West Coast rain forest theme. The original field house has been replaced by a building that houses a caretaker's

residence, public toilets and storage space for park activities. A creative children's playground has been added, but the original swings and the sandbox are still in use. The teeter-totters were removed in 2002.

Chaldecott swamp has long since been drained — and redrained — and replaced by playing fields that receive year-round use. No trace can be seen of Lake-at-the-Head Creek (Kh'ahtsulek), which once wound its way through the park on its route to the north arm of the Fraser River.

Balaclava Park

In December 1930, the parks board was faced with the major task of assigning names to nine parks or park sites in the Point Grey district and 23 in the South Vancouver district that had come under its jurisdiction the previous year. One of the parks was named after the street commemorating the Battle of Balaclava, fought during the Crimean War in 1854. Balaclava Park is an L-shaped park of 4.21 hectares between 29th and 31st Avenues. Its other boundaries are Balaclava and Carnarvon Streets and the lane behind Blenheim Street.

A misunderstanding over the expropriation of one lot in the middle of Balaclava Park culminated in a legal case. In December 1928, the municipal council of the Corporation of Point Grey passed a bylaw to acquire this lot, which belonged to Alexander McGregor. In February 1932, the City of Vancouver authorized the payment of $450 to McGregor. But the payment was never made, as city hall could not find his address and later it was believed, erroneously, that he had died. In the meantime, the city continued to send him a notice every year for land taxes that he dutifully paid — not realizing from his home in Scotland that his land back in Vancouver had already been expropriated and was now part of Balaclava Park.

Not until after McGregor's death on 16 October 1938 did the error come to light. His heirs in Scotland claimed the $450 authorized payment plus interest at 6 percent from 1928 as well as the refund of taxes, amounting to $255. Negotiations took place and D.E. McTaggart, the city's lawyer, said that "a good conscience would return the $450," as the city had been using the lot for some years. Eventually a compromise was reached between the city and Mr. McGregor's heirs that was acceptable to all concerned.

In 1932, relief workers were employed at Balaclava Park as well as Stanley Park and Kitsilano Park, according to parks board minutes. Four-year-old Pat (Ledgerwood) Birch, who lived at Blenheim and 30th in the spring of 1936, said that some of her earliest memories are of walking near the park with her mother and seeing big piles of underbrush and huge stumps burning in the clearings. She remembered the strong smell of smoke in the air. Over half a century later, Birch recalled, "I was terrified!"

In May 1938 a playground was constructed at the park, and in June 1953 a field house was approved. In 1954 as Vancouver was gearing up for the British Empire Games, a running track was installed. In 1956 Roger Bannister, John Landy and other athletes ran from UBC, where they were billeted, through the University Endowment Lands to Balaclava Park to practise for the mile race. Hugh Stewart remembers being at the British Empire Games Stadium and witnessing the race when both Bannister and Landy broke the four-minute mile.

Balaclava Park now has a rugby and softball field, a quarter-mile cinder track oval as well as a 40-yard-square cricket pitch in the middle of a soccer field. Like many others in Vancouver, it is a multi-purpose park. This can lead to conflicts, as the following news item highlights. Under the headline "Balaclava Going to the Dogs," the *Vancouver Courier* reported in March 1999 on the ongoing negotiations between dog owners and the parks board. Stephen Rybak, a dog owner, said that owners were willing to set up a "dog watch" program to ensure that dog walkers picked up after their dogs, which he hoped would deal with concerns expressed by Balaclava Park's rugby players. As in the case of Mr. McGregor's heirs, negotiations and compromises continue to solve problems in Dunbar's parks.

Memorial West Park

Dunbar's busiest park is Memorial West Park. Tennis, lawn bowling, baseball, soccer, a children's playground and a busy community centre make it the hub of the community. Comprising 7.50 hectares (equivalent to four city blocks), it is bounded by Dunbar and Wallace Streets and stretches from 31st to 33rd Avenue.

Memorial West Park has had several name changes. A letter from the Point Grey Chamber of Commerce was read at the Vancouver Park Board meeting on 8 August 1929, referring to the fact that "Memorial Park was previously called Dunbar Park by the former Point Grey Municipality." In the late 1920s the municipality of Point Grey renamed it Memorial Park in memory of soldiers killed in World War 1. When Point Grey amalgamated with Vancouver in 1929, however, the park became Memorial West Park to distinguish it from Memorial Park at 41st Avenue and Prince Albert Street, which then became Memorial South Park.

In 1928 just over $2,500 was set aside for Memorial Park Pavilion in the middle of the park. At the pavilion men in suits and women in hats and summer finery sat on deck chairs and enjoyed the beautiful flower beds. A checkers game nearby became quite popular. A group of men would congregate in silence around the perimeter where two men, standing on alternating black and white squares embedded in the ground,

Aerial view of Memorial West Park looking west, February 1962, with the community centre. Photo by George Allen Aerial Photos Ltd. Courtesy of the Vancouver Board of Parks and Recreation. ▶

would move the wooden pieces from square to square with a metal rod. The black and white squares are still in place behind the field house — waiting to be resurrected.

The year 1929 was a busy one at Memorial West Park. The sum of $3,400 was spent on clearing and upgrading the northeast area. More land was ploughed and graded, and the heavy rocks that were removed were used for the rockery area around the steep slopes of the running track. Walkways through the park were paved and some planting was done. In 1932 relief workers were once again employed — this time to build the field house.

Parts of Kh'ahtsulek or Lake-at-the-Head Creek could still be found in Memorial West Park in the 1940s. Near 33rd and Highbury was a large pond where children played and sailed model boats, and where dogs went swimming. Ten-year-old Vivien Warr, newly arrived from England with her parents in 1948, recalled vividly her first winter in Vancouver and her first attempts at ice skating. Encouraged to join on to the end of a string of skaters playing crack the whip, she remembers hanging on for dear life as she was flung around the pond.

The northwest corner of the park has always been forested. Elaine Schretlen recalls playing there as a child from the late 1950s through the mid-'60s. "There used to be this huge stump and, honest to goodness, ten of us could hold hands around the stump of this tree. We'd clamber up on the stump — three or four of us could be on it at one time — and we'd

Jubilee Queen Peggy Moyls with her entourage at Memorial West Park, 12 August 1936. Dressed in her coronation gown and with an escort of Royal Canadian Mounted Police, she was crowned by Mrs. Gerry McGeer, the wife of Vancouver's mayor. A flypast of monoplanes of the Royal Canadian Air Force followed. At just the right moment, a long ribbon descended from one of the monoplanes bearing a message for Peggy: WISHING YOU A HAPPY CORONATION AND A LONG REIGN. Courtesy of Ian McGlashan. ▾

Dunbar/West Point Grey float on 16th Avenue approaching Crown Street with Lord Byng High School in the background. Peggy Moyls is on the float while Major E.A. Boulden is in an open car behind the float. Courtesy of Peggy Moyls. ▶

play for hours. Across the street on 31st there was a house with a turret that looked like a castle. We used to have a fantasy that it was our castle, and we were kings and queens. I was so sad when they took the stump away. It gave us hours and hours of entertainment. Our imaginations would just go completely wild!"

In the fall of 1954 a group of local citizens came together and decided that it was time Dunbar had a community centre in Memorial West Park. Until then the Dunbar Community Hall (formerly called the Point Grey Community Hall) was located on the east side of Dunbar Street between 29th and 30th Avenues at 4476 Dunbar. It was housed on the second floor of a brown shingled building behind the Dunbar Table Supply store.

One of the most successful fundraisers was organized by John Berry and Gerry Hughes. The student body at Lord Byng High School was approached and the result was a one-evening blitz in which 100 adult volunteers each drove four students on a house-to-house canvas. The fundraising was done in a record-breaking 11 months.

When the new Dunbar Community Centre opened on 1 November 1958, Lord Byng student reporter Ross Munro wrote in an issue of Lord Byng's *Scarlet and Grey* newspaper: "Thousands of people have been shown through the centre by the staff. They have seen the gymnasium, craft room, games room, car work-shop, room for roller-skating. . . ." Celebrations continued, and on 8 November 750 people attended a very successful dance.

In her 1995 president's address, Margaret Wall recalled: "A memory that all founding members agree upon is that Rae McLean was the driving force behind getting the Centre built. Between her and her mother,

Margaret Adamson, I gather that our founders had no leisure time on their hands in which to get into mischief." Volunteers have always played a major role in the Dunbar Community Centre. Doug Trounce and Bruce Louie started out as student volunteers and both eventually became board members. John Berry and Joe Loughlin each served 25 years or more as board members, and Margaret Wall has remained on the board since 1972.

Almost 25 years after being built, the centre was expanded in the 1980s to include a fitness centre with a whirlpool and sauna, racquet and squash courts, an elevator for the disabled, a seniors lounge, and a new entrance, lobby and office. On 25 February 1987, the Community Juice Bar opened, a joint project of Stong's Markets and the Dunbar Community Association. Rooms at the centre originally intended for a single purpose were in 2006 multi-purpose rooms. The large room on the lowest floor, for example, housed a playschool co-operative, table tennis and dog obedience classes.

Malkin Park

Named for the man who donated the land to the City of Vancouver in 1948, Malkin Park is bounded on the north and south by 43rd and 45th Avenues. Its eastern boundary is Balaclava Street, and its fourth boundary is behind the houses bordering the east side of Blenheim Street. Two natural springs in the grassed area of the park help create a bog environment and constant drainage problems. A third spring at 41st Avenue and Balaclava Street was originally the source of a tributary that flowed through the park and emptied into Lake-at-the-Head Creek.

William Harold Malkin, an importer and merchant, was born in England in 1868 and arrived in Vancouver in 1895. He was mayor of Vancouver for the years 1929 and 1930 — the first mayor after amalgamation. One of his election slogans was "When you vote for Malkin, you vote for law and order, civic morality and fairness to labour."

In 1910 Malkin purchased land bounded by Blenheim, Balaclava, Marine Drive and what is today the southern boundary of Crofton House School. On this estate he built a mansion called Southlands. Towards the end of 1948 he made a gift of the northern part of his land — 2.4 hectares — to the city with the understanding that it was to be used as a "natural park." Years earlier, in 1934, he had made another significant contribution to the citizens of Vancouver when he had donated money, in memory of his wife Marion, for the construction of Malkin Bowl in Stanley Park.

On 13 May 1963, the Vancouver School Board requested 1.6 hectares of Malkin Park in order to build a school, but its request for such a large

▲ Coyote warning signs such as this one at 41st Avenue and Camosun Street were installed throughout the Dunbar area in 2000. The "Shared Trail" sign reflects the fact that members of the Southlands Riding Club have improved and expanded the trails, many of which were originally used by horseback riders from the Clinton stables. Courtesy of Joan Tyldesley.

tract of the park was promptly turned down by the parks board. A few years later Kerrisdale Elementary School Annex was built, utilizing the road allowance for 43rd Avenue as well as a narrow strip of land on the northern part of the park — considerably less land than originally requested. A one-acre playing field to the south of the school was also developed at this time on land leased by the school board.

By 1973 reports began to surface at the parks board of building projects underway in the southern part of the park. Tree houses, in various stages of construction, were reported to be occupying 12 of the larger alder trees, and interlacing paths through the dense undergrowth had been opened up by neighbourhood children. When the city tried to clear part of the park in 1973, the attempt was promptly stopped by neighbours. After a public meeting, a resolution was passed to designate the southern half a "natural area." Hamish Kimmins, a professor of ecology at UBC, said at the time that the park was an environment unique to the City of Vancouver and that removal of understorey plants and extensive drainage projects would destroy the lush wetland vegetation prized by birds.

Malkin Park continues to be a favoured location for birds. Red alders, maples and willows offer an excellent tree habitat, while elderberries, thimbleberries and salmonberries provide a good source of food. Hummingbirds nest here, thriving on the nectar of the salmonberry and thimbleberry bushes during their breeding season, and band-tailed pigeons roost at night in the tall alders, in which they build their flat stick nests. One study reported that 63 species of birds were observed regularly and 20 species were known to nest in Malkin Park.

Musqueam Park

The largest park in Dunbar is Musqueam Park, comprising just over 24 hectares. Before amalgamation it was known as Georgia Park, but in December 1930 it was renamed. The western section of the park is located south of Marine Drive between Salish Drive and Crown Street. The eastern section is south of 46th Avenue between Crown and Alma Streets. Much of the park is forested with second-growth cedar and maple trees. Trails connect it with Pacific Spirit Park on the northwest, with the north arm of the Fraser River on the south, and with Deering Island Park on the southeast. Sports fields are located in the eastern section of the park adjacent to Alma Street.

In October 1952, the parks board was urged by a group of nearby property owners to expand Musqueam Park when they heard rumours that a drive-in theatre might be located adjacent to the park — a plan favoured neither by the Musqueam Indian Band nor by the neighbours. Park extensions were again underway in February 1963 and March 1964.

On three occasions between 1963 and 1966 the parks board used some of its funding from city council for additional land acquisitions for Musqueam Park.

Musqueam Creek, earlier known as Tin Can Creek, once flowed from 16th Avenue through Pacific Spirit Park into a small lake near the Musqueam Indian Reserve before emptying into the Fraser River. Barrie Lindsay remembered childhood fishing expeditions in the 1940s to the creek. "Tin Can Creek had lots of salmon in the late summer and early fall. There were also lots of cutthroat trout, which we could occasionally catch with string, bent pins and worms. I never remember catching a salmon on a hook, and we hadn't caught on then to the more traditional and efficient Native method of removing a salmon from a stream."

Today the creek is part of a joint project by the Musqueam Indian Band and the David Suzuki Foundation to protect and rehabilitate the waters of both Musqueam and Cutthroat Creeks so that salmon can once again spawn there. Willard Sparrow, a Musqueam Band member who lived near Musqueam Creek, said that once there were so many coho and chum you could hear the salmon spawning in the creek before you could see them. In 1997, six coho and six chum spawned.

Musqueam Marsh Nature Park

In August 1988, after considerable environmental activism by concerned citizens, city council voted to turn the area directly south of Musqueam Park between 48th and 50th Avenues into a nature park and amalgamate it with Musqueam Park. This is the Musqueam Marsh Nature Park, which is only 0.7 hectare in size. Here in early spring little green shoots can be seen pushing their way up through the earth; then suddenly, about three weeks later, the whole area is carpeted with wild lily-of-the-valley. Nearby a wild clematis climbs up a giant oak tree, a chestnut tree towers over a clump of vine maples, stands of trembling aspen whisper in the wind, Oregon grapes cluster under tall western red cedars, and enormous cherry trees and bigleaf maples indicate previous human habitation.

Wildlife abounds in the surrounding marsh-bog and ditches. Members of the Vancouver Natural History Society identified 21 different kinds of birds during their annual bird count in December 1983, including a Virginia rail, a red-tailed hawk, a rough-legged hawk and a winter wren. Many other birds put in an appearance during the spring, summer and fall. In 1985 Katherine Beamish identified 15 different types of plants in the area, including red ozier dogwood, bishop's mitre, skunk cabbage and thimbleberries.

Artist Jack Darcus took this photo of himself with a monkey hugging his head and two fawns at his feet in 1968 in what later became Musqueam Marsh Nature Park. Darcus looked after injured animals — bear cubs, deer, birds — for the Stanley Park zoo. One afternoon in the late '60s, neighbours Paul and June Binkert were sitting in Darcus's kitchen having coffee with him when an unusual noise was heard coming from the bathroom. Darcus opened the bathroom door so they could see his latest recovering visitor, and there in the bathtub was a bald eagle eating a raw chicken. Courtesy of Jack Darcus. ▶

Once a fisherman lived here in a small house. When he died in 1964 the city took over the property and rented it from 1964 to 1971 to Jack Darcus, a struggling artist and an animal lover. When Darcus left, the city tore down the house, and blackberries have since obliterated all signs of it. Rufous-sided towhees scratch beneath the vines, flickers screech from nearby treetops, and an occasional flycatcher makes a sweeping dive for food.

Heron Trail branches off near Alma Street and 48th Avenue and leads west to a pond where sticklebacks dwell, water boatmen dart about on the surface of the water and an occasional brown muskrat has been seen. In 1987 and 1988 a tall white-haired gentleman who lived near the marsh, Paul Binkert, cut trails through the woods and introduced neighbours and nature lovers to the proposed Musqueam Marsh Nature Park.

"When we first came here in 1964 it was so exciting to be able to open the windows and hear the frogs croaking in Musqueam Park. But now we hardly ever hear them — only very faintly on rare occasions. It's part of the worldwide phenomenon," said June Binkert. In 2003 the West Southlands Ratepayers Association restored a pond and some of the wetland area, and the Save Our Parkland Association erected a small plaque beside the pond, naming it "June's Pond."

Deering Island Park

A short bridge at the south end of Carrington Street leads to Deering Island Park in the Fraser River — Vancouver's only park located on an island. The park is at the western end of the island; the remainder of the island is occupied by large houses built in the late 1980s. An interesting slough at the northwest end of the park is home to many birds, including a green-backed heron.

Deering Island has had several name changes. It was originally called Deering Island after John Deering, who wanted to build a cannery there at the beginning of the twentieth century. It has also been called Mole Island, after early settlers. Many fishermen referred to it as Willis Island; others called it Middle Island. When B.C. Packers purchased this tidal sedge island, its name reverted to Deering Island.

In 1984 B.C. Packers put Deering Island up for sale, and two years later the Vancouver Park Board presented Vancouver City Council with plans to acquire the whole or part of Deering Island for park purposes. Council had other plans and decided that all the land on this narrow, alluvial island should be developed for residential purposes. Only through tremendous work and lobbying by local community and environmental groups was the westernmost tip of the island and the foreshore near it acquired for park purposes. The official dedication took place in November 1998.

Dunbar's Downtown Park

A new park appeared in 1998 to honour two Dunbar residents. It is located on Beach Avenue between Hornby and Howe Streets in downtown Vancouver. The 0.25-hectare May and Lorne Brown Park is named after the only husband and wife team to serve on the Vancouver Park Board. Lorne Brown served as a park commissioner in 1967 and 1968; May served as a park commissioner from 1973 to 1976 and as a city councillor from 1976 to 1986, the year she was made a member of the Order of Canada. The two worked tirelessly to preserve the University Endowment Lands as parkland and to improve community recreation organizations (see also chapters 3 and 6).

May Brown with park commissioner Allan Featherstonhaugh on the left and Mayor Philip Owen on the right at the official opening of the May and Lorne Brown Park in 1998. Courtesy of May Brown.

Former and Future Parks

In December 1930, Quesnel Park and Tarahil Park were both listed as park sites in the former Corporation of Point Grey. Blenheim Lodge, a home for seniors, now occupies the triangular piece of land at 16th and Quesnel, originally set aside for Quesnel Park. A pond there would freeze over in the winter, to the delight of local ice-skaters. In the early 1940s Joan (Ferguson) McLeod and her friends dug underground forts and tunnels there. They also built fires and roasted potatoes in the burning embers.

Tarahil Park was located in the area originally referred to as Blenheim Flats and later as Southlands. It was part of a 0.4-hectare plot set aside for a road allowance. Later it was sold for housing, and the monies realized went to acquire parkland in other areas of the city. The road allowance near 3180 West 55th Avenue was sold to Bernice Ramsay, a keen equestrian, who used it as pasture for her horses and built a panabode house for herself.

Another park — an unofficial one — also disappeared. It was cleared by Japanese people who worked on Celtic Island in the fish-processing plant, enabling them to escape the plant's strong smells and noise for some peace and quiet. They erected a small bridge joining Celtic Island with the mainland and built a few picnic tables and benches where they could eat and rest. By 1915 they were no longer working at the plant, and brambles and weeds reclaimed their little refuge. Celtic "Island" no longer exists. The narrow body of water separating the island from the mainland was gradually filled in, and Celtic Avenue is located where once the waters of a slough separated the island from the mainland.

Dunbar's Western Environment

The large forested environment on Dunbar's western rim, once known as the University Endowment Lands, was transferred from the provincial government to the Greater Vancouver Regional District in 1989 and renamed Pacific Spirit Park. A competition for naming the park had been won by Sherry Sakamoto, who wrote in her winning entry: "It is the gateway to the Pacific and the spiritual ground to becoming one with nature."

All Vancouverites can rejoice that this 809-hectare park was preserved. Many alternative plans for the area had been suggested in the past. In the early 1950s, a large area was cleared of stumps and designated for residential development. Within the last 50 years, plans were being considered at various times for a cemetery, for a townhouse development on the edge of Camosun Bog and for light industry.

Fortunately, none of these plans materialized and the park was not occupied by *Homo sapiens*. Instead, it is home to 34 species of mammals, including the northern water shrew, the spotted skunk, the western big-eared bat and, in recent years, the coyote. Ten types of amphibians and reptiles, including the Pacific tree frog, the northern alligator lizard and the red-backed salamander, are found here, in addition to 113 species of birds. These include great blue herons (B.C.'s largest nesting colony), bald eagles, great horned owls, pileated woodpeckers, cedar waxwings, tiny rufous hummingbirds and the larger Anna's hummingbirds. Some of the latter shun warmer southern climates to remain year round in Pacific Spirit Park or Dunbar, where they are a welcome winter sight to residents who keep hummingbird feeders full during the coldest months.

Camosun Bog

On the eastern edge of Pacific Spirit Park is the oldest bog in the city of Vancouver. Camosun Bog is a unique example of a bog within a forest within a city. It covers 15 hectares between 17th and 25th Avenues. In 1997 a boardwalk was completed that stretches from the western end of 19th Avenue to the western end of 21st Avenue. In 2005 a connecting boardwalk was built that provides a self-guided tour through the heart of the bog — a fascinating walk back through history to the end of the last ice age some ten thousand years ago, when this area started out as a sedge marsh. Eight thousand years later it evolved into an extensive sphagnum peat bog, much more extensive than the one that exists today.

Bog Advocate

In 2001 Laura Super, a Grade 12 student at Lord Byng, prepared a submission on the work of the Camosun Bog Restoration Group for the Green Legacy division of the Canadian Museum of Nature. Super's exhibit about protecting rare plants was launched at the museum in June 2002, to travel across Canada for three years. Laura comments: "My love for Camosun Bog started during my elementary school years. My school was a block away from the bog and I spent many lunch breaks frolicking in it. During these early years I did not realize how lucky I was to have ready access to such a natural gem. Then as I edged into high school and learned about biomes, I began to understand the bog's significance. In the summer of 2000, for an anti-graffiti project, a group of friends and I painted a mural of the Camosun Bog on the

wall of the local Shoppers Drug Mart [28th and Dunbar]."
Photo courtesy of Joan Tyldesley.

The area around the bog was logged in the early 1900s and was further devastated by a major fire in 1919 that burned the entire area from 19th to 29th Avenue. The trees in the bog area date from 1919. Hunters once shot deer and pheasants in this part of the forest. Families headed out to the area as early as the 1920s to cut their Christmas trees and haul them home on wagons or sleds. Hundreds of Dunbar children played here and, until the 1970s, learned to ice-skate on what they called the lily pond.

Needless to say, the bog — which took thousands of years to evolve — was adversely impacted not only by increased human activity but also by construction of streets, houses, storm sewers and elementary schools. In 1929 a major drain was installed at Crown Street and King Edward Avenue. In 1975 earth fill from the excavation of Sedgewick Library at UBC was deposited at the western edge of the bog. It was only as a result of action by Dr. Bert Brink and other concerned citizens that the bog was not entirely lost at this time. Nearby development has lowered the bog's natural water levels considerably until there is danger that the bog cannot survive.

In spite of human encroachment, the bog still supports a number of distinctive plant species. These include insect-eating plants called sundews; sphagnum moss, one of the oldest living plants in the world; Labrador tea, a plant with fuzzy leaves that absorb water; cloudberry, a plant that has survived since the glacial era; and the Arctic starflower, a rare plant at this latitude.

Positive steps were taken in the winter of 1990–91 when the Vancouver Natural History Society sponsored the removal of 250 large hemlock trees from the vicinity of the bog by means of helicopter logging. In 1995 the Camosun Bog Restoration Group was formed and has been actively working with the Greater Vancouver Regional District to restore and preserve this rare ecosystem. In 2003 the Enviro-Club was founded by students Tarasch Rawjee and Bruce Huang at St. George's School to work towards the betterment of the environment. One of the major projects of the club was helping the long-time volunteers in the restoration of Camosun Bog. The introduction of new areas of sphagnum moss is speeding up the process for recreating the original bog ecosystem. Informative signs now outline the bog's history. In the words of the preservationists, "This unique bog must be considered a Dunbar treasure for all of Vancouver to visit and enjoy" (Brown, Taylor & Woodcock 27).

Commercial Nurseries

Dunbar residents have always taken a keen interest in gardening, and H.M. Eddie & Sons Ltd. — or "Eddie's Nursery," as it was commonly called — was the source of many of the original roses, fruit trees and flowering bushes that beautified the newly landscaped gardens of Dunbar Heights in the 1930s.

Eddie's Nursery was truly a family business. Henry M. Eddie (1881–1953), who trained in horticulture in Scotland, emigrated to Canada in 1910 and started his first nursery in the Sardis-Chilliwack area. In 1930 he opened a retail sales centre at the junction of West 41st Avenue and Southwest Marine Drive on land he leased from the Musqueam Band. Musqueam Creek ran through the nursery and salmon swam up the creek on their way to spawn. He was world-renowned for propagating roses and received many horticultural awards, including two gold medals from the National Rose Society of England for new rose introductions: "Poly Prim" and "Gordon Eddie." He also hybridized and introduced the disease-resistant white dogwood "Eddie's White Wonder," which received many international awards and has become famous wherever dogwoods are grown.

The flooding of the Fraser River in 1948 destroyed years and years of work and experimentation by the Eddies at their Sardis location. For three months the entire grounds of the nursery — where $200,000 worth of young plants including the new dogwoods were being grown — lay under 12 feet of the muddy floodwaters. Only one plant survived — a grapevine! Fortunately, a young "Eddie's White Wonder" dogwood was grow-

▲ In the late 1940s, Henry Eddie, his wife Myrtle and their daughter Rosemary stand in front of their newly renovated home and office building at Eddie's Nursery at West 41st and Southwest Marine Drive. Courtesy of the Eddie family.

Rosemary, Henry Eddie's daughter (left), and Myra, artist Sam Black's daughter, photographed in the tulip garden at Eddie's Nursery in May 1959 on the day of their graduation dinner and dance at Lord Byng High School. The display garden at Eddie's Nursery attracted visitors from all over Vancouver. Courtesy of the Eddie family. ▸

ing in Eddie's Gilbert Road nursery off Steveston Highway; all future stock came from this dogwood.

John Young, who lived across the street from H.M. Eddie's house at 4049 West 39th Avenue, described some neighbourly advice he received on pruning roses. "I used to have roses beside the sidewalk, and one spring day while I was pruning them, Mr. Eddie came out to do some work in the yard, so when I stood back, he said, 'What are you doing there, Mr. Young?' I said, 'Oh, I just pruned the roses.' He said, 'When are you going to start?' I said that I thought I was finished! He laughed and said, 'Here, give me your pruners.' Then he cut them down. 'You leave two nodes above, that's all.' He was the foremost authority on roses in North America. I sure had good roses that year." Young also recalled H.M. Eddie's musical abilities: "On New Year's Eve he used to play the bagpipes. We would have a party at Mac Robinson's, another neighbour. At midnight we would hear him coming down the street with the bagpipes so we would all come out, everybody in the neighbourhood, and we would walk behind him singing 'Auld Lang Syne.'"

In 1940 H.M. Eddie's son, Henry Eddie, moved from Sardis to the Dunbar location with his family; he managed the nursery until it closed in 1972. They lived in a cottage at the nursery until 1951, then moved to their new home at 4050 West 41st Avenue, on a large undeveloped triangle of land they had purchased from the city. A request at this time to move their office building to this location was refused.

One of the original "Eddie's White Wonder" dogwood trees was planted on the grounds of Henry Eddie's home, where it flourished for many years. In 1973 Henry Eddie sold his home, but before doing so he received permission from the new owner to move the dogwood, since two new houses were planned for the site where it grew. VanDusen Gardens was delighted to accept the tree. It was moved successfully and is now about 12 metres high and 4.5 metres wide. It can be found west of Rhododendron Walk in the western native garden, near the fence on 37th Avenue.

"Eddie's White Wonder" was selected as Vancouver's centennial tree in 1986. Its pure white blossoms can be seen on many boulevards in May and June as well as in front of the Dunbar Library, where a tree was planted in 2001 by the Dunbar Residents' Association.

A letter to the editor of the *Vancouver Courier* in 2003 suggested that every family moving into the Dunbar area should be given a Reddie apple tree, another famous propagation by H.M. Eddie. Elizabeth Fletcher, who bought H.M. Eddie's home, reported that the Reddie apple tree he planted in his own backyard was still thriving in 2006 and producing bushels of delicious apples every year. She chuckled when she recalled one of Henry Eddie's employees at the nursery. "She almost hated to part with any of the plants in her care. She would question you as to the exact place you intended to put each plant. Sometimes it almost seemed as though she wanted to come home with you just to make certain you knew what you were doing!"

In the 1920s and early '30s Charles Armstrong owned a nursery at 3830 West 19th Avenue that extended on either side of his house. He published three volumes entitled *The Aesclepiads* about the family of milkweed plants found throughout the world. Some species in Africa were used as arrow poison; other species in North America were eaten with buffalo meat. Today, the native B.C. garden of Frank and Erin Skelton occupies almost the same site as this early nursery.

Hyland Barnes started a nursery business in the 1930s that sold bulbs, trees and shrubs at 2993 Marine Drive. In the 1940s he moved his business and home to 3250 West 48th Avenue. Barnes was known to the Eddie family and was respected by them as a person who had a good background in horticulture and who was always searching for new and unique plants that could be grown successfully in the Vancouver climate.

In 1916, in the days of horse-drawn carriages, James Murray opened a general store at Kingsway and McKay at which people could buy grain, horse bridles, fruit trees and general merchandise. His granddaughter, Susan Murray, related the following story about him. "James was an enthusiastic and energetic young man, willing to try new things. Once while he was trimming a currant bush he took cuttings and tried to root them.

▲ H.M. Eddie and Sons Ltd. catalogue, 1946–47. Courtesy of the Eddie family.

All the cuttings grew and the following spring the plants looked so good that a neighbour wished to buy some. James thought perhaps there was some money to be made in the nursery business."

In 1938 James and his wife Jean opened Murray Nurseries Ltd. at 2893 West 41st Avenue. At James's death, the management of the company passed to his youngest son, John. In September 1955 John purchased several acres of land at 3140 West 57th Avenue and in 1972 Murray Nurseries moved to this location. Landscape construction was a big part of their success through the '70s, but by the 1990s the garden centre sales were increasing steadily. Betty Murray, a third-generation Murray horticulturist, received her degree in agriculture from UBC in 1993 and was general manager until the summer of 2004, when she moved to Nanaimo. In 2005 John, now in his eighties, once again became both owner and general manager. The nursery was by this time one of Vancouver's best-known garden centres. But in 2006 the family sold the land previously occupied by the nursery. Flowers, shrubs and trees will soon be replaced by stables, horses and houses. John Murray will continue to pursue his life-long interest in horticulture on the Sunshine Coast.

Southlands Nursery at 6550 Balaclava dates from the 1950s, when it opened as a wholesale business in the landscaping field. In 1989 it changed ownership and for the next four years was known as Jones Nursery. In 1992 Thomas Hobbs, who had operated a florist shop in Kerrisdale, purchased the business. His creativity is now focused not only on raising, arranging and marketing flowers, but also on writing about them. *Shocking Beauty*, published in 1999, emphasizes the outstanding visual effects one can create growing flowers. The development of the nursery has been the fulfillment of a lifelong dream for Hobbs, who, at the age of six, says he decided that plants were the best things in the world and growing them the best occupation.

In the rural area of Southlands small nurseries open for business sometimes for only a few weeks or months each year. A wide variety of plants and shrubs thrive here in good growing conditions and in close proximity to an abundant supply of manure from neighbouring horse stables.

Private Gardens

A meticulously landscaped garden surrounded the home of Mr. and Mrs. Charles Wilson on their five-acre estate at King Edward Avenue and Balaclava Street. Wilson, a former city alderman who arrived in Vancouver in 1886, acquired the land prior to a trip he and his wife made in 1913 to New Zealand. Parts of the low stone wall bordering King Edward still exist as well as four large cedars where 26th Avenue was later put through. These trees shielded the pasture, the chicken coops and the stable to the south of the main house.

The Wilsons chose a monkey puzzle tree as the focal point in the centre of their large front lawn and surrounded it with yellow daffodils. These trees had recently been brought north on a ship from San Francisco. Another unusual tree for the times was the basswood or linden tree planted to the west of the house. Sufficient space was left for the tree to grow to its full height of 37 metres and for visitors to enjoy its yellowish, fragrant flowers.

Many years later Mrs. Wilson recalled, "The land was subdivided about 1933 at the bottom of the awful Depression. My neighbours came with tears in their eyes . . . as the lovely old garden with beautiful trees was being bulldozed down. We shed a few tears ourselves." The rear of the considerably altered Wilson house stands at 3223 West 26th Avenue.

In the Depression years the Sisters of the Convent of the Sacred Heart had a thriving orchard of 1.25 hectares of land south of Chaldecott Park between 27th and 28th. The area to the west of the orchard was all bush. Bruno, the convent's permanent gardener, lived in a small cottage on the northeast corner of the grounds until his death in 1937. Al Schretlen had fond memories of picking cherries, apples and plums there during his summer holidays in the 1930s. "I enjoyed it because I could eat as much as I wanted. The crops were fantastic as the soil was very good."

By the 1930s, Dunbar was rapidly losing its vacant lots, and pockets of rural atmosphere were not always appreciated. Many housewives, for example, still kept chickens. Carole Rochford recalled that her mother had a chicken run in the 1930s and they always had fresh eggs. Barbara (Allan) Forbes remembered walking with her mother in the late 1930s to the 3400 block on 16th Avenue to see a herd of goats grazing on what would later become the central boulevard. Don Wilson, who lived on the north side of the 16th Avenue hill, knew several neighbours who raised rabbits to supplement their diet in the 1930s.

Slightly to the west, Duncan and Margaret Campbell of 3961 West 21st Avenue bought many of their standard rose bushes and fruit trees from Eddie's Nursery on Marine Drive. They also grew a wide variety of vegetables — some of which were stored for winter use in a pit in the garden lined with tarpaper. The fruit was processed in glass Mason jars in a large copper canner; the jellies, jams, preserves and whole fruit were then stored in the cellar for winter consumption.

Margaret (Campbell) Moore recalled her parents' garden in the 1930s and '40s when the lot beside their house produced Byng and Queen Ann cherries, crabapples, green transparent apples, Bartlett pears, Anjou winter pears, raspberries, red and black currants, red and green gooseberries, strawberries, grapes, peaches (which later got peach leaf curl), a wide variety of vegetables, and beds and beds of flowers.

Garden Clubs

Early in World War II, citizens were urged to "Plant a Wartime Garden" to grow food for their own tables. Victory gardeners in Vancouver, New Westminster, and North and West Vancouver produced some 31,000 tons of fresh vegetables and fruits in the year 1943 (Martin 129–30). Victory Gardens sprouted up throughout the Dunbar area in former flower beds, on boulevards and beside fences in back lanes; and proud owners — adults and children alike — enjoyed producing their own fruit and vegetables. Victory Garden competitions were organized, and ribbons and rosettes were awarded in numerous categories for "Best in the Show."

In 1930 Mary and Lyall McGlashan and their two young children, Ian and Betty, moved into a house at 3565 West 22nd Avenue. Lyall loved flowers, especially chrysanthemums, and began cultivating exhibition-type mums in the fall of 1934, which he displayed in the window of his store, the Scottish Ham Curers, at 4245 Dunbar. Jack McGlashan (not related), superintendent of grounds at UBC and an expert on the cultivation of chrysanthemums, encouraged Lyall to contact customers who had expressed an interest in growing chrysanthemums, and he offered to speak to them on the subject of "How to Grow Mums."

In early March 1937, young Ian and Betty McGlashan began selling tickets door to door for the talk at 25 cents for three tickets. On the appointed evening in March, 70 people were seated in the Canadian Legion

An open garden in full bloom with spring bulbs in the 3900 block of West King Edward during "Dunbar in Bloom," 2000. Courtesy of Joan Tyldesley. ▶

Hall near Alma Street to hear John McGlashan lecture on the finer points of cultivating chrysanthemums. Others arrived without tickets and had to be turned away, as the hall was full. At this inaugural meeting of the Point Grey Amateur Chrysanthemum Association, 62 joined the men-only group. The first official show of chrysanthemums was in October 1937, in the Dunbar Community Hall. The club has met continuously ever since, making it one of the oldest garden clubs in British Columbia. Lyall McGlashan was its first president.

By the 1980s and 1990s, club membership had begun to decline, and a drastic move was taken in 1998. For the first time in its lengthy and illustrious history, women were permitted to join the Point Grey Chrysanthemum Association. (The word "Amateur" had been deleted from the club's official name 10 years before.) As Ian McGlashan remarked, "It was a move in keeping with the times. It was decided that women would enhance the club membership."

In March 2002, exactly 65 years after its inception, Elaine Graham of Richmond became the first woman president of the association. "When I went to my first meeting I was a little surprised to find I was the only woman in the room. But the guys gave me such a warm welcome that I never thought about it much after that." By 2002 the club was meeting monthly at VanDusen Gardens and membership was once again on the rise.

On 19 February 1962, Jack Airey recruited some of his neighbours, and the inaugural meeting of the Dunbar Garden Club was held. Forty people, predominantly men, were present. According to Margaret Airey, Jack's widow, many women had far too many responsibilities at home to attend meetings. The business portion of the initial meeting closed with the auction of a potted tulip donated by the president. The proceeds — 50 cents — became the first deposit in the club's treasury. Mr. Burdock of Ortho Agricultural Chemicals was the speaker that evening. He showed a film entitled *The Manly Art of Lawnmanship* and donated garden chemicals to the club for the raffle that took place the following month.

In the 1980s, membership declined, but Heather Northcote kept the club alive for some five years by offering her home for monthly meetings. In 2006 the Dunbar Garden Club was once again a thriving club, with more than 90 members.

During the annual Salmonberry Days festival, Dunbar gardeners celebrate "Dunbar in Bloom" and share their gardens with the community. In the year 2000, 20 gardens were open on two days in May. Visitors could view a Japanese garden, a garden with a pond and desert plants, a garden featuring a ravine, a native West Coast garden and even a secret garden.

Outstanding trees go hand in hand with outstanding gardens, and Dunbar has more than its share of both. Gerald B. Straley's 1992 book *Trees of Vancouver* includes the names of trees found in private gardens in

▲ Jack Airey was the first president of the Dunbar Garden Club. Courtesy of Margaret (Newton) Airey.

the Dunbar area. Among them are the eastern redbud tree on the east side of Highbury Street between 19th and 20th Avenues, a pair of Japanese red pines in a garden on Kevin Place off 29th Avenue, a Dawson's magnolia tree on the southeast corner of 41st Avenue and Southwest Marine Drive, and a monkey puzzle tree at 23rd and Wallace. A very large Garry oak — B.C's only native oak tree — is located on the west side of Dunbar Street between 19th and 20th Avenues.

Sidewalks, Street Trees and Boulevards

Before sidewalks were made out of concrete, they were dirt paths. Then came wooden boards laid crosswise and nailed to logs. Louise (Cornish) Van Unen recalled these wooden sidewalks from the days when she ran errands for her mother from the 3900 block of West 33rd Avenue to Dunbar Street. Sometimes the wooden planks would split and the nails would come loose. If you weren't careful, one end of the plank could spring up and hit you on the leg. By 1919, the Corporation of Point Grey had a reputation as an area with good regulations for landscaping and the laying of concrete sidewalks. The dates embedded in the concrete sidewalk at the end of each block show the expansion of Dunbar.

The year 1924 was a particularly busy one for laying concrete sidewalks in the Corporation of Point Grey. On one evening alone, 23 bylaws were read by the municipal council for concrete sidewalks four feet wide. These were to be undertaken as part of the local improvement plan. Concrete curbs came many decades later, and some blocks along Crown and Blenheim Streets still had the original dirt verges in the year 2006.

In 1950 Leslie and Susan Walker ride their tricycles in the 3500 block of 29th near Dunbar. Curbs had yet to come on many streets in the 1950s. Courtesy of Leslie (Walker) Deeth. ▶

◄ A canopy of cherry blossoms on Highbury Street looking north to the mountains, spring 2002. Courtesy of Larry Moore.

By 2000, corners on curbs were being made more accessible to wheel-chair and stroller users.

In 1927, the Point Grey municipal council authorized the purchase of 2,500 trees to be planted on boulevards and 4,000 seedlings to be planted in a nursery at a cost of $2,165. At the first meeting following amalgamation in January 1929, the Vancouver Park Board drew up a list of bylaws governing boulevard improvements, and Vancouver City Council began providing funds for maintaining boulevards and for buying hundreds of new trees that were planted in the Dunbar area.

Owing to the Depression, in 1933 the parks board was forced to eliminate boulevard and street work. By 1939 boulevard trees were being planted as a relief project, but not until December 1946 — a year after the end of World War II — were funds available again for general boulevard and tree work.

In the 1920s and '30, large trees such as mountain ash, chestnuts and elms were planted on the boulevards, but by the 1950s and '60s smaller ornamental trees were being planted. The bright red berries of the mountain ash, or rowan berry tree, that had originally been planted on West 19th and West 21st Avenues near Pacific Spirit Park attracted birds, and they in turn deposited the rowan berry seeds in Camosun Bog. The descendants of these early boulevard trees were among the trees removed by helicopter from Camosun Bog in 1990–91 to restore the bog vegetation.

96	ash
43	beech
25	beech, European
432	birch, European
42	birch, paperbark
48	black locust
16	camellia, false
31	catalpa
103	cedar
28	cedar, deodar
1,365	cherry
299	chestnut
5	chestnut, pink
31	cottonwood
292	crabapple
76	cypress
15	dogwood
46	dogwood, Pacific
450	elm
142	fir
25	fir, Douglas
5	ginkgo
123	hawthorn
19	hemlock
14	holly
35	honey locust
19	hornbeam
31	ironwood, Persian
57	Japanese silver bell
69	katsura
12	laburnum
136	linden
16	liquid ambar
166	London plane
66	magnolia
1,796	maple
637	oak
29	pear, flowering
79	pine
1,128	plum
77	rowan (mountain ash)
68	spruce
8	tulip
10	walnut

In 2001 there were 8,347 street trees in Dunbar/Southlands, representing 277 species and cultivars. Paul Montpellier, city arborist, provided the list at left, which reveals the valuable legacy on Dunbar streets and boulevards. During the 1990s, 1,272 new trees were planted in the neighbourhood, and 754 dead and diseased trees were removed. People from across the city and around the world come to enjoy Dunbar's boulevard trees as well as the quiet of the neighbourhood and the beauty of the gardens.

Several businesses on Dunbar help to beautify the boulevards. Mc-Dermott's Body Shop has maintained a colourful floral display for many years on 29th Avenue. Dunbar Chevron station adds a green touch at 39th and Dunbar. On 27th Avenue west of Dunbar, a stately pink chestnut tree towers over the boulevard; in the lane behind the stores, a tall magnolia with white blossoms is watched over by the staff at Olinda's and by residents and owners of the building. Farther west on 27th Avenue, a garden bench welcomes visitors to relax and enjoy the flowers, shrubs and palm tree by St. Philip's Church.

Traffic-calming bulges on the corners of boulevards and in roundabouts add another opportunity for creative gardening. Many are waterwise gardens and are being maintained by local residents. Shrubs on a traffic calmer in the middle of the street and flower beds beside the liquor store brighten the intersection at 18th and Dunbar.

Preserving the Legacy

As the twentieth century unfolded, parks became more and more important as vacant lots disappeared, as traffic increased, as ditches and swamps were drained, and as safety in the woods became a factor. Parents began to supervise their children's activities more closely, and community teams began to replace neighbourhood games. Dunbar's parks have become multi-purpose areas where everyone can gather. In addition to the area's many parks, Dunbar residents have easy access to trails in Pacific Spirit Park, sandy beaches on Burrard Inlet, a natural foreshore on the Fraser River and four golf courses on the southern boundary.

The north arm of the Fraser River on Dunbar's southern doorstep represents a largely untapped recreation resource. Possibilities exist for creating new parklands and greenspaces there in the twenty-first century. The waterfront, including the Dyke Trail along the north arm of the Fraser River, is gradually becoming part of the Fraser River Greenway Walk, which could extend east to Fraser River Park, to Marpole and beyond.

Guiding all decisions to do with Dunbar parks since the 1930s has been the Vancouver Park Board, now called the Vancouver Board of Parks and Recreation. To their dedication, their visionary views, their hard work

and their persistence, the people of Dunbar owe a tremendous debt. Dunbar residents can look back even further to thank the citizens who served on the parks committee of the Corporation of Point Grey before 1929, who diligently assembled the lands that have become Dunbar's present-day parks. The city planner from Chicago, Harland Bartholomew, also made a valuable contribution in 1928 when he drew up his Bartholomew Report for park areas in Point Grey.

With vigilance and foresight, residents can continue to enjoy the parks, gardens, boulevards and natural environments passed on by previous generations, and can preserve and enhance them for future generations.

CHAPTER 12

Respecting Nature's Legacy

Pam Chambers, Shelagh Lindsey, Peggy Schofield
and Helen Spiegelman

I n physical terms, Dunbar is a collection of streets, homes, churches, schools and other structures that meet the community's needs and reflect its character. But Dunbar is also the land that lies under the streets and lawns of the neighbourhood. It is the hidden streams that once flowed in forested ravines on the southern slopes of Point Grey and still flow underground out of sight. It is the trees and shrubs that grow in yards and parks, and the migratory and resident wildlife that derive food and shelter from them.

Every human settlement exists as part of a natural environment, and Dunbar is no exception. The fresh water that flows from taps, fuel for heat, electricity for appliances, telecommunications for connectivity to the outside world, treatment of wastes — these are all an essential part of the neighbourhood's functioning. The development of the infrastructure that provides these day-to-day environmental services is part of Dunbar's history, even though the infrastructure is shared with the larger community. These services connect Dunbar residents with nature and with other neighbourhoods in unexpected ways.

The Land Beneath

The streets and lawns of Dunbar are perched on top of a rolling expanse of rocky sediments deposited by glaciers that entombed the entire Lower

Mainland under two kilometres of ice until as recently as some 15,000 years ago. As the glaciers melted, sand and silt were deposited in layers, which can still be seen in the steep cliffs on the tip of Point Grey above Wreck Beach. These sandy cliffs were rapidly eroding during the 1970s, a natural process that continues despite efforts to control it. (The cliffs could still erode several tens of metres, endangering the Museum of Anthropology on the UBC campus.)

All this was explained to an interested group of Dunbar residents by geologist John Clague during a nature walk held in May 2003. Clague had just co-authored a book, *Vancouver: City on the Edge*, which describes the region's "dynamic geological landscape." His book explained another interesting souvenir of the glaciers that can be found in Dunbar: huge isolated boulders, too large to have been brought by people into the neighbourhood. These, he explained, are "glacial erratics," released from the ice and deposited about 14,000 years ago in the spots where we still see them today. A split boulder the size of a small house fills the entire backyard of a home on Southwest Marine Drive, overlooking the former McCleery farm.

In contrast to the "upland domain" of Dunbar Heights, the Southlands area is characterized by geologists as a "modern lowland domain." This means that the soil farmed by the McCleerys, the Magees and the Moles was created more recently than the soil on Dunbar Heights. Terry Slack gathered maps indicating the changes in the Southlands geology since the last ice age. He said that about 7,500 years ago the Fraser River delta began building on what was then a seafront below the present New Westminster. About 5,000 years ago, the north arm of the Fraser River was formed. It is thought, he said, that about 4,000 years ago coho and chum salmon from the ice-free Columbia River began to colonize the many creeks draining into the North Arm. Southlands was at this time a maze of drying channels and mudflats, the beginning of the rich soils we find there today. After the pioneers started building their flood-control dikes along the river, this build-up of soil ended.

The Trees Above

After the ice retreated, the land that had been shaped by the glaciers regenerated with life. It was recolonized by plant and animal species that had continued to thrive farther south during the Ice Age. By the time the written history of Dunbar begins in the last half of the nineteenth century, old-growth forests of western hemlock, Douglas fir and western red cedar covered the Point Grey peninsula. The first of the tall trees on the south slope of Point Grey were felled about 1880. By the time the municipality of Point Grey was established 30 years later, all of the ancient forests there had been reduced to slash. "The whole territory," wrote Point

◄ This huge glacial erratic, deposited 14,000 years ago, today fills the back garden of a home on Southwest Marine Drive. The home overlooks the former McCleery farm on the Fraser River. The children perched on the rock in this photo, taken in the early 1920s, are Betty (McCleery) McQueen and her brother Kenneth, who spent their childhood on their great-uncle's farm.Courtesy of Betty McQueen.

Grey reeve J.A. Paton in *British Columbia Magazine* in 1911, "was a mass of fallen burnt timber and second growth."

This happened to be the same year that "Botany John" Davidson (1878–1970) arrived in Vancouver from Aberdeen, Scotland. Davidson would become one of the most celebrated naturalists in British Columbia, eventually making his home in Dunbar. His extraordinary career is described in a book written in 1993 about the first 75 years of the Vancouver Natural History Society, a society he co-founded.

By the time he arrived in British Columbia, Davidson had gained knowledge of botany at the University of Aberdeen, rising from the ranks of "boy-attendant" to perform all the duties of an assistant professor and be put in charge of the university's botanical museum. Yet because he never received a formal academic degree, he was passed over for an official position as an assistant professor. Leaving his wife and children to follow later, Davidson set off for British Columbia. In this young province, with its huge botanical endowment and scarce pool of credentialed experts, Davidson immediately received an appointment as British Columbia's first provincial botanist and was assigned the job of surveying B.C.'s plant species. He enlisted the help of nearly 200 correspondents — ranchers, surveyors and teachers — and made many journeys himself into the mountains and the wilderness, collecting more than 700 native species. He planted samples of each species on a piece of provincial land that was set aside on the Colony Farm at Essondale, establishing the first botanical garden in Canada. The garden attracted botanists from across the country.

When funding for the garden was withdrawn during the First World War, the government assigned Davidson's collection, now numbering between 20,000 and 30,000 herbs, shrubs and trees, to the new University of British Columbia, even before a department of botany was established. Davidson proceeded to clear the land, which at the time was almost completely covered in slash, and re-established the garden there. Early in 1916, he was awarded a faculty position as an "instructor of botany" at UBC, where he remained until his retirement in 1945. (In the year of his retirement, Davidson and his second wife, Edna, settled in Dunbar, calling their home Braeriach after a peak in Scotland's Cairngorm Mountains. Davidson lived here until his death in 1970.)

It was in 1918 that Davidson helped found the Vancouver Natural History Society (VNHS), an offshoot of the active B.C. Mountaineering Club. The VNHS held field trips and illustrated talks for members and the public. The respected "Professor Davidson" was already much in demand as a speaker at schools and community functions. He presented such an inspiring talk at the Point Grey Municipal Hall in Kerrisdale in 1915, titled "Wild Plants and Their Relation to the Beautification of

"Why are there hemlocks in Dunbar but not in Europe?" asked John Worrall, UBC professor emeritus of forest sciences, on a Salmonberry Days walk. Answer: When the glaciers covered the northern half of the planet, hemlocks remained only in Central America and the Mediterranean region. When the glaciers melted, the hemlocks began to spread northward again. In Europe, however, the returning hemlocks were blocked by the Alps, which run east-west. North American hemlocks encountered no such barrier because the mountain ranges run north-south.

Second-growth hemlock in Pacific Spirit Park. Photo by Cleo Wong.

"Botany John" Davidson was B.C.'s first provincial botanist. UBC Botanical Garden's scholarly journal *Davidsonia* is named in his honour. Courtesy of Liz Rowley, curator of Davidson's papers. ▶

Point Grey," that a group of Kerrisdale volunteers planted nearly 300 native bigleaf maples that still stand on East and West Boulevards.

Later, Davidson was the instigator of an official Arbour Day in Vancouver. The call for an Arbour Day was prompted by logging practices in British Columbia's forests, which Davidson characterized as "commercialized vandalism." He described the urgency of public concern in a speech in 1929:

> Soon after the outbreak of war in 1914, when every loyal citizen was considering the prevention of waste, or the utilization of waste products, it was realized that our method of logging caused the loss of hundreds of thousands of young trees, which were destroyed to permit the removal of larger and more valuable trees. The younger trees were left on the ground to dry or rot, along with the slash of the larger trees, and these together constituted a dangerous fire menace which for the past

number of years has been draining the wealth of the Province for present and future generations.

It was evident that the conscience of the people should be awakened[.] There was danger of the history of forest depletion in the east repeating itself in the west[.] But the problem was[:] how were we to arouse the people to the wastefulness of our so-called modern method of logging — commercialized vandalism? (quoted in Peacock 18)

The rows of stately trees that line the streets of Dunbar are a legacy of Davidson's and the Arbour Day Committee's work. When city council adopted the Arbour Day Bylaw on 12 March 1917, the parks board was given responsibility for planting and maintaining trees on public boulevards. Today the Vancouver Board of Parks and Recreation looks after 130,000 street trees of 600 different species. (For more on the street trees of Dunbar, see chapter 11.)

The street trees in Dunbar have been protected by the parks board since 1917, but until 1994 the city exercised no control over trees on private property. These include remnants of Point Grey's ancient forest as well as important specimens planted by earlier generations. During the 1980s, environmental activists in Dunbar, Kerrisdale and other neighbourhoods complained to the city about the loss of mature trees that was occurring during that decade's development boom. As large houses with multi-car garages replaced smaller structures, many trees were removed from residential lots. In response to public concern, city council in 1994 adopted Private Property Tree Bylaw No. 7347, requiring property owners to obtain a permit to remove trees over a certain size. The bylaw limited such removals to one tree per year and required the planting of replacement trees (although trees could still be removed without a permit to make room for larger buildings).

In 2004 the Dunbar Residents' Association held a contest in conjunction with its annual Salmonberry Days environmental festival to identify the tallest tree in Dunbar. The purpose was to raise consciousness and begin an informal inventory of the neighbourhood's heritage trees. One of the three winners that year was a native Douglas fir measuring 44 metres in height, growing in the ravine near Blenheim Street and Marine Drive, in the area where Lake-at-the-Head Creek flows above-ground.

Just as Dunbar gardens sometimes host native trees that fall victim to their own success and are culled by property owners who prefer sunny gardens, the natural forest at Dunbar's edge is subject to invasion by garden plants that over time can crowd out native species. Decades of roadside dumping along the forest edges introduced common garden plants into Pacific Spirit Park, including Himalayan blackberry, English ivy, periwinkle, archangel and Japanese knotweed. Margaret Moore noticed that the rowan trees planted by the parks board on the boulevards of her block produced juicy berries that were carried off by birds each fall, re-

▲ Bert Brink, a UBC instructor and conservation activist, blew the whistle on the dumping of fill near Camosun Bog. Photo by Laurence Brown.

sulting in the widespread occurrence of rowan trees in Camosun Bog and in the forests of Pacific Spirit Park. English holly trees were sowed in the forest by the same method. In response, Tom Nichols began to organize local work parties under the aegis of the Pacific Spirit Park Society's vegetation group to remove blackberries, holly and ivy. Denis Underhill and Ed Chessor joined in the effort. The work parties grew larger and more frequent, and other neighbourhoods began similar efforts in their own pockets of wilderness, including Jericho Park in Kitsilano and Renfrew Ravine in southeast Vancouver.

Experts and Elders

After John Davidson's term as president of the Vancouver Natural History Society ended in 1937, the presidency passed to another Dunbar resident, a high-school botany teacher and avid outdoorsman named Charles F. Connor, who held the post until 1941. Liz (Parker) Rowley, curator of the John Davidson papers, remembered Connor as "the bee man" who kept hives in his garden at 3222 West 36th Avenue, where he lived for 40 years. According to Rowley, Connor was a great help to other bee-keepers who had trouble with bees swarming.

Both Charles Connor and John Davidson inspired a generation of younger naturalists. One was Vernon C. (Bert) Brink, who led VNHS field trips for 50 years and knew Connor and Davidson well. Brink observed that these two early Dunbar naturalists, Connor and Davidson, were of similar temperaments: "Both took their religious faiths seriously and sometimes argued heatedly about matters botanical or religious." Like Davidson, Brink taught at UBC, instructing students in botany, biology and agronomy. His second career, as an activist in support of conservation, has been recognized with many awards, notably the Order of British Columbia (1990) and the Queen's Jubilee Medal (2002).

Bert Brink's greatest gift to the people of Dunbar was in 1972, when he along with other UBC faculty members blew the whistle on the dumping of fill excavated for the construction of UBC's underground Sedgewick Library onto cleared land on the northwestern edge of Camosun Bog. The dumping was halted, preventing further loss of what, a generation later, would be recognized as an important and rare habitat within Vancouver's borders. As detailed in chapter 11, another retired professor in Dunbar, Laurence Brown, built on Brink's work by organizing a long-lasting community project to restore and preserve the heart of Camosun Bog.

Many university teachers and researchers, both active and retired, have been a mainstay of Dunbar's environmental festival, Salmonberry Days, coming back year after year to lead interpretive nature walks in their subject specialty. These include UBC botanists Wilf Schofield, Shona

Ellis and Carl Douglas, ornithologist Jamie Smith, entomologist Judy Myers, forest scientist John Worrall, geologists Ted Danner and John Clague (from Simon Fraser University), and mycologist Paul Kroeger. In addition, Terry Taylor came from neighbouring Point Grey to share his encyclopedic knowledge of plants. Paul Jones, an artist and naturalist, moved with his wife from Dunbar to Kerrisdale in the early 2000s but continued to lead bird walks in Pacific Spirit Park each year during Salmonberry Days.

Many of Dunbar's environmental activists could be described as elders — people who can provide insights that come only from long life experience. Such is the case with Denis Underhill, who grew up in Dunbar and then raised a large family here. After his wife passed away in the late 1990s, Underhill began spending time in Camosun Bog helping with the restoration activity. He soon became one of the "Heroes of the Bog," sharing a reservoir of accumulated knowledge, ranging from plant identification (he identified a new variant of blueberry unique to Camosun

▲ Looking north in 1973 onto the Camosun Park oval and playing field at 16th Avenue and Discovery Street just west of Queen Elizabeth Elementary School. The large scarred area in the lower right is where fill from the construction of Sedgewick Library at UBC was dumped on the ecologically sensitive Camosun Bog. Determined protest from the community led by Prof. Bert Brink successfully halted the dumping. In 2006, the disturbed area was covered with mature alders and cottonwoods. Courtesy of the Vancouver Board of Parks and Recreation.

Denis Underhill, 2005, tagging shrubs in Camosun Bog. Photo by Laurence Brown. ▶

Bog) to practical techniques for removing invasive species and propagating bog species. In 2005 Vancouver mayor Larry Campbell recognized the work of the "Crazy Boggers" with the Mayor's Environmental Achievement Award.

Connecting Young People with Nature

Camosun Bog has always had a special appeal to young people (even Denis Underhill played in the pond there as a child). In recent years young people have used it as a laboratory for school projects, as a project for community service and sometimes as a Saturday morning outing before the weekend soccer game. Laura Super joined the Crazy Boggers while still a high-school student, then brought along friends who spent hours on their knees in the peat with other community volunteers, weeding invasive species from the bog. In 2003 Super was awarded the GVRD's first Gordon Smith Scholarship in recognition of her work as a young environmentalist (see also page 363). Laura Winter, who lived on West 24th Avenue, worked in Camosun Bog as part of the Catching the Spirit summer youth program, as well as with the region-wide GVRD Parks Forum, receiving a Youth Stewardship award for her contributions. The St. George's School Enviro-Club also cleared and replanted sections of the bog.

The Dunbar Salmonberry Days festival was founded because of an unexpected exchange between local conservationists and "soccer mums

◀ Camosun Bog work party, 2002. Left to right: Garth Thomson, Pat Wilson, Denis Underhill, Tara Johnson and Laurence Brown. Courtesy of Laurence Brown.

and dads" in the winter of 1997. The Dunbar Soccer Association was seeking approval for high-power lighting at the Southlands Elementary School playing field, so that the teams could hold practices after school on dark winter evenings. Terry Slack and Helen Spiegelman questioned whether the lights would have an impact on the nesting herons in Pacific Spirit Park. "What herons?" was the response. Slack and Spiegelman resolved that night to organize a nature festival in an effort to help children growing up in Dunbar become better acquainted with the wildlife in their backyards. Dunbar Salmonberry Days was launched the following spring. Children's events during that first festival included Peggy Schofield's workshops where children helped make huge papier mâché models of a frog and a dragonfly. In coming years there would be regular "pond dips" organized by UBC lecturer Karen Needham. Each year more and more children would tag along with their parents on the nature walks, learning the names of local wild plants and trees.

The papier mâché wildlife created by children in 1998 were carried in a small parade, the Lake-at-the-Head "creek walk," held as part of Salmonberry Days that year. Terry Slack guided the procession through the back streets and lanes of Dunbar, following the course of the buried creek that runs from Camosun Bog to the north arm of the Fraser River. Along the way, the group passed a construction site where builders were having difficulty pouring the foundation for a new garage because the hole kept filling with water from the buried creek, still flowing underground.

The soccer field lighting was eventually installed at Southlands school, but it was specially designed to illuminate the field with mini-

Saturday bog buddies pose for a photo in November 2006. Left to right: Samuel Tobert, Meg Tobert, Alina Cook and Colin Cook. Photo by Brian Woodcock. ▼

Junior Forest Wardens

The Junior Forest Wardens were organized by the B.C. Forestry Association in 1929, offering many boys in Dunbar an opportunity to learn more about forestry and develop an appreciation of the outdoors. Thelma Lower, whose sons were members of the group at Lord Byng High School, commented: "In their red shirts and caps they participated in all civic parades and royal occasions. They also took part in industrial displays of truck logging equipment at the Pacific National Exhibition." The emphasis in the 1930s was on conservation and preventing forest fires, with summer camps at Point Atkinson and in the North Shore mountains.

Junior Forest Wardens Stewart Chambers (centre) and two friends on Seymour Mountain, not in uniform this day. Courtesy of Pam Chambers.

mal spillover to the woods. Southlands school is home to the *Salmon Wall* (see photo page 15), a colourful mural created in 1995 in a partnership between Musqueam artist Debra Sparrow and the school community.

Preserving Local Wetlands

Not far from Southlands school is a location where Professor John Davidson took his UBC students on field trips during the 1930s and 1940s. He took students to this spot because of the extraordinary variety of plants, including medicinal herbs, growing there. It was also the watershed of Musqueam Creek, where wild salmon returned in great numbers until very recent times. In 1984 an alert citizen in the area observed city trucks dumping fill at the road-ends of West 48th, West 49th and West 50th Avenues. The city's intent, it turned out, was to fill the city-owned wetland and put new residential properties up for sale, just as had been done at other locations on Dunbar's western edge (see chapter 6). Local residents immediately organized a public meeting at the Marineview Chapel for citizens to pose questions and voice concerns to the city planning department.

Salmonberry Days

In 1998, the Dunbar community began staging a month-long neighbourhood environmental festival each May called Salmonberry Days. Naturalists, city engineers and other environmental experts lead walks and give talks on subjects relating to Dunbar's natural history and environmental services. The festival brings global environmental issues down to the local level and helps make natural history part of the neighbourhood's "lore."

Salmonberry Days organizers, 2004. Back row, left to right: Helen Spiegelman, Terry Slack, Kathy Parmley, Tony Molyneux. Front row, left to right: Linda MacAdam, Peggy Schofield, Sonia Wicken. Missing: Sharon Slack, Ling Leung, Elaine Knapp-Fuller. Photo by Wendy Turner.

It was apparent at the meeting that no one except the "concerned citizens" seemed to be aware of the ecological value of the land. Neighbours formed the West Southlands Ratepayers' Association and organized a guided tour of the area. The walk was led by the late Paul Binkert, a noted mountaineer and conservationist, his wife, June, and another important Dunbar/Southlands environmental activist, Wendy Turner. The proposed subdivision did not go forward. In 1988, council approved the amalgamation of the land into Musqueam Park. Later, one of the ponds in the marshy area was restored and today provides natural drainage of a nearby sports field.

June Binkert, Wendy Turner and Terry Slack were founders and long-time members of the Fraser River Coalition. This group's focus was on the lower reaches of the river, which have been subject to serious impacts from urban development. One such development is the Vancouver International Airport, which is located on critical migratory pathways of both birds and fish. When a large expansion of the airport was initiated in 1976, Turner began convening weekly meetings at her home that continued for 27 years. During this long airport development process, the citizens group examined reports and prepared public comments on behalf of the wildlife and estuary habitat affected by the development. Because of their work, the airport was required to mitigate noise emanating from

This cartoon was created by Annette Shaw in 1987 in support of the campaign to save the Musqueam wetlands from housing development. Courtesy of Annette Shaw. ▸

its new runway operations, and the Sea Island Conservation Area was established as a wildlife habitat to replace habitat destroyed by the development. Dunbar resident Meg Brown, who led the work on airport noise during these years, continued on as a member of the yvr Advisory Committee on Noise. In 2005 Turner and Binkert, members of the airport's Environmental Advisory Committee, learned of plans for yet another new airport runway development, and have begun to research the possible impacts.

The Fraser River Coalition also teamed up with the Fraser Basin Council (a non-profit body funded by several levels of government) to organize an important conference held in New Westminster in April 2002. The symposium, titled *The Changing Face of the Lower Fraser River Estuary*, brought together experts from many disciplines to consider the future of the river. They helped set the stage for co-operative action to protect the river estuary that has played such an important role in Dunbar/Southlands' history.

Defenders of the Sturgeon

More than one hundred years ago, in 1894, a campaign to protect a fish called the Fraser River white sturgeon was being waged by the Stó:lō people. On 12 March of that year, the Department of Indian Affairs

◀ Dunbar/Southlands environmentalists celebrate the opening of a new park on the Fraser River. Left to right: Wendy Turner, Terry Slack and June Binkert. Pictured with them is Kerrisdale resident Johanna Albrecht, who led a campaign for a tree-protection bylaw in Vancouver during the 1990s. Courtesy of June Binkert.

received a petition signed by 158 Native people from several Fraser River communities, including Musqueam. The purpose of the petition, in the words of spokesman Captain John of Soowahlie, was to "enter protest against the wholesale slaughter of sturgeon in the Fraser River." It was signed by many chiefs and sub-chiefs, including Musqueam chief Johnny Quie-que-aluck. The Native groups' initiative was supported — to no avail — by a letter from the Fraser Valley Indian Agent, Frank Devlin. Then in 1914, Native and non-Native fishermen together lodged a complaint to the federal government about alleged overfishing of the white sturgeon. But this protest also went unheeded, and a take of many thousands of pounds of sturgeon was authorized by the Department of Fisheries. The sturgeon became so depleted that today they are an imperilled species, "red-listed" by the Committee on the Status of Endangered Wildlife in Canada. In 1998, wheelchair athlete Rick Hansen threw his support behind the white sturgeon, founding the Fraser River Sturgeon Conservation Society. Terry Slack, who recounted this history, is one of the society's most active members, tagging and releasing fish so their habits and movements can be better understood. Slack himself is a semi-retired commercial gillnet fisherman, no longer able to rely on fishing because of the depletion of the salmon stocks.

Ideas that Changed the World

Along with the environmentalists already mentioned, Dunbar has been home to some famous activists who started global movements. The Dun-

bar living room of Jim and Marie Bohlen, in the 3500 block of West 19th Avenue, was a meeting place for the small group of people who founded the pioneer environmental organization Greenpeace. Jim Bohlen was an American engineer who, after working for a defence contractor in New Jersey, became disillusioned with American policies. He and his wife Marie immigrated to Canada in 1967, where Jim found employment at UBC. In 1969, the Bohlens joined with Irving Stowe and others to form the Don't Make a Wave Committee to stop the nuclear tests in Amchitka, Alaska. Looking for a way to intervene on a practical level, Marie conceived the brilliant idea of sailing a boat up to Amchitka to confront the Americans during the tests.

Believing with Margaret Mead that a small group of people could make a difference, the Bohlens joined with other activists such as Bob Hunter and Ben Metcalfe to charter a halibut seiner, the *Phyllis Cormack*, which set off to Amchitka. Although seven tests had been planned for Amchitka, only three were carried out; the U.S. government had to admit that the others were cancelled as a result of public pressure. The Bohlens' project demonstrated the combined power of non-violence and the media in capturing the public imagination. The Bohlens sold their home in Dunbar in 1974 to establish a homestead on Denman Island called the Greenpeace Experimental Farm.

Another Dunbar resident whose ideas are changing the world is William E. Rees, founder and long-time head of UBC's School of Community and Regional Planning. Rees and a talented graduate student named Mathis Wackernagel developed a way to bring his work in human ecology and ecological economics down to earth, creating a measurement tool to demonstrate the impact of human activities on the natural environment. With this tool, which he called "ecological footprint" analysis, he could measure the demands on the environment of different activities and show that if everyone around the world lived as we do in North America, we would require four planet Earths to supply our needs. Rees and Wackernagel's book outlining the concept was published in 1996 and has been translated into many languages, helping raise awareness of the need to change the way we live in order to live within the Earth's means.

Two locally famous citizens in Dunbar have been mentioned many times in this book. Sharon Slack grew up on a small family farm in Blenheim Flats. In the early 2000s she was appointed head gardener at the City Farmer organic demonstration garden on Maple Street. Sharon also created a garden at her home on West 33rd Avenue that produces food and ornamental plants using every inch of space of the 33-foot lot, including the top of the carport. In her spare time, she tends public plantings in neighbourhood "corner bulges" such as the one at 33rd and Wallace, which she planted with drought-resistant native species.

Terry Slack was raised in a floathouse on the Fraser River booming grounds until he was in Grade 4, when the family moved to Blenheim Flats. Terry's name has been intimately linked to Fraser River conservation activities and the early history of Dunbar/Southlands, which he painstakingly researched at the city archives. Terry's basement is filled with salvaged lumber that he uses to create a variety of products, ranging from benches he installed along the riverside trails in Southlands (including one next to Celtic Slough that is dedicated to his father) to children's games that teach about nature. More than once, Terry has enticed visiting celebrities to support his important local causes by presenting them with hand-crafted wooden penny banks shaped like sturgeon and salmon. In 2004, he presented such a souvenir to primatologist and conservationist Jane Goodall, and in 2005 to U2 musician Bono.

Building a Modern City

Even when the local landscape was no more than "a mass of fallen burnt timber and second growth," the founders of the municipality of Point Grey had a vision of the modern city they wanted to create. They set about to design their new residential suburb with "forethought and wis-

▲ June Binkert has been an effective advocate for habitat conservation through many organizations, including the Fraser River Coalition and Save Our Parklands Association. A legacy of her work in Dunbar is "June's Pond" in the restored wetland in Musqueam Park. Photo by Steven Lemay.

dom in its planning." J.A. Paton, who served as reeve of the new municipality (a position similar to mayor) did not underestimate the challenge of the task. "Point Grey," he wrote matter-of-factly, "having outlived its usefulness as a logging camp, was to be kicked, cuffed and knocked into the semblance of a city suburb" (Paton 734).

To finance sewers, water, roads and other modern improvements, the new municipal government asked voters to support money bylaws. First came an assessment for roads to "pave the way" for development and settlement (and more ratepayers). "With the settler," Paton pointed out, "came the demand for further tokens of civilization — water, sewerage and better means of transportation." In 1910 the Point Grey council submitted several bylaws to the voters, asking for, among other things, $500,000 for water and $250,000 for a sewage system. All the measures passed. "The passing of those measures," wrote Paton, "assured those intending to settle in this new municipality that their comfort would be looked after." By 1925, the *Point Grey Gazette* reported that there were 79.3 miles of sewers, 25 miles of gas mains and 147 miles of water mains in Point Grey.

The mid-twenties was also the time when Dunbar Heights was beginning its peak period of development. The sewer system was extended into Dunbar, gradually replacing septic tanks, but as late as 1947, the area of southwest Dunbar bounded by 36th, 29th, Wallace and Camosun Streets was still not served by the sewer system. According to a news report at the time, a delegation from the Southwest Dunbar Community Association "urged the [sewer] extension," claiming that "septic tank seepage is becoming a health menace in the thickly populated area." The citizens were told, however, that the work might not be included in the following year's sewer construction plan. Acting mayor Charles Jones noted that "already $125,000 has been spent in the Dunbar district on sewers." Alderman Jack Price reportedly commented that "there are other areas with conditions just as bad as in the Dunbar district," reminding the Dunbar homeowners that in some other areas "it is necessary to flush the ditches with a hose because of septic tank seepage" ("Dunbar May Wait"). As recently as 1964, when June and Paul Binkert moved into their panabode house on West 50th in Southlands, they had to rely on a septic tank because local sewer lines were still not completed.

CONSTRUCTION OF THE HIGHBURY TUNNEL

At the time the Binkerts arrived in Southlands, a massive $19-million infrastructure project had just been completed to eliminate the discharge of raw sewage into English Bay, False Creek and Burrard Inlet. A new 4.2-kilometre sewer main carried sewage from the entire northern drainage of Vancouver as well as parts of Burnaby to the north arm of the Fraser

◀ Open cut at the south end of
the Highbury Tunnel in the early
stage, just before excavation.
Courtesy of Greater Vancouver
Regional District.

River and thence, via an underwater crossing, to a new sewage treatment
plant on Iona Island. The sewer main, called the "Highbury Tunnel," is
the largest structure in Dunbar, although it is invisible because it is deep
underground for most of its length. Construction of the tunnel took four
years and cost much wear and tear on both workers and the Dunbar
community.

The firms selected to construct the tunnel were Northern Construction and J.W. Stewart — firms that had carried out the removal by explo-
sion of the marine hazard Ripple Rock near Campbell River in 1958.
Before the work began, inspectors canvassed the entire length of Highbury Street, making note of pre-existing cracks in people's walls and
foundations so as to protect the city from unfounded damage claims.
Later, when the drilling was occurring close to the surface, there were

some complaints. Residents said they could hear the pounding even when it was as deep as 60 or more metres below them. One resident reported a cracked toilet bowl. In other homes, foundations cracked. Nigel Gow, who bought his house on Highbury Street in 1962 after the construction was complete, said he had heard that before construction the city had bought several houses south of Marine Drive on Highbury to minimize disruption to residents during the process.

First, 16 pilot holes were drilled at strategic sites along Highbury Street. Exploratory drilling indicated a problem that would plague the construction process: high groundwater levels in the silty glacial soil meant the tunnel would have to be drilled essentially underwater. A series of deep wells about 20 centimetres in diameter had to be drilled along Highbury Street at about 30-metre intervals; they were fitted with pumps that would operate continuously once the tunnel excavation began. One of these wells lies under a manhole in Memorial Park near 33rd Avenue and Highbury, going 70 metres deep, straight into the tunnel below. At times of exceptionally heavy rainfall, some neighbours claimed to smell sewer gas, hear eerie sounds and see the manhole cover rise up and hover over its base. Retired regional district engineer John Rome has noted, however, that the cover is tethered with a clamp underneath and is in no danger of flying off.

Once the wells were drilled, the tunnel was excavated from both ends at the same time. When the "North Heading" and the "South Heading" connected in the middle on 12 September 1962, they were only half an inch off, despite the troubles that had plagued the project.

Excavation of the North Heading from the initial open cut near Highbury and West 6th commenced on 18 February 1960. For the first 1400 metres, the tunnel went mostly through rock, without untoward incident. But beyond that point the workers ran into silt and clay, which impeded their progress. Work was stopped on 23 November 1960. Meanwhile, the South Heading encountered excessive water flows from the saturated silty soil soon after construction began on 13 April 1960. For nine weeks, submersible pumps operated continuously to keep the excavation area clear, but the water flows became excessive and the excavation was stopped. After additional measures were taken to control the water, the work resumed, only to stop again on 3 November 1960. Because of the problems and delays at the South Heading, and a further 1300 metres of difficult ground ahead, a decision was made to change the procedure.

From that point forward the design of the tunnel was changed from a horseshoe shape, which is easier to construct, to a cylindrical shape that provides safer working conditions. This required the acquisition of two circular shields, ordered from Britain, to support the ground around the tunnel face and protect the workers from falling debris. Harold

Mulrooney, who worked on the tunnel construction, described the process in great detail, remembering it as if it were yesterday:

> They brought this big "mole" in — we just called it a jumbo. But you had to seal it in. It took them a month to set the thing up. They had all these plates made, 15 plates made the circle and they were 18 inches wide and 3 feet long and just a slow curve so that 18 [of them] would make a complete circle right around. You went ahead 18 inches, pulled your rams back, put in a ring of steel around you, and put the rams against the steel, and that would anchor it. Then you would push ahead another 18 inches. If you saw the water coming in, you went and jacked the air pressure up another half a pound or a pound.

As Mulrooney noted, the workers were now working under pressurized conditions in an effort to exclude water. Compressors and air locks raised the air pressure in the tunnel to twice the ordinary atmospheric pressure. The problem with this procedure was that the workers were likely to suffer, as deep-sea divers do, from decompression sickness, commonly called "the bends." There was a decompression chamber on site to raise the ambient pressure for a worker at the start of the shift and to lower it very slowly at the end, but many workers still suffered from the bends.

Harold Mulrooney described the effect: "To go in there is not too

Member of the excavation crew sitting in the air lock chamber underground where the air pressure was raised or lowered gradually. Pressure in the underground work area was kept at twice the ordinary atmospheric pressure to prevent flooding by groundwater. There was an additional decompression chamber at the surface in case of need. Courtesy of Greater Vancouver Regional District. ▼

▲ The finished tunnel in 1963, diameter 9.5 feet (3 metres). The track for the work train and the tubes along the sides would be removed before the tunnel was put into operation. Courtesy of Greater Vancouver Regional District.

much — but if you got the flu or something, or a cold, or if you got sinus trouble, you soon had problems. You never get any air because you can't stand the pain! It used to hit me in my knees. Some people — Ray DeCosse, for example — it would take him in the head and he couldn't stand up. He would just fall over."

Hans Meyer was a lock-tender, opening and closing the door of the decompression chamber. He described the chamber as 20 to 25 feet long, with benches on either side. The workers would read during the decompression period and were not allowed to smoke. If a worker got the bends in spite of these precautions, he was sent to a special chamber at Vancouver General Hospital. Dr. E.S. (Ted) Robinson, a specialist who lived nearby, was frequently consulted on these occasions. According to Mrs. Robinson, when a worker needed extra care a loud buzzer sounded, which could be heard in their bedroom. They always knew then to expect a knock on the door requesting the doctor to head over to tend the injured worker. Sometimes the call came in the middle of the night.

In spite of the pressurized drilling, cave-ins occurred. Sometimes work had to be halted for as long as two weeks until the wet runoff subsided. In the 5700 block of Highbury (near West 41st), John Hopkins recalled that a driveway across the street suddenly collapsed into a deep chasm — seconds after the owner had backed his car out. This happened because water rushing along the outside of the tunnel took the soil away. Dump trucks worked far into the night, filling the hole with loads of gravel.

Tunnel workers Bill Field and Harold Mulrooney recalled the remarkable things they saw in the railcars amidst the excavated sand and gravel: parts of petrified trees, seashells and huge boulders, all constituents of the glacial moraine on which Point Grey is situated. Field said that he brought home some clay, and his son found it quite workable and used it to create a life-size bust of astronaut William Shepherd.

Dave Killeen, who was a child at the time, recalled watching the drilling every day on his way to elementary school. On one particularly wet and gloomy day one of the workers said to him: "Don't ever become a driller unless you're strong and stupid."

Lock-tender Meyer described the working hours: "From the time that I was hired I had to work six days a week, Monday to Saturday. We worked in three shifts — day, afternoon and graveyard — so everybody had to take turns in graveyard. I'd never worked nights, so it was a new experience." When the union came in, the workers became hourly employees earning $1.25 an hour, soon raised to $2.50 an hour, which seemed astronomical at the time. Drillers received $3 per day extra pay as compensation for the more dangerous work. Harold Mulrooney recalled that workers smoking in the tunnel saw their cigarettes burn very quickly because of the extra oxygen.

Shirley Drab, living near the south end of the tunnel, was up with her infant one night and looked out to see the workers coming out of the end of the tunnel in a railcar, their headlamps lit, eerily appearing over the top of the fence in the blackness. Then they all turned off their lights — it was the end of their shift.

Today, maintenance inspections of the Highbury Tunnel are a challenge because of the length of the structure. In 1985 three GVRD employees including engineer John Rome inspected the tunnel by walking its entire length, a distance of 4.2 kilometres. The space is confined, with temperatures of about 28 degrees Celsius; there are no points of egress except the extreme north and south ends. During the inspection the flow of raw sewage had to be temporarily diverted into the ocean. In 2001 the tunnel required inspection again, but public standards no longer tolerated the approach used in 1985. GVRD staff designed a raft-mounted, unmanned video inspection system, but it was unable to provide a complete and detailed inspection. In 2003 a team of consultants from Aqua-Coustic Remote Technologies and Frontier Geosciences devised an apparatus that used sonar systems, remote vehicles, closed-circuit TV and computer data management to carry out "continuous, real-time inspection" of the entire tunnel. The process generated 160 gigabytes of digitized information about the tunnel's condition and found no visible structural defects.

THE END OF THE PIPE

Pam Chambers and her late husband, Stewart Chambers, who served on the North Fraser Harbour Commission for several years, attended the opening in 1963 of the new Iona Island sewage treatment plant, where the Highbury Tunnel ends. The harbour commission's small patrol boat was pressed into service to take dignitaries out to the opening ceremony. Among them was Lieutenant-Governor Gen. George Pearkes, VC. Pam remembered Pearkes as a rather fun-loving person. "He was just about in stitches as to what he could say in the speech expected of him that would sound reasonably dignified in the circumstances. He managed, of course."

The new sewage treatment facility on Iona Island was controversial. Chuck Davis commented: "Residents of Richmond were really unhappy with the decision to put [the treatment plant] there: they wanted Vancouver to keep its own sewage." But the site was chosen, according to the Greater Vancouver Regional District (GVRD), because it provided "good tidal flushing action." The Iona plant was designed to provide primary treatment only, reducing the suspended solids and biological oxygen demand of the sewage by about half before discharging the effluent into the Strait of Georgia. Twenty-five years after the plant opened, the GVRD spent $40 million to construct a deep-sea outfall, which Davis noted "improved the quality of water at nearby Sturgeon Banks." The outfall is 7.5 kilometres long and consists of two 8-foot-diameter concrete pipes supported by a sand and gravel jetty. However, the tidal flushing action intended to disperse the sewage at the end of the outfall has had the unintended consequence of seriously eroding the jetty, costing ratepayers up to $100,000 each year in repairs. The Iona plant has been expanded six times since it was commissioned. In 2001 more than 200 billion litres of waste-water were treated at the plant, which serves 600,000 people. This works out to 913 litres of waste-water per day for each person.

REBUILDING AN AGING SYSTEM

As noted earlier, the first municipal sewage lines were built in Point Grey around 1911, and the system was gradually expanded, with the last sewers installed around the middle of the twentieth century. All of the original sewers in Vancouver, as well as the Highbury Tunnel, were built as combined sewers, carrying both sanitary sewage from toilets and sinks and storm water runoff from roofs and paved surfaces — the accepted practice at the time the systems were built. During heavy rainfall, however, the volume of storm water runoff becomes too large for the Iona sewage treatment plant to handle, and the sewers overflow into the Fraser River and other receiving waters through special outfall pipes installed for this purpose. (There are two such outfalls in Southlands, at the foot of Dunbar and at the foot of Macdonald.) These events are called "combined sewage overflows" or CSOs.

In the early 1960s, Vancouver began gradually rebuilding its aging sewer system, replacing the combined sewers with separate storm water and sanitary pipes. The city's Infrastructure Reconstruction Program provides for the replacement of about 1 percent of the system annually, based on an anticipated 100-year life for the new pipes being constructed. Trucks and crews carrying out this work can frequently be seen in the streets of Dunbar. The total cost for replacement of sewers, city-wide, was projected to be over $1 billion, or $14 million per year.

NEW STORM WATER SOLUTIONS

Along with the program to install a separated system for sanitary sewage and storm water, the city began to encourage measures that direct storm water into the ground rather than into the sewer system. For instance, "permeability guidelines," included as part of the new RS-5 single-family zoning introduced in Dunbar in 1996, require that at least 60 percent of the surface of a residential lot be "permeable" so that rain can soak in.

In the early 2000s, the city introduced a pilot project to further relieve pressure on the sewer system. Participating homeowners received a subsidy towards the cost to disconnect their downspouts from the sewer system and allow the water from the roof to percolate naturally into the earth. The program was expected to save the city money by reducing sewage treatment costs, while also reducing the incidence of CSOs and the potential for flooding.

Also in the early 2000s, the city conducted pilot studies for a new "country lane" paving system as an alternative to conventional lane repaving. Specially designed permeable paving provided a sturdy surface for vehicles, yet allowed rain to soak into the ground rather than flow into storm sewers. By 2005, Dunbar still had no official country lanes, but on 30 July of that year Vancouver mayor Larry Campbell and dignitaries from other levels of government visited Dunbar for the official opening of Vancouver's "first sustainable street." In a news release, the city announced: "A typical curb-and-gutter street [Crown Street, south of Marine Drive] has been redesigned into one that is traffic-calmed with minimal impermeable surfaces and a naturalized storm water management system." During a sneak preview of the Crown Street improvements during Salmonberry Days 2005, a sudden downpour of rain demonstrated the naturalized drainage system in action.

Important beneficiaries of the Crown Street improvements are the fish in Musqueam Creek, which flows into the north arm of the river near the Musqueam reserve. The Musqueam Ecosystem Conservation Society and the David Suzuki Foundation started a rehabilitation project at the creek in 1997. In 1999, Terry Point, a Musqueam who grew up near the creek, led a Salmonberry Days walk explaining the restoration project and also reminiscing about playing in the area as a boy. By 2005 seventy wild salmon had returned to the creek, up from only 12 in 1996. In the new "sustainable street" system on Crown Street, runoff from the street containing grease, oil and other pollutants runs into a "swail" (a shallow ditch with reinforced permeable sides) and pollutants are filtered by vegetation before they reach Musqueam Creek or the Fraser River.

There are more than 50 formerly salmon-bearing creeks in Vancouver. Most have been culverted to run underground, as has Dunbar's Lake-at-the-Head Creek, despite their critical importance to migratory fish.

SOMEONE ELSE'S BACKYARD

Between 1944 and 1966 Dunbar's garbage along with garbage from the rest of the city was deposited in a ravine in southeast Vancouver, formerly a favourite place for local children to play. (E.G. Perrault, who grew up near the Kinross Creek ravine, remembered that the neighbourhood kids dammed the creek one summer "and for one solid week we went to the ravine every single day to skinny-dip in a pool of our own making that was full of darting fingerlings.") For over 20 years, five days a week, trucks delivered garbage to the "Kerr Road Dump," eventually filling the wild ravine to a depth of 49 metres. When the landfill finally closed for good in 1967, the fill began to settle, and the release of methane gas from the buried garbage made the land unsuitable for development. In the end, the land was left to regenerate in a natural state and designated as a park, today known as Everett Crowley Park. In 2004 and 2005, groups from Dunbar visited the park during Salmonberry Days and were able

◄ In 2002 a resident of Olympic Street rescued some 1930s hand-cut cedar shingles that were headed for the landfill. He used them to make siding for his children's playhouse. Courtesy of Peggy Schofield.

to see how the site holding Dunbar's garbage was now being reclaimed and restored by local volunteers.

Since 1967, Dunbar's garbage has been trucked to a new landfill located at Burns Bog. This is a natural peat bog like Camosun Bog, but 4 000 hectares in size (as large as 10 Stanley Parks). It will be filled with garbage to a height of 39 metres by the time the facility closes in 2045.

Curbside recycling began in Dunbar in 1990. Helen Spiegelman remembered that the city's recycling program put a local volunteer, John Gilbert, out of business. Gilbert collected newspaper from Dunbar households free of charge for several years in his red pickup truck, earning modest returns by selling the paper to a paper company. When the city's program reached Dunbar in 1990, it made Gilbert's service redundant.

▲ Helen Spiegelman worked for many years with the Recycling Council of British Columbia and is a co-founder of Dunbar's popular Salmonberry Days. Photo by Steven Lemay.

In 2006, Dunbar residents were issued new containers for their garbage and yard waste, which would be collected using a mechanical arm on a truck instead of by workers lifting cans and bags by hand. Householders were given a range of different-sized containers from which to choose. No longer would there be a flat rate for everyone; those who chose the smaller containers would pay less.

WATER, WATER EVERYWHERE

All of the water that flows through taps in Dunbar comes from Capilano Creek in North Vancouver. The first water system to tap into this abundant source was built by a private company, the Vancouver Waterworks Company, in 1886–89. That early water system consisted of seven miles of riveted steel main that brought water under the First Narrows into the new townsite of Granville. In the early 1890s the city bought the system from Vancouver Waterworks and began to provide water service as a public utility. It would be at least another 20 years before piped water came to Dunbar. In 1910 Point Grey voters approved a money bylaw to spend $500,000 for water. Point Grey reeve J.A. Paton wrote: "An overall plan for Point Grey's water system was laid out by a firm of engineers hired by the municipality. Surveys were made of the entire municipality, steel pipe and suitable fittings were ordered, tenders were called for and let for the trenching and laying [of pipes], and the work went on" (Paton 736).

Almost immediately, water shortages occurred during the summer droughts. In 1911 the Point Grey council approved a contract for construction of the three-million-gallon water reservoir on Little Mountain, which was built the same year. In 1926, water was made a regional utility managed by the Greater Vancouver Water District (GVWD).

For many years after the water system was established, the Capilano watershed was being heavily logged by the Capilano Timber Company. In 1924, John Davidson, who was mentioned earlier in this chapter, gave a fiery speech warning citizens of the threat to the water supply when a watershed was logged indiscriminately. He reminded his audience of the value of a good water supply: "We cannot over-estimate the value of a reliable source of cold, fresh water, furnished by slowly melting snows percolating through the sandy, gravelly soil and cool shady forests to the water intakes; Vancouver is in an enviable position in this respect." Davidson went on to describe the devastating effects of logging that had occurred in Mosquito Creek — damage he had predicted 10 years earlier:

> Within two years, a large scar made its appearance, trees, gravel and rocks were washed down; at least one of the houses [in the area] was smashed by falling trees; debris temporarily dammed the creek, washed out the bridge and its supports of rock, and deposited sand, gravel, rocks and trees all along the lower part of the valley. Spring freshets are

now an annual menace, the erosion continues, the end is not yet. The scar can now be seen from Vancouver and is increasing year by year. Other scars are beginning, and will soon be in evidence from this side; the "writing on the wall."

In his speech, Davidson warned that "[w]hen the citizens of Vancouver realize the necessity of the trees on the mountain slopes for the maintenance of this supply, they will not tolerate any interference with the timber or any part of the watershed. . . ." The speech was printed as a pamphlet and widely distributed, sparking an investigation of the effects of logging in the Capilano watershed and, eventually, the slow phasing out of the devastation. On 4 December 1933, the *Vancouver Province* reported that "the last log on the Capilano was taken out two weeks ago" (cited in Peacock 36).

Davidson's views about logging in watersheds were shared by the man who served as the GVWD's water commissioner from 1926 to 1952, Ernest Albert Cleveland. Cleveland negotiated a Crown lease with the province that would protect the watersheds from logging. After Cleveland left the GVWD, however, views changed. In March 1967, the water district's Crown lease was amended to allow logging. And so logging resumed in the North Shore watersheds until a new generation of environmentalists raised the alarm. In May 1999, renowned mountaineer John Clarke gave a multimedia slide show in Dunbar, telling his audience where the neighbourhood's water comes from and why he and many other concerned citizens were opposing GVWD-sanctioned logging in the watersheds. In May 2002 the water board bowed to public pressure and cancelled the agreement that allowed logging.

Perhaps because of the logging, the tap water in Dunbar has often appeared cloudy, especially after periods of heavy rain. In October 2000, Health Canada linked "turbidity" with gastrointestinal disease. The GVWD water quality report for 2000 found that on up to 48 days during the year the water from the Capilano reservoir (which serves Dunbar) exceeded the Health Canada turbidity standard. In November 2001 the GVWD introduced a Water Turbidity Index to monitor the cloudiness of the region's water.

Not only is water *quality* a major concern, but so is a reliable *supply*. In the early 1960s, Vancouver's water system experienced a loss of water pressure as a result of both urban growth and water demand from other parts of the region. To solve this problem, the city established eight "pressure zones" with systems to maintain the correct pressure in each zone. Nevertheless, solutions that solve water allocation will not solve problems of water supply. In the Salmonberry Days 2005 newsletter, the Dunbar Residents' Association raised the question whether the neighbourhood would face "long dry summers ahead," citing GVWD information that the total storage capacity of both the Capilano and Seymour reservoirs is insufficient to meet current water demands in the summertime. "Our region experiences a drought each summer," the newsletter explained. "We rely on heavy winter snowpacks high in the North Shore Mountains to replenish our water reservoirs once the winter rains stop. Because of recent weather patterns and the growth of the region's population, the summer reservoir levels have dipped very low in recent years."

Sprinkling restrictions were introduced in Vancouver as long ago as the 1960s and were reintroduced in 1993 as part of a Water Shortage Response Plan. Metering of water continued to be discussed as a way to change historic attitudes that water is a "cheap resource in plentiful supply." The city offered householders rain barrels at a subsidized cost in an effort to conserve water.

The city's actions illustrate the change in thinking that has occurred since a century ago, when the municipality of Point Grey was making its rapid transition from clear-cut to modern "City Beautiful." Although city and regional utilities provide Dunbar with essential community services that make urban life comfortable and pleasant, residents tend to forget that the infrastructure providing these community services is tied inextricably to the natural environment. With the help of environmental activists down through the years — including the Dunbar residents mentioned in this chapter — the public is becoming more aware of the link between their community and the natural world that supports it. Like our houses, our streets and other neighbourhood facilities, our environmental infrastructure reflects changing times and changing values. At the dawn of the twenty-first century, both civic and regional governments are beginning to design infrastructure that acknowledges and works more effectively with nature.

Acknowledgements

The Dunbar Residents' Association is indebted to our major funders for this project: the B.C. Heritage Trust, the Young Canada Works in Heritage Institutions (in partnership with the Heritage Canada Foundation), the Vancouver Historical Society, VanCity Savings Credit Union, Brian Wood, and the Dunbar Community Centre. Our publisher, Ronald Hatch of Ronsdale Press, was faithful and patient through several extensions of our contract and revisions of the text. We offer special thanks to our steadfast copy editor, Naomi Pauls, whose faith in the project never wavered. We also acknowledge Hannes Barnard, who helped with research about the Highbury Tunnel; Ian Carter, who brought the project to life; Imbi Harding, who gave her support to the project in its early stages; Beryl March, who wrote the preface and the initial draft of chapter 2; Trevor Martin, for his expertise in the preparation of photographs; Louise Phillips, who fine-tuned maps; and Jo Pleshakov, who submitted grant applications, among other important tasks. We are grateful to Ron Simpson, who worked closely with Peggy Schofield to develop the base maps. We acknowledge the Schofield family, who directed their grief into support for this project, both tangible and moral, that helped to make this book a lasting memorial to Peggy.

We also wish to thank the following organizations for their not inconsiderable assistance: the Anglican Church of Canada's Archives of the Diocese of New Westminster, BC Hydro Information Services, B.C. Sports Hall of Fame and Museum, British Columbia Archives, City of Richmond Archives, City of Vancouver Archives, City of Vancouver Engineering Services, City of Vancouver Planning Department, Dunbar Business Association, Dunbar Community Centre, Dunbar Evangelical Lutheran Church, Dunbar Heights United Church, Eaglequest Golf Centre, Greater Vancouver Regional District, Hodgson/Sharman Collection, Kerrisdale Elementary School, Lacrosse Hall of Fame, Lord Byng Secondary School, McCleery Golf Club, McDermott's Body Shop, Musqueam Golf and Learning Academy, Point Grey Golf and Country Club, the *Province*, Queen Elizabeth Annex, Queen Elizabeth Elementary School, Shaughnessy Golf and Country Club, Southlands Riding Club, UBC Library's Rare Books and Special Collections, UBC Museum of Anthropology, United Church of Canada, Vancouver Board of Parks and Recreation, *Vancouver Courier*, Vancouver Museum, Vancouver Public Library's Special Collections, Vancouver School Board.

The following long list of additional individual contributors to this book speaks to the community effort that went into its production:

Betty Abbot, Sherry Abramson, Rosalind Addison, Edward Affleck, Margaret Airey, Satoru Akazawa, Betty Albinson, Fred Albinson, Eve Alexander, Anna Allman, Len Amiel, Pam Ana, Rosario Ancer, Laura Anderson, Pastor Mark Anderson, Bruce Anthony, Richard Archambault, Rae Archer, Joan Ashley, Susan Askew, John Atkin, Alma Attwaters, Phyllis Aune, Ralph C. Bagshaw, Douglas Baker, Jonathan Baker, Tony Bardsley, Maureen Beddoes, Mike Beddoes, Bryan Belfont, Edith Bernard, Ken Bernard, John Berry, Jack Betteridge, June Binkert, Pat Birch, Millie Bjarnason, Harry Blight, Graham Blyth, Charles Blythe, Cori Bonina, Ifon Boone,

▲ Betty (McCleery) McQueen was the living link to our neighbourhood's early history during the production of this book. Confessing a lifelong interest in history, Betty has been the keeper of her family's records and photos and the favourite stories that have been passed down through the generations. During many hours of interviews and informal conversations, she was able to invoke the spirit of the pioneer families that worked the land along the north arm of the Fraser River when British Columbia was a young province.

Pat Bourque, James (Ed) Bowman, Clarice Brewill, Vernon (Bert) Brink, Joyce Bromley, Dorothy Brown, Laurence Brown, May Brown, Bob Bruce, Willi Bruegger, Germaine Brunskill, Joan Buckham, Shirley Buie, Michael Bullock, Angus Bungay, Bonnie Burnell, Colleen Butchart, Doris Campbell, Irene Carter, Mary Ann Carter, Melva Carter, Paul Carter, Hilda Catherall, Edith Chambers, James Chambers, Pam Chambers, Chris Chan, Eddie (Senyow) Chan, Ruth Chang, Ken Charko, Andrew Charles, Stephen Chatman, Robert Chesterman, Beverly Chew, Harold J. Chisholm, Gwen Chiu, Elaine Chretten, Leila Chu, John Church, Shirley Church, Jack Claridge, Lloyd Claridge, Margaret Claridge, Norman Claridge, Margaret (Peg) Clark, Jean Clarke, Vivien Clarke, Sally Clinton, Nora Cobbin, Joy Coghill, Marnie Connal, Ross Connal, Catherine Connell, Barbara Constantine, Karen Cooke, Tanya Cooke, Stan Cornish, Bette Cosar, Merva Cottle, Dana Coukell, Pat Cowen, Jacqueline Cowley, Beverly Ann

Craig, Carl Cramer, Pat Crawford, Brian Creer, Peggy Creighton, Angela Crompton, Clare Cruise, Don Cupit, Tracy Dafoe, Fred Dalla-Lana, Patsy Damms, W.R. (Ted) Danner, Jack Darcus, Greg Dash, Edna Davis, Janet Davis, Victor Daykin, Laura De Jong, Linda Debreli, Leslie Deeth, Michel Desrochers, Andy Devine, Beverly Dickie, Rosemary Dickinson, Lee Dobson, Ron Docherty, Betty Done, Terry Dougan, Barry Downs, Barry Drummond, Glen Drummond, Jack Duggan, Marion Dunn, Kaye Earle, J. Henry Eddie, Jill Edgar, Douglas Edwards, Gail Edwards, Betty Edwardson, Tom Elliott, Jon Ellis, Henry Ewert, Tim Fanning, Haakon Feilum, Sandy Ferrin, Dianne Filer, Donald Fisher, Lena Fisher, Elizabeth Fletcher, Paul Flucke, Audrey Folland, Norman Folland, Linda Fong, Barbara Forbes, Sarah Forbes, Lissa Forshaw, Grant Frame, Ian Fraser, Marion Funell, Lorraine Furness, Betty Galata, Karen Gale, Assaf Gal-Or, Orion Garland, Doug Gayton, Sheila Gear, Kathleen German, Erika Gerson, Bruce Gibson, Mary Gillard, Sue Girling, Betty Gjertsen, Jessica Glesby, Katherine Glover, Tsuneharu Gonnami, Glenn Gourlay, Douglas Gowe, Neil Gowe, Ronald Gowe, Elaine Graham, Ian Graham, Ivy Granstrom, Larry Grant, Marissa Grant, Tom Grant, Wendy Grant John, June Grasdal, Jude Grass, John MacLachlan Gray, Delbert Guerin, Victor Guerin, Paula Gustafson, Susan Hage, Nichola Hall, Lisa Haller, Ken Halverson, Vernon Halverson, Eric Hamelin, Douglas Hamilton, Leslie Harlow, Cole Harris, Teddy Harrison, Ivy Hatton, Brent Hawkins, Muriel Hawley, Catherine Hawthorne, Ken Hayden, Earl Hayter, Clista Heather, Pauline Helliwell, Sandra Herd, Sheila Herman, Fred Herzog, Bernard A. Heskin, Keith Higgins, Joyce Hiland, Ken Hildebrand, Ross Hill, Ehleen Hinze, Jeffrey Ho, T.K. Ho, Vincent Ho, Lea Holz, Susan Hooge, Joanne Hopkins, John Hopkins, Jean Hopkins, Catherine Howard, Jane Hubbard, Paul Hughes, Fred Hume, Edmund (Ted) Hunt, Helen Hunt, Elizabeth Hunter, Joan Hunter, Russell Hunter, Penny Hurt, Ruth Hutton, Robin Inglis, Keith Iwasaki, Bilkish (BJ) Jaffer, Thomas Jakeway, Patricia Jamieson, Erroll Jang, Andrée Jantzen, Deborah Jennings, Valerie Jerome, Kenneth Jessiman, Gordon Jinks, Lionel Jinks, Elizabeth (Betty) Johnson, Kay Johnson, Nancy Johnson, Brad Johnston, Jacqui Johnston, David Jones, Gwynneth Jones, Marjorie Jones, Robert (Bob) Jones, David Joyce, Laszlo (Les) Jozsa, Salman (Sal) Kassam, Jim Kelly, Howard Kelsey, Peter Kendall, Robert (Bob) Kendrick, Sonny Kent, Walter Kerchum, Jack Kermode, Larry Killam, Dave Killeen, Lorraine Kirkpatrick, Shirley Knight, Victor Kolstee, Pauline Kot, Fakroon Lakdawalla, Norma Landstrom, Carol-Ann Lang, Keith Langergräber, Lou Lanser, Jean Lathwell, Lori-Ann Latremouille, Alma Lawrence,

Ann Lawrence, Richard Lawrence, Graham Laxton, Susan Lazar, Terri Le Claire, Ernie Lee, Sheila Lee, Joyce Lee, Amy Leigh, Steven LeMay, Ling Chuen Leung, Barrie Lindsay, Shelagh Lindsey, Eunice Liversidge, Dianne Longson, Thelma Lower, Elizabeth Lucas, Dean Lundy, Anndraya Luui, Donald Luxton, Mary Lynch, Dan Maas, Linda MacAdam, Helen MacDonald, Joan MacDonald, Murdo Mackenzie, Rea MacNeil, John MacPherson, Taya Maki, James (Jamie) Malkin, Jess Malmgren, Norman Mann, Jim Marlon-Lambert, Diane Marshall, Jennifer Marshall, Roz Marshall, Dave Martin, Sarah Matossian, John McBryde, Stephanie McClellan, Bill McConnell, Jeremy McDaniels, Bernice McDonough, Sheila McGivern, Ian McGlashan, Angus McIntyre, Art McKay, Jean McKelvy, Alan McKenna, Moir McLagan, Tayce McLagan, Patricia McLean, Bruce McLellan, Edith McLellan, Robert McLellan, Joan McLeod, Jim McPherson, Joan Elizabeth (Betty) McQueen, Steve McTaggart, Spence McTavish, Steve McVittie, Audrey Meek, Jeanette Mende, Farouk Meralli, Barbara Mercer, Crista Merrari, Hans Meyer, Tiffany Michas, James Miller, Melita Miller, Milroy family, Gayle Mitchell, Jennifer Mitchell, Peggy Mizuguchi, Katherine Monk, Ena Montador, Mer Montador, Patricia Montpellier, Paul Montpellier, Amuri Moore, Larry Moore, Margaret Moore, Robert D. Morrisette, Marion Morrison, Don Morrow, Barbara Mount, Ben Moyls, Betty Murray, John Murray, Susan Murray, Val Murray, Joan Nazif, Toireasa Nelson, Nada Nesin, Steve Nesin, Eldo Neufeld, Tom Nichols, Eric Nicol, T. (Ed) O'Brien, Cornelia Oberlander, Shelagh O'Dwyer, Airlie Ogilvie, Linda Ohama, Paul Ohanessian, Midge Oke, Peter Ommundson, Toni Onley, Audrey Ostrom, Toni Owen, Bob Pabla, Muriel Pacheco, Donald Paterson, Geraldine (Gerry) Patrick, Kim Pechet, Maureen Pepin, Thelma Perrault, Katherine Pettit, Susan Phillips, Betty Pierson, Craig Pinder, Patricia (Pat) Pinder, Kay Plumbley, Ozzie Plumbley, Rose Point, Susan Point, Raymond Polder, Nora Polson, Jack Pomfret, Marilyn Pomfret, Susan Pond, Alice Porter, Marion Postgate, Marie Pottelberg, Raymond Poulter, Manly Price, Jocelyn Pritchard, Richard Rajala, Keith Ralston, Sharon Randle, Daryl Rankine, Mary Raphael, Tarasch Rawjee, Eva Redmond, Harold Redmond, Bill Rees, Kathleen Richardson, Alice Richmond, John Richmond, Frank Robertson, Helen Robinson (née Sutherland), Helen Robinson (née Welsh), Dr. Edward (Ed) Robinson, Carole Rochford, Edith Rodgers, John Rome, Elma Rome, Lisa Ronmark, David Rose, Robert (Bob) Ross, Bill Rossum, Karen Rossum, Cathy Rourke, Elizabeth (Liz) Rowley, Susan Roy, Harry Rumley, George W. Runcie, Jack Rush, Elfleda Russell, Candace Ryding, Diana Sanderson, Derek Sankey, Harkirpal S.

Sara, Frederick Schipizky, Maddy Schmelcher, Matt Schmelcher, Peggy Schofield, Al Schretlen, Elaine Schretlen, Avis Schutz, Julia Scott, Joan Seidl, Brian Self, Brian Seymour, Vic Sharman, Alan Shaw, Annette Shaw, Bernice Shaw, Ronald (Ron) Shearer, Margaretta Shirkoff, A. Siemens, Lillian Simpson, Ron Simpson, Dave Sinclair, Healey Sinclair, Frank Skelton, Sharon Slack, Terry Slack, Bessie Smith, Cecilia Smith, Diane Smith, Frank Smith, Gerald R. Smith, Gordon A. Smith, Karen Smithson, Sheila Smyth, Pastor Ken Sorensen, Debra Sparrow, Jerilynn Sparrow, Edna Sparshu, Helen Spiegelman, Jane Stahl, Charlotte Stenberg, Mel Stevens, Carrie Stevenson, Vic Stevenson, Barry Stewart, Hugh Stewart, Laura Super, Arnold Sveistrup, Jennifer Sweeney, Maureen Sweeney, Ildiko Szabo, Jean Tannahill, Norman Tarbuck, Rosemary Taylor, George Tedlock, Helen Thom, Betty Thornton, Ching Tien, Peggy Tingey, Joyce Tiplady, Lillian Tiro, Janet Tomkins, Bill Tong, Doug Trounce, Elmer B. (Al) Tryon, Betty Turner, Joan Tyldesley, Jean Tyson, Hitoshi (Tosh) Ujimoto, Arthur Unsworth, Marie Unsworth, Pastor Darcy Van Horn, Louise Van Unen, Cathy Varsek, Doug Vincent, Jean Vivian, Mark Vulliamy, Jennifer Wade, Rollie Wakeman, Pat Waldron, Dana Walker, Angie Walkinshaw, Gordon Walkinshaw, Margaret Wall, Vivien Warr, Ian Wasson, Eric Water, Thelma Waters, Victor Waters, Wendy Waters, Don Watters, Helen Weatherall, William (Bill) Weatherall, Gordon Weatherill, Elliot Weisgarber, Anna Welbourne, Byron Welch, Claire Wensveen, Yvonne Wheatley, Dell Whelan, Robert Whyte, Sonia Wicken, Mark Wickstead, Alison Wigton, Irene Wiland, Elfleda Wilkinson, Al Williams, Carol Williams, Audrey Wills, Madlyn Wills, Don Wilson, Ron Winkelman, J. Morley (Padam) Wiseman, Pam Withers, Tara Wohlberg, Brian Woodcock, Joy Woolfrey, Mark Wright, Ewald Wuschke, Ewald Wuschke Jr., Ken Wuschke, Maria (Mary) Wuschke, David Yanor, Mitsuo Yesaki, John Young, Margaret (Peg) Young, Wally Young, Victoria Zabolotny, Jamie Zagoudakis, Franklin Zahar, Marly Zell.

Each of the people and organizations mentioned (as well as several we are sure to have missed) contributed something important. Personal memories, hours of volunteer effort, financial and in-kind donations large and small, old family photos, patient advice and guidance, support and encouragement continued to be offered over the seven long years that it took to complete this project. Sadly, some of the people on this list left us before they could see this book and accept our gratitude for the confidence they placed in us to help them tell the story of our neighbourhood. The authors hope that this effort, despite inevitable errors and omissions, will open the door to more stories.

Sources

Interviews were conducted by the chapter author unless otherwise noted.

Chapter 1: The First People

The author acknowledges with thanks all her Musqueam interviewees, the elders and the staff at the band office, who extended every courtesy to her when she was seeking information for this chapter. Susan Roy read a late draft of this chapter, and her expert revisions were appreciated.

REFERENCES

Amoss, Pamela. *Coast Salish Spirit Dancing: The Survival of an Ancestral Religion.* Seattle: University of Washington Press, 1978.

Barnett, Homer C. *The Coast Salish of British Columbia.* Westport, Conn.: Greenwood Press, 1955.

Borden, C.E., and D. Archer. "Archaeological Salvage at Musqueam Northeast DhR-4, Vancouver, B.C." In *Archaeological Salvage Projects, 1973,* compiled by William J. Byrne. Mercury series. Archaeological Survey of Canada, Paper No. 26. Ottawa: National Museums of Canada, 1974.

——. "Musqueam Northeast Archaeological Salvage Project." In *Archaeological Salvage Projects, 1974,* compiled by Roscoe Wilmeth. Mercury series. Archaeological Survey of Canada, Paper No. 36. Ottawa: National Museums of Canada, 1975.

Carlson, Keith Thor, ed. *A Stó:lō–Coast Salish Historical Atlas.* Vancouver: Douglas & McIntyre; Chilliwack, B.C.: Stó:lō Nation, 2001.

Challenger, Winnifred Mole. "Henry Mole: A Pioneer of B.C." Transcript of Henry Mole's diary entries and author's summaries of entries, 1862–1917. Typescript, n.d.

Conner, Daniel C.G., and Doreen Bethune-Johnson. *Our Coast Salish Way of Life: The Squamish.* Scarborough: Prentice-Hall, 1986.

Francis, Daniel, ed. *Encyclopedia of British Columbia.* Madeira Park, B.C.: Harbour Publishing, 2000.

Guerin, Arnie. "Native Situation during the 1930's: An Interview with Arnie Guerin, Musqueam Indian Reserve, B.C.," by Michael Windjack. History 303 essay and cassette, 1983. UBC Library, Rare Books and Special Collections.

Harris, R. Cole. *The Resettlement of British Columbia: Essays on Colonialism and Geographical Change.* Vancouver: UBC Press, 1997.

——. *Making Native Space: Colonialism, Resistance, and Reserves in British Columbia.* Vancouver: UBC Press, 2002.

Holm, Margaret. "Prehistoric Northwest Coast Art." M.A. thesis, University of British Columbia, 1990.

Johnson, Elizabeth Lominska, and Kathryn Bernie. *Hands of Our Ancestors: The Revival of Salish Weaving at Musqueam.* Vancouver: UBC Museum of Anthropology, 1986.

Kew, J.E.M. "Coast Salish Ceremonial Life." Ph.D. thesis, University of Washington, 1970.

Knight, Rolf. *Indians At Work: An Informal History of Native Indian Labour in British Columbia.* Vancouver: New Star Books, 1978.

Macdonald, Bruce. *Vancouver: A Visual History.* Vancouver: Talonbooks, 1992.

Maclachlan, Morag, ed. *The Fort Langley Journals, 1827–30.* Vancouver: UBC Press, 1998.

Matson, R.G., and Gary Coupland. *The Prehistory of the Northwest Coast.* San Diego: Academic Press, 1995.

McDonald, Robert A.J. *Making Vancouver: Class, Status, and Social Boundaries, 1863–1913.* Vancouver: UBC Press, 1996.

McDonald, Robert A.J., and Jean Barman, eds. *Vancouver Past: Essays in Social History.* Vancouver: UBC Press, 1986.

Musqueam Indian Band [Web site, cited 3 August 2004]. www.musqueam.bc.ca.

Pojar, Jim, and Andy MacKinnon, eds. *Plants of Coastal British Columbia including Washington, Oregon and Alaska.* Vancouver: Lone Pine Press, 1994.

Weightman, Barbara. "The Musqueam Reserve: A Case Study of the Indian Social Milieu in an Urban Environment." Ph.D. thesis, University of Washington, 1972.

Wynn, Graeme, and Timothy Oke, eds. *Vancouver and Its Region.* Vancouver: UBC Press, 1992.

INTERVIEWEES AND CONTRIBUTORS

Charles, Andrew. Personal interview. 25 August 1999.

Chu, Leila (née Yung). Conversation with Keith Langergräber. 8 February 2003.

Davis, Janet (née Guerin). Conversation with Pam Chambers. 9 December 2004.

Fong, Linda (née Chan). Personal interview. 23 January 2001.

Grant John, Wendy (née Sparrow). Personal interview. 17 January 2003.

Guerin, Delbert. Personal interview. 6 March 2004.

Harris, Cole. E-mail. 18 March 2004.

Point, Rose (née Pettis). Personal interview. 20 September 2000. Conversations. 2003–04.

Rome, John. Conversation with Peggy Schofield. 2003.

Sparrow, Jerilynn. List of medicinal plants. 2003.

Chapter 2: Early Settlement and Industry

The author acknowledges the important contributions of Beryl March to this chapter. Beryl conducted most of the research, produced the initial draft and provided close editing of subsequent drafts.

REFERENCES

Bell-Irving, Elizabeth. *Crofton House School: The First Ninety Years, 1898–1988.* Vancouver: Crofton House School, 1988.

Challenger, Winnifred Mole. "Henry Mole: A Pioneer of B.C." Transcript of Henry Mole's diary entries and author's summaries of entries, 1862–1917. Typescript, n.d.

City of Vancouver. Base Map 194 ® 1960. Revised 1974.

Coney, Michael. *Forest Ranger, Ahoy! The Men — The Ships — The Job.* Sidney, B.C.: Porthole Press, 1983.

Downs, Art. *Paddlewheels on the Frontier: The Story of B.C. Sternwheeler Steamers.* Cloverdale, B.C.: B.C. Outdoors Magazine, 1967.

[Doyle?]. Letter from owner of Celtic Cannery complaining of "deplorable condition" of the fishing industry, 1902. Doyle Papers, UBC Library, Rare Books and Special Collections.

Doyle, Henry. "The Rise and Decline of the Pacific Salmon Fisheries." B.Sc. thesis, University of British Columbia, 1957.

Kahrer, Gabrielle. *A Mosaic of Destinies, A Mosaic of Landscapes: The History of Pacific Spirit Regional Park, 1860s to 1950s.* Vancouver: Greater Vancouver Regional Parks, 1991.

Klassen, A., and J. Taversham. *Exploring the UBC Endowment Lands.* Vancouver: J.J. Douglas, 1977.

Lyons, Cicely. *Salmon, Our Heritage.* Vancouver: Mitchell Press, 1969.

Matthews, James Skitt, comp. "Early Vancouver; a collection of historical data, maps, and plans made with assistance of pioneers of Vancouver between March & December 1931" [typescript]. Vancouver: City Archives, 1932.

McCleery, Fitzgerald. *Diary of Fitzgerald McCleery: Earliest Settler (North Arm, Fraser River): Vancouver, 1862–1866: Who, Together with his Brother Samuel, Were the First European Settlers upon the Site of Vancouver* [contains diaries only in typescript]. Vancouver: City Archives, 1940.

Morton, J. *The Enterprising Mr. Moody, The Bumptious Captain Stamp: The Lives and Times of Vancouver's Lumber Pioneers.* Vancouver: J.J. Douglas, 1977.

Musqueam Indian Band. "Sparrow (1990)." [Cited 3 October 2005]. www.musqueam.bc.ca/Sparrow.

Rajala, Richard A. "The West Coast Salmon Rush." *Legion Magazine*, November/December 1999.

Scholefield, Ethelbert Olaf Stuart, and F.W. Howay. *British Columbia from the Earliest Times to the Present.* Vancouver: S.J. Clarke, 1914.

"$600,000 Midnight Fire Razes City Warehouse." *Vancouver Daily Province*, 22 May 1950, 1.

Sparrow, Ed. Letter to Indian Agent Ball, September 28, 1938. RG 10, Indian Affairs, Series C-VI, Vol. 10900. File Title: Vancouver Agency — Fisheries — General (1923–1939). National Archives of Canada.

Thomas, Sandra. "Something Fishy Going On with Tiny Eulachons." *Vancouver Courier*, 26 May 2005.

Tottori-Kenjin History Book Committee, ed. "A Brief History of Tottori-Kenjin Doshikai and Its Members." Published by Tottori-Kenjin Doshikai History Book Committee for the organization's centennial anniversary. Typescript, 2002.

White, Kayce. "Kerrisdale." In *The Greater Vancouver Book: An Urban Encyclopedia*, edited by Chuck Davis, 101. Surrey, B.C.: Linkman Press, 1997.

White, William L. "Tools of Power." In *Raincoast Chronicles Six/Ten.* Collector's Edition II, edited by Howard White, 180–93. Madeira Park, B.C.: Harbour Publishing, 1983.

Widen, Ted G. "Celtic Shipyard 1899–1988." History 205 essay, University of British Columbia, 1988.

Yesaki, Mitsuo, and Sakuya Nishimura. *Salmon Canning on the Fraser River in the 1890s.* Vancouver: Peninsula Publishing, 2000.

INTERVIEWEES AND CONTRIBUTORS

Brink, Vernon C. (Bert). Conversation with Beryl March. March 2002.

Chan, Eddie. Personal interview by Peggy Schofield. 18 December 2002.

Chu, Leila (née Yung). Conversation with Keith Langergräber. 9 February 2003.

——. Personal interview by Peggy Schofield. March 2003.

Cruise, Clare. Telephone conversation. 2004.

Fong, Linda (née Chan). Personal interview by Peggy Schofield. 23 January 2001.

Hamilton, Douglas. E-mail to Helen Spiegelman. 9 June 2005.

Jones, Bob. Personal interview by Peggy Schofield. 17 August 2000.

McQueen, Betty (née McCleery). Personal interview by Pam Chambers. 1 February 2000. Conversations with Helen Spiegelman. 2005, 2006.

Point, Rose (née Pettis). Personal interview by Peggy Schofield. 15 January 2003.

Rajala, Richard. Telephone conversation with Helen Spiegelman. 21 March 2005.

Slack, Sharon (née Bain), and Terry Slack. Personal interview by Toireasa Nelson. 29 August 1999.

Chapter 3: Forging a New Community

REFERENCES

"Alvensleben, Gustav Constantin Alvo von." *The Encyclopedia of British Columbia*, edited by Daniel Francis, 14. Madeira Park, B.C.: Harbour Publishing, 2000.

British Columbia from the Earliest Times to the Present. Vol. 4, *Biographical*, s.v. "Fitzgerald McCleery," 980–84. Vancouver: S.J. Clarke Publishing, 1914.

Challenger, Winnifred Mole. "Henry Mole: A Pioneer of B.C." Transcript of Henry Mole's diary entries and author's summaries of entries, 1862–1917. Typescript, n.d.

Charlton, Gerard. "The Changing Face of Dunbar." Dunbar Residents' Association newsletter, June 2006, 1.

City of Vancouver Archives, Bruce Russell collection, Add. MSS. 836, Loc. 589-F-5 file 2, Dunbar Community Survey, ca. 1970.

Crowhurst, Fred. Newspaper clipping, n.d. Vancouver Public Library, Special Collections. Vancouver, B.C. — Districts — Dunbar.

Davis, Chuck. "Alvo (Gustav Konstantin) von Alvensleben." In *The Greater Vancouver Book: An Urban Encyclopedia*, edited by Chuck Davis, 841. Surrey, B.C.: Linkman Press, 1997.

"Donald MacLaren." The Aerodrome — Aces and Aircraft of Word War I [Web site, cited 24 October 2005]. www.theaerodrome.com/aces/canada/maclaren.

"Dunbar, Southlands Residents to Seek Planning Area." *Vancouver Courier*, 21 February 1974.

Dunbar Residents' Association. Minutes of a meeting held at Lord Byng Secondary School auditorium on 28 November 1991.

"First Dunbar Resident." Newspaper clipping, n.d. Vancouver, B.C. — Districts — Dunbar. Vancouver Public Library, Special Collections.

King, William Lyon Mackenzie. Quoted in *Colombo's Canadian Quotations*, edited by John Robert Colombo, 306. Edmonton: Hurtig Publishers, 1974.

Kluckner, Michael. *Vanishing Vancouver.* Vancouver: Whitecap Books, 1990.

Macdonald, Bruce. *Vancouver: A Visual History.* Vancouver: Talonbooks, 1992.

Mackie, Richard Somerset. *Island Timber.* Victoria: Sono Nis Press, 2000.

McDonald, Robert A.J., and Jean Barman. *Vancouver Past: Essays in Social History.* Vancouver: UBC Press, 1986.

Paton, J.A. "A History of Point Grey Municipality." Collection of articles written for the *Vancouver Sun.* Call number FC 3845 SP63 P38. City of Vancouver Archives.

Ralston, Keith, et al. *A Study of Point Grey Municipality.* History paper, University of British Columbia, 1974–75. City of Vancouver Archives.

"Ratepayer Group for Southlands." *Vancouver Courier*, 15 November 1973.

Reksten, Terry. *The Illustrated History of British Columbia*. Vancouver: Douglas & McIntyre, 2001.

Sara, Iqbal Singh. "Fundamentalist: Rejoinder by Sardar Iqbal Singh Sara" [on-line]. *SikhSpectrum.com*, no. 5, October 2002.

Walker, Elizabeth. *Street Names of Vancouver*. Vancouver: Vancouver Historical Society, 1999.

"Who Runs the City — Voters or Bureaucrats?" Dunbar Residents' Association newsletter, Fall 2005.

Wynn, Graeme, and Timothy Oke. *Vancouver and Its Region*. Vancouver: UBC Press, 1992.

INTERVIEWEES AND CONTRIBUTORS

Baker, Jonathan. E-mail to Peggy Schofield. 12 September 1998.

Belfont, Bryan. Personal interview by Pam Chambers. 6 April 2000.

Blythe, Charles. Personal interview by Pam Chambers. 3 May 2001.

Brown, May (née Adams). Personal interview by Pam Chambers. 21 July 2001.

Chambers, Edith and James. Personal interview by Susan Phillips. 1981.

Chan, Eddie. Personal interview by Peggy Schofield. 18 December 2002.

Chisholm, Harold J. Letter to Peggy Schofield. 17 July 2000.

Chu, Leila (née Yung). Personal conversation with Keith Langergräber. 8 February 2003.

Daykin, Victor. Written observations re: Japanese families at Celtic. n.d.

Dickinson, Rosemary. Telephone conversation with Pam Chambers. 21 March 2005.

Edwards, Douglas. Personal interview by Peggy Schofield. 25 August 2002.

Fong, Linda (née Chan). Personal interview by Peggy Schofield. 23 January 2001.

Harlow, Leslie (née Adam). Personal interview by Pam Chambers. 14 November 2001.

Hawthorne, Catherine. Personal interview by Pam Chambers. 19 March 2005.

Jones, Marjorie (née Tryon). Personal interview by Peggy Schofield. 27 March 2001.

Leung, Ling Chuen. Personal interview by Peggy Schofield. 3 October 2000.

Lindsey, Shelagh. Conversation with Pam Chambers. n.d.

MacDonald, Helen. Personal interview by Peggy Schofield. 9 August 2000.

Malkin, James (Jamie). Personal interview by Pam Chambers. 9 March 2000.

Marshall, Diane. Personal interview by Peggy Schofield. 16 March 2001.

McQueen, Betty (née McCleery). Personal interview by Pam Chambers. 1 February 2000. Personal interview by Peggy Schofield. 4 December 2002. Telephone conversation with Helen Spiegelman. 8 November 2005.

McVittie, Steve. Conversation with Pam Chambers. 11 March 2005.

Mitchell, Gayle (née Johnson). E-mail to Peggy Schofield re: Dr. E.V. Johnson.

Montador, Mer. Personal interview by Peggy Schofield. 6 July 2001.

Morrisette, Robert D. Letter to Peggy Schofield. 6 March 2002.

Redmond, Eva (née Twaites). Personal interview by Pam Chambers. 21 September 1999.

Richardson, Kathleen. Telephone interview by Pam Chambers. 7 August 2002.

Rochford, Carole (née Mitchell). Personal interview by Peggy Schofield. 10 August 1999.

Ross, Robert (Bob). Personal interview by Peggy Schofield. 29 December 2003.

Sara, Harkirpal Singh. Letter to Peggy Schofield. 2001.

Slack, Sharon (née Bain). Telephone conversation with Pam Chambers. 31 January 2005.

Smith, Gerald R. Telephone conversation with Pam Chambers. 24 March 2005.

Spiegelman, Helen. E-mail correspondence with various DRA members. 1997–2001.

Tien, Ching. Personal interview by Pam Chambers. 26 November 2001.

Tryon, Elmer B. (Al). Personal interview by Peggy Schofield. 15 August 2000.

Waters, Thelma and Victor. Personal interview by Pam Chambers. 1 May 2001.

Wicken, Sonia (née Palisniuk). Personal interview by Pam Chambers. 10 March 2005. Telephone conversation with Helen Spiegelman. 30 November 2005.

Wilkinson, Elfleda (née Langford). Personal interview by Peggy Schofield. 7 May 2001.

Zabolotny, Victoria. Personal interview by Peggy Schofield. 9 March 2000

Chapter 4:
Commercial Development through the Decades

REFERENCES

Aird, Elizabeth. "Taking On the Big Guys." *Vancouver Sun*, 6 July 1996, H3.

Aufiero, Gennaro. Obituary. *Vancouver Sun*, 9 January 2001, D8.

Barrett, Tom. "Land Sharks Feasted in a Frenzy as Suburbs Exploded." *Vancouver Sun*, 27 October 1999, C9.

Bennett, Paul, Pierre Fallavier, and Ian Fisher. "Dunbar's Commercial Areas: Room for Improvement?" Term project, Planning 540, Community and Regional Planning Dept., University of British Columbia, 1997.

Broadfoot, Barry, Rudy Kovach, Fred Herzog, et al. *The City of Vancouver*. Vancouver: J.J. Douglas, 1976.

Bucci, Paul. "B.C. Towns Devastated by Patriotic Rush to Fight in the Great War." *Vancouver Sun*, 6 November 1999, B1.

Coppard, Patricia. "City Accused of Wasting Money on Community Liaison Job." *Vancouver Courier*, 25 August 1999, 7.

Davis, Chuck, ed. *The Greater Vancouver Book: An Urban Encyclopedia*. Surrey, B.C.: Linkman Press, 1997.

Davis, Gary, and Kim Harris. *Small Business: The Independent Retailer*. Houndsmills, U.K.: Macmillan, 1990.

Diggins, Joyce. "Touring Vancouver's West Side." *Vancouver Courier*, 30 November 1983, 36.

——. "Around Dunbar." *Vancouver Courier*, 7 December, 1983, 36.

——. "Historical Journey Continues." *Vancouver Courier*, 14 December 1983, 18.

Dunbar Community Vision. Vancouver: City of Vancouver Planning Department, 1998.

Dunbar-Southlands: A Community Profile. Vancouver: City of Vancouver Planning Department, 1994.

Fleming, Francis. "At Century's End, Spare a Thought to Labourers Past." *Vancouver Sun*, 31 December 1999, A21.

Fong, Petti. "Vancouver Checks Out First." *Vancouver Sun*, 21 June 1997, H1, H5.

Hall, Jamie. City Limits (various columns). *Vancouver Sun*, 1999.

Janigan, Mary. "The Buzz on E-Biz." *Maclean's*, 1 April 2002, 28–30.

Johnson, Mike, and Terry Johnson. "History of Vancouver, 1922." Architecture 425 essay, University of British Columbia, 1967.

Jones, Deborah. "Try Thinking Outside the Big Box Occasionally." *Vancouver Sun*, 6 April 2002, A23.

Kluckner, Michael. *Vancouver: The Way It Was*. Vancouver: Whitecap Books, 1984.

Lang, Carol-Ann. Jack Lang obituary. *Vancouver Sun*, 7 December 1999, D7.

Macdonald, Bruce. *Vancouver: A Visual History*. Vancouver: Talonbooks, 1992.

Mak, Eunice, and Lidio Daneluzzi. *Dunbar-Southlands Community Profile*. Vancouver: City of Vancouver Planning Department, 1979.

McDonald, Robert A. J., and Jean Barman, eds. *Vancouver Past: Essays in Social History*. Vancouver: UBC Press, 1986.

Miller, Chris. "Dunbar St. Faces Taxing Problem." *Vancouver Courier*, 7 June 2000, 13.

——. "Dunbar Residents Group Says City Not Listening to Zoning Concerns." *Vancouver Courier*, 21 November 2001, 15.

Mitchell, David, and Shari Gradon, eds. *British Columbia's Business Leaders of the Century*. Vancouver: Business in Vancouver Media Group, 1999.

O'Brien, Larry, and Frank W. Harris. *Retailing: Shopping, Society, Space*. London: David Fulton Publishers, 1991.

Putnam, Margaret. "Smart New Suburban Shop in Vancouver." *Modern Hairdressing and Beauty Culture*, April 1941, 12–13.

Slack, Terry. "The Booming Babies." *Vancouver Sun*, December 1999.

"Trends and Futures in the Retail Grocery Business in Vancouver: A Dialogue." Proceedings of a conference held 10 May 2000. City of Vancouver Community Services (draft), 7 September 2000.

UBC Annual Report 2003–2004. Vancouver: University of British Columbia.

Vancouver and B.C. business directories, 1925–96. Vancouver: Various publishers. City of Vancouver Archives; UBC Library, Rare Books and Special Collections; Vancouver Public Library, Special Collections.

Vancouver Local Areas 1971–1981. Vancouver: City of Vancouver Planning Department, August 1985.

Vancouver Local Areas 1996. Vancouver: City of Vancouver, Community Services, March 1999.

Vogel, Aynsley, and Dana Wyse. *Vancouver: A History in Photographs*. Vancouver: Altitude Publishing, 1993.

Walker, Elizabeth. *Street Names of Vancouver*. Vancouver: Vancouver Historical Society, 1999.

Wuschke, Ewald. "The Safeway Story." *Southlands News*, September 1974, 1–3.

Wynn, Graeme, and Timothy Oke, eds. *Vancouver and Its Region*. Vancouver: UBC Press, 1992.

INTERVIEWEES AND CONTRIBUTORS

Amiel, Len. Telephone interview by Peggy Schofield. 9 April 2002.

Archer, Margaret. Personal interview by Peggy Schofield. 5 July 2001.

Belfont, Byron. Personal interview by Pam Chambers. 18 May 2000.

Blight, Harry. Personal interview. 2 April 2000.

Bonina, Cori (née Rossum). Personal interview. 21 September 2000.

Bowman, James (Ed). Personal interview. 15 January 2002.

Brunskill, Germaine. Personal interview. 5 March 2004.

Carter, Melva (née Carscadden). Telephone conversation with Pam Chambers. 29 March 2000.

Chan, Eddie. Personal interview by Larry Moore and Peggy Schofield. 17 January 2003.

Chang, Ruth. Personal interview. 25 October 2002.

Charles, Andrew. Personal interview by Peggy Schofield. 25 August 1999.

Church, John. Personal interview by Peggy Schofield. 9 August 2002.

Church, Shirley (née Yeo). Personal interview by Peggy Schofield. 9 August 2002.

Claridge, Jack. Personal interview. 12 December 1999.

Claridge, Margaret (née Nicholson). Personal interview. 2 November 1999.

Cornish, Stan. Personal interview. 3 November 1999.

Coukell, Dana (née Logie). Personal communication. 29 October 2001. Personal interview. 14 June 2005.

Cowen, Pat. Personal interview. 15 October 1999.

Craig, Beverly Ann. Personal interview by Pam Chambers. 25 July 2001.

Dalla-Lana, Fred. Personal interview by Imbi Harding, Peggy Schofield and June Binkert. 10 May 2001.

Damms, Patsy (née McQueen). E-mail to Peggy Schofield. 20 June 2000.

Dougan, Terry. Personal interview. 4 March 2002.

Fisher, Lena (née Pheasey). Personal interview. 21 November 2002.

Fong, Linda (née Chan). Personal interview. 17 January 2003.

Forshaw, Lissa. Personal interview. 5 March 2002.

Funell, Marion (née Tulloch). Personal interview by Joan Tyldesley. 11 August 2001.

German, Kathleen. Personal interview by Pam Chambers. 15 January 2002.

Gowe, Ronald N. E-mail to Peggy Schofield. 18 November 2001.

Halverson, Vernon. Personal interview by Peggy Schofield. 8 August 2000.

Heather, Clista (née Davis). Personal interview. 2 July 2000.

Heskin, Bernard A. Letter to Alice Richmond. 3 October 2001.

Ho, Jeffrey. Personal interview. 27 March 2003.

Hubbard, Jane (née Pyatt), and Thelma Perrault. Personal interview by Peggy Schofield. 2 April 2001.

Hunter, Joan. Personal interview by Margaret Moore. 4 February 2000.

Jaffer, Bilkish (BJ). Personal interview. 12 September 2000.

Jakeway, Thomas George. Interview notes, "Remembering Dunbar" meeting, Keith Ralston, moderator. 25 May 1999.

Jinks, Gordon and Lionel. Personal interview by Peggy Schofield. 16 March 2001.

Kassam, Salman. Personal interview. 12 September 2000.

Kendrick, Robert W. E-mail to Helen Thom. 12 March 1999. E-mail to Larry Moore. 14 April 1999.

Killeen, Dave. "Remembering Dunbar" meeting, Keith Ralston, moderator. 25 May 1999.

Lindsay, Barrie. Personal communication to Margaret Moore. 27 October 1999.

Longson, Dianne (née Walker). Personal communication. 25 September 1999.

MacDonald, Helen. "Remembering Dunbar" meeting, Keith Ralston, moderator. 25 May 1999.

Macdonald, Joan. Personal interview. 1 March 1999.

McGlashan, Ian. Personal interview. 13 August 2002.

McIntyre, Angus. Personal communication. 2 August 2002.

McLean, Patricia. Telephone interview by Joan Tyldesley. 29 July 2001.

McQueen, Betty (née McCleery). Personal interview by Pam Chambers. 1 February 2000.

Mercer, Barbara. Personal interview. 4 March 1999.

Merrari, Crista. Informal interview. 2004.

Montador, Ena. Personal interview by Peggy Schofield. 23 October 1999.

Moore, Margaret (née Campbell). Personal interview. 6 September 2000.

Ommundsen, Peter. E-mail to Peggy Schofield. 22 July 2002.

Pinder, Craig. Personal interview. 28 February 1999.

Porter, Alice. Personal interview by Peggy Schofield. 12 June 2000.

Poulter, Raymond. "Remembering Dunbar" meeting, Keith Ralston, moderator. 25 May 1999.

Ralston, Keith. Moderator, "Remembering Dunbar" meeting. 25 May 1999.

Randle, Sharon (née Eddie). E-mail to Peggy Schofield. 10 January 2003.

Raphael, Mary. Personal interview. 4 March 1999.

Richmond, Alice. Letter to Peggy Schofield. 24 October 2001.

Robertson, Frank Alan. Personal interview by Peggy Schofield. 28 January 2000.

Robinson, Helen (née Sutherland). Personal interview by Peggy Schofield. 25 February 2001.

Robinson, Helen (née Welsh). Personal interview. 15 October 2001.

Rochford, Carole (née Mitchell). Personal interview by Peggy Schofield. 10 August 1999.

Schofield, Peggy. Interview materials and source documents. 1998–2002.

Schretlen, Al. Personal interview by Peggy Schofield. 15 August 2000.

Slack, Sharon (née Bain), and Terry Slack. Personal interview by Toireasa Nelson. 25 August 1999.

Smith, Bessie (née Whyte). Personal interview. 1 March 1999.

Smith, Frank. Personal interview by Margaret Moore. 29 March 2000.

Sveistrup, Arnold. Personal interview. 9 May 2000.

Thom, Helen. Personal interview. 1 March 1999.

Tryon, Elmer B. (Al). Personal interview by Peggy Schofield. 15 August 2000.

Tyldesley, Joan. Written correspondence. 4 August 2001.

Wakeman, Rollie. E-mail to Peggy Schofield. 14 November 2001.

Weatherall, William. Personal interview. 15 February 2000.

Wiland, Irene. Letter to Peggy Schofield. 10 July 2001.

Williams, Al. Personal interview. 7 March 2003.

Williams, Carol. Telephone interview. 19 May 2006.

Wood, Brian. Telephone interview. 15 August 2000.

Woolfrey, Joy. E-mail correspondence. 10 November 2002.

Wuschke, Ewald. Personal interview. 28 October 1999.

Yanor, David. Telephone interview. 11 May 2000.

Chapter 5:
Transportation in a Classic Streetcar Suburb

In addition to the following sources, various issues were consulted of the following: the *B.C. Electric Employees' Magazine* and *The Buzzer* (published by the B.C. Electric Railway Company and courtesy of B.C. Hydro Information Services), the *Point Grey Gazette* (available at the City of Vancouver Archives), the *Province*, and the *Vancouver Sun*.

REFERENCES

Clampitts, Coiret. Interview by Major J.S. Matthews, 3 December 1931. "Early Vancouver; a collection of historical data, maps, and plans made with assistance of pioneers of Vancouver between March & December 1931," vol. 1, p. 232. City of Vancouver Archives.

Ewert, Henry. *The Story of the B.C. Electric Railway.* North Vancouver: Whitecap Books, 1986.

Macdonald, Bruce. *Vancouver: A Visual History.* Vancouver: Talonbooks, 1992.

Mellis, William K. Interview by Major J.S. Matthews, 2 July 1940. "Early Vancouver," vol. 6, p. 2. City of Vancouver Archives.

Rowling, Henry S. Interview by Major J.S. Matthews, 13 April 1933. "Early Vancouver," vol. 5, p. 155. City of Vancouver Archives.

Vancouver's Trolley Buses, 1948–1998. Vancouver: B.C. Transit, 1998.

Walker, Elizabeth. *Street Names of Vancouver.* Vancouver: Vancouver Historical Society, 1999.

Warner, Sam Bass, Jr. *Streetcar Suburbs: The Process of Growth in Boston (1870–1900).* 2nd ed. Cambridge, Mass.: Harvard University Press, 1962.

Wilson, Mr. and Mrs. C.H. Interview by Major J.S. Matthews, 17 September 1937. "Early Vancouver," vol. 5, p. 321. City of Vancouver Archives.

Wilson, Hugh, Andrew Wilson, and the B.C. Hydro Power Pioneers. *Gaslights to Gigawatts: A Human History of BC Hydro and Its Predecessors.* Vancouver: Hurricane Press, 1998.

Wynn, Graeme, and Timothy Oke, eds. *Vancouver and Its Region.* Vancouver: UBC Press, 1992.

INTERVIEWEES AND CONTRIBUTORS

Albinson, Fred. Personal interview by Larry Moore. 22 August 2003.

Bowman, James (Ed). Personal interview. 24 July 2002.

Cowen, Pat. Personal interview. December 1999.

Crawford, Pat. B.C. Hydro Information Services.

Gowe, Ronald N. E-mail to Peggy Schofield. 18 November 2001.

Graham, Ian. Personal interview. 2002.

Harlow, Leslie (née Adam). Personal interview by Pam Chambers. 14 November 2001.

Holz, Lea. Personal interview. 1 August 2002.

Hubbard, Jane (née Pyatt). Personal interview by Peggy Schofield. 2 April 2001.

Jessiman, Kenneth. Personal communication to Peggy Schofield. n.d.

Jinks, Gordon and Lionel. Personal interview by Peggy Schofield. 16 March 2001.

Jones, Marjorie (née Tryon). Personal interview by Peggy Schofield. 27 March 2001.

Lundy, Dean. Telephone interview by Peggy Schofield. 19 November 2002.

MacKenzie, Murdo. Personal communication. 2002

Malkin, James (Jamie). Personal interview by Pam Chambers. 9 March 2000.

McGlashan, Ian. Telephone interview. 10 September 2002.

McPherson, Jim. Personal interview by Peggy Schofield. 31 May 2000.

McQueen, Betty (née McCleery). Personal interview by Pam Chambers. 1 February 2000.

Montador, Ena. Personal interview by Peggy Schofield. 23 October 1999.

Moore, Larry. Personal interview. 2002.

Pierson, Betty (née Clarke). Telephone interview. 10 September 2002.

Robertson, Frank Alan. Personal interview by Peggy Schofield. 28 January 2000.

Slack, Sharon (née Bain), and Terry Slack. Personal interview. 29 July 2002.

Stevens, Mel. Personal interview. 22 July 2002.

Tryon, Elmer B. (Al). Personal interview by Peggy Schofield. 15 August 2000.

Vivian, Jean (née McLean). Telephone interview. 10 September 2002.

Waters, Victor. Personal interview by Pam Chambers. 6 September 2001.

Chapter 6: The Residential Landscape

REFERENCES

Bartholomew, Harland, and Associates. *A Plan for the City of Vancouver, British Columbia, including Point Grey and South Vancouver, and a General Plan of the Region*. Vancouver: Vancouver Town Planning Commission, 1929.

Binkert, June. "Some Dunbar Homes in Their Settings: Walk #2." Typescript (for Salmonberry Days), 1998.

Carlson, Keith Thor, ed. *A Stó:lō–Coast Salish Historical Atlas*. Vancouver: Douglas & McIntyre; Chilliwack, B.C.: Stó:lō Nation, 2001.

Ellis, Jon. "Complaints about Big Houses." Dunbar Residents' Association newsletter, February 2004.

Higgins, Keith. "Naïve Readings/Vancouver Special" [posting to Internet blog]. [Cited 15 August 2005]. www.tatlin.com/naivereadings/index.php?cat=3.

———. Vancouver Special [Web site, cited 15 August 2005]. www.vancouverspecial.com.

Kluckner, Michael. *Vanishing Vancouver*. North Vancouver: Whitecap Books, 1990.

Luxton, Donald, ed. *Building the West: The Early Architects of British Columbia*. Vancouver: Talonbooks, 2003.

Macdonald, Bruce. *Vancouver: A Visual History*. Vancouver: Talonbooks, 1992.

McAfee, Ann. "City Plan." In *The Greater Vancouver Book: An Urban Encyclopedia*, edited by Chuck Davis, 245–46. Surrey, B.C.: Linkman Press, 1997.

McGeogh, Gerry. "Heritage Revitalization Agreement and Designation — Morrisette Farmhouse, 5503 Blenheim Street." Report presented to Vancouver City Council, 20 March 1998.

Mitchell, Katharyne. *Crossing the Neoliberal Line: Pacific Rim Migration and the Metropolis*. Philadelphia: Temple University Press, 2004.

Pettit, Barbara Ann. "Zoning and the Single-Family Landscape: Large New Houses and Neighbourhood Change in Vancouver." Report presented to Vancouver City Council. Typescript, 1993.

———. Quoted in "Home Improvements," by David Carrigg. *Vancouver Courier*, 11 March 2003.

Wackernagel, Mathis, and William E. Rees. *Our Ecological Footprint: Reducing Human Impact on the Earth*. Gabriola Island, B.C.: New Society Publishers, 1996.

Whitlock, Rob. "Secondary Suites" [on-line]. Report presented to Vancouver City Council, 27 January 2004. [Cited 11 August 2005]. www.city.vancouver.bc.ca/ctyclerk/cclerk/20040301/p2.pdf.

Williams, Robert. "Recommended Design Guidelines for Domestic Dwellings on Lots less than 25 Feet in Width, RS-1 Schedule." Typescript, 1981.

Windsor-Liscombe, Rhodri, curator. *The New Spirit: Modern Architecture in Vancouver, 1938–1963*. Montreal: Canadian Centre for Architecture; Calgary: Nickle Art Gallery, University of Calgary; Vancouver: Vancouver Art Gallery, 1997.

Wynn, Graeme. "The Rise of Vancouver." In *Vancouver and Its Region*, edited by Graeme Wynn and Timothy Oke, 69–145. Vancouver: UBC Press, 1992.

INTERVIEWEES AND CONTRIBUTORS

Albinson, Fred. Phone conversation. April 2005.

Archambault, Richard. Interview by Pam Chambers. 4 July 2001.

Bourque, Pat. Interview by Peggy Scofield and Imbi Harding. March 2001.

Brown, May (née Adams). Personal interview by Pam Chambers. 21 July 2001.

Chisholm, Harold J. Letter to Peggy Schofield. 17 July 2000.

Claridge, Jack. Personal interview by Larry Moore. 12 December 1999. Personal interview by Margaret Moore. 18 May 2004.

Downs, Barry. Personal interviews by Peggy Schofield and Imbi Harding. March 8 & 30, 2001.

Ellis, Jon. Conversations. April 2005.

Forshaw, Lissa. Telephone conversation with Helen Spiegelman. May 2005.

Grant, Tom. E-mail to Helen Spiegelman re: last log house in Dunbar. 29 April 2005.

Hall, Nichola. Telephone interview by Helen Spiegelman. 28 August 2005.

Higgins, Keith. E-mails to Helen Spiegelman. 27–28 April 2005.

Killam, Larry. Interview by Peggy Schofield. 18 January 2001.

Luxton, Donald. E-mail to Helen Spiegelman. 28 July 2005.

McQueen, Betty (née McCleery). Conversations. 2005, 2006.

Oberlander, Cornelia (née Hahn). Interview by Peggy Schofield. 4 May 2000. Letter to Shelagh Lindsey. n.d.

Watters, Don. Interview by Peggy Schofield. 6 September 2001.

Chapter 7: People and Places in the Arts

REFERENCES

Affleck, Edward L. "A History of the Knox Operatic Group/Dunbar Musical Theatre." Typescript, 1992.

Alexander, John. "Joe's Passion: Lawrence Books." *Amphora* (Alcuin Society) 128 (Autumn 2002): 16–18.

Challenger, Winnifred Mole. "Henry Mole, a Pioneer Gentleman of British Columbia." Typescript, 1970.

"City's Record-Making Artist." Undated, unattributed newspaper clipping about Peter Sager found between pages of a 1938 Lord Byng High School annual.

Gilmour, Clyde. "Talked Chaplin into Movies, John H. Boothe Retires." Major J.S. Matthews clipping collection, 14 June 1951. City of Vancouver Archives.

Gold, Kerry. "Vancouver Artist Onley Honoured by Isle of Man." *Vancouver Sun*, 6 May 2002, B6.

Gustafson, Paula. *Salish Weaving*. Vancouver: Douglas & McIntyre, 1980.

Wyatt, Gary, ed. *Susan Point, Coast Salish Artist*. Vancouver: Douglas & McIntyre, 2000.

Wyman, Max. "The Dance Scene." In *The Greater Vancouver Book: An Urban Encyclopedia*, edited by Chuck Davis, 694–96. Surrey, B.C.: Linkman Press, 1997.

———. "At 80, Weisgarber Moves On." *Vancouver Sun*, 4 December 1999, E17.

INTERVIEWEES AND CONTRIBUTORS

Affleck, Edward. Telephone interview. 17 March 2000.

Ancer, Rosario, and Victor Kolstee. Personal interview. 6 February 2001.

Archambault, Richard. Personal interview. 4 July 2001.

Baker, Douglas. Personal interview. 4 April 2000.

Belfont, Bryan. Personal interview. 6 April 2000.

Binkert, June. Conversation. 13 May 2002.

Bullock, Michael. Personal interview. 28 November 2001.

Bungay, Angus, and Lori-Ann Latremouille. Personal interview. 1 December 2001.

Charko, Ken. Personal interview. 28 November 2001.

Chatman, Stephen, and Tara Wohlberg. Personal interview. 10 April 2000.

Chesterman, Robert. Personal interview. 14 November 2000.

Clark, Margaret (Peg). Personal interview. 13 March 2000.

Clarke, Jean (née Parker). Telephone interview. 1 February 2001.

Coghill, Joy. Personal interview. 30 March 2000.

Connell, Catherine. Personal interview. 6 November 2001.

Cosar, Bette. Personal interview. 30 April 2001.

Craig, Beverly (née Barkley). Personal interview. 25 July 2001.

Darcus, Jack. Personal interview. 11 December 2001.

Edgar, Jill. Personal interview. 14 February 2000.

Feilum, Haakon. Telephone interview. 27 April 2002.

German, Kathleen. Personal interview. 15 January 2002.

Gray, John MacLachlan. Personal interview. 11 October 2000.

Gustafson, Paula. Conversation. 13 May 2002.

Harlow, Leslie (née Adam). Personal interview. 14 November 2001.

Hatch, Ronald. Personal interview. 9 May 2000.

Jones, David, and Kim Pechet. Personal interview. 8 May 2000.

Jones, Gwynneth. Personal interview. 28 January 2000.

Jozsa, Laszlo. Personal interview. 1 December 2000.

Lawrence, Ann. Conversation. 10 May 2002.

Malkin, James (Jamie). Personal interview. 9 March 2000.

Marshall, Roz. Personal interview. 15 March 2000.

McQueen, Betty (née McCleery). Personal interview. 1 February 2000.

Miller, James and Melita. Personal interview. 15 November 1999.

Mitchell, Gayle (née Johnson). E-mail to Peggy Schofield re: George Tedlock. 20 October 2002.

Nicol, Eric. Personal interview. 16 February 2000.

Onley, Toni. Personal interview. 14 March 2000.

Point, Susan. Personal interview. 17 November 2001.

Polson, Nora (née Borrowman). Personal interview. 2 June 2001.

Poulter, Raymond. Telephone interview. 20 November 2001.

Pritchard, Jocelyn. Personal interview. 11 January 2000.

Redmond, Eva (née Twaites). Personal interview. 21 September 1999.

Rowley, Elizabeth (Liz) (née Parker). Personal interview. 13 March 2001.

Schipizky, Frederick. Personal interview. 1 December 2001.

Schofield, Peggy. Personal interview. 14 April 2000.

Schretlen, Elaine (née Ellefson). Personal interview by Peggy Schofield. 3 December 1999.

Smith, Cecilia. Letter and Theatre Under The Stars program to Pam Chambers. February 2002.

Smith, Gordon A. Conversation with Pam Chambers at Emily Carr Institute. 7 April 2005.

Smithson, Karen (née Weisgarber). Personal interview. 27 March 2000.

Sparrow, Debra. Personal interview. 23 February 2001.

Thornton, Betty. Telephone interview. November 2001.

Tien, Ching. Personal interview. 26 November 2001.

Turner, Betty (née Allan), and Susan Lazar. Personal interview. 22 January 2000.

Waldron, Pat, and Audrey Wills. Personal interview. 16 May 2000.

Weisgarber, Elliot. Personal interview. 10 January 2000.

Wiseman, J. Morley (Padam). Personal interview. 10 August 2000.

Zagoudakis, Jamie. Personal interview. 19 February 2000.

Chapter 8: Sports and Recreation

The following archival resources were consulted: the B.C. Archives, the B.C. Sports Hall of Fame and Museum, the Dunbar Community Centre archives, the Lord Byng Secondary School archives, the Vancouver Maritime Museum, the main branch of the Vancouver Public Library, and the UBC Museum of Anthropology.

REFERENCES

Brook, Paula. "Golden Girls Show Their Mettle in Run for the Cure." *Vancouver Sun,* 3 October 2001, B2.

Campbell, Blake. *Dunbar Lawn Bowling Club: Brief Historical Review of the First 50 Years Plus One, 1927–1977.* Vancouver: Dunbar Lawn Bowling Club, 1977.

Culbert, Lori. "Adventure in Ultimate Frisbee." *Vancouver Sun,* 18 August 2001, B6.

Dheensaw, Cleve. *Lacrosse 100.* Victoria: Orca Book Publishers, 1990.

"Dunbar Soccer Boasts more than 500 Players." *Vancouver Courier,* January 1972.

Dunlop, Donald, and Ron Shearer. *Don't Make Mistakes! Play Perfectly!* Vancouver, 1980.

Fischer, Gertrude. *The Complete Book of Golden Retriever.* New York: Howell Book House, 1980.

Golden Gazette II. Dunbar Community Centre publication, Summer 2001.

Granstrom, Ivy. Obituary. *Vancouver Sun,* 19 April 2004.

Hamblin, Barry. "Schoolboy Cricket No Game for the Sissies." *Vancouver Sun,* 27 March 1957, 16.

Hanna, Dawn. "Keeping the Green." *Vancouver Courier,* 22 February 2004, 1–7.

"Horse Lovers from the Lower Mainland." *Vancouver Sun,* 5 April 1952, 28.

Long, Wendy. "Disabled Athletes Honoured." *Vancouver Sun,* 28 April 2001, G6.

Lord Byng High School annuals, 1937, 1938, 1939. Courtesy Pam (Seivewright) Chambers.

Mackin, Bob. "Blind Octogenarian Still Setting Running Records." *Vancouver Courier,* 21 July 2001.

"Meanderings of Steelheads in Point Grey." *Daily News Advertiser,* 1 December 1912.

O'Connor, Naoibh. "Bird's Eye View." *Vancouver Courier,* 4 February 2004.

Oke, Midge. "Why I Paddle Dragonboats." *Dig It in Dunbar.* Dunbar Garden Club newsletter, October 1999, 7–8.

Our Yesterdays, 1914–1968. Vancouver: Dunbar Heights United Church of Canada, 1968. Printed by the Vancouver Training Workshop for the Handicapped.

Retrospect: The Story of St. Philip's Anglican Church, Vancouver, 1925–1975. Vancouver: St. Philip's Anglican Church, 1975.

Riessner, Sylvia. "Southlands: Barns and Bales in the Big City." *Pacific Horse,* April 1996.

Shaughnessy Golf and Country Club. Vancouver: Shaughnessy Golf and Country Club, n.d.

"Southlands Riding Club." Historical article prepared by club members, n.d.

Steele, R. Mike. *The First One Hundred Years: An Illustrated Celebration.* Vancouver: Vancouver Board of Parks and Recreation, 1988.

"Swing Your Honey and Promenade Home." *Western News,* 29 March 1973.

Thomas, Alister, ed. *Paddle Quest: Canada's Best Canoe Routes.* Erin, Ont.: Boston Mills Press, 2000.

"Vancouver's Old Streams." From revised edition, 1989. Originally printed in *Waters,* journal of the Vancouver Aquarium (1978): 3.

White, Silas. Sports entries in *The Encyclopedia of British Columbia,* edited by Daniel Francis. Madeira Park, B.C.: Harbour Publishing, 2000.

INTERVIEWEES AND CONTRIBUTORS

Albinson, Betty (née McLean). Personal interview. 20 April 2002.

Albinson, Fred. Personal interview. 20 April 2002.

Bardsley, Tony. Telephone interview. 14 November 2000.

Barnard, Ken. Telephone interview. 10 March 2001.

Betteridge, Jack. Telephone interview. 10 June 2001.

Brown, Dorothy. B.C. Golf Museum. Personal interview. 23 June 2004.

Buckham, Joan (née Crawford). Personal interview. 4 May 2001.

Burnell, Bonnie. Telephone interview. 6 February 2003.

Carter, Ian. E-mail. 10 September 2001.

Carter, Irene (née Forker). Personal interview. 9 June 2000.

Carter, Mary Ann (née Sheller). Personal interview. 19 November 2002.

Claridge, Jack. Personal interview. 18 May 2004.

Claridge, Lloyd. Personal interview. 18 March 2002.

Clinton, Sally (née Anders). Personal interview. 9 October 2000.

Cornish, Stan. Personal interview by Larry Moore. 3 November 1999.

Creer, Brian. Personal interview. 8 March 2002.

Creighton, Peggy. Telephone interview. 22 August 2000.

Cupit, Don. Telephone interview. 5 November 2000.

Dobson, Lee (née Davenport). Telephone interview. 10 October 2002.

Drummond, Glen. Telephone interview. 22 January 2003.

Duggan, Jack. Telephone interview. 7 July 2004.

Forshaw, Lissa. Telephone interview. 24 March 2002.

Fraser, Ian. Telephone interview. 15 June 2003.

Furness, Lorraine. Telephone interview. 17 February 2003.

Gayton, Doug. E-mail to Peggy Schofield. 5 December 2001.

Gowe, Douglas. Telephone interview. 23 January 2003.

Gowe, Ronald N. E-mail to Peggy Schofield. 18 November 2001.

Granstrom, Ivy. Personal interview by Peggy Schofield. 2 August 2000. Telephone interview by Margaret Moore. 8 May 2003.

Grass, Jude (née Fuller). Telephone interview. 11 July 2004.

Heather, Clista (née Davis). Personal interview by Larry Moore. 2 July 2000.

Ho, T.K. Telephone interview. 22 February 2005.

Hughes, Paul. Personal interview. 13 April 2003.

Hume, Fred. Personal interview. 5 March 2003.

Hunt, Edmund Arthur (Ted). E-mail. 10 March 2003.

Hunt, Helen (née Stewart). Personal interview. 9 February 2003.

Hunter, Joan. Personal interview by Peggy Schofield. 28 August 1999.

Hutton, Ruth (née Carley). Telephone interview. 22 January 2003.

Iwasaki, Keith. Personal interview. 28 December 2002.

Jang, Erroll. Personal interview. 6 February 2003.

Jinks, Gordon and Lionel. Telephone interview. 5 December 2002.

Johnston, Jacqui (née Kubiski). Telephone interview. 4 May 2002.

Joyce, David. Letter. 20 March 2001. Personal interview. 24 June 2004.

Kelly, Jim. Personal interview. 11 February 2003.

Kelsey, Howard. Personal interview. 9 December 2002.

Kent, Sonny. Telephone interview. 15 January 2003.

Kermode, Jack. Telephone interview. 5 January 2003.

Knight, Shirley (née Pike). Telephone interview. 5 March 2003.

Kot, Pauline. Telephone interview. 22 November 2002.

Landstrom, Norma (née Johnston). Personal interview. 14 March 2002.

Laxton, Graham. Letter. 14 September 2000.

Lindsay, Barrie. E-mail. 10 February 2000.

Malmgren, Jess. E-mail via Vancouver Public Library. 7 May 2004.

Mann, Norman. Telephone interview. 10 September 2002.

Martin, Dave. Telephone interview. 10 September 2002.

McBryde, John. Telephone interview. 4 February 2003.

McDonough, Bernice (née Mack). Letter. 12 August 2000.

McKay, Art. Personal interview. 8 February 2001.

McLellan, Bruce. Personal interview. 12 September 2001.

McTavish, Spence. Telephone interview. 16 January 2003.

Meek, Audrey. Personal interview. 5 April 2002.

Mitchell, Gayle (née Johnson). E-mail to Peggy Schofield re: George Tedlock. 20 October 2002.

Neufeld, Eldo. Telephone interview. 7 January 2003.

Ostrom, Audrey (née Burdon). Personal interview. 12 May 1999.

Paterson, Donald. Telephone interview. 5 February 2003.

Pepin, Maureen (née Sankey). Personal interview. 8 June 1999.

Plumbley, Kay (née LeClair). Personal interview. 19 October 2000.

Point, Rose (née Pettis). Personal interview. 10 May 2002. Personal interview by Peggy Schofield. January 2004.

Pomfret, Jack. Personal interview. 22 March 2001.

Pomfret, Marilyn. Telephone interview. 15 January 2001.

Postgate, Marion. Telephone interview. 6 January 2003.

Robinson, Helen (née Welsh). Personal interview. 8 May 2001.

Rodgers, Edith (née Hine). Personal interview. 9 August 2000.

Rush, Jack. Personal interview. 17 March 2000.

Sankey, Derek. Personal interview. 8 September 2001.

Schmelcher, Madeleine (Maddy) (née Shaw). Personal interview. 10 May 2003.

Schretlen, Elaine (née Ellefson). Telephone interview. 20 November 2002.

Schutz, Avis (née McGee). Personal interview. 10 July 2001.

Scott, Julia (née Neames). Personal interview. 7 June 2001.

Self, Brian. Personal interview. 17 February 2005.

Shearer, Ronald (Ron). Telephone interview. 21 July 2001.

Slack, Sharon (née Bain). Personal interview. 23 July 2002.

Slack, Terry. Personal interview. 28 May 2001.

Smith, Diane (née Harper). Personal interview. 9 March 2000.

Smith, Frank. Personal interview. 29 March 2000.

Smithson, Karen (née Weisgarber). Letter to Pam Chambers. 14 May 2000.

Smyth, Sheila. Letter. 19 March 2002.

Stenberg, Charlotte. E-mail. 17 September 2001.

Stewart, Barry. Telephone interview. 21 January 2003.

Thom, Helen (née Hurlston). Personal interview. 7 July 2000.

Trounce, Doug. Telephone interview. 6 February 2003.

Tyldesley, Joan. Personal interview. 14 May 2004.

Van Unen, Louise (née Cornish). Telephone interview. 10 November 1999.

Vivian, Jean (née McLean). Telephone interview. 5 June 2002.

Wakeman, Rollie. Telephone interview. 8 January 2003.

Walkinshaw, Angie. Telephone interview. 15 September 2002.

Weatherall, Helen (née Wolrige). Personal interview. 28 January 2003.

Wicken, Sonia (née Palisniuk). Personal interview. 4 April 2002.

Winkelman, Ron. Personal interview by Larry Moore. 6 June 2002.

Withers, Pam (née Miller). Personal interview. 6 July 2002.

Young, John. Telephone interview. 2 August 2004.

Young, Margaret (Peg). Telephone interview. 22 January 2003.

Chapter 9: School Days

The authors appreciated access to the following school archives during their research: Kerrisdale Elementary School, Lord Byng Secondary School, Queen Elizabeth Elementary School and Queen Elizabeth Annex. Information collected about Magee Secondary School, Point Grey Secondary School, Prince of Wales Mini School and Point Grey Mini School was not included in the final chapter as these schools were deemed to be outside the neighbourhood boundaries. Information about these schools resides in our archival collection.

REFERENCES

Barman, Jean. *Growing up British in British Columbia: Boys in Private Schools*. Vancouver: UBC Press, 1984.

Bell-Irving, Elizabeth. *Crofton House School: The First Ninety Years, 1898–1988*. Vancouver: Crofton House School, 1988.

Gosbee, Chuck, and Leslie Dyson, eds. *Glancing Back: Reflections and Anecdotes on Vancouver Public Schools*. Vancouver: Vancouver School Board, 1988.

Hamilton, Valerie L. *The Schools of Vancouver*. Vancouver: Vancouver School Board, 1986.

Knickerbocker, Nancy. *No Plaster Saint: The Life of Mildred Osterhout Fahrni*. Burnaby: Talonbooks, 2000.

McDonald, Robert A.J., and Jean Barman, eds. *Vancouver Past: Essays in Social History*. Vancouver: UBC Press, 1986.

Rink, Deborah. *Spiritual Women: A History of Catholic Sisters in British Columbia*. Vancouver: The Sisters' Association, Archdiocese of Vancouver, 2000.

Rose, Elizabeth A. *Point Grey School: The First Fifty Years, 1929–79*. Vancouver: Vancouver School Board, 1978.

Waites, Kenneth Arthur, ed. *The First Fifty Years: Vancouver High Schools, 1890–1940*. Vancouver: Vancouver School Board, 1943.

INTERVIEWEES AND CONTRIBUTORS

Abbot, Betty (née McGlashan). Personal interview by Peggy Schofield. 31 May 2001.

Abramson, Sherry. Personal interview by Peggy Schofield. 31 July 2001.

Addison, Rosalind. Written account to Peggy Schofield. 10 August 2003.

Alexander, Eve. Conversation with Peggy Schofield. 4 April 2000.

Allman, Anna (née White). Personal interview by Peggy Schofield. 10 January 2001.

Bowman, James (Ed). Telephone interview by Joan Tyldesley. 12 July 2002.

Catherall, Hilda. Personal interview by Pam Chambers. 2 November 2001.

Chambers, Pam (née Seivewright). Telephone interview by Joan Tyldesley. 27 November 2002.

Chan, Chris. Written account to Peggy Schofield. 12 September 2002.

Chiu, Gwen. Telephone interview by Joan Tyldesley. 9 January 2003.

Church, Shirley (née Yeo). Personal interview by Peggy Schofield. 9 August 2002.

Cornish, Stan. Personal interview by Larry Moore. 3 November 1999.

Cowen, Pat. Personal interview by Margaret Moore. 15 October 1999.

Cowley, Jacqueline (née Chevalier). Personal interview by Peggy Schofield. 2 September 1999.

Cramer, Carl. Telephone interview by Peggy Schofield. 9 December 2002.

Defoe, Tracy. Personal interview by Peggy Schofield. 3 July 2001.

Edwards, Douglas. Personal interview by Peggy Schofield. 25 August 2001.

Filer, Dianne (née Livingston). E-mail to Peggy Schofield. 3 April 2002.

Folland, Audrey and Norman. E-mail to Peggy Schofield. 2 May 2002.

Fong, Linda (née Chan). E-mail to Peggy Schofield. 10 January 2003.

Forbes, Barbara (née Allan). Written account to Margaret Moore. 10 July 2002.

Forshaw, Lissa. E-mail to Peggy Schofield. 10 May 2002.

Funell, Marion (née Tulloch). Personal interview by Joan Tyldesley. 11 August 2002.

Gillard, Mary. Written account to Peggy Schofield. 1 June 2000.

Girling, Sue (née Rae). E-mail to Peggy Schofield. 9 November 2001.

Glover, Katherine (née Carpenter). E-mail to Peggy Schofield. 30 September 2002.

Golata, Betty (née Moulton). Written account to Peggy Schofield. 13 August 2001.

Gonnami, Tsuneharu. Telephone interview by Joan Tyldesley. 25 November 2002.

Grant John, Wendy (née Sparrow). Personal interview by Peggy Schofield. 17 January 2003.

Grasdal, June (née Aubrey). E-mail to Peggy Schofield. 12 September 2002.

Harlow, Leslie (née Adam). Telephone interview by Pam Chambers. 14 November 2001.

Herd, Sandra. Personal interview by Peggy Schofield. 22 June 2001.

Herman, Sheila. Personal interview by Peggy Schofield. 8 June 2001.

Hinze, Ehleen (née Bohn). Personal interview by Karen Cooke. 26 August 1999.

Hopkins, Joanne and John. Personal interview by Peggy Schofield. 16 September 2002.

Hubbard, Jane (née Pyatt). Personal interview by Peggy Schofield. 2 April 2001.

Jennings, Deborah. Personal interview by Peggy Schofield. 23 January 2003.

Jerome, Valerie. Personal interview by Peggy Schofield. 31 December 2002.

Kendall, Peter. Personal interview by Peggy Schofield. 30 September 2002.

Killam, Larry. Personal interview by Peggy Schofield. 18 January 2001.

Latremouille, Lori Ann. Personal interview by Peggy Schofield. 1 December 2001.

Liversidge, Eunice (née Wilson). Telephone interview by Joan Tyldesley. 14 September 2001.

Luui, Anndraya (née Louie). E-mail to Peggy Schofield. 3 October 2000.

MacNeil, Rea. Telephone interview by Joan Tyldesley. 14 June 2002.

McDaniels, Jeremy. E-mail to Peggy Schofield. 4 September 2001.

McGivern, Sheila (née Fitzpatrick). E-mail to Peggy Schofield. 17 September 2001.

McIntyre, Angus. Personal interview by Peggy Schofield. 8 July 2002.

McLagan, Tayce. Personal interview by Peggy Schofield. 15 May 2001.

McQueen, Betty (née McCleery). Telephone interview by Peggy Schofield. 26 November 2002.

Meralli, Farouk. Written account to Peggy Schofield. 16 September 2002.

Montpellier, Patricia. Written account to Peggy Schofield. 8 August 2003.

Nazif, Joan. E-mail to Peggy Schofield. 7 September 2002.

Oberlander, Cornelia (née Hahn). Personal interview by Peggy Schofield. 4 May 2000.

Ogilvie, Airlie. Personal interview by Peggy Schofield. 22 January 2002.

Pacheco, Muriel (née Schofield). E-mail to Peggy Schofield. 10 October 2002.

Perrault, Thelma. Personal interview by Peggy Schofield. 2 April 2001.

Pottelberg, Marie. E-mail to Peggy Schofield. 18 October 2000.

Rankine, Daryl (née Muir). Telephone interview by Joan Tyldesley. 17 July 2002.

Richmond, John. Personal interview by Peggy Schofield. 9 July 2001.

Robertson, Frank Alan. Personal interview by Peggy Schofield. 28 January 2000.

Schmelcher, Madeleine (Maddy) (née Shaw). Personal interview by Peggy Schofield. 11 October 2000.

Schretlen, Elaine (née Ellefson). Personal interview by Peggy Schofield. 23 November 2000.

Smyth, Sheila. E-mail to Peggy Schofield. 20 July 2002.

Stenberg, Charlotte. Personal interview by Peggy Schofield. 16 November 2000.

Stevenson, Vic. Personal interview by Peggy Schofield. 8 September 2000.

Sweeney, Jennifer. E-mail to Peggy Schofield. 9 October 2002.

Thom, Helen (née Hurlston). Personal interview by Joan Tyldesley. 26 November 2002.

Tomkins, Janet. E-mail to Peggy Schofield. 11 October 2000.

Tryon, Elmer B. (Al). Personal interview by Peggy Schofield. 15 August 2000.

Ujimoto, Hitoshi. Personal interview by Peggy Schofield. 19 July 2002.

Varsek, Cathy. Written account to Peggy Schofield. 11 May 2002.

Waters, Wendy. E-mail to Peggy Schofield. 27 September 2002.

Wensveen, Claire. Telephone interview by Joan Tyldesley. 30 November 2002.

Wheatley, Yvonne (née Goddard). E-mail to Peggy Schofield. 29 October 2001.

Whelan, Dell (née Cooney). E-mail to Peggy Schofield. 11 January 2003.

Yesaki, Mitsuo. Telephone interview by Joan Tyldesley. 14 November 2002.

Chapter 10: Neighbourhood Churches

Sincerest thanks to all who answered questionnaires and provided information and photographs for this chapter. Many are or knew the pioneers whose strong personalities and sense of community, vision and faith contributed to the establishment of Dunbar's places of worship.

REFERENCES

Anderson, Dr. Frank H., and Janet Anderson. "Historical Recollections of the Dunbar Heights Regular Baptist Church." Typescript, 13 July 2000.

Anglican Church of Canada. Archives of the Diocese of New Westminster, Vancouver School of Theology, UBC. Bob Stewart, curator.

Commemorative Album, Immaculate Conception Parish, Golden Anniversary, 1924–1974. Vancouver, 1974.

Commemorative Album, Immaculate Conception Parish, 75th Anniversary. Vancouver, 1999.

Cronin, Kay. *Cross in the Wilderness.* Vancouver: Mitchell Press, 1960.

Dunbar Evangelical Lutheran Church. Archival records. 2000–2001.

"Dunbar Evangelical Lutheran Church, 50th Anniversary 1943–1993." Typescript, 1993.

Dunbar Evangelical Lutheran Church, Twenty-fifth Anniversary, 1943–1968. Vancouver, 1968.

Inglis, Robin. "St. Philip's Anglican Church, Vancouver: The Past 25 Years. An Historical Essay." Typescript, 1999.

Jamieson, Mrs. Alex. Transcript of an interview conducted by Miss Alice Philip, 1975. United Church of Canada Archives, Vancouver School of Theology, UBC.

Leahy, Father J.A., SJ. "Sixtieth Anniversary." Typescript, 27 April 1984.

MacGregor Ministries. "The Emissaries of Divine Light (Ontologists)" [on-line]. [Cited 4 February 2003]. www.macgregorministries.org/cult_groups/emmisaries _divine_light.

Oliver, J. Russell. "A Message to Those of the 'Knox' Family Serving with H.M. Forces." Typescript, 12 October 1943.

Our Yesterdays, 1914–1968. Booklet, Vancouver, B.C., 1968. Dunbar Heights United Church archives.

Retrospect: The Story of St. Philip's Anglican Church, Vancouver, 1925–1975. Vancouver: St. Philip's Anglican Church, 1975.

Richards, Dr. John. "Historical Sketch, Dunbar Heights Regular Baptist Church." Typescript, March 1982, with supplementary information by Pastor Don Ekstrand, 1991/92, and Pastor Darcy Van Horn, 1999.

Schretlen, K. Elaine. "History of the Crib Scene at Immaculate Conception Parish." Typescript, January 1995.

Spears, Gilbert J. "Historical Record of Dunbar Heights United Church." Typescript, 1950.

Stewart, Agnes M. "Annual Report of Ladies Aid Society for 1914." Typescript, 1914.

"Suburbanites Plan Commodious Unit." *Vancouver Sun,* 21 August 1926.

"2,000 Watch Fire Destroy Church Hall in Kerrisdale." *Province,* 24 March 1975.

Tyldesley, Joan. "Youth Activities at Knox United Church." Typescript, 2002.

United Church of Canada. Archives, Vancouver School of Theology, UBC. Doreen Stevens, curator.

INTERVIEWEES AND CONTRIBUTORS

Abbot, Betty (née McGlashan). E-mail to Peggy Schofield. 7 September 2002.

Anderson, Pastor Mark. Telephone conversations. 2000.

Anthony, Bruce. Letter. 11 November 2000.

Archambault, Richard. E-mails, telephone conversations and photo discussion. 2000–2001.

Ashley, Joan Winnifred. Questionnaire. July 2000.

Aune, Phyllis Mary Morgan. Questionnaire. 2000.

Bagshaw, Ralph C. Questionnaire. 2000.

Bernard, Edith Marie. Questionnaire. 25 August 2000.

Butchart, Colleen (née Dundee). Personal interview. 18 October 2000.

Campbell, Doris. Information. 2004.

Carter, Paul. Youth group questionnaire. 2001.

Chambers, Pam (née Seivewright). Telephone conversations and research. 2000.

Charles, Andrew. Personal interview. 24 August 2000.

Chisholm, Harold J. Questionnaire. Letter to Peggy Schofield. 17 July 2000.

Edwardson, Betty. Telephone conversations. 2000–2001.

Gear, Sheila. Notes, information, access to Dunbar Heights United Church archives. 2000–04.

Gjertsen, Betty. Questionnaire and photos. 8 November 2000.

Hamelin, Eric, and youth group. Questionnaire. 2001.

Harrison, Teddy. Youth group questionnaire. 2001.

Inglis, Robin. Telephone conversations. 2000–2001.

Jakeway, Thomas George. Questionnaire and personal interview. 2000.

Jamieson, Patricia Winnifred. Questionnaire. July 2000.

Lathwell, Jean. Telephone conversations. 2000.

Lawrence, Alma Martha. Questionnaire. 2000.

Lawrence, Richard Curtis. Questionnaire. 2000.

Le Claire, Terri. Immaculate Conception Parish secretary. Assistance and access to church records. 2000–2001.

Lower, Thelma. Correspondence re: Couples Club. 14 March 2000.

Matossian, Sarah, and youth group. Questionnaire. November 2000.

McClellan, Stephanie. Youth group questionnaires. October–November 2000.

McConnell, Bill. Telephone conversation, letter and photo. September 2000.

McKenna, Alan. Tour of Knox United Church. 2000.

McLagan, Moir. Tour of Knox United Church. 2000.

Mende, Jeanette Marie. Questionnaire. 2000.

Mitchell, Gayle (née Johnson). E-mail to Peggy Schofield. 20 October 2002.

Nelson, Toireasa J. Research. 2000.

Pond, Susan Lorraine. Questionnaire. 2000.

Poulter, Raymond. Questionnaire and sketch of Hunter Presbyterian Church. July 2000.

Runcie, George W. Questionnaire. 12 February 2000.

Rush, Jack. Questionnaire and personal interview. 2000.

Simpson, Lillian. Questionnaire. 2000.

Sinclair, Dave. E-mail to Peggy Schofield. 17 August 2001.

Sorensen, Pastor Ken. Dunbar Evangelical Lutheran Church. Conversations and research assistance. 2000.

Sparshu, Edna. Questionnaire. 2000.

Stevenson, Vic. Research. 2000.

Sweeney, Jennifer. E-mail to Peggy Schofield re: Father Leahy. 8 October 2002.

Sweeney, Maureen. E-mail to Peggy Schofield. 7 September 2002.

Unsworth, Marie and Arthur. Questionnaire. 2000.

Van Horn, Pastor Darcy. Telephone conversations. 2000.

Waters, Thelma and Victor. Personal interview by Pam Chambers. 1 May 2001.

Welch, Byron. Letter in response to questionnaire plus photos. 29 September 2000.

Williams, Al. E-mail to Peggy Schofield. 16 March 2002.

Chapter 11: Parks, Gardens and Boulevards

REFERENCES

Askew, Susan. "History of the Dunbar Garden Club." *Dig It in Dunbar*, 2 February 2000, 5–7.

Baker, Nadia, Patrick Lilley, Toshiko Sasaki, and Heather Williamson. "Investigation of Options for the Restoration of Camosun Bog, Pacific Spirit Park." Thesis submitted in partial fulfillment of the requirements for Environmental Studies 400, University of British Columbia, 2000.

Bartholomew, Harland, and Associates. *A Plan for the City of Vancouver, British Columbia, including Point Grey and South Vancouver, and a General Plan of the Region.* Vancouver: Vancouver Town Planning Commission, 1929.

Bennett, Peppi. "Beautiful Trees Make City Unique." Letter to the editor, *Vancouver Courier*, September 2000.

Brown, Laurence, Terry Taylor, and Brian Woodcock. "The Restoration of Camosun Bog." *Discovery*, Vancouver Natural History Society, 28, no. 1 (Summer 1999): 27.

Bruce, A. Cromar. "City Could Send Him Tax Notices, but Didn't Know Where to Pay Debt." *News Herald*, 21 November 1939.

Burrows, Matthew. "It's a Wicket, Wicket World." *Vancouver Courier*, 16 July 2000.

Cutter, D.C. *Malaspina and Galiano*. Vancouver: Douglas & McIntyre, 1991.

Gold, Kerry. "Dunbar Residents Realizing Water Park Dream," *Vancouver Courier*, 7 June 1995, 9.

Greater Vancouver Regional District Parks. Management Plan. Prepared by GVRD Parks, West Area, November 1991.

Johnson, Pat. "Balaclava Going to the Dogs." *Vancouver Courier*, 10 March 1999, 3.

Jones, Carolyn. "Henry M. Eddie and His Famous Dogwood." *VanDusen Bulletin*, March 1995.

Kahrer, Gabrielle. *A Mosaic of Destinies, A Mosaic of*

Landscapes: The History of Pacific Spirit Regional Park, 1860s to 1950s. Brochure. Vancouver: GVRD Parks, 1991.

Macdonald, Bruce. *Vancouver: A Visual History*. Vancouver: Talonbooks, 1992.

MacNeill, Ian. "Musqueam Bog to Be Spared." *Vancouver Western News*, 11 November 1987.

Martin, Carol. *A History of Canadian Gardening*. Toronto: McArthur & Company, 2000.

McGlashan, J. Lyall. "The First Year of Point Grey Amateur Chrysanthemum Association." In *Point Grey Amateur Chrysanthemum Association*, 1987.

Point Grey Amateur Chrysanthemum Association: 50 Years 1937–1987 and Still Growing Strong. Alan Croll, past president; Ian McGlashan, secretary. Booklet published by club members in 1987.

"Saving the Last City Salmon Stream." *VanCity Enviro-Fund in Review*. Vancouver: Musqueam Indian Band/ David Suzuki Foundation, 1997–98.

Steele, R. Mike. *The First 100 Years: An Illustrated Celebration*. Vancouver: Vancouver Board of Parks and Recreation, 1988.

Straley, Gerald B. *Trees of Vancouver: A Guide to the Common and Unusual Trees of the City*. Vancouver: UBC Press, 1992.

"Vancouver's Old Streams." From revised edition, 1989. Originally printed in *Waters*, journal of the Vancouver Aquarium (1978): 3.

Whysall, Steve. "Up Close and Personal." *Vancouver Sun*, 15 June 2001, EI.

INTERVIEWEES AND CONTRIBUTORS

Abbot, Betty (née McGlashan). Telephone interview by Peggy Schofield. 25 July 2001.

Airey, Margaret (née Newton). Personal interview. 5 February 2003.

Albinson, Betty (née McLean). Personal interview. 5 March 2003.

Albinson, Fred. Personal interview. 5 March 2003.

Askew, Susan (née Pook). Personal interview. 27 February 2001.

Bernard, Ken. Telephone interview. 9 October 2001.

Binkert, June. Personal interview. 3 October 2001.

Birch, Pat (née Ledgerwood). Personal interview. 19 May 2002.

Bromley, Joyce. Personal interview. 17 June 2001.

Brown, May (née Adams). Personal interview by Pam Chambers. 21 July 2001.

Buckham, Joan (née Crawford). Personal interview. 14 May 2000.

Chambers, Pam (née Seivewright). Personal interview. 2 June 2002.

Claridge, Lloyd. Personal interview. 18 February 2000.

Claridge, Margaret (née Nicholson). Personal interview. 20 June 1999.

Claridge, Norman. Telephone interview. 20 February 2000.

Cobbin, Nora (née Moon). Personal interview. 29 April 2001.

Cornish, Stan. Personal interview by Larry Moore. 3 November 1999.

Cowen, Pat. Personal interview. 8 October 1999.

Damms, Patsy (née McQueen). Telephone interview. 14 March 2000.

Darcus, Jack. Telephone interview. 14 September 2005.

Dash, Greg. Vancouver Park Board. Personal interview. 20 March 2004.

Desrochers, Michel. Vancouver Park Board. Telephone interview. 15 September 2005.

Dickie, Beverly (née Brooks). Telephone interview. 4 June 2001.

Eddie, J. Henry. Personal interview by Margaret and Larry Moore. 29 October 2002.

Fletcher, Elizabeth (née Atkinson). Telephone interview. 20 May 2002.

Forbes, Barbara (née Allan). Personal interview. 15 June 2000.

Gale, Karen (née Tang). Personal interview. 23 November 2001.

Graham, Elaine. Personal interview. 12 March 2002.

Lindsay, Barrie. Telephone interview. 23 September 2001.

MacAdam, Linda. Telephone interview. 6 April 2002.

McGlashan, Ian. Personal interview. 14 August 2002.

McKelvy, Jean. Telephone interview. 15 June 2000.

McLeod, Joan (née Ferguson). Telephone interview. 9 May 2002.

Meek, Audrey. Personal interview. 20 March 2002.

Montpellier, Paul. E-mail. 31 July 2000.

Murray, Betty. Telephone interview. 2 October 2005.

Murray, Susan. E-mail. 3 October 2005.

Nichols, Tom. Personal interview. 30 March 2002.

Patrick, Geraldine. Personal interview. 25 November 1999.

Rochford, Carole (née Mitchell). Telephone interview. 2 May 2000.

Rush, Jack. Personal interview. 17 March 2000.

Schmelcher, Madeleine (Maddy) (née Shaw). Personal interview. 24 September 2001.

Schretlen, Al. Telephone interview. 12 October 1999.

Schretlen, Elaine (née Ellefson). E-mail. 14 May 2000.

Scott, Julia (née Neames). Personal interview. 14 October 1999.

Shaw, Alan. Telephone interview. 16 March 2000.

Shaw, Bernice. Telephone interview. 16 March 2000.

Skelton, Frank. Personal interview. 27 February 2001.

Slack, Sharon (née Bain). Personal interview.
  18 February 2002.
Slack, Terry. Personal interview. 25 May 2001.
Smith, Diane (née Harper). Personal interview.
  18 September 1999.
Smyth, Sheila. Letter. 19 March 2002.
Stewart, Hugh. Telephone interview. 22 October 2000.
Super, Laura. Telephone interview. 21 August 2004.
Thom, Helen (née Hurlston). Personal interview.
  14 March 2001.
Tingey, Peggy (née Moyls). Letter. 14 July 2000.
Van Unen, Louise (née Cornish). Telephone interview.
  14 November 1999.
Vulliamy, Mark. Vancouver Park Board. Personal
  interview. 11 August 2004.
Walker, Dana. Vancouver Park Board. Personal interview.
  29 June 2004.
Wall, Margaret. Personal interview. 16 June 2001.
Warr, Vivien. Personal interview. 18 November 1999.
Wasson, Ian. Personal interview. 27 September 2000.
Wilson, Don. Telephone interview. 8 June 2000.
Young, John. Telephone interview. 20 April 1999.

Chapter 12: Respecting Nature's Legacy

The authors wish to acknowledge Hannes Barnard, who
helped extensively with the research on the construction
of the Highbury Tunnel.

REFERENCES
Camosun Bog Restoration Group [Web site, cited 20 No-
  vember 2005]. www.naturalhistory.bc.ca/CamosunBog/
  about_threats.
Carlson, Keith Thor, ed. *A Stó:lō–Coast Salish Historical
  Atlas.* Vancouver: Douglas & McIntyre; Chilliwack,
  B.C.: Stó:lō Nation, 2001.
City of Vancouver. "Annual Report 2003, Solid Waste
  Division" [on-line]. [Cited 20 November 2005].
  www.city.vancouver.bc.ca/engsvcs/solidwaste/PDF/
  ann_report2003.pdf.
——. "Canada's First Sustainable Street Opens in
  Vancouver with Green Municipal Funds Support."
  News release, 2 August 2005 [on-line]. [Cited
  20 November 2005]. vancouver.ca/ctyclerk/
  newsreleases2005/NRcrownstreet.htm.
——. "Environmental Residential Lane — 'Country
  Lane' Treatment" [on-line]. [Cited 20 November 2005].
  http://vancouver.ca/engsvcs/streets/admin/improve
  ments/improvementTypes/countryLane.htm.
——. "Plan for the Can: Automated Collection of
  Garbage and Yard Trimmings" [on-line]. [Cited
  20 November 2005]. http://vancouver.ca/engsvcs/
  solidwaste/autocollect/index.htm.
——. "Waterworks Construction" [on-line]. [Cited
  20 November 2005]. http://vancouver.ca/engsvcs/
  watersewers/water/construction.htm.
——. "Waterworks History" [on-line]. [Cited
  20 November 2005]. http://vancouver.ca/engsvcs/
  watersewers/water/history.htm.
Clague, John, and Bob Turner. *Vancouver: City on the
  Edge.* Vancouver: Tricouni Press, 2003.
Davidson, John. "The Hand-Writing on the Wall."
  Presidential address, Vancouver Natural History
  Society, 1 October 1924.
Davis, Chuck. "The Greater Vancouver Regional
  District." *The Greater Vancouver Book* [Web site, cited
  20 November 2005]. www.discovervancouver.com/
  GVB/gvrd.asp.
"Dunbar May Wait." 10 September 1947. Major
  Matthews Collection, Add. MSS. 54. Street and Place
  Names Cards, 508-E-2. Dunbar Heights, Card 4. City
  of Vancouver Archives.
Dunbar Residents' Association. "Dunbar Salmonberry
  Days, 2003." Spring newsletter and event calendar.
Duthie, Dave. "Iona Island Wastewater Treatment Plant
  (WWTP), Jetty Repair (2005) Construction." Report to
  GVRD Waste Management Committee, 17 March 2005.
Evergreen Foundation. *Everett Crowley Park: Paradise
  Reclaimed.* Vancouver: Evergreen Foundation, 1997.
Glavin, Terry. *A Ghost in the Water.* Vancouver: New Star
  Books, 1994.
Greater Vancouver Regional District. Sewerage: Iona
  WWTP [Web site, cited 20 November 2005].
  www.gvrd.bc.ca/sewerage/iona.htm.
Greenpeace. "Greenpeace Founders" [on-line]. [Cited
  20 November 2005]. http://archive.greenpeace.org/
  comms/vrml/rw/text/def/founders.html.
Hermanson, Sally, and Graeme Wynn. "Reflections on
  the Nature of an Urban Bog." *Urban History Review /
  Revue d'histoire urbaine* 34, no. 1 (Fall 2005 automne):
  9–27.
Macdonald, Bruce. *Vancouver: A Visual History.*
  Vancouver: Talonbooks, 1992.
Paton, J.A. "The Story of Point Grey." *British Columbia
  Magazine* 7 (1911): 734–37.
——. "Some Information about Point Grey." *Point Grey
  Gazette,* 19 December 1925.
——. "Point Grey Interests Are Its Citizens' Interests."
  Dunbar News, 22 September 1927.
Peacock, Jim. *The Vancouver Natural History Society,*

1918–1993. Vancouver: Vancouver Natural History Society, 1993.

Society Promoting Environmental Conservation. "New GVRD Water Index Recognizes Turbidity Hazard in Water Supply." News release, 1 November 2001 [on-line]. [Cited 20 November 2005]. www.spec.bc.ca/news/news.php?newsID=102.

———. "SPEC to Cooperate with GVRD on No-Logging Policy for Vancouver Water Supply." News release, 13 December 1999 [on-line]. [Cited 20 November 2005]. www.spec.bc.ca/news/news.php?newsID=33.

Spiegelman, Helen. "Oh, the Taxes We Waste on Our Waste." *Vancouver Sun*, 9 March 1995, B3.

Trendell-Whittaker, Peggy. *In Our Backyard.* Vancouver: Whitecap Books, 1992.

Wackernagel, Mathis, and William E. Rees. *Our Ecological Footprint: Reducing Human Impact on the Earth.* Gabriola Island, B.C.: New Society Publishers, 1996.

Ward, Doug. "Trash Talk." *Vancouver Sun*, 23 August 1997, C4.

Weyler, Rex. *Greenpeace.* Vancouver: Raincoast, 2004.

Yang, Wilbert. "GVRD 2002 Solid Waste Recycling and Disposal Figures." Report to Waste Management Committee, 4 February 2004.

INTERVIEWEES AND CONTRIBUTORS

Binkert, June. Conversation with Beryl March. 2002. Telephone conversations with Peggy Schofield to 27 March 2003.

Brink, Vernon C. (Bert). Conversation with Beryl March. 2002.

Brown, Laurence. Conversation with Pam Chambers. 20 June 2003.

Gowe, Ronald N. E-mail to Peggy Schofield re: Highbury Tunnel. 18 November 2001.

Lower, Thelma. Letter to Vivien Clarke. 2000.

McTaggart, Steve. Conversation with Helen Spiegelman. 23 September 2005.

O'Brien, T. (Ed). Telephone conversation with Pam Chambers. 2 April 2003.

Redmond, Harold. Personal interview by Pam Chambers. 29 January 2000.

Rowley, Elizabeth (Liz) (née Parker). Telephone conversation with Pam Chambers re: C.F. Connor. n.d.

Slack, Sharon (née Bain), and Terry Slack. Personal interview by Toireasa Nelson. 25 August 1999.

Spiegelman, Helen. Personal interview by Peggy Schofield. 19 October 2002.

Watters, Don. Personal interview by Peggy Schofield. 6 September 2001.

About the Authors

PAM CHAMBERS (née Seivewright) was raised in Dunbar after her family moved there in 1931. She attended Lord Kitchener and Lord Byng schools, and graduated from UBC in 1943. Following a short career as a social worker and a long career as a private piano teacher, she has worked seriously as an artist since 1994. A recipient in 1997 of Volunteer Vancouver's Community Service Award, she has been president of the Vancouver Youth Symphony Society, president of the Community Arts Council of Vancouver and volunteer coordinator of the Artists in our Midst Dunbar/Kerrisdale group.

VIVIEN CLARKE, born in Regina, Saskatchewan, and raised in Victoria, B.C., has been a resident of Dunbar since 1986. She is a graduate of the University of Victoria and taught high school in Kelowna, B.C., and Montessori preschool and kindergarten in Vancouver. Married to Patrick Clarke, Vivien has one daughter, who attended Kitchener Elementary and is now a UBC graduate. Recently retired from employment with the VanDusen Botanical Garden Association, Vivien is now a volunteer guide at VanDusen, a master gardener, part-time garden designer and an active member of Dunbar Evangelical Lutheran Church.

SHELAGH LINDSEY grew up in Toronto. Born in 1926, she attended the University of Toronto, where she honoured in philosophy and graduated in 1948. After some false starts, she very sensibly returned to school, taking an advanced degree in communications at Stanford University. She joined the Sociology Department at the University of Manitoba in 1967. In 1972, she was invited to join the Department of Environmental Studies in the Faculty of Architecture. Upon returning to Vancouver in 1979 she became an adjunct professor in the School of Architecture at UBC, where she taught Meaning in Architecture and Meaning and Behaviour in Landscape. She retired to community service in 1995.

BERYL MARCH is a long-time resident of Dunbar. In 1946 she and her husband, John, bought an uncleared lot on Wallace Street above Marine Drive. They designed and gradually built their home, moving into it in 1951. Beryl had a distinguished career as a professor of poultry science at the University of British Columbia, serving as Dean of the Faculty of Agricultural Sciences in 1984–1985 and, following her retirement in 1986, being appointed Professor Emerita.

ANGUS McINTYRE has had a lifelong interest in public transportation. Three years after graduation from Point Grey High School in 1966, he started work as a trolley bus driver with B.C. Hydro. He is a director of the Vancouver-based Transit Museum Society, which is dedicated to the preservation and operation of vintage transit vehicles. Angus also volunteers as a motorman and conductor on old B.C. Electric interurbans at the Downtown Historic Railway along False Creek. He has been a Dunbar resident for more than 25 years and currently drives the No. 7 Dunbar trolley bus route.

LARRY F. MOORE is Professor Emeritus of Organization Management in the Sauder School of Business at the University of British Columbia, where he taught and conducted research for more than 30 years. For many years he was a volunteer consultant to Volunteer Vancouver and was designated an honorary member of the Western Association of Directors of Volunteers. He has lived in the Dunbar area since 1965, is a keen gardener, birdwatcher, cyclist and skier, and is fascinated by Dunbar's commercial history and development.

MARGARET MOORE (née Campbell) has lived all her life in the house in Dunbar that was built by her father in the mid-1920s. She started Grade 1 when Queen Elizabeth School first opened, continuing on to Lord Byng, UBC and a career in teaching. She married Larry Moore and they had four children who attended the same schools. Her interests include gardening, history, Scottish country dancing, canoeing, genealogy and grandchildren — not necessarily in that order. She is a member of the Dunbar Garden Club.

PEGGY SCHOFIELD was born in the United States. She and her Nova Scotia–born husband Wilf Schofield arrived in Vancouver in 1960, settling in Dunbar in 1965 to raise three daughters. After many years of involvement in the arts, the Dunbar business district and the Dunbar Residents' Association, Peggy became interested in local history when the City of Vancouver led a "visioning" process to find out what the community wanted for its future. It occurred to her that a knowledge of local history was the best foundation for decisions about the future. She made a commitment to the "Documenting Dunbar" project and subsequently, despite a serious illness, served as the volunteer coordinator of this book until her death in January 2005.

HELEN SPIEGELMAN and her husband George and their two boys moved to Vancouver from Seattle in 1978, settling in Dunbar in 1987. She joined the Dunbar Residents' Association board of directors in 1995 and was also active in Neighbour-to-Neighbour, a city-wide coalition of neighbourhood associations. She and two other women campaigned for seats on city council in 1999 under the banner Neighbourhoods Matter. She has also served on the boards of environmental organizations, including the Society Promoting Environmental Conservation, the Recycling Council of B.C. and the Pacific Spirit Park Society.

JOAN TYLDESLEY was born in Vancouver and spent most of her early years in Dunbar, from the late 1940s through to the 1960s. She attended Kerrisdale Elementary School, Lord Byng High School and the University of British Columbia. Later, she taught for 13 years at Kerrisdale Annex. Now retired, she lives just outside the Dunbar area but still considers herself a part of the community and enjoys many of the pleasures she delighted in as a child, from blackberry picking to browsing in the Dunbar Public Library.

Index